The Muslim Question and Russian Imperial Governance

INDIANA-MICHIGAN SERIES IN RUSSIAN AND EAST EUROPEAN STUDIES
Alexander Rabinowitch and William G. Rosenberg, general editors

ELENA I. CAMPBELL

The Muslim Question and Russian Imperial Governance

INDIANA UNIVERSITY PRESS

Bloomington and Indianapolis

This book is a publication of

Indiana University Press
Office of Scholarly Publishing
Herman B Wells Library 350
1320 East 10th Street
Bloomington, Indiana 47405 USA

iupress.indiana.edu

Telephone   800-842-6796
Fax   812-855-7931

© 2015 by Elena I. Campbell
All rights reserved

Manufactured in the United States of America

Cataloging information is available from the Library of Congress.
ISBN 978-0-253-01446-7 (cloth)
ISBN 978-0-253-01454-2 (ebook)

1 2 3 4 5 19 18 17 16 15

For my family

Contents

Acknowledgments   ix
Note on Transliteration   xiii
Abbreviations   xv

Introduction: Understanding the "Muslim Question" and Its Changing Contexts   1

Part 1. The Emergence of the Muslim Question   19

1. The Crimean War and Its Aftermath: The Question of Muslim Loyalty and Alienation   21

2. The Challenges of Apostasy to Islam   33

3. "What Do We Need from Muslims?" Combating Ignorance, Alienation, and Tatarization   54

4. "In Asia We Come as Masters": The Challenge of the Civilizing Mission in Turkestan   84

5. Dilemmas of Regulation and Rapprochement: The Problem of Muslim Religious Institutions   106

Part 2. The Muslim Question during the Era of Mass Politics   135

6. Challenges of Revolution and Reform   137

7. The Muslim Question in the Aftermath of the Revolution   154

8. "Solving" the Muslim Question   170

9. World War I   195

Conclusion: Could the Muslim Question Have Been Solved?   215

Notes   225
Bibliography   265
Index   290

Acknowledgments

My research for this book began in the early 1990s at St. Petersburg State University, where I grew interested in the history of the Orthodox church and religion in tsarist Russia. Participation in a special seminar taught by Boris Nikolaevich Mironov helped me connect these interests to the problems of empire, but it was my work in the seminar of Boris Vasil'evich Anan'ich that led me to "discover" the "Muslim Question" in Russian historical documents and inspired me to uncover the various meanings of this problem. As my *nauchnyi rukovoditel'*, Boris Vasil'evich gave me intellectual freedom while also teaching me the craft of history, instilling in me a passion for archival research, and encouraging me throughout the many years of my work on this project. I have also benefited greatly from the advice and insights of colleagues at the St. Petersburg branch of the Institute of Russian History of the Russian Academy of Sciences (since 2000, the St. Petersburg Institute of History; RAN) and the history department of the European University at St. Petersburg. My special gratitude goes to Viktor Moiseevich Paneiakh and Mikhail Markovich Krom who broadened my training, as well as Boris Ivanovich Kolonitskii, Rafail Shalomovich Ganelin, and Vladimir Vikent'evich Lapin for sharing their rich knowledge and understanding of imperial Russian history. Participating in the research seminar at the European University was invaluable in working on my project.

I have benefited greatly from discussing my work at a series of international seminars that explored the regional dimension of imperial rule in Russia. I have appreciated the vibrant intellectual atmosphere created by the organizers Jane Burbank, Mark von Hagen, Peter Savel'ev and Anatoly Remnev, and by the participants Nailya Tagirova, Ekaterina Pravilova, Irina Novikova, Francine Hirsh, Leonid Gorizontov, Shane O'Rourke, Nikolai Ssorin-Chaikov, Rustem Tsiunchuk, Paul Werth, Willard Sunderland, Charles Steinwedel, Aleksei Volvenko, and Sviatoslav Kaspe. I am especially thankful to Willard Sunderland for his excellent comments at the early stages of my book's development. Jane Burbank invited me to the seminar "Empires, States, and Political Imagination" at the University of Michigan, and introduced me to interdisciplinary and comparative thinking about empires in world history, broadening my intellectual horizons. I am grateful to the Davis Center at Harvard University, where I was able to commence work on my book project. Terry Martin invited me to the historians' workshop. John LeDonne shared with me his encyclopedic knowledge of Russian history, his passion for research, as well as showed his personal kindness. Wladimir Berelowitch invited me to the École des hautes études en sciences sociales, where I found an excellent audience for early versions of my work. I gratefully acknowledge support from my colleagues at the history department of the University of Washington. Glennys Young offered insightful suggestions and inestimable support. The participants of the assistant professors' writing group—Purnima Dhavan, Adam Warren, David Spafford, Shaun Lopez, Florian Schwartz, Charity Urbanskii, and Noam Pianko—provided comradeship and valuable comments on parts of my book. I acknowledge the useful suggestions of the anonymous reviewers of my manuscript and the valuable editorial help from Sigrid Asmus, Audra Wolfe, Janet Rabinowitch, and Joyce Rappaport. I am especially thankful to William Rosenberg of the University of Michigan, who brought the American and Russian academic worlds closer to each other. His guidance, generous help, and encouragement have sustained me through the long process of writing this book.

The research for this book has been accomplished with the assistance of archive personnel in Russia, Ukraine, Uzbekistan, Germany, and France. I especially want to express my gratitude to Galina Georgievna Lisitsyna and Irina Gurkina from the European University, for their help in obtaining access to the Russian archives. I am thankful to Anastasiia Romanova for her friendship and for sharing her knowledge of the collections of libraries in St. Petersburg. The support of Farit Mubarakshevich Mukhametshin, the former ambassador of the Russian Federation in Uzbekistan, helped me gain access to the Central State Archive of the Republic of Uzbekistan. I am very grateful for the kindness and help of the personnel of the State Archive in the Autonomous Republic of Crimea and the Political Archives of the Federal Foreign Office in Berlin. Special thanks to Wladimir Berelowitch, Juliette Cadiot, Alain Blum, and Dmitrii Gouzevitch from the Centre d'Études des Mondes Russe, Caucasien et Centre-Européen who directed me to and enabled me to see the A. Topchibashev's collection. Oksana Igorevna Morozan, director of the Central State Archive of Documentary Films, Photographs, and Sound Recordings of St. Petersburg; Rustem Arkad'evich Tsiunchuk, professor at the Kazan Federal University; El'mira Iskhakovna Amirkhanova, head of the Manuscript and Rare Books Division of the N. I. Lobachevskii Library at the Kazan Federal University; and Aleksander Papushin, director of the Web-based *Great Russian Album* were very helpful in providing photographs and permissions for publication.

The research for this book was partially funded by the Moscow Social Science Fund, the Kone Foundation in Finland, and the Soros Foundation. A Royalty Research Fund Award and a Junior Faculty Award at the University of Washington contributed to additional archival research and writing of the book. An unexpected yet appreciated gift came from employees at the Citizens Bank in Charlevoix, Michigan, who kindly offered me one of their empty offices when I needed space away from my busy household to work on my book during a summer in northern Michigan.

Parts of chapter 5 were published as "The Autocracy and the Muslim Clergy in the Russian Empire (1850s–1917)," in *Russian Studies in History* 44, no. 2 (Fall 2005): 8–30. I thank the publishers for permission to reprint the material.

Finally, throughout many years my family has provided a tremendous support to me and my book project. I give special gratitude to Scott Campbell, my husband, for his understanding and inexhaustible optimism as well as the maps that he has made for this book. Our children, Masha and Kolya, have brought new dynamics and meaning into our lives. Their curiosity about and cheerful support of "mama's book" as well as their boundless love gave me strength to complete my work. This, however, would never have been achieved without the help and encouragement of my parents, Zinaida Pavlovna and Ivan Ivanovich Vorob'evy and my in-laws, Kay and Larry Campbell.

Note on Transliteration

For personal names, place names, and terms, both Russian and non-Russian, mentioned in Russian sources, I have maintained Russian-language transliteration patterns according to the Library of Congress system, with some modifications. I have omitted the final Russian soft sign in oft-used words and names, as, for example, Kazan', Den', Sevastopol' and oblast.' I have used "j" instead of "zh" or "dzh" in non-Russian words, such as Andijan and Azerbaijan. I have also used a more common "y" instead of "iu" and "ii" in personal names such as like Yusuf and Dostoevsky.

I have retained the dates as they were found in Russian documents, according to the Julian calendar, which was twelve days behind the Gregorian calendar in the nineteenth century and thirteen days behind in the twentieth. The Julian calendar was in use in the area of the Russian empire until February 1918.

Abbreviations

Published Sources

PSZ   Polnoe sobranie zakonov Rossiiskoi imperii
        (Complete Collection of the Laws of the Russian Empire)
SZRI   Svod zakonov Rossiiskoi imperii (Law Digest of the Russian Empire)

Government Institutions

MVD   Ministerstvo vnutrennikh del (Ministry of Internal Affairs)
DDDII   Departament dukhovnykh del inostrannykh ispovedanii
        (Department for Religious Affairs of Foreign Confessions)
MNP   Ministerstvo narodnogo prosveshcheniia (Ministry of Public Education)
MID   Ministerstvo inostrannykh del (Ministry of Foreign Affairs)

Archival References

f.—fond—collection
op.—opis'—inventory
d.—delo—file
l., ll.—list, listy—(leaf, leaves)
ob.—oborot (verso)

The Muslim Question and Russian Imperial Governance

Introduction

Understanding the "Muslim Question" and Its Changing Contexts

This study is an inquiry into Russian thinking about what was historically known as the "Muslim Question"—in Russian, *Musul'manskii vopros*. Although Russian tsars had ruled over Muslim subjects as early as the sixteenth century, the "Muslim Question" emerged only in the second half of the nineteenth century and became a highly contested issue among educated Russians, both outside and within the government. During the last decade of the tsarist regime, it also became the subject of state policy. While recent studies have examined imperial Russia's Muslim communities as well as government policies toward Islam, the "Muslim Question" itself has never been carefully explored. It has, therefore, not been clear under which circumstances the question was formulated, let alone how this issue was understood by the educated Russian public and government officials, or what specific solutions they brought to bear upon it. What role did the debate on the "Muslim Question" play in the development of Russian policies toward Islam? Why did the issue remain contested and unresolved until the very end of the empire?

This book attempts to address these questions by taking the notion of the "Muslim Question" itself as an object of historical analysis. Since the concept was used by historical actors in late imperial Russia, I will henceforth refer to it as a historical term without quotation marks surrounding it. As articulated in the nineteenth and early twentieth centuries, the Muslim Question comprised a complex set of ideas and concerns that centered on the problems of reimagining and governing the tremendously diverse Russian empire in the face of challenges presented by the modernizing world. I suggest that in order to understand Russian policy toward Islam and especially Russians' views of and anxieties about Muslims after the Crimean War (1853–1856), we need to view the subject not only within the framework of Western European orientalist discourse and colonial practice but also within the larger context of a modernizing imperial society. Approached in this way, the Muslim Question also sheds light on the nature, possibilities, and consequences of state-sponsored reform in late imperial Russia. Focusing on the fundamental problem of "what to do about the Muslims" foregrounds the importance of the specific contexts of the empire—including the interaction of those contexts—within which the state's ambitious attempts to rebuild the Russian social and political structures took shape.

* * *

The prominent Slavophile publicist I. S. Aksakov wrote in 1864, "We have an infinitude of questions [*voprosy*]—a whole forest of [them], so many that one can become perplexed, but what about answers? There are hardly any, or perhaps just a few. . . . Although we talk and begin with much excitement, it is very rare for us to agree about anything."[1] Aksakov's comments describe the new era in Russian history that followed the Crimean War, a time that experienced fundamental social transformations and discussions about Russia's future development. This discussion evolved in terms of *voprosy*, a word that conveys the notion of problems in need of "solutions." An increased public awareness of the empire's many "questions," perceived as new types of problems produced by rapidly changing social conditions, represented a new way of comprehending social reality and was a novel phenomenon in autocratic Russia. And, as Aksakov's own statements indicate, while many educated Russian public and state figures shared the reformist spirit, they differed in their understandings of the essence of the empire's problems and the premises upon which Russia's successful transformation would be based. The Muslim Question was among those many new problems that emerged in the public and bureaucratic consciousness in the years following the Crimean War. Although each question followed its own trajectory, collectively they emerged as a subject of public and government discussion in response to the multiple challenges of state-driven modernizing efforts and empire and shared certain common features.

The Russian empire had evolved as a geographically bounded but culturally diverse hierarchical confessional state, with the Orthodox church officially enjoying "predominant" status. Imperial Russia featured an estate-based social structure, serfdom, imperial patriotism based on loyalty to the dynasty, and a well-established system of autocratic government resistant to the waves of European revolutionary change. Russia's humiliating defeat in the Crimean War exposed the deficiencies of the existing order, and, as S. Iu. Witte, minister of finance from 1893 to 1903 and later chairman of the Committee of Ministers, put it, "opened the eyes of those who were able to see."[2] Russia's defeat by the alliance of the Ottoman empire with Britain and France pushed the country's educated elites to identify the most urgent domestic problems as "questions" and to undertake far-reaching reforms designed to revitalize the empire so that it could better defend itself and compete in an increasingly imperial world.[3] The resulting Great Reforms represented a turning point in Russian history. Like the previous Russian state-driven reformist projects, the Great Reforms of Alexander II were oriented toward Western European models, but this time the transformations went deeper and challenged the very principles upon which the Russian imperial state had heretofore relied.

In the 1860s, the Peasant Question—the problem of serfdom and the peasants' lot—was the primary concern of the Russian-educated public and government officials. The emancipation of about twenty million serfs in 1861 opened a new era of integrating Russia's "lower classes" (*nizy*) into the structures of the state and transforming the empire's diverse system of estate-based obligations and privileges.[4] This trend toward societal integration also characterized the reforms of the judiciary, local self-government, the educational system, and the introduction of universal military service that followed the emancipation of the serfs. These transformations were conceived in terms of "progress" and "enlightenment," "fusion" (*sliianie*) and "rapprochement" (*sblizhenie*). The new institutions of self-government and justice implied the need for an intellectually developed, conscious, and socially engaged population. Thus, to pursue these reforms, the government had to appeal to its subjects' patriotism and a sense of responsibility to the state: concepts that engaged the notion of citizenship.

With the introduction of elected offices arose the so-called Constitutional Question, a problem that centered on popular participation in politics. The reforms challenged not only the system of autocratic government, but also the structures of the confessional state. The Clerical Question raised the problem of the Orthodox church, an institution that required comprehensive reforms to maintain its influence among the more mobile and educated population while competing with other confessions and emerging secular ideologies.[5] An equally important and related question concerned the privileged status of the Orthodox church and the limits of imperial tolerance toward other religious groups, which in turn gave rise to any number of confessional questions.[6] The very natures of officially ascribed confessional affiliation, and religious belief, as well as the question about the role of religion in a modernizing society were under debate.[7] The Great Reforms were thus both a product of the modern age and a state-guided attempt at modern transformations. As such, they brought new challenges while also making educated Russians increasingly aware of the distinctive times in which they lived, engaging them in a debate about the meaning of tradition and progress.

The emancipation of the serfs and the other reforms of the 1860s also forced educated Russians to reconceptualize the problem of empire, including its policies on the borderlands. The universal projects of integration and enlightenment met up against the empire's cultural diversity and regional variations in imperial governance, and raised questions about the nature and limits of imperial citizenship.[8] The emergence of the *narod* (the "common people") as a new element in social and political life challenged traditional imperial policies that had been based on cooperation with non-Russian elites and on the preservation of the status quo in imperial Russia's expanding frontiers.[9] The dismantling of the traditional social order, the development of new educational system and means of communication, along with the emergence of a public sphere, created possibilities for reimagining the nature and the boundaries of imperial communities and the empire as a whole.[10]

The imperial modernization project assigned the state an active role in bringing transformations to its diverse subjects. At the same time, social reforms supported the emergence of new types of educated Russian imperial actors on the borderlands. For these new agents, determining the place of Russians and non-Russian minorities in a modernizing empire, understood as the Russian cause (*russkoe delo*) and the Alien cause (*inorodcheskoe delo*), became complementary spheres of social engagement and initiative.[11] In the multicultural Russian empire, however, educated Russians were not alone in their efforts to reevaluate their own condition and role in imperial relations. This process took place in concert with their interactions with non-Russian elites, who also came to rethink the nature of their communities and their place in a modernizing empire and world at large.

At the time of the Great Reforms, the challenges presented by the empire's changing borderlands were themselves shaping the ways that educated Russians reconceptualized imperial relations and the goals of the reforms. The Russian defeat in the Crimean War, in fact, took place on the empire's culturally diverse border regions of Crimea and the Caucasus, and thus brought questions about Muslim alienation, empire, and reform to the forefront of the attention of the Russian public and the government. The 1863 rebellion in Poland was another eye-opening event.[12] The armed rebellion itself, with its massacre of Russian soldiers said to be peacefully sleeping in their barracks, along with pro-Polish sentiments in Britain and France that raised the possibility of European intervention into Russian–Polish relations, inflamed patriotic sentiment in Russia, reconfigured the Russian reform agenda in the western provinces, and stimulated debate on the problems of the borderlands and the empire's non-Russian peoples. The Polish rebellion was the first "modern" national movement to shake the Russian empire and make a forceful impact on the minds of the Russian elites. It thus stimulated the development of Russian national consciousness and created a prism through which the empire's other non-Russian borderlands would henceforth be perceived.

Public attempts to question the empire's borderland policies had begun, however, well before the Polish rebellion and were stimulated by factors outside the empire, including the revolutionary events of 1848 that challenged Russia's multinational western neighbor, the Habsburg empire. The most famous attempt to draw attention in Russia to borderland policies was *Pis'ma iz Rigi* (Letters from Riga), composed by the Slavophile publicist Iu. F. Samarin (1819–1876). Written in Riga in 1846–1848, where Samarin participated in the government's inspection of this city, the *Letters* passionately criticized what he perceived as isolation of the Baltic provinces, the result, he claimed, of imperial policies in the region. The problem, formulated as the Baltic Question, was also related to the Peasant Question; in this connection it emerged earlier than the other so-called alien questions because peasants in the Baltic provinces had been emancipated prior to their Russian counterparts and had thus become a new player in the social and political life of the region.

Samarin's *Letters* were too critical to be published under the repressive regime of Nicholas I. Instead, the work was circulated privately among limited circles of educated society and officials in St. Petersburg and Moscow. Samarin was consequently imprisoned,[13] as the tsarist government feared open discussion of these issues because they challenged established imperial relations in the Baltic provinces. Such criticisms did not achieve wide resonance until after 1863, when the relaxation of censorship opened the way for the creation of an influential press. This invigorated, if still fledgling, public sphere came to play an important role in the formulation and discussion of vital questions of the day, helping to redefine the nature of politics in tsarist Russia. It was here that the pressing new questions related to Russian political and social life could now be publicly raised and discussed.

The influential editor of *Moskovskie vedomosti* and *Russkii vestnik*, M. N. Katkov (1818–1887), and the editor of the Slavophile *Den, Rus,* and *Moskva,* Aksakov, were particularly galvanized by the Polish rebellion of 1863, and each played an important role in shaping public and governmental debate on these issues.[14] The Polish Question occupied a central place in these discussions, providing a framework within which other alien questions could be raised and debated. For example, in September 1863, while addressing the Polish Question in *Moskovskie vedomosti,* Katkov commented on the opening of the Finnish Seim. Although he recognized that relations between Finland and Russia had never been strained, he nevertheless emphasized the "abnormality" of Finland's special status within the empire, implying that the situation could present a potential threat to state unity.[15] While the government sought to prevent public criticism of the special imperial status of Finland, and the Finnish Question was not a frequent topic of concern until the 1880s, the Jewish Question quickly assumed a prominent position in the discussion.[16] With reference to the Baltic provinces, by the late 1860s, despite the government's attempts at prevention, public discussion commenced about the perceived alienation of the Baltic provinces from Russia. Attention was paid to the privileges of the Baltic barons and the perceived domination of German culture. These topics became conceptualized as the Baltic Question.[17]

In this new psychological and sociopolitical environment, Samarin's earlier criticism of Russian borderland policy became more relevant. Aksakov was strongly influenced by Samarin, for example, in Aksakov's own discussion of the Baltic Question.[18] In 1882, Aksakov began to publish Samarin's *Letters* in his newspaper *Rus,* while also calling for the publication in Russia of Samarin's other work, *Okrainy Rossii* (Russia's Borderlands), which had been published abroad in 1868–1872. In 1883, Katkov followed Aksakov in *Russkii Vestnik* by formally introducing the broader reading public to the Muslim Question.[19]

By this time, the more general term *inorodcheskie voprosy* (alien questions) had also became common in public and bureaucratic discussions, both reflecting and contributing to important changes in thinking about the empire. While the contents of individual questions varied, all addressed a fundamental problem: how could the traditionally heterogeneous character of the empire be reconciled with the challenges and needs of a modernizing state? With the unification of Germany and Italy well under way, educated Russian elites recognized that the Russian empire could only compete with its European rivals if it achieved a greater degree of internal cohesion. But what principles should constitute the foundation of that unity?

The formulation of alien questions signaled an important shift toward viewing non-Russian minorities as a special category of subjects who represented a challenge to the empire's unity and required the development of specific and appropriate policies. As historians have noted, throughout the second half of the nineteenth century the modes of classifying the empire's diverse populations were undergoing change. One important sign of this process was the gradual expansion of the legal category of *inorodtsy* (aliens) to include the entire non-Russian population of the empire.[20] While religion and social estate remained fundamental concepts, Russia's governing institutions and educated elites made increasing use of the category of ethnicity (*narodnost'*) and of the more politicized category of nationality (*natsional'nost'*).[21] The use of these new categories, which differentiated the empire's communities by language as well as by religion and way of life, implicitly reflected changing perceptions about integration and the character of the empire. But perhaps more importantly, to conceptualize distinct groups as nationalities meant to ascribe to them a distinct spirit and a trajectory of development toward some form of political autonomy. The nationalistic way of thinking politicized religion, Russia's traditional category of difference, thus presenting a challenge to the rulers of the multiconfessional imperial state. Geography also played an important role in the ongoing reconfiguration and reconceptualization of the Russian empire.[22]

Many educated Russians now came to conceive of the Russian empire as a complex set of territories consisting of a "central core" (*tsentral'noe iadro* or *korennaia Rossiia*) that "inherently belonged" to Russians, surrounded by a ring of borderlands incorporated into the empire at different times and populated largely by aliens. Both concepts, however, of aliens and Russians, remained contested notions. Nor was there a clear answer to the question of where to draw the boundaries between the Russian core and the alien borderlands. The areas that came to be viewed during the course of the nineteenth century as the core were highly diverse spaces in both cultural and social terms, and so were the borderlands.

The continental character of the tsarist empire helped to shape a sense of Russia's unique relationship between the central core and the borderlands. In contrast to Western empires' overseas colonies, the Russian imperial borderlands were often viewed by educated Russians as a "continuation of Russian territory."[23] The geographical continuity of the empire's territory seemed to predetermine the future of the borderlands—they would merge with the center. At the same time, particularly following the Polish rebellion and the emergence of nationalistic ideologies within the empire, educated Russians began to emphasize cultural otherness as a serious political problem: a threat to the integrity of the empire, an obstacle to reforms, and a challenge to the developing project of defining and strengthening the Russian core.

The emergence of alien questions also highlighted—perhaps inadvertently—the need to define the very meaning of Russianness, but even more importantly the path Russians themselves should choose in a modernizing empire. The alien questions were thus also inextricably intertwined with an even more fundamental Russian Question. And how could it be otherwise in an empire as culturally and ethnically diverse as Russia's? Especially in the transitional areas between the core and the borderlands, this interconnectedness became especially explicit.

The most important of these transitional areas was the Volga–Ural region. It was with reference to this region, therefore, that the Muslim Question was first raised and clearly articulated. The Muslim Question emerged as a prism through which Russian public, church, and state figures could understand and debate the notions of confession, nationality, citizenship, reform, and empire itself. And it was with respect to the Tatar inhabitants of these lands that the Muslim Question acquired its highly complex and contested nature, as we will see.

* * *

The expansion of the tsarist state into regions populated by Muslims had begun as early as the sixteenth century and continued in stages through the next three hundred years. As the result of this expansion, Muslims lived in different provinces throughout the Russian empire. The southeastern imperial borderlands—the region from the middle of the Volga to the Ural Mountains, Central Asia, the Caucasus, and the Crimean peninsula—were populated by large compact Muslim communities. Geographic location, demography, timing, and the nature of their incorporation into the empire, as well as their diverse histories before the Russian conquest, also made Russian Muslims a heterogeneous group.

The annexation of Kazan khanate in the sixteenth century brought the first large group of Volga Muslims into the empire.[24] They faced religious persecution while Christianization was employed as a mode of integration. As the result of this campaign, thousands of Tatars accepted baptism. By the end of the eighteenth century, in contrast, when the Russian empire extended its rule to Crimea and began its penetration into the Caucasus and the steppe region, the imperial system was built, on the one hand, by limited religious tolerance and the state's regulation of non-Orthodox confessions, and, on the other hand, non-Russian elites' loyalty to the ruling dynasty. The active Christianization campaign among Muslims was stopped. The state recognized Islam as a tolerated faith and patronized the creation of Islamic hierarchical establishments on the eastern frontier in Ufa (1788) and in Crimea (1794). While pursuing toleration, however, the imperial state remained committed to maintaining the dominant position of the Orthodox church.

Although the tsarist government had been preoccupied with matters related to Islam and Muslims for almost three centuries, the Muslim Question as such emerged only after the Crimean War. The issue brought to the fore a complex set of problems quite different from those that had long been posed by the actual existence of a Muslim population within Russia's borders. Shaken by the war and the Polish rebellion, the Russian educated elites became increasingly concerned about what they perceived as Crimean and Volga Muslims' alienation and ignorance. The Great Reforms that followed the war introduced ideas of enlightenment, integration, and citizenship and were extended to the Volga region and Crimea, thus raising a question about a new place for Muslims in a modernizing society. At the same time, Russians' awareness and perceptions of the Muslim Question were also formed in response to another challenge—the apostasy movement of the baptized Tatars in the Volga region that reached its peak during the reform era. The latter development demonstrated the apparent vitality of Islam and the weakness of the "dominant" Orthodox church.

The emergence of the Muslim Question reflected some educated Russians' growing concerns about Muslims and the unity of the Russian state. As we will see, there was no consensus among contemporaries as to the essence of this question, which remained fraught with multiple and evolving interpretations. The Russian debates on the Muslim Question revealed anxieties not only about Muslims but also, and to an even greater extent, about Orthodox Russians. The search for "solutions" thus presented a challenge not only to the state's traditional policies toward Islam but also to the very principles of Russian autocratic governance.

The question of what to do with Muslim subjects who were already controlled by the state became more complicated in the second half of the nineteenth century, as a result of the Caucasian War (officially ended in 1864) and imperial conquests in Central Asia. By 1881, these conflicts had brought a large group of nonintegrated Muslims into the empire's realm. At the same time, the total number of Muslim subjects dramatically increased, amounting to nearly 17 million by the beginning of the twentieth century, and forming the largest non-Orthodox population of the empire. The violence of the conquest and the military resistance of the new Muslim subjects to imperial rule signaled to the Russian ruling elite the danger presented by a nonintegrated Muslim population. At the same time, the conquests of the second half of the nineteenth century in Asia also raised the question of whether Russia might itself become an even stronger power, one as influential as other European empires who ruled over substantial Muslim populations. Given that the inclusion of this large new group of Muslims began during the Great Reforms, their very presence sharpened arguments about these tasks among Russians themselves. Moreover, by the 1880s, as we will see, an emergent Muslim modernist intelligentsia was itself confronting Russians with their own projects of Muslim enlightenment and integration into the empire. They contested Russians' efforts to define and direct government policy toward Islam in the non-Russian borderlands. As a consequence, it was also during this time that an alarming vision of the Muslim Question began to emerge in the periodical press and government documents.

The attempted assassination of Alexander II in 1866 and the actual assassination of the tsar in 1881 shook the Russian state and society. The new tsar, Alexander

III, came under the influence of a diverse group of journalists and officials who were critical of the Great Reforms and hostile to the establishment of representative institutions advocated by Westernizers oriented toward Europe. The opposing arguments of Slavophiles about Russians' special path of development found new resonance, albeit in a distorted form. Katkov and K. P. Pobedonostsev (1827–1907), Alexander III's tutor and the new ober-procurator of the Holy Synod, effectively formulated the ideology of the new reign. The ideology essentially brought together the initially opposing concepts of state nationalism, as articulated by Katkov, and the romantic nationalism of the Slavophiles, with their emphasis on Orthodoxy. At the core of this "new course" was the idea of autocracy as a native political institution of Russia, an ideological concern about the "Russian" character of the empire, and the role of Russia as a Slavic nation defending Slavs subjugated by Muslims on the Balkan peninsula. As Richard Wortman has demonstrated, a "national myth" emerged as the framework of the new reign, with pre-Petrine Russia used as a point of historical reference.[25] Although the new ideology had a Slavophile flavor, the borrowing from Slavophile thought was selective. Slavophile ideas about representation in the form of an Assembly of the Land (*zemskii sobor*), with freedom of conscience and speech, noninterference of bureaucracy into private life, local initiative, and revitalization of the Orthodox parish, were rejected.

Instead, the new government of Alexander III tried to adapt the reforms to the idea of national autocracy (*narodnoe samoderzhavie*).[26] Some of the reforms were revised. Others, such as the introduction of political representation, religious tolerance, and reform of the Orthodox church, were simply dropped from the regime's agenda. Instead, the state embarked on a program of rapid industrial development while leaving the foundational structures of the empire intact. Although the Orthodox church officially maintained privileged status within the empire and the Russian language was increasingly used by the state as a means of imperial integration, the Orthodox church remained subordinated to the state, Russian Orthodox peasants were still not fully emancipated, and educated Russians were not the ruling nationality. The state's efforts to modernize the empire along a native path had important implications for how the Muslim Question emerged and was perceived by the educated Russian within and outside the government.

* * *

It was only, however, after Russia experienced another crushing military defeat in the war against Japan (1904–1905), and went through the turbulence of revolution, that the Muslim Question fully came to the fore of public and government attention. In the last decade of the old regime, the topic became one of the most polemical and highly charged issues in the periodical press, in the Duma, at missionary congresses and conferences, and in special government commissions. This increased awareness of the complex of issues subsumed under the concept of the Muslim Question, and especially the Russian anxieties related to them, developed in response to several factors.

Most important was that the revolutionary moment of 1905–1907 itself force-fully reopened an extended set of questions, many of which had been raised during the 1860s and 1870s without being resolved. The introduction of modest forms of democracy in 1906 transformed the issue of integration into a question of the meanings and limits of imperial citizenship. Now the ongoing Russian debate on how to modernize the empire and strengthen its unity had to take into consideration not only the empire's cultural diversity, but also the political claims made by the Muslim intelligentsia.[27] At the same time, a new problem formulated as the Nationality Question (*natsional'nyi vopros*) became an important issue of political life. Liberal Muslim politicians called for equal rights for what they imagined to be a "Muslim nationality." They confronted educated Russians with the question: "Are Muslims just an alien confessional group, or fellow citizens?"

The limited expansion of religious tolerance and the official recognition of apostates as Muslims exacerbated the Orthodox–Islam rivalry. Russian anxieties concerning the Muslim Question consequently increased and became more varied after the conservative turn in 1907 when many of the reforms of 1905 were scaled back. The intellectual and political changes taking place in the wider Muslim world, including the Young Turk Revolution in 1908 and the Iranian Constitutional Revolution of 1905–1911, as well as the spread of pan ideologies (pan-Turkism and pan-Islamism) contributed to these fears. The political polarization of imperial society and, finally, the internationalization of the empire's nationality questions during World War I added further complexity to the Muslim Question in the eyes of educated Russians, as we will see. The debate on the Muslim Question seemed to come full circle when Russians again went to war against Europe's leading power and its Turkish ally. Once again, the issue centered on whether Muslims were, or even could be, loyal to Russia. Now, however, the Muslim Question was even more heavily freighted with what had always been its complementary problem: the still unresolved Russian Question.

*   *   *

This volume thus analyzes not only how proposed solutions to the Muslim Question varied over time, both locally and at the imperial center, but also how perceptions of the question itself developed in the changing contexts of the Russian empire. As a developing set of ideas and their associated values, what came to be called the Muslim Question was an elastic concept, an unsettled discursive issue with various meanings and definitions. In most cases, though, Russians evoked its rhetorical power to articulate fears and anxieties as much about Muslims as about the state and themselves. These cases are the focus of this study. What follows is not a comprehensive examination of all existing attitudes toward Muslims in late imperial Russia, nor a detailed narrative of Russian policies toward Islam. Instead, the volume focuses on thinking about Russian Islamic policies as they were formulated as part of a broad debate on what was known as the Muslim Question from the Crimean War to the end of the imperial state in 1917.

This book is divided into two parts. The first explores the emergence of the Muslim Question in the aftermath of the Crimean War by focusing on the circumstances under which Muslims came to be viewed as both a confessional and a political problem. Collectively, the chapters in Part 1 demonstrate the underlying tensions that characterized Russians' views of the Muslim Question and their implications for the formation of Russian Islamic policies. Chapters 1 and 2 explore how Russians raised the issues of Muslim loyalty and alienation during and after the Crimean War, reconceptualized the problem of apostasy and Islam, and came to formulate the Muslim Question as one of Muslims' alienation and domination. Chapter 3 analyzes how this perception played out in state schooling policy and then explores how the emergence of a Muslim modernist movement complicated, for many, the Muslim Question itself. Chapter 4 examines the tensions embedded in Russian thinking about the Muslim Question as they were revealed in Russian responses to the Andijan uprising of 1898 in Turkestan. Part 1 ends by asking, in chapter 5, how the concerns associated with the Muslim Question challenged the existing models of state policies toward Muslim religious institutions.

The second part of the book then addresses how the perceptions and definitions of the Muslim Question changed during and after the revolutionary upheavals of 1905, which brought fundamental changes to the structures of Russian governance. Chapter 6 explores how the expansion of religious tolerance and the nod to representative government offered by the tsar in the October Manifesto shifted the dimensions of the Muslim Question onto new theoretical and practical foundations. The conservative turn associated with Prime Minister P. A. Stolypin's government reform in 1907 brought an official reconceptualization of the goals and nature of state-sponsored modernization that, as chapters 7 and 8 will suggest, had implications for turning the Muslim Question into an urgent and highly contested issue. Chapter 9 takes the story into the period of World War I. It demonstrates how the war experience reinforced official perception of the Muslim Question while exacerbating the antagonism among the debate's participants. The volume concludes with a retrospective review and analysis that asks why the Muslim Question remained a contested issue and was not "solved."

The research for this book draws on a wide range of published and archival sources. The first group of sources includes materials produced by those government agencies that dealt directly with the Muslim Question. Religion was traditionally a primary marker of identity among Russia's imperial subjects, and was one of the state's instruments of rule. Issues concerning the Orthodox population as well as the relations of the Orthodox church to other confessions of the empire were concentrated within the Holy Synod, created by Peter the Great in 1721. The state system of supervision of confessional matters of the empire's other tolerated denominations, including Islam, took shape during the ministerial period when the Department for Religious Affairs of Foreign Confessions (*Departament dukhovnykh del inostrannykh ispovedanii*) was established within the Ministry of Internal Affairs (MVD) in 1832.[28] As the life of Russia's imperial society became increasingly complex, the responsibilities of the department diversified and came to include supervision of the institutions of Muslim ecclesiastical administration, construction of mosques, appointments of Muslim clergy, and conversions; however, it also watched political and social movements among the Muslim population of the empire. By the twentieth century, the Department for Religious Affairs of Foreign Confessions was the key government institution that generated and accumulated material on the Muslim Question.

Beginning in the 1860s, when mass education became a top priority of the state, the Ministry of Public Education became another key institution for shaping policies and attitudes toward Russia's Muslims. In the twentieth century, the "moods" of the Muslim population also became the subject of attention of the Department of Police at the MVD. Muslim regions annexed by the empire in the second half of the nineteenth century, the Caucasus and Central Asia, both fell into the jurisdiction of the War Ministry. In the 1860s, the Asian Department at the Main Staff was created to deal with the military administrative organization of the Caucasus and Central Asia, but also of the Orenburg region and Siberia as well as military–diplomatic relations with neighboring Asian countries. The intensification of the eastern direction of Russia's foreign policy made the matters related to Islam the focus of attention of the Asian Department of the Ministry of Foreign Affairs.[29]

The necessity for interministerial dialogue on political issues related to Islam had long been recognized by the government. This issue became especially urgent after the conservative turn in 1907. To discuss the Muslim Question, special interministerial committees were created at the MVD in 1910 and 1914. It had been anticipated that these committees would be convened periodically, but this hope was thwarted by the pressures of World War I and the 1917 revolution. Finally, the State Duma, created in 1906, was another institution whose abundant archives also related to the discussion of the Muslim Question.

This book is based on the documentation produced and accumulated by the relevant central and local government agencies preserved in the state archives in St. Petersburg, Moscow, Simferopol, Kazan, and Tashkent. Important materials include internal and interdepartmental correspondence, reports and special notes, journals of government committees, drafts of legal documents, and other preparatory materials. In my analysis, I combined them with the published official documents. On the eve of World War I, and especially during the war, the status of Islam in Russia became the focus of attention of the German government, which in turn intensified Russia's concerns about its Muslim population. The materials studied for this theme are located in the Political Archive of the German Foreign Office in Berlin.

Finally, the press also played a crucial role in raising and articulating the Muslim Question in Russia, and thus periodicals of various political orientations have constituted another important source. In preparing this study I have made use of published and unpublished writings by Orthodox missionaries, educators, academic

Orientalists, and representatives of Muslim modernist intelligentsia, all of whom were involved in the Russian debate on the Muslim Question, along with a variety of relevant diaries, letters, and memoirs that helped provide a better understanding of its subjective dimensions.

A range of important secondary literature has also helped shape my work. A number of scholars have paid particular attention to the study of nineteenth-century Russian projects concerning the cultural integration of the empire's diverse subjects; such scholarship has demonstrated that these attempts were rarely successful.[30] At the same time, valuable studies by historians of the western borderlands have explored imperial Russian policies as they were understood and articulated by the state's agents themselves.[31] By examining Russification from this perspective, for example, scholars including Theodore Weeks, Aleksei Miller, Mikhail Dolbilov, and Darius Staliūnas have challenged a previously dominant view of it as a rigid policy, concluding instead that Russification was inconsistent and controversial.[32] My study builds on this scholarship while suggesting that we also need to examine further how educated Russians within and outside the government came to formulate and perceive various alien questions themselves. Along with transcending traditional narratives of oppression or cooperation, asking this question should allow us better to understand the very formation of imperial policies and the range of actual tensions the process involved. One aspect of these tensions had to do with the anxieties about Islam that characterized educated Russians' attitudes toward the empire's Muslim population from the second half of the nineteenth century onward. Adeeb Khalid and others have argued that Russians' fears and hostile attitudes toward Muslims are best understood through a European discourse of Orientalism that justified Western colonial domination.[33] Alexander Morrison has equated Russian Islamophobic paranoia in Turkestan with British attitudes toward Islam.[34] Robert Geraci's insightful analysis of public debate on the cultural assimilation of non-Russian ethnic minorities in the East has led him to conclude that Russian authorities (especially after 1905) demonstrated their "instinct for separating East and West" and that this attitude "was stronger than their professed aspirations to bridge two world areas."[35]

Another valuable strand of scholarship, including work by Nathaniel Knight and David Schimmelpenninck van der Oye, has pointed out that, due to Russia's own complex identity, Russian Orientalist discourse was not monolithic and did not maintain a consistently hostile attitude toward the Orient.[36] Moreover, as Vera Tolz has recently suggested, the Russian school of orientology rejected the notion of an East–West dichotomy, in some ways anticipating postcolonial scholarship, particularly Edward Said's critique of Europe's perceptions of the "Orient."[37] This volume's discussion of the Muslim Question confirms the complexity of Russian anxieties and views. Fears of Islam in late imperial Russia were also mixed with hope. Muslims were viewed as both threats and models. The book also emphasizes the relationship between this complexity and the specific context of the Russian empire's modernization projects in which Russians' engagement with Muslims took shape, and is central to its understanding. It was this context that largely explains the often contradictory and indecisive Russian views and policies toward Islam in the last decades of the tsarist regime.

This approach to the Muslim Question should also allow further insight into the broader processes of reform in late imperial Russia, although that is not the study's focus. Understandably, much of the scholarship on the politics of reform has focused on autocracy and its institutions.[38] Grounding an analysis of the reforms in the debate on the Muslim Question highlights the importance of the imperial context in which Russia's modernization projects were articulated, and allows us to ask how, for example, Russia's unique imperial setting may have set the stage for interaction and competition between different projects of reform and ideologies of Russian and non-Russian nationalism. At the same time, the various ways the Muslim Question was addressed should allow us to learn more about the origins and nature of different versions of Russian nationalism themselves.[39]

This book also hopes to contribute to studies of Russia's confessional system and the imperial state's religious policies. The work of Robert Crews has demonstrated how Russia's confessional system and politics helped to integrate the Muslim population successfully into the larger structures of the empire.[40] Here I have shifted the emphasis toward the tensions produced by the imperial confessional order that, I argue, lay at the heart of the Muslim Question throughout the last decades of the imperial regime.[41]

Finally, as we have noted, the Russian empire was a diverse yet interconnected polity.[42] The political framework of the empire facilitated the interactions of different Muslim groups, both with each other and with other ethnoreligious imperial communities. And as we will see, it was the dynamic and nature of these interactions that became a matter of concern for many educated Russians within and outside the government. The empire was also tied together through the imagination and administrative practices of the Russian ruling elite. For example, the experience of imperial rule in other borderlands and in respect to other non-Orthodox groups had some effect on how educated Russians perceived issues related to Islam, while the encounter with Islam played an important role in the development of Orthodoxy. It is hoped, therefore, that the lens of the Muslim Question will also allow us to visualize Russian–Muslim relationships in a larger picture of a multiconfessional empire more generally.

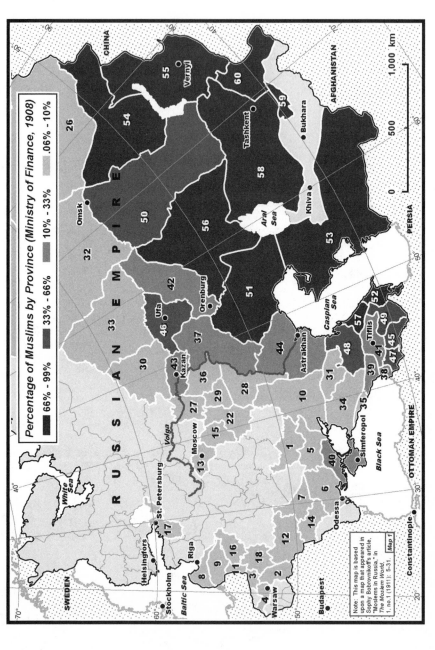

A Percentage of Muslims by Province (excluding the Khanate of Khiva and the Emirate of Bukhara). Based upon a map that appeared in Sophy Bobronikoff's article "Moslems in Russia," *The Moslem World*, 1, no. 1 (1911): 5-31. Created by Scott Campbell.

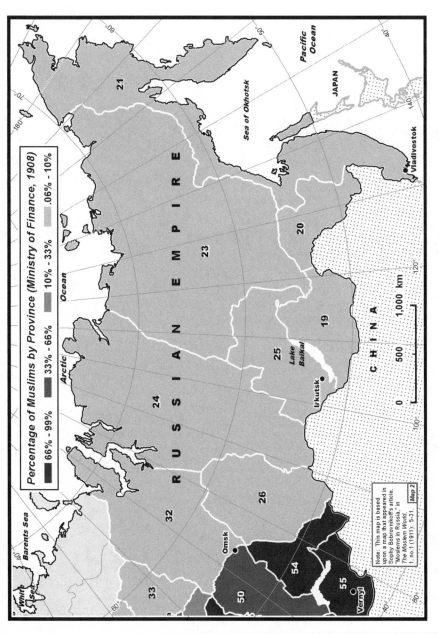

A Percentage of Muslims by Province (excluding the Khanate of Khiva and the Emirate of Bukhara). Based upon a map that appeared in Sophy Bobronikoff's article "Moslems in Russia," *The Moslem World*, 1, no. 1 (1911): 5–31. Created by Scott Campbell.

#	Province	% Muslim	Group		#	Province	% Muslim	Group
1 -	Khar'kov	0.06%	.06%–10%		31 -	Stavropol	4.39%	.06%–10%
2 -	Siedlce	0.08%	"		32 -	Tobolsk	4.47%	"
3 -	Lomza	0.08%	"		33 -	Perm	4.96%	"
4 -	Warsaw	0.08%	"		34 -	Kuban	5.38%	"
5 -	Ekaterinoslav	0.09%	"		35 -	Chernomorsk	5.41%	"
6 -	Kherson	0.09%	"		36 -	Simbirsk	8.63%	"
7 -	Kiev	0.09%	"		37 -	Samara	10.37%	10%–33%
8 -	Courland	0.09%	"		38 -	Batum	11.12%	"
9 -	Kovno	0.11%	"		39 -	Kutaiss	11.12%	"
10 -	Don	0.12%	"		40 -	Tauride	13.14%	"
11 -	Suwalki	0.14%	"		41 -	Tiflis	17.98%	"
12 -	Volhyniia	0.16%	"		42 -	Orenburg	22.66%	"
13 -	Moscow	0.23%	"		43 -	Kazan	28.75%	"
14 -	Podoliia	0.23%	"		44 -	Astrakhan	30.60%	"
15 -	Riazan	0.27%	"		45 -	Erivan	42.47%	33%–66%
16 -	Vilna	0.28%	"		46 -	Ufa	50.03%	"
17 -	St. Petersburg	0.29%	"		47 -	Kars	50.16%	"
18 -	Grodno	0.37%	"		48 -	Tersk	52.18%	"
19 -	Zabaikal'skaia	0.48%	"		49 -	Elisavetpol	62.96%	"
20 -	Amur	0.54%	"		50 -	Akmolinsk	64.43%	"
21 -	Primorskaia	0.57%	"		51 -	Ural'sk	74.15%	66%–99%
22 -	Tambov	0.58%	"		52 -	Baku	82.05%	"
23 -	Yakutsk	0.70%	"		53 -	Zakaspiisk	88.07%	"
24 -	Enisseisk	0.86%	"		54 -	Semipalatinsk	89.71%	"
25 -	Irkutsk	1.48%	"		55 -	Semirechensk	90.18%	"
26 -	Tomsk	2.12%	"		56 -	Turgai	90.99%	"
27 -	Nizhnii-Novgorod	2.62%	"		57 -	Daghestan	94.69%	"
28 -	Saratov	3.92%	"		58 -	Syr-Darya	96.37%	"
29 -	Penza	3.98%	"		59 -	Samarkand	97.62%	"
30 -	Viatka	4.27%	"		60 -	Ferghana	99.09%	"

Part One
The Emergence of the Muslim Question

1 The Crimean War and Its Aftermath

The Question of Muslim Loyalty and Alienation

The Crimean War (1853–1856) proved to be the moment of truth for Nikolaevan Russia. Its humiliating outcome forced Russia's educated elites to identify the empire's problems and recognize the need for fundamental transformations aimed at modernizing and restoring Russia's position in the ranks of European powers. Historians have studied the role of the Crimean War as a catalyst for the reforms of Russia's social institutions: serfdom, justice, local self-government, education, and military service.[1] More recently, scholars have also turned their attention to the impact of the Crimean War on the development of Russian nationalistic discourse, a discussion in which Orthodoxy occupied an important place.[2] As this chapter suggests, the experience of the war and its aftermath also played a significant role in stimulating and shaping educated Russians' thinking about borderland policies and Russian–Muslim relations in particular.

The Crimean War represented the culmination of a continuing struggle among the empires of Europe, aimed at safeguarding their interests in the regions of the Black and Mediterranean seas. The proximate cause of the military conflict was a religious dispute between Russia and France over the privileges of the Orthodox and Catholic churches in Christian holy sites located in Palestine, which was then ruled by the Ottoman empire. The war began in October 1853, when the Russian emperor Nicholas I, countering Napoleon III's championship of the Catholic cause, sent his army to the Danubian principalities in order to assert his right to intervene on behalf of Orthodox Christians living under Ottoman power. A year later, France, Britain, and Sardinia joined the war on the Ottoman side against imperial Russia. The fighting took place on several fronts: on the Baltic Sea, the White Sea, the Pacific Ocean, and the Caucasus, but the main conflict was centered on the Crimean peninsula, where the allied forces attempted to capture the Russian naval base of Sevastopol.[3]

As we will see, the war destabilized Russia's multiconfessional empire, provoked social anxieties, and raised questions about "trustworthiness" and "alienation" of Muslims in the Crimea and Volga regions. While the war provided a stimulus to the Russian empire's final subjugation of the Caucasus and further expansion into Central Asia, these actions tremendously increased the number of Russia's nonintegrated Muslim subjects. At the same time, the war brought into motion large-scale transformations of the empire's social and political system that ultimately raised questions about a potential new place for Russian Muslims in a modernizing imperial society.

Wartime Anxieties: Are Tatars "Trustworthy"?

In the preface to his archive-based study, *Tavricheskaia guberniia vo vremia Krymskoi voiny* (*The Tauride Province during the Crimean War*; 1905), A. I. Markevich (1855–1942), a schoolteacher and historian of Crimea, wrote that the war brought a great number of terrible sacrifices and hardships to the diverse population of the Crimean peninsula. But among these, most importantly, the population of this borderland, which had been annexed to Russia only seventy years earlier, had "to prove its close and indissoluble connection with the great Russian state."[4]

The annexation of the Crimean peninsula by the Russian empire occurred in stages that culminated in 1783 when Catherine II ordered an invasion of the khanate of Crimea, which led to the deposition of the khan. The population of this new borderland region was culturally diverse, consisting of Turkic-speaking Muslim Tatars and nomadic Nogays as well as a non-Muslim minority made up of Karaim Jews, Christian Armenians, Georgians, and Greeks. The former khanate was administratively integrated into the empire, and became Tauride province. Though many Tatars moved to the Ottoman empire during the conquest and the Russian government encouraged the colonization of Crimea by non-Muslims, the region's population remained diverse and included a significant portion of Muslims. By the time Crimea was annexed, the Kazan Tatars had already been under Russian rule for more than two hundred years. The experience of Russia's first encounter with Muslims in the sixteenth century, however, had largely been one of religious confrontation; the incorporation of Crimean Muslims took place during a different era, when Catherine II extended religious tolerance to Muslims and began to integrate their religious institutions into the state. Catherine's organization of religious administration in Crimea served as a model for integrating Muslim spiritual leaders, first in the Volga–Ural region and later in Transcaucasia.[5]

The Crimean khans had been Ottoman vassals, and their subjugation to Russia marked an important point in the history of Russian–Ottoman rivalry over the control of the successor states of the Golden Horde. The Russian annexation of Crimea was thus a crucial event in international relations. Russia's arrival on the Black Sea, along with the ongoing decline of the Ottoman empire, helped produce one of the most significant international dilemmas of the nineteenth century. The Eastern Question generated intense struggle between Russia and the major powers of Europe over influence in the Ottoman territories. The Crimean War represented a culminating point in the escalation of this struggle. It was there on the

Crimean peninsula that Russia received a blow to its imperial ambitions and faced a threat to the very integrity of the state.

Nicholas I's manifesto of 20 October 1853 presented the idea of defending Orthodoxy as Russia's official justification for the war.[6] The eruption of the war fuelled patriotic sentiments cast in religious terms among some educated Russians. A well-known example of such is found in the writings of M. P. Pogodin (1800–1875), a historian and publicist from Moscow who advocated Russian liberation of the Balkan Slavs from Turkish rule and encouraged a seizure of Constantinople. He also presented the war as a historical conflict between Orthodoxy and Islam.[7] In Russia's Black Sea region, the war mobilized local Orthodox clerics. Among them, the archbishop of the Kherson–Tauride diocese, Innokentii (Borisov; 1848–1857), was the most prominent preacher and enthusiastic supporter of the cause of Eastern Christians living in the Ottoman empire. In his sermons, delivered in Odessa and the various cities of Crimea, Innokentii interpreted the Crimean struggle as a holy war.[8]

The war also strengthened anxieties and tensions among the empire's religiously diverse communities. These anxieties grew especially strong among the various Christian groups and Muslim Tatars of the Crimean peninsula as the region became transformed into a war zone. The Muslim elites' declaration of loyalty to the tsar reassured the Tauride provincial administrators.[9] Even at the beginning of the war, however, rumors about a "hostile spirit" (*vrazhdebnyi dukh*) and "antipathy" (*neraspolozhenie*) among Crimean Tatars toward Russians and other Christians, as well as an "alarmist mood" (*trevozhnoe sostoianie*) of the local Christian population, reached Nicholas I. In November 1853, the war minister V. A. Dolgorukov requested that local authorities investigate these rumors.[10] The Third Section of His Imperial Highness's Chancellery (the political police) investigated the reports, saying that gunpowder and lead were stored on the estates of the Tatar *murzas* (nobles), and that Tatars rendered assistance to the enemies. No evidence was found that these reports were true. Similarly, no evidence supported rumors about Muslim Tatar plans to attack Christians during church services or to kill and rob the Christian population.[11]

In February 1854, the head of the Tauride chamber of the Ministry of State Property informed the Tauride governor that Tatars were obeying the authorities and did not yet warrant the government's mistrust.[12] At the same time, he could not guarantee the future tranquility of the population, and recommended strengthening the Russian military presence in certain villages of the Crimean peninsula.[13] A few months later, the Tauride governor-general, V. I. Pestel, wrote to the head commander of Russian forces in Crimea, Prince A. S. Men'shikov, stating that "the residents of all the places along the path of the Russian troops forgot the differences of their origins and joined as one Russian family" to greet the soldiers.[14]

The authorities' concerns about Tatars' "trustworthiness" (*blagonadezhnost'*), understood above all as obedience to the government, increased with the expectation of the enemy's invasion of the peninsula and especially after enemy troops landed in Evpatoriia at the beginning of September 1854. Men'shikov failed to prevent the landing of the allied forces and could not defend Crimea. The allied troops defeated the Russian army at Alma Heights and marched toward Sevastopol.[15]

The population of the coastal region left their homes in panic. Thousands of Tatars arrived in allied-occupied Evpatoriia.[16] In turn, local officials reported on what they interpreted as a "change in mood" (*peremena v nastroenii*) and unrest among Tatars after the enemy landed.[17] They pointed to instances of Tatar "treason," such as the spread of hostile rumors, assistance to the enemy, assaults on Russian officials, and robberies of Russian noble estates and state property.[18] At the same time, official documents recorded examples of generous donations to and support for the Russian army and the government by Tatars of different social origins, as well as cases of Muslims assisting Christians.[19] The Tatars, along with other Crimean residents accused of untrustworthiness (*neblagonadezhnost'*) and bad behavior (*durnoe povedenie*), were exiled to the Russian internal provinces, while those who demonstrated political loyalty to the throne and fatherland were awarded medals.[20] The war shook the Crimean multiconfessional society and aggravated tensions between its diverse communities, presenting imperial authorities with the challenging task of dealing with both the supposedly hostile mood of the Tatars and the alarmist state of the Christian population. Along with responding to the anxieties generated by the local Christian population, government authorities also had to handle cases in which Tatars were subjected to hostilities, terror, and marauding by Cossacks, Greeks, and Russians.[21]

The uncertainties and anxieties of war were echoed in the culturally diverse Volga–Ural region, which had been a part of the empire for longer than Crimea. In the Orenburg and Viatka provinces, rumors circulated among the Russian population about the Muslim landowner and officer S. Tevkelev having instigated a rebellion among his own Muslim peasants; he was said to have provided them with gunpowder. Local gendarmes received information about secret directions from the Orenburg mufti (the head of a state-sponsored hierarchical Muslim establishment) to the mullahs to pray in their mosques for the Turkish sultan and his troops. At the same time, in Samara province, Tatars spread rumors about a governmental plan to use force to baptize Muslims.[22] Local authorities were unable to confirm rumors about the subversive actions of the Tatars, and instead reported on the general tranquility and obedience of the local population. In May 1854, for example, the civil governor of Viatka province reported to the minister of the interior that "in Tatar mosques the appropriate prayers for the health and well-being of the Russian imperial family and for the success of the Russian army in the ongoing war are being recited."[23]

Overall, neither the rumors nor the denunciations concerning Tatar sympathies toward Turkey managed to shake the government's trust in the Muslim spiritual and social elite. The Orenburg governor-general wrote as follows about the antigovernment intentions ascribed to Tevkelev:

It is unlikely that the rich landowner is associated with such activities, as he owns a few hundred Muslim souls; these actions would first of all not benefit Tevkelev himself, because he would be the first to incur losses from the rebellion of his own peasants. In addition, over his entire service up until now there has been no reason to suspect him of any feelings others than those of a loyal subject.[24]

The subsequent appointment of Tevkelev in 1865 as head of the Muslim Ecclesiastical Assembly in Ufa was proof of the government's trust in him.[25]

During the war, imperial authorities approached Crimean Tatars with increased suspicion, viewing them as a security risk.[26] At the same time, some officials realized the importance of preserving order among the borderland's religiously diverse communities as well as of maintaining a sense of trust among Muslim Tatars. The rumors spread by both local Christians and Muslims were not only sources of officials' information and anxieties, but in the government's view also represented a form of unrest among the population that could be harmful to the existing confessional and social status quo and political stability of the empire. Therefore, local authorities not only investigated reports about Tatars' "treason," but also tried to suppress the circulation of unverified denunciations, and in certain cases hindered the very process of investigation.[27] Although, as the imperial authorities themselves recognized during the war, in many cases Tatars were arrested and exiled on the premise of false accusations, some local officials tried to prevent the criminalizing of Tatars en masse and worked to deescalate tensions between the local communities.[28]

The Crimean War ended with the Treaty of Paris on 30 March 1856. On 26 August of that year, the day of his coronation, the new emperor, Alexander II, issued a charter in which he expressed gratitude to the "loyal subjects" (*vernopoddannye*) of all the estates of Tauride province for their sacrifices to the "holy cause of the fatherland" (*sviatoe delo otechestva*). The imperial charter was delivered to Simferopol, where it was received "by the province and district marshals of nobility, cities' mayors, *volost* heads [*volostnye golovy*], deputies from Crimean colonists, and Tauride's mufti with honorary Muslim clergy."[29] After a reception at the governor's house, the charter was transferred to the Simferopol cathedral of Alexander Nevskii.

Yet the end of the war and the foreign occupation on the Crimean peninsula brought new challenges to the local population and imperial authorities. Immediately after the war, Russian military authorities received information about the attempts of some 4,500 Tatars from Balaklava to move to the Ottoman empire.[30] Local officials brought this matter to Alexander II, who ordered them not to create obstacles for the emigration of the Crimean Tatars. Their voluntary relocation might, he advised, serve as a "favorable circumstance to get rid of the harmful population."[31] As several historians noted, the new governor-general of New Russia, A. G. Stroganov, reinterpreted the tsar's statement by presenting the Tatars' departure as "necessary" instead of just "advantageous."[32] Soon, requests for emigration came from Volga Tatars as well.

The Crimean War and Its Aftermath 25

The provisions of the peace treaty forced Russia to cede the mouth of Danube River and part of Bessarabia to the Ottomans, accept the neutralization of the Black Sea, and give up its claims to protect Orthodox Christians living in the Ottoman empire—all serious blows to educated Russians' sense of their state's role as an imperial power.

The end of the Crimean War, however, allowed Russia to expand its influence in the Caucasus and then Central Asia. In 1859, Russian troops commanded by Prince A. I. Bariatinskii captured the legendary Imam Shamil (1797–1871), thus ending the organized resistance of Muslim tribes in the eastern Caucasus.[33] Fighting in the western Caucasus continued until 1864 and was especially brutal. The establishment of Russia's domination in the Caucasus caused a mass exodus of the Muslim population, especially Circassians, to the Ottoman empire. Alan Fisher estimates that between 1855 and 1866, at least 500,000 Muslims left their homelands in Crimea and the Caucasus.[34]

In response to the Crimean defeat, educated elites in Russia sought to restore their empire's status as a great power by identifying and addressing domestic "ills." This internal examination was carried out in an international environment hostile to Russia, one that had only worsened after the Polish rebellion of 1863. The emigration of the tsar's Muslim subjects to the Ottoman empire also resonated in Europe. The mass departure of Tatars and the simultaneous influx of a new Christian population, including refugees from the Ottoman empire, to Russia in the wake of the Crimean War altered the confessional balance between Christians and Muslims in Crimea. As Mara Kozelsky argues, the decline of Islam allowed some Russians to reimagine Crimea as a locus of Russian religious identity and paved the way for the Christianizing process.[35] But not all Muslims left the empire. While attempting to modernize Russia's social and administrative institutions, educated Russians both inside and outside the government turned their attention to the problem of imperial governance of the empire's Muslim population.

In this context of modernization, wartime concerns about Tatars' trustworthiness were now reconceptualized as issues of Muslims alienation and rapprochement with Russia. If discussions in the developing press are any indication, this interpretation resonated with the broader public. The issue of integrating Muslim subjects into the imperial polity became especially acute when Russia officially ended its long war in the Caucasus in 1864 and began its military conquest of Central Asia.

Why Are Muslims Alienated?

The role of Tatars during the Crimean War, cases of mutinies and assistance to the enemy in Crimea, and resistance to recruitment in the Volga region, together with subsequent Muslims' emigration, demonstrated to the government and to the educated Russian public both the alienation of Muslims and the political danger this alienation represented for the stability of the empire.[36] In the wake of increased levels of Tatar emigration to the Ottoman empire, both during and after the Crimean War, the issue of alienation became the primary means through which Russian commentators came to understand the Muslim Question. In leading contemporary journals, published government reports, memoirs, and, finally, scholarly studies, Tatar emigration—though not a new phenomenon—acquired the status of a political and socioeconomic problem. [37] During the war, emigration was perceived as a blessing by the government, but afterward it seemed to reach such tremendous levels that it was accused of causing a catastrophic depopulation of Crimea, a region seen as a precious pearl in the crown of the Russian tsars. As one observer put it, there was an impression that "all the Tatar people left Crimea."[38] The economic decline of the empire's borderland particularly concerned contemporaries. The mass flight of Russian Muslim subjects also came to be perceived as damaging to the self-image of Russia as a civilized European country, as well as to Russian diplomatic efforts to protect Christians living in the Ottoman empire.[39]

Many government reports and articles on emigration questioned why Tatars were leaving Russia. Some looked to perceived Muslim religious fanaticism as an explanation. The confessional view of Islam as a religion hostile to Orthodoxy served to some Russians to explain both Tatar "mutinies" during the war and their emigration to the Ottoman empire, which Kazan archbishop Antonii (Amfiteatrov) in 1867 conceptualized as Tatar "coldness to the Russian cause, absence of patriotism and sympathy toward the Russian people and the government," thus merging confessional and patriotic discourses.[40] Wartime religious rhetoric that identified Russian patriotism with Orthodoxy consequently served to associate treason with Islam.[41]

The secular nationalist press galvanized by the Polish rebellion of 1863 and, later, by the struggle of Balkan Slavs for independence, similarly accused Tatars of hostility to Russians. *Moskovskie vedomosti* and *Novoe vremia* labeled Crimean and Kazan Tatars, along with Germans, Poles, Finns, and Jews, as dangerous separatists. The newspapers repeated the wartime rumors about the intentions of the Crimean Tatars to slaughter Christians and intimidated their readers with the possibility of a religious war inside the empire. At the same time, *Vestnik Evropy*, founded in 1866 by a liberal writer, M. M. Stasiulevich, condemned the general distrust of Tatars that began to emerge after the Crimean War. The journal attributed unrest among Tatar peasants during the war to the unsatisfactory conditions of their lives, pointing out that not a single Tatar nobleman crossed over to the enemy side.[42] The journal warned that viewing non-Russians through what it called "confessional" and "ethnic" lenses did not jive with the goal of political unification of Russian citizens.[43]

Published government reports and eyewitness accounts also provided evidence for the view that not all Tatars were "traitors, deserters, and robbers." As E. I. Totleben, a military engineer and key figure during the defense of the Russian naval base of Sevastopol, wrote in a memorandum, "some cases of Tatars' treason" during the war were exaggerated and led to the false conviction that Tatars were "hostile," "dangerous," and "fanatical."[44] Lieutenant-General G. I. Levitskii, in his semiofficial report on Tatar emigration, called for a "fair evaluation of the Tatar people."[45] He stated that individual cases of treason displayed during the war could be contrasted with the "hundreds of examples of rare honesty and loyal duty" of the Tatars—something that was not always demonstrated by the Russian population.[46] In his explanation of Tatar emigration, Levitskii played down the role of perceived religious fanaticism and focused instead on the Tatars' poor economic conditions and government policies that encouraged Tatar departure. In response to accusations lodged against the Tatars, Levitskii stated that it made no sense to demand "supernatural valor and self-sacrifice" from a "conquered people who have with us nothing in common in religion, language, customs, morals, and manners; who are oppressed and who did not forget what they had been formerly and what they are now."[47]

The problem of Muslims' perceived alienation became more acute and complicated as the government launched a series of fundamental social reforms in the 1860s–1870s. The reformers thus faced the following questions: Could reforms ease Muslims' alienation and tie them to Russia? Should and could the government's universal projects of integration be adapted to Muslims' confessional needs and the peculiarities of their lifestyle? The introduction of universal military conscription in 1874, which was one of the major modernizing projects, provoked new anxieties among Tatars as well as concerns among Russian officials who anticipated a new wave of Tatar emigration. General S. M. Vorontsov, who had participated in the Crimean War, was dispatched to Crimea by the tsar to gain an understanding of reasons for Tatar emigration and to prevent the departure of the "population necessary for the region" by explaining the special conditions of military service for Crimean Tatars.[48] Vorontsov reported that the promise to ease military service for Tatars by creating a special squadron in Crimea guaranteed the freedom of Islam and therefore calmed down the majority of the Tatar population. He believed that reconciliation between Tatars and Russians was feasible, and he attempted to rehabilitate Tatars in the eyes of the tsar.[49]

In 1876, the Ministry of Internal Affairs established a commission whose purpose was to find ways to prevent mass emigration of Crimean Tatars to the Ottoman empire. The commission's members blamed emigration on what they saw as the national peculiarities and religious fanaticism of the Tatars. At the same time, the commission criticized the government for its inconsistent emigration policies. The commission noted that "after a hundred years, Tatars were not merging with the Russians, as if constituting a supplementary state to Russia, and were instead sympathizing with Turkey."[50] In its discussions about land issues, schooling, and the easing of military service for Crimean Tatars, the commission's report indicated its members' recognition of reasons other than religion for Tatars' emigration, and offered evidence that some Russian officials had already articulated that the government's policy should aspire to integrate Muslims in Russia more thoroughly.[51]

Muslim petitions for emigration from the Volga–Ural region, although not as profuse as the quantity from the Crimean peninsula, also encouraged the authorities to think about why Muslims chose resettlement.[52] As N. P. Ignat'ev, the Russian ambassador to Istanbul, wrote, "If the Volga Tatars did not have the desire to move away from Russian rule during the time of conquest of the Kazan and Astrakhan khanates, it is incomprehensible why such an idea could be conceived and would develop in our time during the present benevolent fatherly reign." Ignat'ev thought that improved governance would prevent Muslims from "seeking a better life in Turkey."[53]

That the final subjugation of the Caucasus in 1864 coincided with a period of social reforms added force to educated Russians' thinking about the empire's Muslims. As with the question of Tatar emigration, the developing press played an important role in making the discourse about Muslims a part of the public domain. General R. A. Fadeev (1824–1883), a participant in military campaigns against Imam Shamil, was among the first to publicly raise (in the 1860s) questions about the goals of the imperial conquest of the Caucasus that had cost Russia such tremendous human and material sacrifice. Fadeev's primary concern was to establish Russia in the leading position in Western Europe and among the Balkan Slavs. He held conservative views about Russia's social and political transformation. As a military writer, he saw the restoration and utilization of Russian military potential as key to establishing Russia's status.[54] This goal influenced his treatment of the Caucasus. His publications about that region attempted to gain public support for the army, clarify the Russian mission in the Caucasus, and establish the importance of the new borderland for the empire. Among Russia's motivations for the long and bloody conflict in the Caucasus, Fadeev stressed the protection of Christian Georgia from the militancy of Islam. Thus, in his view, the subjugation of the Caucasus represented the culminating moment of Russia's struggle with Islam. It advanced Russia further into the Muslim world and forced Russia to confront the problem of deciding the future of Asia, a turn of events that would affect the country's position vis-à-vis Europe.[55]

Russia's victory in the Caucasus was also celebrated by the influential nationalistic journalist, editor, and public figure M. N. Katkov. At the beginning of Alexander II's reign, Katkov advocated liberal reforms on the pages of his *Russkii vestnik*. His influence reached its peak following the Polish uprising of 1863, when he opened a debate on the Polish Question and other alien questions, defended the empire's unity, and established himself as a champion of Russian national interests. It was during this time that his *Moskovskie vedomosti* became one of the most widely read newspapers in Russia.[56] In an editorial on 27 May 1864, he wrote: "The Grand Duke, Viceroy, reports: 'The Caucasian war is over. Not a single rebellious tribe left in the Caucasus.' Joyful news! This is a new glorious page in the chronicles of the current tsar's reign and a new brilliant success bestowed on him by God! "[57] For Katkov, as for Fadeev, the conquest of the Caucasus fulfilled a historical task for Russia. Like Fadeev, Katkov justified Russian conquest by the need to protect Christian Georgia. In the Caucasus, he saw a land historically connected to ancient Greece and Kievan Rus. Katkov especially emphasized the importance of Christianity for the Caucasus's past, thus implicitly suggesting that it was Russia's mission to restore this ancient religious tradition.[58] But what was the place of the native Muslim population within this conception? Katkov only in passing mentioned what he called the "voluntary relocation" of the mountaineers to the Ottoman empire; he meant this to be a response to British criticism of Russian emigration policies.[59]

Driven by security considerations, in the last phase of the Caucasian War the Russian military command forced the "troubled" Muslim tribes out of their homelands in the western Caucasus, either to the plains of the Kuban River or to the Ottoman empire as a way to "pacify" the region.[60] Fadeev, in his *Pis'ma s Kavkaza* (*Letters from the Caucasus*), published by *Moskovskie vedomosti* in 1864–1865, justified this strategy by pointing to the lack of sufficient time to change the attitudes of what he referred to as "barbarian people, from time immemorial independent, hostile, armed, protected by the unapproachable landscape and influenced by interests hostile to Russia."[61]

While large numbers of Circassians and other Muslim tribes left, the vision of the Caucasus without its native Muslim population was, of course, a utopian one. The regulation of emigration, as well as of return to Russia, became a burden for both the Russian and Ottoman authorities.[62] Not all Muslims were openly hostile to Russia or were willing to leave. The tremendous suffering experienced by Circassians who had been forced to leave their homelands was noted by both Russian authorities and the public, and gave the European press reasons to criticize Russia's methods of conquest. These circumstances forced educated Russians to ask the same questions they asked of the Crimean and Volga Tatars: What makes Muslims hostile to Russia? Would it be possible for Russia to turn the alien Muslim population into loyal subjects of the tsar?

Even some members of the Russian military expressed doubts about the wisdom of removing Muslim populations. In 1863, V. A. Frankini, the military advisor at the Russian embassy in Istanbul, wrote to D. A. Miliutin, the Minister of War: "England is bragging that it is the first Muslim power in the world, but Russia also has a lot of Muslim subjects whose number is growing every day. In pushing away the Muslim population of the Caucasus, Russia admits her powerlessness to deal with them, thus cutting off one head of her two-headed eagle and betraying her character as an Asian power." Frankini explained that the Russian Caucasus needed mountaineers and that Islam, if ignored by the state, would not present an obstacle to the mountaineers' transformation into Russian subjects.[63] The issue of the mountaineers' "rapprochement" with Russia by means of what one author called "European religious tolerance" (*evropeiskaia veroterpimost'*) for Islam became the subject of public discussion in the pages of *Voennyi sbornik*, one of the most popular liberal journals of the reform era.[64]

Yet Russians' anxieties about Muslims' "political trustworthiness" would not go away. The Russian experience in the Crimean War and the Caucasus left a deep suspicion of Muslims among the ruling elite. These anxieties became stronger in the mid-1870s, as the Balkan people's struggle for independence from the Ottoman empire reached its peak. This movement stimulated pro-Slavic sentiments in Russia that were influential in convincing Alexander II to embark on a new military conflict with the Ottoman empire—the Russo-Turkish War of 1877–1878. Again, as during the Crimean War, rumors circulated about Tatars' "hostile mood" toward Russians, challenging the public order as well as recent government attempts to transform it. In the Volga region, the heads of the Simbirsk and Kazan gendarmerie, however, could find no proof behind these rumors and reported that the Tatar population was tranquil.

It was the rumors that "incited one nationality against another," rather than actual "Tatar political reliability," that concerned the Orenburg governor-general, N. A. Kryzhanovskii. In 1877, in response to his concerns, the Ministry of Internal Affairs requested that censors and editors in Moscow refrain from publishing news about the "hostile mood of the Muslim population of our eastern and southern provinces toward the Russian population and about alleged hostile clashes and collisions."[65] At the same time, reports about the "tranquility of the population and its submission to the government" no longer seemed to be enough. In 1877, the head of the Simbirsk gendarmerie, F. M. von Bradke, reported that although there had not been any serious movement among the Tatars of Simbirsk province, he could not guarantee their devotion to Russia were there to be a war with Turkey. "Tatar people," he wrote, "have been conquered by Russia since time immemorial, but they remain the same Tatars as they were a long time ago, with the same fanaticism of their faith." In his opinion, in a situation of aggravated interempire competition, the cultural differences between Muslims and Russians could turn out to be politically dangerous for the state.[66]

The Lasting Legacy of the Crimean War

Russia's experience of the Crimean War and its aftermath thus played a crucial role in bringing the empire's Muslim subjects, and the problems of empire more generally, to the center of public and government attention. Neither rumors about Muslim hostility to Russians nor concerns about Muslims' trustworthiness were entirely new, given the long history of the empire's multiconfessional society. What was new, though, was the way that these issues were reconceptualized in the wake of the conflict. Only after the Crimean War did Russian educated society and the government "discover," and then become increasingly concerned about, what many came to perceive as the alienation of Crimean and Kazan Tatars. As one commentator noted, Tatars lived with Russians as "random roommates" (*sluchainye sokvartiranty*), not entering into "close relations as is expected from citizens of the same fatherland."[67] The reported cases of Muslims' "treason" during the Crimean War and the mass emigration to Turkey seemed to substantiate this view.

The reformist spirit of the 1860s challenged the existing model of imperial governance, which privileged stability over social transformation, relied on cooperation with loyal Muslim elites, and used military force to suppress undesirable rumors or relocate "troubled" Muslim communities from the borderlands. In contrast, reform-minded Russians saw Muslims as a "useful" population that could contribute to the country's economic development and, if successfully integrated, could strengthen Russia's image as a modern imperial power. Thus, reform-era ideas about the wider integration of a heterogeneous empire into a united whole reoriented imperial governance toward the goals of enlightenment and rapprochement of the supposedly alienated Muslims with Russians.

Yet, as the discussion of the reasons for Muslims' untrustworthiness and alienation demonstrated, the policy of integration faced some constraints. By so closely connecting faith with political allegiance, this discussion crystallized the problematic issue of Russia as an Orthodox state governing a multiconfessional empire. Those Russians who associated Orthodoxy with Russian patriotism and imperial mission drove Muslims into an intrinsic alien position that was only fortified by anxieties related to another military campaign against Turkey and Muslim popular resistance to the reforms. The continuous military expansion of the empire and the forceful inclusion of new Muslim peoples into the state, first in the Caucasus and later in Central Asia, presented a challenge to the goals of imperial integration while also intensifying some Russians' fears of Islam. These constraints shaped the way problems related to Muslims and the goals of Russian policies were articulated in late imperial Russia. The problem of Muslims' perceived alienation was an especially acute issue in the Crimea and Volga regions, since the major modernizing projects of the reform era were extended to these territories, thus including local Muslims in the empire's transforming core. But it was also there, in the Volga region, that Muslims had a long history of being a part of the empire's confessional order with the Orthodox church as a predominant confession. To understand the implications of this experience for Russians' understanding of the Muslim Question, we need to discuss how educated Russians responded to another serious challenge—the "apostasy" of Orthodox converts to Islam.

2 The Challenges of Apostasy to Islam

In the period immediately after the emancipation of the serfs, when government policies embraced both the integration of Muslims and the larger project of modernization, Russians received a new blow. Thousands of baptized Tatars in Kazan province renounced their affiliation with Orthodoxy and petitioned to be officially recognized as Muslims. Reaching its peak in 1866, the so-called apostasy movement spread to neighboring provinces and involved other non-Russian communities, both baptized and animists. In the changing political context of a Russian empire shaken by defeat in the Crimean War and the Polish rebellion of 1863, and simultaneously challenged by its victories in the Caucasus and Central Asia, the problem of apostasy took on new meaning. It helped Russians to "discover" that, having been subjects of the Russian tsars for three hundred years, the Muslims of the eastern provinces of European Russia continued to preserve their religion, language, and culture and had successfully resisted outside (Russian Orthodox) influences. Viewed in the new political atmosphere, the cultural "isolation" of the empire's borderland people seemed politically dangerous. Moreover, Islam suddenly appeared to be a vigorous rival to the state church, a dynamic force successfully drawing the surrounding population into its orbit and challenging the reformist premises of the government plan for modernization within the established framework of the empire.

Apostasy to Islam, as well as church and government efforts to combat it, has been the subject of several studies that approach these issues from the perspective of local identity politics and imperial governance in the Volga–Ural region.[1] Yet Russian responses to apostasy deserve more attention because of the role they played in conceptualizing the Muslim Question, and hence, the ways state policies toward Muslims were reformulated in late imperial Russia. Educated Russians within and outside the government sought to understand Islam's appeal to both the baptized and the animists. This chapter examines how Russian answers to this question illuminate shifting visions of apostasy and Islam and additionally highlight tensions that underlined reformist efforts within the imperial context. As recent studies have demonstrated, the challenge of apostasy made educated Russians increasingly hostile to Islam.[2] In paying attention to local circumstances as well as to the changing imperial context, this chapter suggests that the new vision of Islam was neither entirely negative nor unanimously accepted by church and state authorities.

A Shifting Vision of Apostasy and a New Understanding of Islam

The issue of "apostates from Orthodoxy," or, as it was also called, the problem of "recalcitrants" (*uporstvuiushchie*), emerged as a result of Russia's confessional and imperial policies. As the predominant state church, Russian Orthodoxy was the only religion permitted to proselytize within the empire's borders.[3] According to Russian law, once baptized into Orthodoxy, new converts and their descendants were not permitted to change their confessional affiliation. Attempts to leave the Orthodox church were identified as apostasy. The relevant law viewed apostasy as a temporary delusion, while an invitation to apostasy ("seduction") was considered a criminal offense.

As the empire expanded, starting in the sixteenth century, church and state authorities attempted to use conversion to Orthodoxy as an instrument of imperial governance and integration, thus significantly enlarging Russia's official Orthodox community. At the same time, from the late eighteenth century, Russian rulers embraced religious tolerance and official recognition of major non-Orthodox confessions as a means of integrating its subjects into the empire. As the result, the dominant Orthodox church found itself in a situation of rivalry with the officially tolerated confessions, while simultaneously facing the difficulty of maintaining minority converts' loyalties. This situation emerged in the empire's western borderlands, where the Orthodox church confronted Catholicism and Protestantism. The main stage for the Orthodox—Islamic rivalry was in the eastern provinces of European Russia, home to the first significant group of Turkic-speaking Muslims subjugated to Russian rule.[4]

The Christianization of Muslim and animist groups of the Volga region was launched following the conquest of the Kazan khanate in 1552; however, it had never been consistently enforced. The state and the church relied on both force and material incentives, such as tax and military exemptions, as well as grants of clothing and money to increase the numbers of converts.[5] At the same time, indigenous uprisings and pragmatic policy considerations forced tsarist authorities to seek different ways of attempting imperial integration and governance. The reign of Catherine II (1762–1796) marked an especially significant change in the state's views and policies toward Islam.[6] Guided by the ideas of the Enlightenment and hoping to secure the sympathies of her Muslim subjects, especially after the E. Pugachev rebellion of 1773–1775, Catherine halted aggressive Christianization in the Volga region.[7] In 1764, the Office of New Converts (a special baptism commission established in 1731 and reorganized in 1740) was closed, and privileges for new converts were eventually abolished. In 1799, the special missionary positions were abolished, and the newly baptized were entrusted to the care of village priests. Catherine also allowed Russian Muslims to open mosques and confessional schools. In 1788, she created the Ecclesiastical Assembly of the Mohammedan Creed (muftiate) in Ufa (*Ufimskoe dukhovnoe magometanskogo zakona sobranie*), later the Orenburg

Mohammedan Ecclesiastical Assembly, thus extending the state regulation of religious life to Islam. This strategy secured the loyalty of the empire's Muslim subjects and provided favorable conditions for further imperial expansion to the East.[8]

The conversions of earlier periods had created baptized communities of Finnic- and Turkic-speaking populations in the Volga region. The new converts presented the Orthodox church with the challenge of keeping these groups within the organization. Orthodox clerics expressed concern about this issue soon after missionary activity began in the Volga region. As early as 1593, the head of the Kazan diocese, Metropolitan Germogen, complained to Tsar Fedor about the state of the diocese:

> In the Kazan and Sviiazhsk districts the new converts live among Tatars, Chuvash, Cheremis [Mari], and Votiaks [Udmurts]; eat and drink with them; don't go to church, don't wear crosses and don't have icons; don't invite the priests into their houses and don't have confessors . . . don't baptize their children . . . don't bury the deceased in the Orthodox cemeteries. . . . After getting married in a church, they are remarried by a Tatar priest [mullah].[9]

He also complained about some Russians who had married non-Christians and converted to Islam. Throughout the eighteenth century the chief Orthodox clerics from Kazan voiced similar complaints.[10]

By the early nineteenth century, the state and the church faced mass petitions for permission to revert to Islam. These efforts usually coincided with the accession of a new emperor to the throne and/or periods of liberalization.[11] Since leaving the Orthodox church was expressly forbidden by law, petitions asking for permission to renounce Orthodox status were routinely turned down by state officials, and priests were dispatched to tend to would-be apostates. The first open mass apostasy occurred in 1802, when newly converted Tatar communities in the Kazan diocese submitted petitions to the tsar, asking permission to be formally recognized as Muslims.[12] In spring and summer 1827, several thousand Tatars from the Volga region submitted a new round of petitions, provoked in this instance by a rumor that the state was now ready to look favorably on these requests.[13] In their petitions, the baptized Tatars justified their requests by claiming that their ancestors' baptisms had either been carried out by force or in exchange for privileges. Some petitioners denied outright that their ancestors had ever been baptized, arguing that their registration in the Orthodox community was the result of mistakes made by local clergy. At the same time, the petitioners were careful to stress that their desire to be registered as Muslims did not diminish their loyalty to the tsar.[14] As in earlier cases, however, the petitions were rejected by the government.

As Paul Werth has demonstrated, the Russian authorities who dealt with the converts' petitions in the 1820s appear to have had little interest in Islam per se.[15] They saw Islam merely as the former religion of the baptized Tatars, and tended to characterize the wish for apostasy as either delusion or superstition. They categorized Islam as similar to animism—the former belief system of the baptized Mari,

Chuvash, and Udmurt peoples who also lived in the Volga region. To correct this situation, the Holy Synod called for the development of missionary activity to target the baptized Tatars.[16]

Following the recommendation of Kazan Archbishop Filaret (Amfiteatrov), a special mission was created in 1830 in the Kazan diocese, but it failed to stop apostasy.[17] The government attempted to root out the problem by resettling apostates in Orthodox villages, but this measure, too, was unsuccessful. Without land or financial support for resettled people, the settlers often scattered; authorities put a halt to the measure in 1841.[18] Meanwhile, the authorities uncovered more apostates in the 1840s. In part, this was because in 1841 the Synod introduced new regulations for the ecclesiastical consistories, according to which the diocese authorities had to be notified about all of the parishioners who had not come for confession for more than two or three years.[19] In 1844, church authorities listed 4,448 apostates in the Spassk and Chistopol districts in Kazan province, a fact that led to the perception that the newly baptized Tatars were in a state of "general revolt" in these districts.[20]

Throughout the reign of Nicholas I (1825–1855), when order and conformity in the religious sphere was a goal of the state's confessional policy, the so-called "religious–moral condition" of these convert groups became a subject of increased attention in clerical and government circles. Pressed by the need to restore religious discipline and order in the eastern borderland, the Nikolaevan state created institutions that addressed the problem of apostasy. One of the most important of these institutions, in terms of redefining apostasy as well as the church's and government's approaches to the Muslim community, was the Kazan Theological Academy, which was reestablished in 1842.[21]

In 1844, the academy began to teach four languages of eastern non-Christian peoples: Turkish-Tatar, Arabic, Mongolian, and Kalmyk.[22] The Kazan University professors A. K. Kazem-Bek (professor of Tatar and Arabic) and A. V. Popov (professor of Mongolian and Kalmyk) were invited to train language instructors for the academy.[23] N. I. Il'minskii (1821–1891), a priest's son from Penza, was among Kazem-Bek's first eleven students.[24] After graduating in 1846, he was hired by the academy to teach the Tatar and Arabic languages.

To understand apostasy and to develop measures to combat it, the Kazan diocese administration turned to the academy for help. In 1848 and 1849, the archbishop of Kazan, Grigorii (Postnikov), dispatched Il'minskii to the villages of the Kazan province involved in the "revolt" to determine the reasons for their apostasy.[25] Il'minskii traveled dressed like a Tatar and took notes in Tatar and Russian, using shorthand German script.[26] The unofficial nature of this trip (it was presented as a scholarly expedition for the study of the Tatar language, which in fact coincided with Il'minskii's academic interests) and Il'minskii's knowledge of the Tatar language and Islam made it possible for him to see the Tatar communities in a new light.[27]

Typically, authorities received information about baptized Tatars through official channels, from court cases and reports from civil authorities and Orthodox clergy.[28] In contrast, Il'minskii, drawing on his field observations and an archival study of the apostasy cases, presented a new kind of report—an ethnographic survey of the Tatars' religious life in the Kazan region. This information was included in his proposal for a Tatar mission, which was drafted in 1849 in conjunction with ongoing discussions about opening missionary divisions at the Kazan Theological Academy.[29] In evaluating the religious condition of the baptized Tatars, Il'minskii divided them into two groups: the "old converts" (*starokreshchenye*) and the "new converts" (*novokreshchenye*). The former had been baptized in the period between the conquest of Kazan and 1740, when the Office of New Converts was opened. At the time of Il'minskii's observations, the majority of these "old converts" either lived among Russians or in separate villages. These conditions, in his opinion, meant that this group of baptized Tatars had become "almost completely accustomed to Russian ways and to Christianity." By contrast, the "new converts" who converted after 1740 and lived with Muslims, demonstrated far less devotion to Christianity. Many secretly performed Islamic rituals and lived a Muslim way of life.[30] Without fail, it was these "new converts" who initiated the apostasy petitions.

In Il'minskii's opinion, the fact that the religious conditions of the baptized Tatars were heavily influenced by external factors, such as where they lived and the relative proximity of neighboring Muslims, was clear proof that these Tatars, despite their conversions, had never become true (*ubezhdennymi*) Christians. Il'minskii noted that in many cases Tatars who converted to Christianity did so not out of a sense of conviction but rather to gain material privileges. Nor did they receive a proper Christian education following their baptism. For their part, their priests cared only about the external (*vneshnii*) side of the faith. They demanded that Tatars not wear skullcaps, and that they wear crosses, perform the sign of the cross, attend church, keep fasting rituals, and perform occasional religious rites, which also imposed an economic burden on the parishioners. For these reasons, Il'minskii concluded that the "apostasy of the new converts was a natural development that deserved to be met with regret and concern rather than blame."[31]

Il'minskii's observations presented a new understanding of apostasy because they drew attention to religious conviction (*ubezhdenie*) as an important aspect of faith. Hence, to solve the problem of apostasy, Il'minskii proposed not punishment but rather the opening of a mission that would transform already baptized Tatars into sincerely convinced Christians.

Along with a new vision of apostasy, Il'minskii proposed a different understanding of Islam. To understand the nature of this shift, we need to consider Il'minskii's personal explanation of his interest in Islamic studies. In his recollections about his former language instructors at the Kazan Theological Academy, Il'minskii remarked on how his acquaintance with Muslim scholars challenged his perception of Tatars and Islam:

I should admit that what interested me was not the Tatar language but rather Professor A. K. Kazem-Bek; I ran into him several times on the street—dressed in original costume, lively, elegant; and I was happy to see him up close and listen to him. . . .
To help with our homework, A. K. promised to send a Tatar tutor, and so one day a Tatar came to our class—a handsome, slender, and rather tall young man, dressed in a *kazakin* [a short caftan] with trousers worn over the boots and no skullcap. . . .
During my childhood in Penza, I had only seen Tatars from the window—they were village people, poor, on skinny horses and during a fair . . . petty tradesmen; . . .
they left no positive impression on me. And suddenly now I see a Tatar of a different sort. This was Makhmudov. He explained Arabic grammar to us. I had heard about Tatar literacy and about literate Tatars before but did not expect them to be so well educated.
I asked Makhmudov: "Did you study at a gymnasium?"
"No," he said.
"In a district school [*uezdnoe uchilishche*]?"
"No."
"Where did you study the grammar?"
"We have our own Tatar schools, and there are few of them in Kazan."
This news utterly amazed me. Makhmudov left us with [an] absolutely pleasant impression.[32]

Il'minskii also observed the power of religious conviction among Muslim believers. Accordingly, he redefined the image of Islam as a vital spiritual force and a serious rival of Orthodoxy.

In 1847, Il'minskii moved into Kazan's Tatar quarter, where he attended a higher Islamic school.[33] His next opportunity to learn about Tatar life and improve his language skills firsthand came in 1848–1849, when Kazan Archbishop Grigorii sent him to Tatar villages to study the apostasy movement. On these trips, Il'minskii had opportunities to talk with Muslims rather than with baptized Tatars who were suspicious of him.[34] The Kazan archbishop also made it possible for him to travel to Egypt and Syria in 1851–1853, where he studied the languages and religion of the Muslim world, and also learned about the state of Orthodoxy and Western Christian missions in Muslim lands.[35] Upon his return, Il'minskii submitted a report to the academy that included his reflections on Islam. He also returned with a collection of books on Islam for the academy's library.[36]

In 1854, with the energetic support of the Kazan archbishop, the Kazan Theological Academy opened missionary divisions against the schism in the Orthodox church (*raskol*), Buddhism, Islam, and animist religions of the Cheremis (Mari) and the Chuvash.[37] Missionary divisions against the Church schism were also established in the three other Russian theological academies.[38] Although missionary divisions against non-Christian beliefs were particular to the Kazan Academy, it was the struggle against the Church schism, rather than Islam, that preoccupied the leadership of the academy and the diocese, as well as the highest ecclesiastical authorities in St. Petersburg.[39]

The anti-Islam and anti-Buddhist divisions were primarily established to train teachers for seminaries and missionaries for dioceses that served non-Russian and non-Christian populations. The curriculum of these divisions included local languages and beliefs, history, ethnography, and missionary pedagogy.[40] After his trip to the Middle East, Il'minskii was hired by the academy's anti-Islam division. Il'minskii taught both Islam and the polemic against it. After getting to know Muslims during his trips to Tatar villages and abroad, however, he considered the polemic against Islam to be ineffective and therefore he focused his instruction on the teaching of Islam and its written sources.[41]

The position of the new anti-Islam division and its professors at the academy, however, was uncertain. The employment of missionary graduates was a persistent problem, given that only a few ecclesiastical seminaries had special missionary divisions, parish priest positions were poorly paid, and special missionary positions did not exist. The anti-Muslim division thus had a hard time attracting students.[42] In addition, anti-Muslim subjects were given the status of a facultative specialization, and were vulnerable to frequent bureaucratic reforms.[43]

The challenges facing the work of the missionary division were addressed by two professors at the academy, Il'minskii and G. S. Sablukov (a specialist in Oriental languages and Islam), in a report written in 1858 in response to the Holy Synod's request for information about measures to be taken against the apostasy of baptized Tatars.[44] As had been the case with the 1849 mission project, the 1858 report by Il'minskii and Sablukov argued that apostasy stemmed from the "mechanical" nature of the Tatars' baptism and the fact that this baptism had not been followed by a true "internal" conversion. But unlike the previous project, the new report also stressed the influence of "Muslim propaganda" on the baptized Tatars, and presented Islam and Muslims as a *serious* threat to Christianity. The report pointed to the Tatars' strong devotion to their religion, which they sought to spread among non-Muslim people through the work of religious schools, mosques, and mullahs.[45] In order to strengthen Christianity among the baptized Tatars, Il'minskii and Sablukov recommended a two-pronged approach, on the one hand suggesting the development of a program of Christian education for the convert communities, and, on the other hand, placing restrictions on the influence of Muslim propaganda.[46] In its missionary plan, the report assigned a special role to graduates of the anti-Islam division. To utilize their professional skills, the report suggested establishing missionary divisions at the seminaries under the supervision of the Kazan Theological Academy.[47] Addressing the current unsatisfactory state of Tatar language instruction at the seminaries, the report noted:

> The Tatar language is currently considered nothing more than a local language, i.e., a dialect [*narechie*] of national minorities, whose faith is limited to a few vague and incomplete legends, and almost all of whom are baptized. However, because of their large population, the distinctness and the strict exclusivity of their faith, preserved in written sources, persistent disposition to Islam, variety of Tatar dialects . . . inner

religious unity . . . and the presence among them of many military and civil officials, landowners, merchants of the first guild and learned mullahs, the Tatars deserve greater attention of the Orthodox clergy.[48]

Nevertheless, neither the call for greater attention to Islam nor Il'minskii's new vision of the Muslim community did much to change the academy's focus on Church schism or its dismissive view of Islam. The academy's new rector, Ioann (Sokolov) (1857–1864), did not favor the missionary divisions. He found the curriculum of the anti-Islam division too broad and suspected Il'minskii himself of what he called "Islamic propaganda." He considered the serious study of Islam as both absurd and a needless distraction that interfered with the essential goal of the division, which was, in his view, "to teach students how to convert Muslims into Christians, not to turn Islam into a system."[49] Archbishop Afanasii (Sokolov) (1856–1866) shared the same views. Neither Ioann nor Afanasii could imagine that Islam deserved serious attention and thought that Il'minskii simply "exaggerated its strength."[50]

During an exam at the academy in 1857 when students were asked to analyze Muslim teaching, Afanasii demanded that the students tell him directly how to disprove certain points of Islamic teaching, instead of describing to him how Tatars themselves proved these points. Il'minskii tried to defend his students by explaining that "Muslims have their own argumentation which they persistently adhere to, and that the most definite and direct, from our [Christian] standpoint, counter-evidence is absolutely powerless," but this response only further angered the archbishop.[51]

In Nicholaevan Russia, civil and church authorities viewed the issue of apostasy from Orthodoxy to Islam as part of the larger problem of religious dissent, akin to issues presented by the Old Believers or other Russian "indigenous" Christian groups (such as the Dukhobors, Khlysty, Molokans, Skoptsy, and Subbotniks) who had broken away from the state-sponsored Orthodox church.[52] The official labels assigned to these groups were problematic, as Old Believers considered themselves to be the true practitioners of Orthodoxy, and so-called sectarians believed that they practiced true Christianity, while apostates to Islam claimed that they were true Muslims. Since conformity in religion was as important to Nicholas as conformity in politics, the question of apostasy from Orthodoxy to Islam was taken up by a Special Committee for the Affairs of Schismatics and Apostates from Orthodoxy. In 1855, the committee instructed the Kazan Consistory to implement a series of harsh measures, including transferring the children of apostates to a custodial board until their parents returned to Orthodoxy, limiting rights associated with the baptized Tatars' social status, and separating wives from husbands if the apostates refused to have an Orthodox wedding ceremony. In 1861, however, confronted with the persistent resistance of the Tatars, the government was forced to stop the implementation of these measures.[53] The period of Great Reforms also marked a broader shift in state policy toward religious dissenters. Alexander II (1855–1881) halted the activities of the Special Committee and the government developed a series of measures aimed to ease some restrictions on Schismatics, hoping to integrate them more successfully into the empire's legal and social order.[54] Nor did the policy of force in relation to religious beliefs in general correspond with the views of the new Minister of the Internal Affairs, P. A. Valuev (1861–1868), who was a proponent of religious toleration.[55]

This shift in official attitude toward religious matters seemed to resonate with Il'minskii's new perspective on the problem of apostasy. In contrast to a requirement to fulfill Christian obligations under pressure of punishment, Il'minskii emphasized internal conversion as a means of fostering Orthodox identity among baptized non-Russians. His attempts to draw the attention of the local church authorities and the academy's leadership to Islam as a serious and vital spiritual force essentially failed, along with his efforts to strengthen the academy's anti-Islam division (which meant professionalization of missionary activities). In 1858, he left the academy for a brief period to serve as an interpreter for the Orenburg Frontier Commission. In 1861, he was hired by the Ministry of Education to assume the newly restored chair of Turkish–Tatar languages at Kazan University, and in early 1870s he left the academy for good.[56] Yet, his vision of and concerns about Islam acquired heightened relevance and reinterpretation within the government and among a broader public in the new social and psychological atmosphere of the post-emancipation period.

The Crisis of Apostasy in the Context of the Reform Era

Along with the gradual government retreat in counteracting apostasy by means of coercion, the reforms of the 1860s set the apostasy issue into a different context. The decentralization of the administration of state peasants and the introduction of judicial statute which considerably limited administrative interventions created conditions that simplified the apostasy but also made it more difficult for the baptized Tatars to maintain their minority status vis-à-vis their Muslim neighbors.[57] Under these more relaxed conditions, apostasy consequently spread across large areas of Kazan and its neighboring provinces by the late 1860s. Entire Tatar villages reverted to Islam. The apostasy movement at this time involved not only "new converts," but "old converts" as well. The wave of apostasy to Islam also affected formerly animist communities, especially the Chuvash and Udmurts. Rumors spread through villages, stating that it was now permissible to practice Islam, and Tatars filed petitions requesting permission to live according to "the belief of [their] fathers." In their petitions, Tatars claimed that even though they were registered as Orthodox, they had practiced Islam for generations and therefore were not apostates from Orthodoxy, but true Muslims.[58] As in the past, the petitions were rejected.[59]

Local civilian authorities refrained from ascribing any serious political significance to these apostasies, viewing them instead as disturbances of social order caused by individuals spreading senseless rumors. For example, files related to one apostasy case in the Kazan district noted that after the Kazan vice governor announced that the tsar had rejected the petition, the Tatars refused to acknowledge the tsar's decision; nevertheless, they agreed to fulfill other state obligations not related to religion.[60] Given that local administrators' principal concern was to re-establish order as quickly as possible, their response usually amounted to finding and then exiling those whom they regarded as instigators of the troubles, and taking promises from the apostates to return to Orthodoxy: that is, to baptize their children and perform Orthodox burial and wedding ceremonies. Mullahs were requested to promise not to perform Muslim rites among the baptized. These measures were not always successful; apostates refused to identify instigators, did not allow priests to conduct missionary work, and refused to promise to return to Orthodoxy. Apostates also doubted that their petitions were rejected by the tsar.[61]

In 1866, Il'minskii, as an expert in the Tatar language, accompanied the Kazan vice governor, E. A. Rozov, on an investigative trip to the apostate villages of Kazan province. The goal of the trip was to announce the tsar's rejection of the apostates' petitions and to convince Tatars to return to Orthodoxy. For Il'minskii, the trip presented an opportunity to explain the apostasy movement to local civil authorities, and eventually to gain their support for his missionary program. In his report, Rozov echoed Il'minskii's views by saying that "it was necessary for 'new converts' to live as Christians not only in name but also in spirit."[62]

In order to turn the baptized non-Russians into "true Christians," Il'minskii suggested emphasizing not "external" baptism but rather a Christian upbringing based on systematic measures that would apply to all baptized but not openly "apostasized" non-Russians.[63] The essence of what was later called the "Il'minskii system" was the religious instruction of children in their native languages with the help of native missionaries, priests, and teachers. The development of this system took place during a time when the Russian government and public was engaged with the question of how to reform the empire's basic social and administrative institutions. Ideas about conscious piety and religious understanding also informed plans for the modernization of the Orthodox church that had been put forth during the era of Great Reforms.[64] But in light of the Muslim threat, the practical realization of these ideas seemed to be most urgent among the non-Russian converts who, borrowing Paul Werth's term, were located "at the margins of Orthodoxy."[65]

The culmination of apostasy in the late 1860s helped Il'minskii draw the attention of the government and public to his missionary projects. The most important of these programs saw the creation of schools for baptized non-Russian minorities. The first of these was the Kazan School for Baptized Tatars, which opened in 1863 when a baptized Tatar, V. Timofeev, who had taught conversational Tatar at the Kazan Theological Academy, undertook the religious instruction of a group of Tatar boys. The next year, Il'minskii received permission to open a private school. Through Rozov, his undertaking gained the interest of the Kazan governor.[66] Il'minskii's efforts also received the support of Kazan's new archbishop, Antonii (Amfiteatrov) (1866–1879), and the curator of the Kazan educational district, P. D. Shestakov.

D. Karakozov's attempt to assassinate the emperor in 1866 stimulated patriotic and religious feelings among Russians, and as a consequence private donations to the school increased.[67] In 1866, the Minister of Education and the Holy Synod ober-procurator, D. A. Tolstoy, visited the school. In 1867, the Brotherhood of St. Gurii (*Bratstvo sviatitelia Guriia*), which included many local religious figures and educators was founded in Kazan; one of its functions was to raise funds for Il'minskii's efforts.[68] Between 1868 and 1870, the school received visits from the tsar's family. These visits brought new donations and more publicity to the school. The Kazan School for Baptized Tatars served as a model for other schools opened for the non-Russian peoples of the Volga region.

Il'minskii paid special attention to the use of colloquial variants of native languages. He modified the Cyrillic alphabet with diacritical marks to create an effective means to communicate Christian ideas to non-Russians while breaking their connection with the written Islamic culture.[69] In 1862, he published a Tatar-language primer (*bukvar'*), translated according to the new system. In 1869, the first liturgy in the Tatar language was served in Kazan. The St. Gurii Brotherhood took responsibility for religious translations, and in 1876 they opened a special translation commission, chaired by Il'minskii.

Linked to the question of translation was another important element of Il'minskii's system—the use of native priests. He explained the need for non-Russians: "A Russian, unless he possesses a deep ethnographic knowledge . . . is not able fully to accommodate himself to *inorodtsy,* even if he speaks their language. . . . But what is difficult for a Russian, unless he has special training, is given to an *inorodets* by nature."[70] Both Archbishop Antonii and the Holy Synod Ober-Procurator Tolstoy favored Il'minskii's suggestion to ordain non-Russian priests, and in 1867 the Holy Synod ruled favorably on this issue, permitting non-Russians to be ordained and exempting them from the obligatory requirement of a seminary education.[71]

The official and public support for Il'minskii's missionary efforts was accompanied by rising social and governmental anxieties about Islam. As we have seen, Il'minskii and other missionary experts on Islam from the Kazan Academy challenged the dismissive attitude held by most local clerics toward Islam as a religious delusion, and instead proposed a new perspective on it as a vital religious worldview based on developed theology and a social force that deserved serious attention. Yet the task of the missionary study of Islam was to understand Islam in order to combat it. The missionaries' evaluation of Islam as a religious ideology was polemical in nature and was based on a critique of the injunctions of the Koran. In their study of Islam as an ideology, missionaries arrived with the assumption that Muhammad was a false prophet and that the Koran was only supposedly divine.[72] Viewed from a confessional standpoint, Islam was not only a false religion, but an anti-Christian one as well.

Difficulties involving cases of Muslim conversion to Christianity, and especially the continuing march of conversions from Orthodoxy and animism to Islam, gave credence to a view of Islam as an "unyielding" (*nepoddatlivaia*) religion and of

Muslims themselves as "the most stubborn enemies of Christianity."[73] The apostasy of 1866 generated fears among missionaries and some church figures that all the non-Russians in the Volga region would turn to Islam. On a local level, the reform of self-government weakened the center's degree of control and seemed to empower Muslim communities and their clerics vis-à-vis their Orthodox counterparts. Seeing this development as advantageous for Muslim propaganda, Orthodox missionaries and church officials urged the government to limit the supposedly growing strength of Islam.

The dismissive attitude of local church authorities toward Islam changed under new Archbishop Antonii, who placed the issue of Islam in the Volga region in a larger imperial perspective. Before coming to Kazan in 1866, Antonii had spent twenty-four years in Kiev and then in Smolensk, where he had served in a series of prominent posts, including as rector of the Kiev Theological Academy and as bishop of Smolensk.[74] Thus, he was in the western provinces during the time of the 1863 Polish rebellion. If transferring from Kiev to Smolensk represented, as Antonii himself admitted, a move from "a similar to similar,"[75] a transfer to Kazan was different. As he wrote to a correspondent in Kiev shortly after his move, "Yes! It was easier to imagine being carried away to Kiev from Smolensk. There, I had the Dnieper flowing to Kiev in front of my eyes. Here, the Volga flows in a different direction. . . ."[76] In another letter from Kazan, he noted that "it is often sad for me to see more mosques than churches, even though there are fewer Muslims here than Orthodox."[77] Antonii's arrival in Kazan shortly after a large wave of apostasy had hit the Kazan diocese led him to see similarities in Kazan, Kiev, and Smolensk. He discovered in Islam a force similar to the Catholic threat that he had known from his service in the western provinces.

In 1867, Antonii presented a report to the Holy Synod that drew attention to the rising strength of the "Mohammedanian spirit" (*magometanskii dukh*) in the Kazan region, whose main sources of support, he believed, were the mullahs and mosques.[78] The archbishop compared "Mohammedanism" in the eastern part of the empire to "Latinism" (Roman Catholicism) in the western provinces, and argued that apostasy to Islam was harmful for both the church and the state. Antonii criticized the state's toleration policy toward Islam, which he believed contributed to strengthening of Islam vis-à-vis Orthodoxy, and called upon state authorities to take restrictive measures with respect to Muslim institutions. Antonii's call for harsh measures toward Islam, however, did not find support among the Ministry of Internal Affairs officials in St. Petersburg. One of the recipients of the report was A. K. Kazem-Bek, the prominent Orientalist in Kazan and then St. Petersburg and the advisor on Muslim affairs at the Department for Religious Affairs of Foreign Confessions. Kazem-Bek disagreed with most of the archbishop's concerns and expressed hope that the government would continue to exercise caution in its relations with Muslims.[79] Nor did the department's director, E. K. Sievers, support Antonii's later demands to apply repressive measures against apostates.[80]

While the MVD officials discouraged Orthodox clergy from relying on repressive measures in religious matters, the press helped local anxieties about Islam reach the broader reading public. The issue of apostasy to Islam as an imperial and hence political problem was publicly addressed by the famous journalist M. N. Katkov. In 1867, Katkov's editorial in *Moskovskie vedomosti* spoke of the "rising spirit of Islam" in Kazan province, a dangerous development that, he claimed, presented a threat to the unity of the Russian state. Katkov blamed the Russian government for not being national (*beznarodnost' vlasti*) and acting instead as what he described as a Tatar Muslim government in the eastern provinces, but also as a German and Polish government in the Baltic and western borderlands. He argued that the government should be Russian by nationality and not give official (and thus political) recognition to non-Russian institutions.[81] In relation to the eastern borderlands, he was essentially providing a critique of what local missionaries came to see as the state's patronizing of Muslim institutions. For Katkov, non-Orthodox beliefs could and had to be deprived of political meaning and combined with the concept of Russian political nationality. It was, however, Katkov's powerful image of the "flaming center of Islam," rather than the idea of the compatibility of Islam with Russian citizenship, that captured the imagination of many Russian readers and was borrowed and further circulated by Orthodox critics.[82]

The problems related to Orthodox mission, apostasy, and Islam were picked up by the new clerical journals that appeared as a result of increased public interest in matters of the church and the revival of clerical journalism in the 1860s. These journals—including *Strannik* in St. Petersburg, *Pravoslavnoe obozrenie* and *Dushepoleznoe chtenie* in Moscow, and *Rukovodstvo dlia sel'skikh pastyrei* in Kiev— were not isolated clerical organs. They were all characterized by their editors' aspirations to turn them into vital (*zhivoi*) organs by raising relevant questions of Russia's social and church life. They were modeled after secular journals, often republished articles from them, and counted lay Russians among their contributors and readers.

In 1869, the Kazan Theological Academy received a new charter, modeled after the liberal University Statute of 1863, that broadened the scholarly and pedagogical freedoms of the academy's professors and introduced new principles affecting the academy's journal, *Pravoslavnyi sobesednik*.[83] The new charter invited the entire academic community to publish by giving them a great degree of freedom in issuing their own works.[84] From the 1870s on, the journal significantly increased its attention to Islam and missions against non-Christians. The authors were often former or current academy professors of anti-Islam subjects.[85] With their new-found independence, the editors widened the journal's editorial perspective and began to address vital issues of the day that found resonance among the broader Russian society. Increasingly, these issues related to the question of the role and place of Muslims, and non-Russians more generally, in the Russian empire.[86]

In 1881, during the accession of Alexander III to the throne after Alexander II's assassination, entire villages of "old converts" refused to take an oath of allegiance as Orthodox subjects.[87] In the new political climate, such actions appeared especially hostile to the state and led some among high-ranking state officials to criticize the government's approach to apostasy and Islam as too lenient. Among those was the new ober-procurator of the Holy Synod, K. P. Pobedonostsev (1880–1905), who believed that the recognition of apostates as Muslims would strengthen Islam vis-à-vis Orthodoxy and advocated the state's support for the church in its struggle against Islam.[88] To many, including Pobedonostsev, the apostasy was not simply a religious issue but a serious political problem.

This perspective was publicly articulated in 1883 by B. M. Iuzefovich (1843–1911), who took it upon himself to formulate, or as he put it, "raise in a correct way," the Muslim Question. The apostasy problem was at the center of his understanding of this issue. Iuzefovich had begun his career in the Vilna military district during the time of the 1863 Polish rebellion and had spent most of his life in the western provinces. In 1880–1881, he participated in the official inspection of the Kazan and Ufa provinces led by Senator M. E. Kovalevskii. On Kovalevskii's request, Iuzefovich prepared a report about the "schooling and alien questions" of the eastern borderlands. Katkov, whose periodicals paid special attention to the non-Russian borderlands, grew interested in this report, which he published in *Russkii vestnik* in 1883 under the title "Khristianstvo, magometanstvo i iazychestvo v vostochnykh guberniiakh" (Christianity, Mohammedanism, and Paganism in the Eastern Provinces). This article, in turn, attracted the attention of Pobedonostsev, who invited Iuzefovich to serve in the Holy Synod under his supervision.[89]

In his article, Iuzefovich argued that the enduring problem of apostasy in the eastern provinces testified to the "fanatical hostility of Muslims toward Christians." He warned that Muslim propaganda and thus the Muslim Question itself could become politicized through the changing geography of the empire: the expansion of the Russian empire in Central Asia, the Islamicization of the Kirgiz (Kazakh) steppe, and the development of better means of transportation, all of which brought Volga Muslims into the larger Muslim world and therefore in contact with other political and cultural centers.[90] Iuzefovich stressed that Russians now dealt not just with Muslims, but with the "Mohammedanian world" (*magometanskii mir*), strong in spirit, with a developed network of religious schools, and united by the Orenburg Ecclesiastical Assembly, which had been created by the Russian government in the eighteenth century.[91] What concerned Iuzefovich was the possibility of political mobilization, perhaps by the Ottomans, against imperial rule over the religiously alienated but now much larger and united community of Russian Muslims.

Iuzefovich thus formulated the Muslim Question not simply as a religious issue, but also as an emerging political problem of "internal fusion" (*vnutrennego sblizheniia*) of Muslims with Russia.[92] Yet, viewed in light of the apostasy issue in the Volga region, the goal of the policy toward Islam, as he formulated it, was twofold: weakening Muslims' "isolation" (*obosoblennost'*) from Russians while at the same time "establishing boundaries to Islam." This was a task, he believed, that belonged to the government as well as the missionaries.

While calling for restrictions toward Islam, Iuzefovich supported Il'minskii's educational approach to apostasy. Yet even this more accommodating approach was not able to resolve the problem of apostasy. Indeed, by the late nineteenth century attempts by baptized Tatars, who were children and grandchildren of earlier apostates, officially to rejoin the Muslim community had become a chronic phenomenon in the Volga region. By occupying an uncertain legal position between Christianity and Islam, this large group of apostates could not conclude legal marriages, were excluded from inheritance, and were not able to prove their age and social status.[93] Faced with this very real problem of governance, some within the Russian government were coming to the realization that a different solution to the problem of apostasy needed to be found.

In 1884, the problems of apostasy and Muslim propaganda were taken up by the Committee of Ministers in conjunction with a report by the governor of Kazan from 1881. The Kazan governor contended that the apostasy movement was influenced not only by Muslim propaganda, but also by the fact that baptized Tatars had frequent contact with Muslims in communal life. Therefore, to protect baptized Tatars from the Muslims, the governor suggested dividing apostates into two groups, based on the time of their original apostasy, and choosing a particular year as a starting point. According to the governor, one group would be officially recognized as Muslim, while the other, still considered Russian Orthodox, was to be separated and treated as a separate community with their own administration. These measures, as the governor saw it, would reduce the number of apostates and consequently make it easier for the police to control them.[94]

This partial solution to the apostasy problem, however, was rejected by a majority of the governors of the northeastern regions, the Holy Synod, the MVD, and the Committee of Ministers. The main reasons for the secular authorities' rejection of this proposal had to do with the practical difficulties of creating separate communities for the apostates, as well as official hesitations about limiting Muslim autonomy.[95] The only solution that the committee proposed, however, was not new—to develop missionary activity and create special schools for those who were officially Orthodox but had begun to cross over to Islam.[96]

In his concluding remarks on the apostasy issue, Pobedonostsev drew on Il'minskii's authoritative opinion. "The apostasy movement," Pobedonostsev noted, "is a recurring problem not only in Kazan province, but almost everywhere in Russia. It is difficult to define with precision the true reason for the baptized Tatars' longstanding and stubborn aspiration for Mohammedanism, but one may suppose that it is related to the mechanical and hasty baptism of the Tatars, who did not have a deep conviction in Christianity's truth and salvation."[97] Though supportive of missionary activity, Pobedonostsev also called to paralyze "those forces that are hostile to Christianity"—thus advocating restrictive measures against Islam.

Without officially rejecting the principle prohibiting conversion from Orthodoxy, the MVD officials were willing to compromise and approved a number of petitions in cases where prior allegiance to Islam could be proved and where there was no evidence of Muslim "propaganda."[98] Even so, the confessional system remained officially intact until 1905. Thus, the unresolved issue of apostasy in the empire's borderlands became conceptualized as the "confessional question," joining a list of other pressing issues and defining the Muslim Question more broadly.

Orthodoxy "Unmasked"

The continuing apostasy movement among the baptized Tatars of the Volga region in the nineteenth and early twentieth centuries demonstrated the vitality of Islam at the same time that it revealed the weakness of Russian Orthodox influence in the region. In their search for an explanation for this situation, missionaries and Orthodox lay observers not only condemned Islam and Muslims; they also critiqued the state of the Orthodox church and contemporary Russian society. Moreover, in addition to serving as a subject of criticism, the resilience of Muslim religious belief also emerged as a subject that allowed a comparison of Muslim and Orthodox communities. As the Muslim Question unfolded in the late imperial period, it evolved to include both the question of what to do about Islam and predicaments of Russian Orthodoxy, past, present, and future.

While Orthodox clerics and missionaries blamed the state for the apostasy movement and what they interpreted as its support of Islam, they also issued complaints against free-thinking Russian educated elites. The missionaries thus had to struggle on two fronts: against Islam and against what they interpreted as the anticlericalism, "religious indifference," and "cosmopolitanism" of the Russian intelligentsia.[99] At the same time, Orthodox intellectuals and some reform-minded members of the clergy and the government returned the favor by raising questions about the state of the Orthodox church and its own responsibility for the spread of Islam.

The so-called "unmasking" (*razoblachenie*) of the Orthodox church's problems in Russia constituted one part of the broader public debates about the impending reforms in the political and social spheres of Russian life, first in the 1850 and 1860s, and then again at the beginning of the twentieth century.[100] Privately circulated notes and published articles in reformist journals recognized the need to reform one of Russia's main institutions—the Orthodox church. Among the issues addressed were the petty condition and poor performance of Orthodox parish clergy, the role and function of laity in local Orthodox communities (the parishes), and the church's role in society and its relations with the state. In turn, great emphasis was put on freedom and public initiative. These problems became especially visible on the empire's borderlands, where the Orthodox church confronted other religions.

Debates about the church's problems became more intense in the wake of the 1863 Polish uprising. The Russian reading public was especially concerned about the fate of Orthodoxy in the western region when the newspaper *Den*, published by the Slavophile Aksakov, reported about powerless, impoverished, and uneducated local Orthodox clergy who were alienated from their parishes and threatened by Polish rebels. Aksakov's publications in *Den* and other newspapers addressed the needs of the Orthodox parish clergy and mobilized the Russian laity to support Russian Orthodoxy in the western region by joining religious brotherhoods.[101] At the same time, his criticism of the bureaucratic character of the Russian Orthodox church created enemies within the church's hierarchy.[102] In the Baltic region, the confrontation with Lutheranism also exposed the needs of the Russian Orthodox parish clergy, the wretchedness (*ubogost'*) of the churches, and the lack of schools.[103] In this way, the non-Orthodox confessions in the empire's borderlands presented not only a threat to Orthodoxy, but were also subjects for comparison and models for reform.

Similar concerns about the state of Russian Orthodoxy were voiced in the eastern part of the empire. Missionaries and lay observers there drew attention to what they saw as a "backward religious-moral" state of the Russian peasants. The priest D. Grigor'ev explained the spread of Islam in the eastern part of the empire in the following way:

> The influence of one tribe over another increases when the convictions of that tribe become the common property of the peoples' consciousness. . . . Mohammedans do not have official missionaries who are paid two thousand rubles per year. Nor do they have rhetorical examples of exhortation and missionary manuals. But they have one great force: a mass of people who have been educated at school and are committed to the propagation of their faith as their holy duty. This force is the reason why Mohammedanism is able to spread so quickly and successfully among the small non-Russian peoples.[104]

On more than one occasion, missionaries noted that for Orthodoxy to be able to spread successfully within non-Russian groups, Orthodox Russians themselves had to demonstrate the superiority of their religion and culture. Yet Orthodox Russians, in the view of the missionaries, often proved to be much less zealous in their faith than Muslims had to be in theirs.[105] The report of the Ufa chapter of the Orthodox missionary society had the following to say in 1891, for example: "In contrast to the Tatars, Russian [peasants] never talk to aliens about their religion; moreover, Russians speak with aliens in broken Russian, adapting Russian terms to the aliens' way of pronunciation. Thus, the alien in speaking with a Russian villager can learn neither the [Russian] language nor the [Russian] faith."[106]

In the view of M. A. Mashanov, a missionary from Kazan, Orthodox Russians were not only passive in spreading their faith and way of life to non-Russian peoples, but they also could be either scornful of or simply uninterested in baptized non-Russians. The comments of one peasant woman captured this attitude perfectly: "A *magometanin* [Muslim] should believe in the Tatar way and a Russian in the Russian way."[107] Much as other observers had, Mashanov also noted that the most ardent Russian proselytizers were Russian Old Believers.[108] Twenty-five years later, in 1900, S. G. Rybakov, an ethnographer and later an official at the Department for Religious Affairs of Foreign Confessions, expressed very little hope in ordinary Russians as culture-bearers among non-Russian peoples. "In the best-case scenario," he suggested, "the Russian masses can impart the surface traits of Christian-Russian life to the *inorodtsy*. At worst, they can impart schism and sectarianism. But they cannot relay the true essence of Christianity."[109]

Missionaries often drew attention to cases in which Muslim influence had affected Orthodox Russians living in remote areas. Consider the following example of cultural transformation among Russians, as described in the missionary journal *Pravoslavnyi blagovestnik:* "Russians know the Tatar language, having learned it from Tatar workers, and will speak it even with aliens who know Russian. . . . [These Russians] attempt to imitate Asiatic customs, dress in the Tatar costume, eat with Tatars everything, including horse meat and, as a joke, even pray with them."[110] This kind of cultural borrowing occurred when Russian peasants lived far from Russian schools and consequently sent their children to Muslim schools.[111] It could also occur when Russians were hired to work for Tatars, when they turned to mullahs for medical help, or as a result of Russian women living with Muslim men.[112]

Religious lay observers discovered not only a lack of missionary zeal among Orthodox Russians, but also their ignorance of religious matters. Compared to Muslims, both Orthodox Russians and non-Russians seemed unfamiliar with the basic tenets of their faith. Iuzefovich reported: "For example, in Russian villages boys aged fourteen–fifteen not only did not know any prayers, but could not even recite the days of the week. This phenomenon is not exceptional, especially in the Ufa province where such a state of affairs could be found in ten out of thirty villages."[113] He blamed the Orthodox village priests for "indifference to their calling and total apathy."[114]

The large number of cases of apostasy among baptized Tatars revealed the unwillingness and inability of the priests to work in non-Russian parishes—which was also a critique of their poor training in non-Russian languages, as well as their indifference toward religious education among convert communities.[115] Again, Muslims served as positive counterexamples and objects of comparison. For example, in 1867, Kazem-Bek, commenting on Archbishop Antonii's accusations against the government in connection with the apostasy issue, contrasted the "instinctive ability" of Muslim clergy to conduct religious propaganda with the complete absence of zeal on the part of Russian village priests.[116] The "helplessness and irresponsibility" of Russian clergy in the struggle with apostasy provided justification for lay believers to take responsibility for the religious–moral development of the baptized non-Russians and Orthodox Russian common folk. As had been the case in the western borderlands of the empire, the founding of the St. Gurii Brotherhood in Kazan in 1867 was an example of these efforts, which in itself represented a significant step in the transformation of the nature of the Orthodox community in Russia. Critics of the Orthodox church's condition also mentioned the inadequate number of churches and priests and what they saw as the "privileges" of Muslims, who seemed to have more autonomy in their religious affairs and more freedom than the Orthodox in opening their mosques and confessional schools. Muslims mullahs were also elected by the community, unlike Orthodox priests.[117]

Il'minskii, too, had noted the superiority of Muslim religious education. In his article "Ex Oriente Lux," written in 1862–1863, but only published in 1901, he suggested that Russian reformers turn not to Western, but to Eastern models of schooling. Anticipating that he would be accused of having a predisposition to Islam (*Musul'manomaniia*), Il'minskii nevertheless drew attention to the positive aspects of Muslim schools: their private character, closeness to the peoples' needs (*narodnyi kharakter*), and absence of bureaucracy.[118] He tried to bring precisely these characteristics to the School for Baptized Tatars that he established in Kazan in 1864.

Thus, by the beginning of the twentieth century, Russian Orthodox reform-minded writers increasingly found themselves not only denouncing Muslim fanaticism and reiterating "Islam's hostility toward Christianity," but also offering positive statements about Tatars' "boundless love for their national schools and religion."[119]

The Legacy of Apostasy

The apostasy issue was a product of Russia's earlier attempts at Christianizing Muslim Tatars and the state's confessional policies that gave privileges to the Orthodox church while simultaneously extending limited religious toleration to Muslims and other non-Orthodox subjects. The Great Reforms challenged the state-controlled confessional system and forced the government to make some concessions to religious minorities, but did not result in fundamental revision of confessional policies. Russian responses to apostasy issues reveal the complexity of modernization in the imperial multiconfessional society as well as the tensions in Russian thinking about this process.

The reforms stimulated an apostasy movement that peaked in the late 1860s, while also mobilizing reform-minded Orthodox missionaries and providing favorable conditions for the development of a new approach to apostasy as suggested by Il'minskii. Il'minski's innovative approach, however, was meant to be executed within the existing confessional system without undermining its foundations. While he recognized the importance of religious conviction, Il'minskii's goal was to bring the subjective beliefs of baptized Tatars into accord with their formal Orthodox status.

At the same time, Il'minksii's approach to the apostasy issue presented an open challenge to the state's Orthodox church. His proposed solutions—conscious Christianity, religious instruction, translations of religious texts and liturgy into native languages, bringing schools and priests close to the people—must be understood in the context of broader discussions of the need to educate the ethnically Russian Orthodox community and reform the Orthodox church. Il'minskii's approach raised fundamental questions about the role of laity and the very nature of the Russian Orthodox community.

In contrast to a dismissive Orthodox clerical view of Islam, Il'minskii also articulated a new perspective on Islam as a dynamic spiritual force and a serious opponent to Orthodoxy. But this view combined the Orthodox view of Islam as an anti-Christian teaching with recognition of the Tatar Muslim community as a vital community of believers. Although Islam was conceived as a serious enemy, its adherents could also provide an instructive example for Orthodox Russians to emulate. Il'minskii recognized the present impossibility of converting Muslims into Christians, but left hope for Christianization in a distant future. To succeed, both the Orthodox church and the Orthodox community had to be revitalized. Yet while some of the church problems were addressed by the Great Reforms, as Gregory Freeze has demonstrated, the ambitious attempt to rebuild the church failed.[120]

Moreover, as many Russian observers both within and outside the church noted, in contrast to its Orthodox counterparts the Muslim community appeared to be empowered by the reforms. As prospects for reform of the church became bleak, the feeling among many Russians was that the formally predominant Orthodoxy was in a disadvantaged situation with respect to its Muslim rival. Furthermore, when viewed in light of the 1863 Polish rebellion and imperial expansion in Central Asia, the perceived rising strength of Islam appeared as a potentially serious political problem. These apprehensions, voiced by some ecclesiastical figures and missionaries, led them to oppose formal recognition of apostates as Muslims, criticize the state's toleration policy toward Islam, and call for the protection of Orthodoxy and restrictions on Muslim institutions.

Il'minksii's more accommodative approach did not solve the apostasy problem. State authorities looked for alternative ways to deal with this issue. Without officially rejecting the principle prohibiting conversion from Orthodoxy, the MVD officials, however, increasingly refused to use coercion in matters of faith and granted apostates their formal Muslim status in certain cases where prior allegiance to Islam could be proved and where there was no evidence of Muslim "propaganda."[121] As Paul Werth has noted, this tendency to compromise continued from the 1880s through the mid-1890s and was primarily motivated by the officials' desire to simplify administration rather than by a commitment to allow the private beliefs of imperial subjects to determine their formal confessional status.[122] Even so, the confessional system remained officially intact until 1905, and the issue of apostasy in the empire's eastern borderlands remained a chronic problem.

This halfway approach had important implications for the ways the Muslim Question was conceptualized in the late imperial period. The government's gradual retreat stimulated further apostasy and there was an increase in baptized Tatars' claims to be recognized as Muslims. At the same time, pressure was put on the Orthodox clerics and missionaries who had to deal with the problem of apostasy on their own. But with no progress in church reform, this was an especially challenging task for the missionaries.

The unresolved issue of apostasy, along with the tensions it produced, came to occupy a central place in Russians' conceptualization of the Muslim Question.

While the defeat in the Crimean War forced Russian society and the government to place the question of Muslims' integration on the reform agenda, the experience of apostasy in the Volga region significantly modified this goal. The rhetoric about easing alienation continued to describe Russian goals toward Muslims. Yet the apostasy and the church's failure to gain new converts among Muslims served to confirm Muslims' intrinsic alien position based on their religion. At the same time, concerns about Islam's domination of Russian Orthodoxy led increasing number of commentators to suggest that the proper solution to the Muslim Question was not integration but containment.

3 "What Do We Need from Muslims?"

Combating Ignorance, Alienation, and Tatarization

The apostasy crisis posed an unsolvable riddle to modernizing Russians: How might Muslims, who simultaneously appeared to be alienated and dominating, be accommodated to the needs of the state? The issue of mass education, a hallmark of modernization, became a primary site of struggle for the Muslim Question in late nineteenth-century Russia. To maintain its status as a modern imperial power, Russia needed literate subjects who were also well integrated into a larger society. The state projects for educating both non-Russians and Russians emerged simultaneously and presented reformers with a number of similar, and similarly difficult, questions: What is the goal of primary education? What place should be given to religious instruction in modern schools? What should the role of the state and local forces be in enlightening the masses? How should the project of universal education be reconciled with the empire's confessional diversity and hierarchies? How might educating Orthodox Russians and Muslims relate more broadly to the issues of nationality and nationalism? Finally, could the perceived ignorance of Muslims and even of Russians themselves be overcome without undermining the confessional and political order?

The issue of educating peasants arose directly from the emancipation of the serfs in 1861. In the culturally diverse eastern borderlands, this empire-wide issue was reformulated as a problem of "education of aliens" (*obrazovanie inorodtsev*). As Russians became increasingly concerned about Muslims' alienation in the wake of the Crimean War, political significance was assigned to the task of enlightenment and to the rapprochement of Muslims with Russians. "What do we need from our Muslims?" asked a contributor to the *Zhurnal Ministerstva narodnogo prosveshcheniia* (*Journal of the Ministry of Education*), who then answered, "that they become less superstitious, less ignorant, that they become closer to the core Russian population, and share their interests with them as citizens of one state."[1] In the Volga region, however, the enduring problem of apostasy, viewed in a context of the reforming and nationalizing empire, acquired new meaning while at the same time affected an understanding of the state's goals with respect to its Muslim populations. Moreover, since among Russians themselves the question of modernizing the empire remained fraught and divisive, there was no one simple answer to the question about what to do about Muslims.

This chapter explores the state's educational projects for Muslims in light of the Muslim Question, aiming to highlight the tensions that characterized the regime's attempts at reform, and its effect on the evolution of the issue. Special attention will be paid to N. I. Il'minskii and his ideas about reform. Recent studies have emphasized his creative project of offering bilingual education for baptized non-Russians while also condemning him for keeping Muslims away from Russian education, attributing this stance to his views of Islam.[2] This chapter underscores the interpretation of Il'minskii's ideas as a particular vision of Russia's renewal and empire that echoed Slavophile ideas. This vision at once challenged, but also, curiously, influenced, the state's efforts in enlightening Muslims and bringing them closer to Russians. As a vision of empire became reconceptualized in modern national terms, Il'minskii's views faced a challenge from the Muslim modernist movement, with which it fell into competition. This chapter considers these various tensions in Russians' developing understanding of the Muslim Question.

Enlightenment and Rapprochement Contested

During the era of the Great Reforms, the state assumed the role of an active agent with respect to its population. While the MVD's Department for Religious Affairs of Foreign Confessions, which had managed the problems of the empire's religious diversity up to this point, understood its mission as supervisory and regulatory rather than transformative, in the second half of the nineteenth century it was the Ministry of Public Education that became the principle government agency charged with articulating a proactive policy approach toward the empire's non-Russian minorities: Muslims were not only to be tolerated, but also were to be culturally transformed.

The principles of state schooling policy for Muslims were developed when D. A. Tolstoy served as Minister of Education (1866–1880). Tolstoy, also the head of the Holy Synod, replaced a liberal A. V. Golovnin and became minister when the autocracy, shaken by D. Karakozov's attempted assassination of Alexander II, was searching for ways to reaffirm state authority and control over social change. Tolstoy thus faced a dilemma: how to alleviate the masses' perceived ignorance without undermining the main principles of the imperial order, the autocracy, and the dominant position of the Orthodox church. In the sphere of primary education, Tolstoy's response was to ensure the teaching of religion and morality along with maintaining a drive toward centralization and ministry control over education. His educational policies faced a particularly great challenge in the borderlands, where education was also to serve as a device for strengthening the empire's unity.[3] This problem was especially acute after the 1863 Polish uprising in the western provinces, where Tolstoy, first in his capacity as the chief procurator and then also as the minister of education, had to organize the defense against the menace of Catholicism.[4] In the eastern provinces, he faced the Muslim Question. Concerned about the rise of apostasy in 1866, Tolstoy, as we have seen, enthusiastically supported Il'minskii's solution to this problem.

At the same time, in his new role as minister of education, Tolstoy took up the issue of universal primary education and in 1866 and 1867 inspected the Kazan and Odessa educational districts. Tolstoy asserted that all of the 1,200,000 Volga Tatars and 100,000 Crimean Tatars were "culturally ignorant" and "alienated" from Russia.[5] Muslims were not entirely unique in this way; the Russian educated elite deployed similar language to describe Russian lower classes, whose education and inclusion into the new societal order was a no less urgent political issue than Muslims' enlightenment and integration. In his report, Tolstoy stated that in the Kazan district, "only children from middle and upper estates enjoyed the fruits of education; the people [narod], both Russian and alien [inorodnyi], were almost entirely deprived of them."[6]

Indeed, the government's turn toward the peasants was accompanied by populist rhetoric that emphasized that the reforming state "awaken the people from their epochal sleep."[7] The government's encounter with Muslim Tatar lower classes occurred as a part of this turn toward the peasants, who were regarded by the reformers as "ignorant" and "lethargic."[8] These views on the development of the peasant classes had their origins in Enlightenment ideals of progress, understood as the universal formula of human development that rose from the lowest to the highest, from superstition to reason and science.[9]

Russian perceptions of Muslims also drew on Western Europeans' concepts about the superiority of their culture in relation to that of the alleged backward Muslim East. During the nineteenth and early twentieth centuries, European scholars, politicians, and publicists debated the reasons for perceived Muslim backwardness and the compatibility of Islam with "progress" and modern culture.[10] Many educated Russians adopted both the idea and the language of a "civilizing mission" toward Asians. But the Russian vision of this mission, as well as of the Muslim Question more broadly, was complicated by the fact that Russia itself was undergoing large-scale, state-sponsored reforms that raised fundamental questions about the limits of these transformations and the meaning of "enlightenment" and "progress." They, moreover, intensified Russians' debate about "native" versus "European" paths for the country's development.

Religion was one of the issues that lay at the heart of these debates. Judged from the standpoint of the values of liberalism and rational secularism circulating at the time, all forms of religion presented obstacles to progress and reform, but "religious fanaticism" (that is, a type of extreme religiosity intolerant to other views) posed a special threat.[11] As the liberal Vestnik Evropy noted, "no single confession could secure itself against religious fanaticism. It could occur in all civilized countries; however, the degree of religious fanaticism was inversely related [obratno proportsional'na] to the level of culture."[12]

Although the question about the place of religion in the modern world was no less relevant for the Russian Orthodox church itself, Orthodox critics of Islam adopted this reformist and secularist rhetoric for the purpose of anti-Islamic po-lemics. For many Russian religious critics, the doctrines of Islam—especially its fatalism—sentenced Muslims to a fate of "backwardness." According to this view, Islam, in contrast to Christianity—which, it was believed, encouraged aspiration to ever higher perfection—failed to offer an ideal purpose or moral guidelines to which its adherents should aspire. The Koran seemed to preserve tradition and to prohibit any changes that deviated from the Sharia.[13] The widespread view among educated Russians—that the teaching of the Koran was the main obstacle to the government's reformist plans, the enlightenment of Muslims, and their rapproche-ment with Russians—proceeded from an assumption about the importance of re-ligion in human lives and of Muslim lives in particular, as well as from an under-standing of Islam that reduced it to the teachings of the Koran.[14]

The notion of Muslim "ignorance" represented the intersection of several dis-courses: Russian reformist and secularist rhetoric, Orthodox anti-Islamic views, and the rhetoric of a European civilizing mission. It thus created the illusion of a unified front of Russian critics of Islam. By accepting the thesis of Muslim igno-rance (just as they had in the case of Russian Orthodox peasants whom they also viewed as backward), reform-minded Russians justified the need to transform and Europeanize Russian Muslims and assigned themselves a leading role in this en-deavor. Moreover, reform-minded Russians felt secure that they were imposing edu-cational systems on what was almost certainly a "lethargic" and "ignorant" com-munity. The encounter with Muslims' schools, however, presented a challenge to this view in addition to revealing uncertainty among Russians about how to an-swer the question: "What needs to be done about Muslims?"

To achieve educational reform for non-Russians, Tolstoy solicited support of local educators and opened the official *Zhurnal Ministerstva narodnogo prosvesh-cheniia* for discussion of the reform. To address the issue, committees were formed in Kazan and Simferopol. The Committee in Crimea, chaired by the Tauride gov-ernor G. V. Zhukovskii, consisted of Russian teachers, officials as well as Muslims, members of the clergy and some *murzas*. The Kazan committee was chaired by the curator of the Kazan educational district, P. D. Shestakov, and included Il'minskii, E. Malov, who was an instructor at the Kazan Theological Academy, and N. Zolot-nitskii, a former editor of *Viatskie vedomosti* and an activist in educating Chuvash.

Both committees set out the problem as Muslim Tatars' alienation from Russia. For the Kazan committee, however, the primary concern was the threat of Muslim propaganda. As the chair of the committee, Shestakov, saw it, the goal of the gov-ernment's educational efforts was to counter Muslim influence among the neigh-boring baptized non-Russians.[15] The committee therefore endorsed Il'minskii's re-cent experiment of introducing Christian education to baptized non-Russians as a model for educational reform. The Il'minskii approach also became a subject of public debate and raised several objections. The most vocal opponent, the priest A. I. Baratynskii, the chair of the Buinsk school board, criticized Il'minskii's reli-ance on native languages to convey Orthodox truths. The critics also claimed that the use of native languages in education would lead to the development of "tribal peculiarities." Closely related to the issue of language instruction was another contentious question, Who should be the leading force in religious–moral education: Russian priests incompetent in non-Russian languages and culture or skilled lay teachers?[16]

Nor did the question about Muslim education have an easy answer. The Russian reformers realized that, in the case of Muslims, they dealt not with a passive, backward, and isolated mass, but with communities that had their own autonomous schools, written language, and literature.[17]

Russian educators interpreted this challenge differently in Kazan and Simferopol. In both regions, many local observers noticed that Tatars viewed education as a religious duty. Although the government lacked exact statistics on Muslim schools, *maktabs*, and *madrases*, the approximate numbers were enough to demonstrate the Tatars' aspiration for learning. As E. L. Markov, the schools' director (*direktor uchilishch*) of Tauride province, reported to the Simferopol committee, even after mass emigration during and after the Crimean war, the Crimean Tatars, who constituted only 17.85 percent of the population in the province, had more schools than the Russian majority.[18] Markov, an educator, historian of Crimea, traveler, and publicist, was an initiator of the Simferopol Committee for Spreading Education among Crimean Tatars and the author of an extensive report that formed the basis of the committee's discussion. He was among those educators who became inspired by the Great Reforms and the idea of transforming Russian subjects into a new type of imperial citizen by means of education.[19] The education of Muslims was part of this project.

From his experiences in Crimea, Markov concluded that Crimean Tatars could not be viewed as "savages" in respect to education; indeed, they possessed something that Russians could learn.[20] Although he was critical of the methods of instruction at Muslim religious schools, he pointed out that Tatars were not as ignorant as the Russians assumed, and, for instance, practiced a rather liberal approach to women's education: Muslim women were allowed into schools not only as pupils, but also as teachers.[21] He stated that the so-called ignorance of the Tatars had less to do with their lack of understanding of the value of education than with what he thought was a "false view" of the essence of education. Markov believed the problem lay with the religious character of Muslim education, as was also an issue with respect to the education of Russian Old Believers and other religious communities.[22] From his perspective, this religious understanding of education posed an obstacle to the government's plans to introduce secular education, and in particular the Russian language. He felt that Muslims considered these to be attempts at Christianization. Nevertheless, Markov was optimistic about the possibility of bringing secular education to Muslims, especially to the Tatars of the southern shore of the Black Sea, whom he characterized as "half-civilized and industrious."[23]

In Kazan, in contrast to Crimea, Il'minskii emphasized the positive religious qualities of Muslim schools, praising, in particular, the informality of the educational process and their closeness to the people. He considered Muslim schools, rather than European examples, as the model for educational reform among Russians themselves.[24] Il'minskii saw the "true" enlightenment in religious education. In general, Il'minskii was apprehensive about bringing the fruits of secular civilization to the popular masses, whether Muslim or Orthodox, and was not interested in a project of educating modern citizens who associate their interests with the state. Instead, he hoped to raise sincerely religious Christians without uprooting them from their native milieu, and saw the key to Russia's renewal in these revitalized local independent communities. But how did Muslims fit into this project? Viewing Christian education as the vehicle to "true" enlightenment and Islam as "hostile to Christianity religiosity," Il'minskii also recognized the tremendous difficulty and near impossibility of changing Muslims' religious beliefs. At the same time, his methods of Christian education gave hope to the possibility of Christianizing Muslims—but only in the distant future. Thus, Il'minskii's answer to the question about Muslim schools was to tolerate them but not to provide them with governmental regulation and reform.[25]

Tolstoy was a champion of Orthodoxy. But he also realized that Christianization was not going to be achieved in the immediate future. Fearing Muslims' possible political alienation, as demonstrated during the Crimean War, and thus pressed by the need to integrate the Muslim masses into the imperial state more successfully as well as to bring them under tighter governmental control, he developed an educational project that was a compromise between these contrasting views of the goals of reform.

The educational project was linked to the confessional system. The ministry's regulations, issued in 1870, viewed non-Russians as divided by their official confessional affiliation and therefore in need of separate educational systems. The schools for baptized non-Russians were centered on Il'minskii's approach to religious–moral enlightenment in native languages. The goal of educating baptized non-Russians was thus to reinforce their Orthodox beliefs as well as to familiarize them with the Russian language. This approach to elementary education was mostly applied in the Volga–Ural region, where schools for baptized Tatars, Chuvash, and Mari had been created after the model of the Kazan school for the baptized Tatars. In 1872, a seminary for training teachers was established in Kazan, with Il'minskii as its director. Yet Il'minskii himself was apprehensive of such an institutionalization of his educational experiment. He was afraid that under government regulations his schools would lose their freedom and the flexibility necessary for the successful struggle against Islam.[26] Therefore, he made efforts to protect the autonomy of his missionary schools. In 1878, however, the Kazan Central school for baptized Tatars, while still maintaining its private status, was transformed into a two-grade rural school. This decision implied that the ministry's regulations for the teaching program and its staff were to be introduced.[27] Il'minskii was not completely satisfied with the regulations' compromise on the use of native languages. This question, along with the issue of the role of Russian priests in Christian education of non-Russians, remained contentious.

Even less satisfying for Il'minskii, and for those who primarily viewed Islam as a threat, were the ministry's provisions concerning Muslim education. The regulations recognized that Muslim Tatars were firm in their beliefs. Therefore, while Islam remained tolerated by the state, Muslims' enlightenment and rapprochement with Russians were to be achieved through Russian education and language, as well as through subjugating their confessional schools to the supervision of the Ministry of Education.

For Muslim communities, the state created elementary schools with Russian as the principle language of instruction. The curriculum was to include penmanship, arithmetic, history, geography, nature study, and Islam (taught in Tatar). To train instructors for these schools, special Tatar teachers' schools were opened in Simferopol in 1872 and Kazan in 1876. The regulations also implied that Muslim communities would pay to open Russian-language classes at their confessional schools. Russian classes were to be a requirement for the establishment of new confessional schools.[28] Tatars resisted these measures, however, by refusing to pay for the Russian classes. Muslim clergy, likewise, viewed the teaching of the Russian language as a step toward baptism.[29] Consequently, the Russian classes had to be introduced by force. In 1875, under pressure from Shestakov, the curator of the Kazan educational district, Tolstoy agreed to provide 800 rubles annually for Russian classes. To attract Muslims to learn the language, the Ministry of Public Education planned to introduce a future Russian language requirement for those Muslims willing to occupy clerical and civil (*obchestvennye*) positions.

Another important aspect of Tolstoy's educational reform was to extend the ministry's control over education. In 1871, the post of inspector for the Tatar, Kirgiz, and Bashkir schools of the Kazan educational circuit was created. In 1874, these schools, as well as the Muslim confessional schools within the district of the Orenburg Ecclesiastical Assembly, were placed under the control of the Ministry of Public Education.[30] Il'minskii opposed these developments on the grounds that government interference in the operation of Muslim schools would detract from the government's efforts to provide Christian education for baptized non-Russians.[31]

But it was Muslims' resistance and government concerns about public order that ultimately stopped the process of turning over Muslim confessional schools to the supervision of the Ministry of Public Education (MNP). The MVD local and central officials worried that radical interference in the life of Muslims could provoke popular discontent. These anxieties grew with the approach of military conflict with the Ottoman Empire—the Russo-Turkish war of 1877–1878. As a result, the State Council considered Tolstoy's proposals about Muslim confessional schools to be "untimely." The idea of special instruction for government inspectors of Muslim schools was also given up; instead, the inspectors were advised to limit their responsibilities to the oversight (*nabliudenie*) of Muslim schools, thus teaching Muslims that such institutions were not free of government control.[32] In 1881, the Ministry of the Internal Affairs also concluded, "Although it is desirable to spread the Russian language among aliens as soon as possible, at the current moment it is more important to avoid a new pretext for unrest."[33] The tsarist authorities did not give up the idea of spreading the Russian language among Muslims and controlling their education, but—fearing "religious fanaticism" and popular discontent—postponed the implementation of the reforms until a more favorable moment.

The assassination of the tsar in 1881 marked a radical shift to the right in the autocratic politics of reform. The new emperor was responsive to Slavophile ideas about the national character of autocracy, even as he sought to reassure the firm power of the state. The government faced the problem of modifying the Great Reforms to suit the new ideology.[34] Tolstoy's system of educating eastern non-Russians was left intact. The changes were more visible, however, in the trajectory of state policy, which increasingly embraced tighter government control, and limited social life.

By 1885, the question of government supervision of Muslim schools was again in sharp focus, this time raised by the tsar in connection with reports from the governors in Kazan and Ufa. In his response, the new Minister of Education, I. D. Delianov (1882–1897), explained that the lack of government supervision of Muslim confessional schools was a consequence not only of administrators' fears of being accused by Muslims of violating the freedom of Islam (the arguments that had been evoked by his predecessors) but also of the "pointlessness" (*bestsel'nost'*) of government inspection so long as these schools would "preserve the peculiar character and the goal of spreading Muslim education." Delianov recognized that the government and the Muslim confessional schools had different educational goals. He pointed out that the aim of government inspection was to improve teaching, a goal that could not be applied by the Russian Christian state to the Muslim schools that could only be tolerated but not improved. According to Delianov, the MNP should be concerned not with the teaching process in the Muslim schools, but with political control. The major responsibility of government inspection, in his opinion, was to ensure that no antigovernment teachings or non-Muslim students penetrated the schools. At the same time, he admitted that if the program of the Muslim schools were to be modified, government inspection would make sense.[35] Delianov suggested returning to the discussion of Tolstoy's projects about language requirements, as well as introducing obligatory Russian language classes at the *madrases*.

By this time, however, Tolstoy, now in his capacity as Minister of Internal Affairs (1882–1889), proposed not to interfere in the teaching process at the Muslim confessional schools, not only because of the resistance of the Muslim clergy, but also because there were scarce finances for this project. Nor did the Ministry of Internal Affairs support the idea of government inspection for such schools in the

Odessa educational district. Again, the resistance of Volga Muslims to the introduction of such inspections, and the government's desire to avoid inflaming what they saw as religious fanaticism, led the MVD to postpone the reforms.[36] The question about inspection of the Muslim schools in Tauride province was raised again in 1900, but it, too, was blocked by the Ministry of Internal Affairs out of fear of popular discontent.

To some extent, Delianov's response evoked ideas previously articulated by Il'minskii. In his note on this issue, Il'minskii considered the law that established inspection, along with a later circular that suspended government supervision of Muslim confessional schools, as representing opposing approaches to Islam. In Il'minskii's eyes, it was the second approach, in which the government removed itself from involvement in Muslim institutions, that represented what he called "the traditional relation of the Russian state to Islam." He wrote that the subjugation of Muslim schools to the Ministry of Public Education inevitably raised a question about the improvement of these schools by the state: "But in what direction should the friendly advice of the inspector go at these schools—pointing out better ways of teaching Islam, or toward something else?" In the former case, Il'minskii argued, the inspector's action would not be in tune with the strict legal notion of religious tolerance, while in the latter case the inspector would find himself in a morally delicate situation. Il'minskii recommended that the government adhere to what he saw as the "traditional" approach toward the Muslim institutions until the baptized *inorodtsy* were enlightened to a level where there would be no reason to fear their apostasy. As he wrote:

> The success in educating Russian people and baptized *inorodtsy* . . . should sooner or later help Muslims voluntarily overcome their centuries-old stagnation. We firmly believe in the superiority of the principles of Russian Orthodox life and are convinced that there is no need for forcible measures against Muslims. Let's devote all our energy and our attention to the Russian schools and the schools for baptized *inorodtsy,* allow these schools enough time to influence baptized *inorodtsy,* and only after that start organizing Muslim schools, but until that time, leave them in their current state.[37]

While hesitant to introduce inspectorship, the government was increasingly fearful that subversive elements and ideas could possibly penetrate into confessional schools. In 1892, the Minister of the Internal Affairs, I. N. Durnovo, issued a circular prohibiting Muslim confessional schools from using printed books not approved by the Russian censors. The circular also required that only Russian subjects who received their education in Russia could become teachers at the Muslim confessional schools.[38] Yet in the absence of actual government control, these measures were difficult to put into practice. The confessional schools remained largely outside government control.

Il'minskii found allies in Delianov and the new Ober-Procurator of the Holy Synod Pobedonostsev. But Il'minskii's influence on the state schooling policy was only partial. Despite the Tatars' initial resistance and Il'minskii's apprehensions about the government-sponsored Russian–Tatar school project, the state system that provided special schools for Muslims where they could receive education in secular subjects, Russian language, and Islam continued to exist in the interior provinces. In some form, it was extended to other Muslim regions in the Caucasus and Central Asia.[39] While the state did not reverse its strategy of supporting religious tolerance and Muslim secular education as a means of integration, in the climate of political reaction of 1880s the tsarist officials became increasingly fearful of the possible implications of this strategy for the stability of the regime. The Tatar teachers' school in Kazan, whose graduates were joining the ranks of the Russian intelligentsia, caused particular concern.

After the tsar's assassination, the primary goal of state educational policy was to ensure political stability. In this environment, Pobedonostsev reversed the trend toward secularization of elementary education for the Orthodox Russian simple folk, *narod*. During his tenure, he increased the clergy's influence in secular schools and brought the expanded network of parish schools under the control of the church, thus creating a school system independent of the Ministry of Public Education.[40] Pobedonostsev's project of elementary education reflected a new ideology that juxtaposed educated elites with the *narod,* who were viewed as profoundly attached to the church and the tsar. These ideas resonated with Il'minskii's distrust of the intelligentsia and his hopes for protecting non-Russian simple folk from the "harms" of civilization.[41] At the same time, Il'minskii's and others' ideas about revitalizing the Orthodox community in order to make it capable of competing with Islam fell on deaf ears, as Pobedonostsev's goal was to revitalize authority, not social institutions. Pobedonostsev denounced the innovations in church life introduced during the era of the Great Reforms. He dismantled parish reform, abolished the right of diocesan clergy to elect their superintendents, and tightened censorship.[42] As Pobedonostsev and others worried that Orthodoxy was losing the "battle," the question of what was needed from the Muslims became even more fraught.

Tatarization versus Russification

The tensions inherent in the government's educational project for Muslims deepened when the state declared Russification (*obrusenie*) as one of the main goals of official educational policy among eastern non-Russians. While the concept of Russification itself entered the vocabulary of many at that time, recent studies have concluded that there was no consistent Russification strategy in late tsarist Russia; Russification had multiple meanings.[43] In the eastern part of European Russia, the understanding of the term was shaded by perceptions about the Muslim Question, which, in turn, was reconceptualized in national terms, acquiring political meaning. The rhetoric of Russification expressed the spirit of the Great Reforms and accompanied the government project of enlightenment and rapprochement of eastern non-Russians by means of schooling. But in the Volga region, it was Tatarization, rather than Russification, that preoccupied the local missionaries and educators. Up until the 1870s, Il'minskii's primary concern had been the apostasy of baptized Tatars and the spread of Islam among their neighbors who were originally believed to be animist: Udmurts, Mari, Chuvash, or shamanist Kazakhs. This problem was often described as Islamicization (*omusul'manivanie*) and Tatarization (*otatarivanie*), a process by which these other groups merged with Muslim Tatars by adopting their faith, way of life, and language.

Il'minksii's thinking about these issues bore resemblance to some of the ideas of the European romantic nationalism that also informed Russian Slavophilism. The romantic influence is evident in the concepts that Il'minskii and his associates adopted to combat Islamicization and Tatarization. One of them was the concept of a unique, organic community held together by a common culture and national spirit, as opposed to one artificially constructed by externally imposed values and bonds. It was believed that this unique national culture could be discovered in the folklore, language, and customs of the common people. Early Slavophiles accomplished this task for Orthodox ethnic Russians, and Il'minskii and his followers undertook a similar effort in relation to eastern non-Russians whose cultures they hoped to protect from Islam and Tatarization.[44]

In the view of Il'minskii and his supporters, both Islamicization and Tatarization enlarged the community of people who professed hostile faith and were alienated from Russia, while at the same time suppressing the distinct non-Russian cultures of the common people. Therefore, this process was often described by Il'minskii's sympathizers as an "artificial" one led by Muslim Tatars who did not seem to have either the cultural or the historical right to play such a role. Il'minskii came to articulate his concerns in such terms in Orenburg, where he had moved from Kazan in 1858 to work as an interpreter for the borderland commission chaired by the famous orientalist, V. V. Grigor'ev. In Orenburg, encouraged by Grigor'ev, he took great interest in the Kazakh language. He soon found that all of the borderland's commission's official correspondence was in the Tatar language. Il'minskii discovered a "people [*narod*] spoiled [*isporchennyi*] by the Tatar culture" and set himself to work to "reconstitute the Kirgiz [Kazakh] . . . vernacular [*narodnyi*] language."[45] He disapproved of what he considered to be "an unscholarly, and unfair, view of the Kirgiz language as some deformed jargon of the Tatar language."[46] Il'minskii learned the Kazakh language from the young Kazakh graduates of the Orenburg Kirgiz School. As he later recalled, it took him a lot of effort to move the language of these men to what he perceived as the true "Kirgiz way," as their language was infiltrated by Tatarisms.[47] As a result of his studies, Il'minskii created a "Kirgiz–Russian dictionary" and a Russian textbook for "Kirgiz schools."

In 1870, Il'minskii wrote to the naval officer Prince E. A. Ukhtomskii:

> I fell in love with Kirgiz, a distinctive language which preserved many traces of the ancient Turkic life style. . . . the Tatar language [*gramota*] threatens to smooth away and destroy the dialectic peculiarities of the Kirgiz language, and I found that using

the Russian language was the only means to preserve the Kirgiz language from Tatarization. The Kirgiz steppe once and for all brought me up to respect the vernacular [*narodny*] language in general, which I started to view as an authentic document for linguistic studies, while the literary language presents a more or less artificial, random, and arbitrary mixture of different languages and dialects. With this radically changed view I returned to Kazan.[48]

For Il'minskii, the linguistic Tatarization of the Kazakhs presented a problem that went well beyond academic debate. Islamicization was an essential part of the process of the Tatarization of the Kazakhs, and led, he believed, to their "fanatical religious hostility" toward the Russian population.[49] Il'minskii criticized the "misconceptions" of the Russian administration about Tatar as the native language and Islam as the native religion of the Kazakhs. He stated that the Tatars had come to Central Asia with the Russians, and that "foreign" (*chuzhie*) influences came from the Russian border areas.[50]

Il'minskii went further: the Islamicization of the Kazakhs was the direct consequence of imperial policy that had entrusted certain non-Russian intermediaries with undue influence in occupied regions. In the eighteenth century, for example, the government employed Tatars as agents in its diplomatic and commercial relations with the khanates of Central Asia and dispatched them to help pacify the steppe and to "civilize" the Kazakhs.[51] In the Kazakh steppe, Tatars were allowed to open mosques and religious schools. In local administration, Tatars were employed as interpreters and copyists. The Tatar language became the official language of Russian correspondence with the Kazakhs. To Il'minskii, Catherine II's reliance on the Tatars and Islam appeared to be a mistake. Once the Russians' imperial agents, the Tatars had become their principal competitors.[52]

Il'minskii's concerns about the Tatarization and Islamicization of the Kazakhs resonated with some of the representatives of the native Kazakh educated elite. The Kazakh ethnographer, historian, and officer of the Imperial Army, Ch. Valikhanov (1835–1865), whose work was admired by Grigor'ev, Il'minskii's superior in Orenburg, reaffirmed Russians' widely held assumptions about the weak roots of Islam among the steppe nomads. Valikhanov argued that preventing the Islamicization and Tatarization of the Kazakhs offered a way to merge them with the Russians.[53]

Tatarization and Islamicization were also of concern to another native Kazakh educator, I. Altynsarin, but his perception of these problems differed from that of Il'minskii. Il'minskii met Altynsarin in Orenburg in 1859 and maintained a correspondence with him for several years. When the Russian government discussed educational policies in the Kazakh steppe, Il'minskii recommended Altynsarin as a Russian liaison, and, after the latter's death in 1889, Il'minskii published his recollections of Altynsarin's activity as an educator, accompanying his writing with letters and official documents. During his career, Altynsarin occupied a number of positions within the local administration. Beginning in 1879, he served as an inspector of Kazakh schools. Like Il'minskii, he advocated for Russian education in the Kazakh language, and was concerned about the Tatarization of the Kazakhs, which he understood to mean the spread of the Tatar language and Islam. In his memoirs, Il'minskii characterized Altynsarin as "a smart, honest, and nice man" with whom he sincerely sympathized. He especially appreciated Altynsarin's "lively inquisitiveness about Russian education and constant thought about the necessity of this education for the Kirgiz."[54] Unlike Il'minskii, however, Altynsarin believed that what he interpreted as the "fanatical" version of Islam propagated by the Tatar mullahs did not correspond with the "true" spirit of the religion, which he accepted as an element of Kazakh identity not in conflict with Russian education.[55]

Altynsarin celebrated his Russian name day, but remained Muslim. He taught Islam at the Kazakh school and created a textbook on Islam for Kazakhs. Altynsarin's combination of Russian sympathies and Islamic faith continued to be a source of surprise and disappointment for some of his Russian colleagues. A teacher who worked closely with him recalled: "While conversing with him, I always forgot that I was talking to a Muslim Kirgiz; indeed, his kindness and way of thinking made it difficult to notice that he was a Kirgiz Muslim."[56] Another Russian teacher wrote of Altynsarin's last days, and described how Islam distanced Altynsarin from his Russian colleagues:

> During his last three days, nobody among the Russians was allowed to see the sick man; only mullahs were sitting next to him and reading the Koran. . . . At the funeral, there were no other Russians except for us, Russian teachers, and even we had to be at a distance: Kirgiz looked at us as if we were unwanted guests at this ceremony. Some even came to us and asked: "What is your business here?"[57]

P. V. Znamenskii, a professor at the Kazan Theological Academy and later Il'minskii's biographer, explained this seeming contradiction between Islam and Russian sympathies by calling Altynsarin "a Muslim-liberal who did not like the narrow fanaticism of the Tatar mullahs and complained that they spoiled Kirgiz brains and language."[58] Altynsarin's views challenged, but ultimately did not change, Il'minskii's views of Islam.

The ordinary Kazakhs who were influenced by the Tatar Muslim culture, however, appeared to be in a situation similar to that of the baptized and animist non-Russians in the Volga–Ural region. Upon his return to Kazan in 1861, Il'minskii became a strong advocate for the religious education of baptized non-Russians in their living (zhivoi), vernacular (narodny) languages as a way to prevent their Islamicization and Tatarization.

The problem of Islamicization and Tatarization gained special attention among educated Russians and the government in the 1860s–1870s when Russification (obrusenie) became the declared goal of official educational policy among eastern non-Russians. In turn, Islamicization and Tatarization came to be viewed by many observers as a potentially politically dangerous alternative to Russification. In response to this shift in official thinking about the goals of imperial policies, Il'minskii positioned his project of combating Islamicization and Tatarization as Russification. In 1871, in his comments on educational reform among the Kazakhs, Il'minskii urged the prevention of Tatar influence among them, claiming that the common people, compared to the aristocracy, were still not deeply affected by Tatar influence and therefore gave hope for Russification, which he understood as the development of ideas "common to all mankind" (*obshchechelovecheskie*), as well as Russian sympathies communicated to them in their native language. As the Kazan missionary M. Mashanov later argued, non-Russians should merge with Russians, but nevertheless might be able to develop "reasonable" sympathy for Russians without breaking moral connection with their co-tribesmen (*edinoplemenniki*).[59]

Il'minskii's views of Russification became a subject of polemic in the 1860s and 1870s during public debates about the educational system of eastern non-Russians. At the center of the debate were new questions about nationality. Did religion or language constitute the essence of nationality? Il'minskii's response was that religion should form the basis for nationality (*narodnost'*), and the Muslim Kazan Tatars, firm in their religious belief and thus nationality, demonstrated this to him.[60] Il'minskii's followers saw his emphasis on Christian enlightenment as a path leading to Russification, a process simultaneously understood as the "internal (spiritual) fusion" of non-Russians with Russians and an effective means for preventing Islamicization and Tatarization.[61]

Il'minskii's opponents did not deny that Orthodoxy was an essential component of Russification. As we have seen, they criticized the participation of lay believers and of native priests in the church's efforts to Christianize non-Russians while also arguing that the use of native languages might lead to the development of a national consciousness, posing an insurmountable threat to Russification. A participant in these discussions and the chair of the Kazan School Council, the priest M. Zefirov, rejected these later concerns by pointing out that non-Russian literature and languages could lead to mental and political separateness from Russians only among those non-Russians who had a history of independent political existence and had already become aware of their national distinctiveness. In his opinion, unlike the Baltic Germans, Poles, or Austrian Czechs, the destiny of the Chuvash and Mari, whom he viewed as "primitive tribes," was either Russification or Tatarization.[62] It was the second alternative that seemed to be especially disturbing. As Il'minskii warned, Islamicization and Tatarization of non-Russians in Kazan province was like a "gangrene, which, if not stopped, could end in fifty or a hundred years with the definite crossing of all our non-Russians to Tatar Muslims."[63]

The goal of creating a strong imperial state, both domestically and internationally, through the modernization of Russian social institutions and governance confronted the ruling elites with the problem of accommodating the empire's tremendous cultural diversity. In the age of emerging nation-states in Europe, educated Russians attempted to reconceptualize their politically centralized, dynastic, multiconfessional empire as a state based on Russian nationality. With Russians assigned an integrative role in the state, *inorodtsy* came to be associated with separatism and potential threats to state unity, and perhaps even more importantly were seen as a challenge to the Russians' "dominant position" in the empire.

The concerns of the Russian elite about the threat of the politicization of cultural differences grew even stronger when projected onto the regions that had culturally mixed populations and occupied spaces between the imagined "Russian core" and the "alien borderlands." It was in relation to these transitional zones that the alien questions, such as those concerning Polish, Finnish, Baltic, and Muslim populations, acquired special sharpness. The "trends of the time" (*tendentsii vremeni*), as N. Kh. Bunge, a prominent statesman and modernizer of the Russian economy under Alexander III, called the ideas of nationality and assimilation, influenced the ways many educated Russians came to perceive the processes of cultural interaction that were unfolding in these frontier zones.[64] The belief in assimilation, according to which smaller peoples were expected to merge with larger ethnicities, tended to justify Russians' hopes that the smaller, non-Russian groups would eventually be transformed through Russification.[65] Yet these hopes were overshadowed by fears that larger, culturally strong non-Russian groups could compete with and even outdo the Russians in their assimilationist abilities. Russians of a nationalist persuasion, whether within the government or as members of the broader public, increasingly expressed such fears in regard to the spread of Polish, German, Finnish, and Tatar influence among smaller groups of neighboring peoples.

In the eastern part of the empire, these concerns were articulated most clearly in the Volga–Ural region, a transitional area occupying a position somewhere between "the native [*korennoi*] Russian lands" and the recently acquired Muslim borderlands. Anxiety over the multinational character of this region, and especially its cultural balance, became particularly pronounced following the Russian conquest of Central Asia and the dramatic increase in the number of Muslim subjects in the southeast part of the empire. When the confessional issues in the Volga–Ural region—specifically with regard to the apostasy of baptized Tatars and the spread of Islam among animist groups—were reconceptualized as a problem of nationality, a host of new meanings was brought to the Muslim Question.

The empire's confessional system made such a transition in thinking possible. The legal scholar M. A. Reisner, who wrote at the beginning of the twentieth century on the issue of religious tolerance in Russia, concluded that Russian religious laws linked confession with the concept of nationality. According to Reisner, Russian confessional policy was based on political considerations. The state did not tolerate different faiths as such, but rather as different nationalities with all their customs, including faith.[66] Viewing religion as a foundation of nationality, the state thus locked religious communities within their ascribed national boundaries. As the concept was formulated in the 1905–1907 report of the Holy Synod, "The Russian remains Russian as long as he is Orthodox, but he becomes a Pole, Tatar, or German, etc. as soon he accepts Roman Catholicism, Islam, or Lutheranism."[67] One's faith defined one's national culture and all the attributes associated with it: language, appearance, and way of life. In 1897, the priest I. A. Iznoskov wrote: "Among the Tatars, the idea of being a Tatar and being a Muslim are inseparable. And so in propagandizing Mohammedanism, they propagandize Tatarness as well. He who accepts Islam also accepts the [Tatar] nationality."[68] For this reason, the Volga Tatars, as strong devotees of their faith, appeared to missionaries and their sympathizers as the most influential transmitters of culture—the "*Kulturträgers* [bearers of culture] of the Muslim east."[69]

If for Western missionaries in Africa and Malaysia the Islamicization of animists meant a loss for the church and possible difficulties for the colonial administration, in the Russian situation this issue went beyond being a mere question of religious conversion. In Russia's nationalizing empire, the Islamicization and Tatarization of animists and baptized non-Russians, and sometimes even of Russian Orthodox peasants who lived among Muslims in remote settlements, became increasingly regarded by educated Russians as a setback for the Russian core-building project, which was itself a work-in-progress.[70] But it was the growth of the Tatar Muslim community, conceptualized as a nationality, that seemed to be especially dangerous to those who feared the mobilizing power of the Tatar historical memory of political independence, and who thus suspected Tatars of political separatism.

The issue of Tatarization was also closely related to concerns about the role and capacity of ethnic Russians as *Kulturträgers* in the East. As several contemporary authors noted, the strength of the core determined the assimilationist processes in the borderlands.[71] The publicist I. S. Aksakov was among those who raised this issue from the Slavophile perspective in relation to the western provinces, which represented, in his opinion, the main arena of the Polish Question. In 1867, he wrote: "If we want them [the western provinces] to become Russified . . . for this we require that Russians themselves everywhere, and especially in the western provinces, be fully Russians, have their Russian dignity, and not for a minute lose consciousness of their national superiority." Aksakov devoted his publicist energy to the situation in the western provinces, which seemed to him especially disturbing, yet in regard to the eastern part of European Russia he once noted in passing: "We don't have worries in the old Kazan tsardom, among Tatars and Cheremis."[72]

Anxieties about the national strength of Russians as compared with Tatars were expressed by local Russian observers as well as participants in the cultural struggle in Russia's eastern provinces. Unlike the western borderlands, the eastern provinces had not been explicitly claimed by Russians as a part of Russia's core or native (*korennaia*) land. At the same time, Russian commentators on the eastern borderlands considered it to be Russia's mission to keep Islam and Tatars within what they considered their historic boundaries and to preserve the smaller, non-Russian tribes from Tatarization. From the Kazan missionaries' point of view, Russian religious vulnerability as revealed in cases of apostasy was proof of the overall unsatisfactory "religious–moral condition" of the Russian population, which was itself further proof of the upsetting weakness of Russian nationality. Russian peasants seemed not only to be vulnerable to outside cultural influences and not capable of assimilating non-Russians, but also were not conscious of the cultural mission assigned to them by educated Russians. As various missionaries mentioned, in addition to their lack of religious enthusiasm and national consciousness, the Russian peasants disdained baptized Tatars, thus complicating missionaries' struggle against Islam and Tatarization.[73] Increasingly, Russian observers identified connections between the issue of Tatarization and what some formulated as the Russian Question. S. S. Larionov, inspector of the Caucasus school district, concluded as follows at the beginning of the twentieth century: "It seems that we, Russians, were not able to become a model for our aliens in the East and [that] gave an opportunity for Islam to triumph. The issue of Tatarization will disappear when we become more educated, when our schools and institutions will serve as the model for the aliens."[74]

But how to make the Russian "core" population a model attractive to *inorodtsy*? What constituted the Russian Question? The issue was deeper than the problem of defining Russianness on the basis of language or religion. It was the question about Russians' own best path for political and social renewal, an issue that remained divisive among educated Russians themselves. Shaken by the revolutionary movement and Alexander II's assassination, some conservative Russians questioned the very role of Orthodox ethnic Russians as the unifying force in the empire. In 1882, K. N. Leont'ev (1831–1891), a diplomat, religious thinker, and also a publisher sympathetic to Slavophile ideas, clearly articulated this view by turning what liberal-minded Russians saw as problems—such as reaction, fanaticism, and backwardness—into positive characteristics that, in his opinion, would contribute to the stability of the Russian state and society. Viewing religion as a guarantor of stability, he noted that instead of true Orthodoxy, the Russification campaign as conducted by representatives of the "Great Russian core" was bringing destructive European progress to the empire's borderlands. As he argued, "liberalism came from Christian countries, not from the Caucasian mountains and Mecca." Thus, he argued, it was the non-Christians and non-Orthodox, firm in their religious beliefs, not Russians, who could save the empire. Leont'ev wrote: "Thanks to God, that Russification is being resisted."[75] Leont'ev's ideal was a heterogeneous and static empire, which should be "frozen" (*podmorozhena*) rather than transformed.

Although contested, the Russification of Muslims through secular education and Russian language remained government policy. Nonetheless, Tatarization increasingly came to attract greater concern both outside and within government circles. Il'minskii's followers, in particular, opposed forceful Russification, which they spelled *обрусение,* in favor of the more natural process of assimilation into Russian culture, spelled as *обрусѣние.*[76] The same distinction was made in relation to the process of Tatarization. Pointing to conditions favorable to Tatarization, missionaries concluded that not only did Tatarization itself imply the imposition of an alien culture on some non-Russian minorities, but also that the quick assimilation of non-Tatars to Tatar culture was not a natural phenomenon (*otatarivanie*), but the result of premeditated and purposeful activity achieved through

Tatar Muslim propaganda (*tatarizatsia*). Conceived in national terms, Tatarization increasingly began to be seen as part of a Tatar Muslim nation-building project and a struggle against the Russian people. The evidence to support this interpretation was the so-called Muslim awakening.

The Challenge of the "Muslim Awakening"

By the beginning of the twentieth century, many Russians admitted that what some considered to be the "ignorant and fanatical Muslim world" had "unexpectedly awakened." N. P. Ostroumov, the director of the Tashkent Teachers' Seminary, described this development as "the conscious movement of Muslims toward universal [*obshchechelovecheskoe*] enlightenment and toward forms of life that accord with modern conceptions of culture and progress."[77] This "awakening" appears to have begun in the 1870s. At that time, Russian perceptions of Islam and of the Muslim Question, along with government attempts in the 1870s to enlighten and integrate Muslims by means of education, met a response that was voiced by an emerging Muslim intelligentsia that had come of age in imperial society, received a Russian or Western European education, and had become imbued with popular notions of progress and duty toward the common folk. To counter Russian criticism of and attempts to overcome Muslim backwardness and isolation, Muslim intellectuals offered their own visions of Muslim identity, enlightenment, and imperial integration.

What was seen as the Muslim awakening presented a new challenge to Il'minskii and his associates. Yet as they regretfully noted, neither the government nor the broader public took the awakening seriously until it began to take on a more overt political character.[78]

The ideas that both indicated and stimulated the Muslim awakening first became known to the broader Russian reading public in the 1880s through the writings of the Crimean Tatar I. Bey Gasprinskii (Gaspirali) (1851–1914).[79] Gasprinskii was born in a Crimean village to the family of a *murza*. After pursuing a traditional religious education in a *maktab*, he studied in a Russian gymnasium, at the Voronezh Military Academy, and later at the military academy in Moscow. During his time in Moscow (1865–1867), Gasprinskii met the editor M. N. Katkov, and through him became acquainted with the concepts of Russian nationalism, liberalism, and political radicalism.[80] In 1867, Gasprinskii returned to Crimea, where he taught the Russian language at Muslim schools. In 1871, he left Crimea and lived in Paris and then in Turkey.[81] Sometime during that period, Gasprinskii conceived the idea of publishing a Turkic language newspaper in Bakhchisarai, Crimea. Several years passed, however, before it became possible to put this idea into practice. After his return to Crimea from Turkey, from 1878 until 1882, Gasprinskii served as the mayor (*gorodskoi golova*) of Bakhchisarai.

In 1881, in Simferopol, Gasprinskii published a brochure in the Russian language entitled *Russkoe musul'manstvo. Mysli, zametki i nabliudeniia musul'manina* (*Rus-

sian Muslims: Thoughts, Notes, and Observations of a Muslim). In this essay, he raised questions about Russian–Muslim relations, government policy toward Muslims, and suggested possibilities that he felt would lead toward state unity in the multiethnic empire. He claimed that the "question about aliens" (*vopros ob inorodtsakh*), and Muslims in particular, had not yet been clarified, and he took it upon himself to start a public debate on this issue.[82] Gasprinskii criticized the Russian state's relations with Muslims, which he thought exemplified the principle of "While I am the master, you pay and live how you wish" rather than being a "fully planned and consistent policy inspired by an idea."[83] At the same time, he criticized the condition of Russian Muslims, which he described as characterized by a "social and intellectual isolation, deep backwardness, dead immobility in all spheres of life, and gradual pauperization."[84] He asked: "Should Muslims and Russians live . . . as random companions [*sputniki*], neighbors, or should they develop closer family relations, like between the children of the great family of peoples [*narody*] of our vast great Fatherland?"[85] Gasprinskii answered his own question by stating that it was not enough for Muslims to be just "loyal citizens" (*vernopoddannye grazhdane*) who lived under the protection of imperial laws, paid taxes, and fulfilled state duties. Such an "official or external connection" had to be supplemented by what he called a "moral connection" (*nravstvennaia sviaz'*) or "conscious sympathy" with Russia. Gasprinskii's call for rapprochement, progress, and a new social consciousness reflected the ideas of the era of Great Reforms that had previously informed the Russian public debate on the alien questions.

Gasprinskii assigned the leading role in rapprochement to educated Russians; however, he envisioned both Russians and educated Tatars (*intelligentsia*) as the future civilizers of the Muslim Orient.[86] At the same time, he pointed to the "weak assimilationist capacities" of Russians while also noting the strength of the Muslim communities that had successfully resisted outside influences.[87] In contrast to the views of Orthodox writers, Gasprinskii explained Muslim "isolation" not by the "hostile spirit of Islam" but by the lack of education and knowledge about Russia among Muslims.[88] He thus advocated for the rapprochement (*sblizhenie*) of Muslims with Russians, which he understood not as assimilation—which he claimed was impossible—but as the "moral Russification [*nravstvennoe obrusenie*] of the Muslims," to be accomplished by improving their education while at the same time allowing them to preserve their cultural identity.[89] Gasprinskii's program presupposed the need to reform traditional Muslim education and to Europeanize the Muslim way of life, and he popularized both goals through his newspaper *Terjuman-Perevodchik* (1883–1914). He also opened a reformed *maktab* in Bakhchisarai in 1884, and publicized his views in numerous trips to Muslim regions of the empire.[90]

Gasprinskii was the ideological founding father of the reformist movement among Russian Muslims—the so-called "new method" (Jadid) movement. This movement attempted to overcome the alleged backwardness of Muslims through the synthesis of cultural Islamic values with the achievements of the West. In declaring that its purpose was the adaptation of Islam to modern society, Jadidism in the Russian empire had much in common with similar reformist movements among intellectuals in other Muslim countries. Like the Russian reform-minded religious and secular critics, the Jadids criticized the condition of contemporary Muslim society, but unlike the Orthodox critics, they saw the reason for Muslim backwardness not in Islam but in the cultural conservatism of the Muslim community.

At the heart of Jadidist reform activity was the transformation of traditional Muslim religious education. To bring innovation to Muslim education and to make it serve the needs of the modern world, Jadids proposed introducing secular subjects into the curriculum and implementing modern methods of teaching and organizing the educational process. The Jadids considered Islam to be the basis of identity for the Muslim community and often referred to Islam to justify their reforms. However, as Adeeb Khalid has noticed, their understanding of Islam had been formulated in the context of a desacralized world.[91] The Jadids made use of new public spaces, such as periodicals, books, schools, charitable societies, theaters, and, later, political organizations, to address the problems of culture and society. This in itself represented a challenge to the old elite's monopoly over cultural production in Muslim society, and as a consequence the Jadids ran into opposition from Muslim traditionalists (kadimists) who accused the reformers of encouraging the destruction of tradition and the debasement of Muslim morality.[92]

Along with their new understanding of religion, the reformers challenged Muslims in Russia to reconsider the boundaries and the nature of Muslim communities in modern national terms. Gasprinskii's appeal to Turkic Muslims to unite on the basis of religion and the Turkic literary language was new, and offered one potential way of imagining a national community that, prior to the beginning of the twentieth century, was mainly a cultural project.

The Muslim reformist movement found resonance among the Volga and Crimean Tatars, Bashkirs, and Muslims in Transcaucasia and Central Asia. In various regions, the susceptibility of Muslims to both reformist ideas and the local peculiarities of the movement was determined by the differing social, economic, and cultural conditions of Muslim life.[93] The spread of Jadid ideas among the Volga Tatars had in many respects been preconditioned by the rapid social and economic changes in European Russia, as well as by the confessional confrontation in the Volga–Ural region. Faced with the challenges presented by modernization, economic competition, as well as the state and church attempts to transform Muslims' cultural identity, Volga Tatar intellectuals, most of whom came from either clerical or commercial backgrounds, took up Gasprinskii's ideas and emerged as the new leaders of the Muslim reformist movement in the Russian empire.

During this same period, the activity of the Volga Tatar reformers created the preconditions for development of a Tatar national consciousness. The interest of local intellectuals in Volga Tatar history, folklore, and language, as seen for example in the activity of earlier Tatar educators such as Sh. Marjani (1818–1889) and K. Nasyri (1825–1902), created the basis for a Tatar national project.[94] However, the territorial and cultural boundaries of this emerging Tatar identity were still unclear and numerous questions remained, such as whether the Tatar nation should develop independently from the broader Turko-Muslim community as defined by Gasprinskii, or whether Bashkir and Tatar national cultures should be considered separately or together.

Gasprinskii's success in receiving government permission for his publications testified that, to at least some extent, his appeal to the Muslim's "enlightened" thinking had convinced some Russian officials. In 1883, the Tauride vice governor justified his approval of *Terjuman* not only on the basis of Gasprinskii's "political reliability" (*blagonadezhnost'*), but also by the usefulness of this newspaper in making the Tatar population "acquainted with the laws and government decrees and breaking their current state of isolation."[95]

The Muslim intelligentsia's concern with progress presented a challenge to preexisting Russian stereotypes of Islam, a fact that became especially apparent in discussions surrounding the problem of the compatibility of Islam with the concept of progress. The emergence of progressive Muslims, and especially their publishing activities, upset the broadly accepted view of a "stagnant Islamic world." In the 1880s and 1890s, following the lead of *Terjuman*, Muslim authors, among them A. A. Devlet-Kil'deev, Murza Alim, and A. Baiazitov, published a number of articles in the Russian press in which they debated with Russian and European critics of Islam. These Muslim writers denied the widespread charges that Islam was fanatical, fatalistic, intolerant of other religions, despotic, polygamist, and tolerant of slavery, and they strove to give the Russian-speaking public a "true sense" of the Koran. "Islam," these authors argued, "neither rejected progress nor was hostile to Western civilization," and they added that "the Koran and Sharia were amenable to all reasonable reforms."[96] Relying on citations from the Koran, the Muslim authors publicly challenged the contention of orientalist scholars and Orthodox missionaries that Islam was incompatible with modern culture. The attempts of Muslim publicists to "rehabilitate the Koran," in turn, provoked reactions from Russian missionaries and orientalists who responded with quotations of their own.

Central to the question of "Islam and progress" was the issue of Muslim–Russian rapprochement and the place of Muslims in a modernizing state. To accept the proposition that Islam was compatible with modern civilization meant an acceptance of the fact that rapprochement with Russians did not require Muslim subjects to give up their Muslim identity. For those Russians who considered Islam to be a religion hostile to Christianity and the empire as a Russian Orthodox state, this perspective was unacceptable on principle, and, not surprisingly, Orthodox missionaries held the view that Islam should not be modernized but rather weakened. The view that Christianization constituted the only means of true enlightenment and rapprochement had to contend with the realization of the difficulty and even impossibility of missionary work among Muslims, which made it difficult to give up the conception of Muslims as a stagnant and ignorant people.

In 1884, in the Slavophile newspaper *Rus,* M. A. Miropiev, a graduate of the Kazan Theological Academy and a teacher at the Turkestan Teachers' Seminary, published a response to Gasprinskii's *Russkoe musul'manstvo* (*Russian Muslims*). Believing Russians were not well prepared to respond to Gasprinskii's concerns about the policies of the Russian state toward Islam, Miropiev took it upon himself to formulate and answer the Alien Question in relation to Muslims. He rejected Gasprinskii's insistence on the need for a "moral rapprochement" based on a respect for Muslim national distinctiveness. Such an approach, Miropiev argued, should only apply to "civilized" nationalities whose cultures did not strongly differ from the Russian. To Miropiev, Muslims were not civilized; he therefore advocated a policy of cultural assimilation. As Miropiev saw it, Islam could not provide a basis for rapprochement and consequently had to be weakened rather than modernized. An assimilationist approach, in Miropiev's view, would lead Muslims to intellectual and moral enlightenment through acquisition of the Russian language and Russian culture—without, however, making any reference to religion (i.e., by ignoring religion).[97]

To Russian critics like Miropiev, Muslim reformist efforts represented not so much a movement toward progress and rapprochement with the Russians, but rather a calculated promotion of Islam and an attempt to unify and "fanaticize" the different Muslim communities within the empire. These critics were especially dismayed by what they saw as the popularization of a positive image of Islam in the Russian press.[98] Ten years after *Terjuman* was launched, V. D. Smirnov wrote that Gasprinskii's newspaper was a valuable source of information from which Russians could learn about the aspirations of Muslim intelligentsia and the state of Islam in Russia. Nevertheless, he took care to point out that instead of promoting state interests, as Gasprinskii had promised when asking for official permission to publish *Terjuman*, the newspaper had become an apologist for Islam.[99]

Smirnov (1846–1922) was born near Astrakhan into the family of a village sexton. He studied at the Perm Ecclesiastical Seminary and then at the St. Petersburg Theological Academy. After studying for one year at the latter, he transferred to the department of Oriental languages at St. Petersburg University. After graduating, Smirnov served as a professor of Turkic languages at the same university and also as a censor of Russian Muslim publications, including *Terjuman*. Il'minskii, who met Smirnov in 1877 in Kazan, had a positive opinion of him as someone who "knew Muslim Tatars, understood the state goals well, and was not partial toward Muslims."[100] The Russian orientalist V. A. Gordlevskii (1876–1956) mentioned Smirnov's belief in the "Russian idea" and his fervent temperament, suggesting that he could be a successful publicist and propagandist.[101] Indeed, Smirnov was not only a scholar of the language, literature, and history of Turkey, but also a publicist who wrote about contemporary Islam and the question of alien education. He took the Muslim intellectuals' criticism of Russian writings on Islam almost personally and became involved in the polemic. Viewing Islam as an intolerant, anti-Christian religion, Smirnov accused Muslim commentators of "poor knowledge of their own religious teaching and history." His criticism was directed not only at progressive Muslim writers who, as he put it, tried to "clear the road for Islam within Russian society," but also at those educated Russians who had become responsive to the new kind of "Muslim propaganda" that, in his view, was striving to achieve a "high standing" for Islam and to create a "party" within the Russian state. Although Smirnov was motivated by his anti-Islamic views (as were other Orthodox critics), his expressed concerns about the progressive Muslim intelligentsia also suggested fears about the possible implications of modernizing Islam in the European sense of political progress for imperial governance of Muslims and their standing vis-à-vis Russians who themselves were denied political rights and freedoms.

Additionally, the attempts of Muslim reformers, as Il'minskii put it, to "strengthen Islam on the rational foundations of the intelligentsia [*na ratsional'nykh i intelligentskykh osnovaniakh*]"[102] once again seemed to reveal the weakness of Orthodoxy. In 1890, Il'minskii, in a letter to N. P. Ostroumov, retold a story about a public religious debate with Baptists in Rostov organized by the Orthodox clerical authorities and reported by the *Ekaterinoslav Eparkhial'nye vedomosti*. Il'minskii wrote: "Jews, Armenians, Russian nihilists, and civilized Tatars came to watch the debate." Mullah Bigiev came to this debate and "bombarded the Orthodox priest with objections and evoked the sympathy of the audience." Il'minskii was very upset about the "presumptuous [*samonadeiannoe*] behavior" of the Orthodox clergy, who only "put themselves in shame and disgraced the Orthodox belief."[103]

Il'minskii was not a proponent of religious polemic with Muslims as a way of proselytizing and did not take part in public debates with "progressive" Muslims. It was Ostroumov, his former student and director of the Teachers' Seminary in Tashkent, who undertook the effort to combat Muslim publicists in the press.[104] Although Il'minskii did not openly participate in the debate, he supported Ostroumov's publications, which he found useful for "exposing the harm and acidity of Islam" (*vrednost' i ekhidstvo*).[105] Ostroumov met with Gasprinskii in Tashkent and corresponded with him and other Muslim publicists. He read issues of *Terjuman* and attentively followed the publications of Russian Muslim authors in other periodicals. Between 1880 and 1914 he published numerous articles and books on contemporary Islam, the Muslim awakening, and the Muslim Question.[106]

Because of the constraints of censorship, Muslim intellectuals responded to Ostroumov's writings in private letters. One letter signed by Murza Alim criticized the biased, one-sided, and hostile view of Islam held by Christian critics. He called instead for the judgment of Islam as well as Christianity from a standpoint of "rationalism" and "science," differentiating between what he called "belief" and "religion." The author also suggested that since Islam was younger than Christianity, Islam in the nineteenth century should be compared with Christianity of the thirteenth century, before the Reformation.[107] The author declared himself to be a "loyal citizen [*vernopoddannyi grazhdanin*] of the Russian tsar and the state." But he disagreed with Ostroumov that religion, and Orthodoxy in particular, should be the binding force in the multiconfessional empire. He pointed out that Christian missionary activity among Muslims had been unsuccessful and only provoked fanaticism and displeasure. Instead, his suggestion was to "reduce these seemingly different religions to one common denominator for all mankind—enlightenment," understood as a "love for the truth and rationalism in religious questions."[108] Enlightenment was the main theme of Gasprinskii's letter to Ostroumov. He wrote that "all holy books were good, but people should become more educated and knowledgeable." Otherwise, any religious teaching would be of little help. He considered intellectual development (*umstvennoe razvitie*) in the native languages of both "uncivilized" Muslims and Russians to be the primary concern. He accused Ostroumov of giving up this goal in relation to Muslims because of what he called the political necessity "to maltreat the subjugated people."[109]

Ostroumov did not reconcile with his Muslim progressive opponents. He continued popularizing the view of Islam as a religion not amenable to progress and hostile to Orthodoxy. Among his works, only *Sarty. Etnograficheskie materialy* (*Sarts: Ethnographic materials*), which expressed a rather optimistic view of rapprochement of the Muslim settled population of Central Asia with Russians, judged the contemporary state of cultural development of the Sarts from a historical, rather than an ideological, perspective. But Orthodox dogmatism was not the only factor that explained Ostroumov's inability to reconcile with his opponents. To Ostroumov, the progressive Muslim intelligentsia and their reformist agenda appeared to be in competition with Russian Orthodox educators, who were themselves attempting to engineer social change as well as guide alien affairs in the eastern part of the empire.

Orthodox writers on the Muslim Question quickly detected nationalistic ideas in the Jadid movement, ideas that, in their view, were helping to reinforce the existing religious isolation and separateness of the Muslim population. As Il'minskii had suggested to the Holy Synod Chief procurator, Pobedonostsev, the Muslim intelligentsia, including "Gasprinskii & Co.," were using slogans of "cultural progress" (*intelligentnyi progress*) to advance a "national-political" point of view that would replace "the traditionally awkward and unseemly fanaticism" of Islam and pave the way for the establishment of a core of Muslim culture in Russia.[110] Il'minskii indicated that it was precisely in Russian educational institutions that Muslims had acquired these nationalist ideas, and that these ideas were in fact much more dangerous than old-fashioned Muslim fanaticism. Il'minskii thus advised Pobedonostsev to be cautious when recommending candidates for the Orenburg Ecclesiastical Assembly: "A fanatic without Russian education and language is considerably better than a Tatar with Russian civilization."[111] Concerned about the spread of "progressive ideas built upon a Mohammedan foundation," Il'minskii stressed what he saw as the "complication of the Muslim Question" in Russia in his letters to Pobedonostsev.[112]

Some of Il'minskii's followers went so far as to suggest that the Jadid movement would lead Muslims down the path to separatism. Among those critics was N. A. Bobrovnikov (1854–1921), a son of orientalist A. A. Bobrovnikov and a graduate of Kazan University. After his father died, N. A. Bobrovnikov was raised by Il'minskii and after Il'minskii's death in 1891 he became the director of the Teachers' Seminary in Kazan. In his survey of the non-Russian population of the Kazan province, published in 1899, Bobrovnikov claimed that the Muslim intelligentsia was cultivating what he termed "conscious aspiration for isolation" or a "separatist movement on the basis of Islam" (*obosobitel'noe dvizhenie*).[113] Bobrovnikov saw the evidence of this trend in Gasprinskii's aspiration to enlighten and unify different Russian Turkic-Muslim communities by means of Islam and, perhaps even more importantly, by what he called an "artificially created" common Turkic language.[114]

In his *Vvedenie v kurs islamovedenia* (*Introduction to the Study of Islam*), in which he later summarized his views, Ostroumov described both Gasprinskii and Il'minskii as missionaries and nationalists.[115] Ostroumov interpreted Il'minskii's efforts to strengthen Orthodox belief among baptized non-Russians through instruction in native languages as a Russian nationalist project that could eventually also involve Muslims. Gasprinskii's "pan-Turkic" nationalist project, in Ostroumov's view, aspired to prevent the eventual assimilation of Muslims and instead promoted their rapprochement with Turkey rather than with Russia. In his view, both Il'minskii and Gasprinskii spread their influence far beyond the areas where they lived through a network of schools and followers, as well as by their active publishing activity.[116] Ostroumov noticed that while Il'minskii's influence was felt mainly in the Volga region, Gasprinskii's followers "seized a much larger region," penetrating into Russian Central Asia.[117]

Ostroumov's and Gasprinskii's conflicting attitudes came into direct competition in Central Asia after Ostroumov took up a position with the Ministry of Education in Tashkent in 1877. From 1883 to 1917, he was the editor of the *Tuzemnaia gazeta,* an official newspaper published in the Sart (Uzbek) language (beginning in 1885 it included a parallel Russian translation) and designed chiefly for the native administration.[118] Viewing his newspaper as a tool for educating natives, Ostroumov published articles about Russia and Turkestan, exposing their history, nature, geography, and politics. He compared the significance of his publishing effort for Turkestan's natives with the importance of *Vedomosti,* the first newspaper for Russians in the eighteenth century.

Although Ostroumov and other graduates of the Kazan Theological Academy were invited to work for the Ministry of Public Education in Turkestan, and Il'minskii, their mentor, was involved in discussions of school policy in Turkestan, neither Il'minskii's system of Christian education nor Orthodox missionary activity was permitted in Turkestan. Nor did Ostroumov's knowledge of Islam and local life guarantee him a stable position within the Turkestan administration. His influence on political decision-making in Turkestan depended to a much greater degree on his success in local politics and his personal connections. Such personal channels were also available to Muslims. In his diary, Ostroumov described cases in which Muslims from other regions of the empire used personal connections with Russian administrators to promote their interests and influence Russian policy toward Islam in Turkestan.[119] It was no accident, then, that Ostroumov's anti-Islam publications were intended for Russian administrators and the educated public who, according to him, "did not have firm [*ustoichivye*] views on alien education" or on the Muslim Question in general.

One of the examples of Muslim influence described by Ostroumov was Gasprinskii's proposal to reform Muslim schools, which he submitted in 1892 to the Turkestan governor-general, A. B. Vrevskii (1889–1898). In this proposal, Gasprinskii addressed the question of how to teach the Russian language to Muslims. He explained the "weak aspiration of Muslims to learning the Russian language" not as a consequence of religious fanaticism and alienation (*otchuzhdeonnost'*), but rather because their lengthy religious education simply left no time for Russian. He thus concluded that in order to achieve success in Russian-language training at Muslim schools, the methods of instruction at religious schools had to be reformed following the example of the new-method schools in Crimea.[120] The governor-general passed the proposal on to V. P. Nalivkin, the Turkestan school inspector, whose recommendation was to reject the advice of "Tatars in general," and Gasprinskii in particular, on principle. First, Nalivkin stated that Gasprinskii was "not competent" to give advice on Central Asian Muslim schools that, in his opinion, differed from schools in Crimea. But perhaps more to the point, Nalivkin considered Gasprinskii's *Terjuman* to be an "anti-Russian" undertaking and doubted Gasprinskii's aspiration to serve the Russian cause in Turkestan. He interpreted Gasprinskii's proposed policy as an attempt to gain influence with Turkestan's Muslims.[121]

Ostroumov called the Tatar intelligentsia's enlightenment and nationalistic project "artificial." In his 1884 memo on the Russian task in Turkestan, he pointed to the "merger" of Russians with the natives as the goal of the Russian administration. By merger he understood not cultural assimilation, but a development of a "sense of economic, every-day, and political connection with the metropolis and the core Russian population."[122] In this project, he asserted, native languages and customs could be preserved without becoming political categories. Similarly, Il'minskii's missionary project, as applied in the Volga region, was viewed by its followers as a way to bring non-Russians closer to Russians without undermining their local identities. Il'minskii's followers preferred "conscious" (soft) Russification to what they called "mechanical" Russification. Therefore, Gasprinskii's nationalist project, which claimed different Turkic peoples for one nation, appeared to the Russian educators and missionaries as a threat not only to the project of merging these peoples with Russians, but also as an attempt to force the suppression of their cultural individuality. Bobrovnikov called Gasprinskii's language program a "brute assimilation of different Turkic dialects into literary Ottoman Turkish."[123] Il'minskii's followers thus felt that they were being attacked on two fronts, by the pan-Turkists as well as by the Russian nationalists, who criticized Il'minskii's use of non-Russian languages and advocated Russian as the means of integration (in Il'minskii's words, "mechanical" Russification).

Il'minskii's followers in Kazan were particularly sensitive to the competition with "new Muslims." Here, Il'minskii's Teachers' Seminary was at rivalry with the Tatar

Teachers' School, both established by the 1870 Ministry regulations. The Tatar Teachers' School seemed to Il'minskii and his followers to signal government support of Islam. They were especially concerned that the school's graduates were responsive to Gasprinskii's ideas about the new-method as well as the all-Muslim literary language. Later, some of the former students of this school would become the leaders of the Muslim cultural and sociopolitical movement in Russia.[124]

Russian educators claimed that they had a special closeness to non-Russian commoners, understood their needs, and possessed the special skills necessary to carry out the mission of their enlightenment and integration into the empire. The graduates of the Tatar Teachers' School contested this assumption. Bobrovnikov described the Tatar Teachers' School as "in direct logical contradiction to the other non-Russian schools," and blamed it for taking strength and energy away from other non-Russian schools."[125] Although he did not believe that the Russian language alone made Muslims into Russians, he opposed the new literary trend propagandized by Gasprinskii and his followers. He claimed that this new language was not understood by the ordinary Tatars and was harmful for them and for Russian–Muslim relations.

As an example, Bobrovnikov referred to the mass disorder among the Tatars in response to the 1897 imperial census. He explained that while the disorder was blamed on Muslim isolation, its real cause was the "muddle-headed" (*bestolkovyi*) translation of the brochure about the census prepared by Sh. I. Akhmerov, an official from the Ministry of Public Education and the inspector of the Kazan Tatar Teachers' School. The translation, according to Bobrovnikov, was into the new literary Turkic language that was not understood by the Tatars. Bobrovnikov suggested that the translators had used this as an opportunity to spread the "new unifying Muslim language," although he did not have facts to prove this intention. To emphasize that it was the Teachers' Seminary, but not the Tatar Teachers' School, that provided the cadres with necessary language skills to communicate with Tatars and be the mediators between them and the government, Bobrovnikov wrote: "The students of the Teachers' Seminary see several mosques from their windows and a *madrasa* is directly alongside the seminary. Therefore, Tatar affairs [*tatarskoe delo*] are near and important for us."[126]

Gasprinskii and his like-minded associates established themselves as Muslim progressives.[127] Not only did they claim that progressive Muslims existed, but also that a successful "Muslim awakening" was a fact. To support this view, in 1901 Gasprinskii in his essay titled *Mebadi-yi temeddün-i Islamiyan-i Rus* (*First Steps toward Civilizing the Russian Muslims*) provided a survey of Muslim cultural advances in Russia, pointing to the continuing increase in publishing, the rising aspiration among Muslims (including women) to higher education, the opening of Muslim theaters, and so on. In his opinion, this Muslim revival testified to "the onset of progress and civilization" within the Islamic world, a change he considered to be "a natural phenomenon bred from within."[128]

Gasprinskii's and Il'minskii's ideas represented efforts to rethink the role and the nature of religion in the face of the pressures of the modern age and the challenges of imperial rule. Both projects claimed to aspire to better integration of Muslims into the empire. Both inspired followers and stirred opposition among their co-religionists. But there were also significant differences. In contrast to Gasprinskii, who viewed progress as inevitable and desirable, Il'minskii was not optimistic about the path of European progress for Russia's future. He rejected the modern period of Russian history and consequently the developments and policies that gave rise to Jadidism. Il'minskii's thinking had more in common with the Slavophile ideas inspired by modern nationalistic ideas built on Russia's opposition to the West.[129] His ideas resembled the Slavophile ideal of a harmonious society with autocracy sanctioned by the moral idea and the religious people freely (without state interference) arranging their lives. The Slavophile concept of Russia as an organic, not a mechanical, community was evoked by Il'minskii and his followers in relation to the ideal of a multiethnic empire as a whole. Their vision appeared to conflict with what Il'minskii's followers saw as Gasprinskii's "artificial" nation-building project. Il'minskii believed in the superiority of Orthodox teaching vis-à-vis Islam, and he hoped that the revitalized Orthodoxy would naturally win the loyalty of the Muslims. Until then, Muslims had to wait, according to Il'minskii. Gasprinskii challenged these expectations. Although in principle they denied the compatibility of Islam with progress, the Orthodox lay-educators in the empire's east recognized the existence of progressive Muslims and interpreted the challenges presented by them as a "complication" of the Muslim Question.

* * *

In the 1860–1870s, as we have seen, the liberal agenda of the state turned its attention to the problem of overcoming what was perceived as the cultural ignorance and alienation of Muslim Tatars. State schooling emerged as a possible solution to this pressing political problem. Government educational projects for the empire's eastern minorities, however, were linked to the state-regulated confessional system. As a result, the tensions that characterized the understanding of the Muslim Question as one of Muslims' alienation and domination were exacerbated instead of resolved. The Orthodox–Muslim rivalry that had previously found expression in the Russian understanding of the apostasy problem had now been implanted into a new institutional framework. The state found itself in the difficult position of pursuing two contradictory agendas, the first aimed at the secular integration of Muslims, and the second at protecting baptized non-Russians from Muslim influence. Without dismantling the confessional system in which the state ascribed subjects an official religious affiliation, the educational project alone could not resolve the issue of apostasy and thus eliminate concerns and tensions related to it. But the special schools that were created for baptized non-Russians and especially the use of native languages, as the critics of Il'minskii feared, were likely to set these non-Russian Christians on a path separate from that of the dominant Russian Orthodoxy. The schooling approach for Muslims also involved potential risks for the autocratic Orthodox state. The state project of Russification of Muslims by means of secular education and Russian language did not anticipate the equalization of Islam with Orthodoxy and the elimination of restrictions based on religion.[130] But in making Muslims "Russian" through education, this approach was likely to produce claims by eventually "Russified" Muslims to be granted the same legal standing as Orthodox Russians. Finally, as Russianness came to be regarded ideologically as the cornerstone of the empire, the problems of apostasy to Islam and of Tatarization evolved into an issue of contested nationality that presented greater challenges as Russia moved into the era of mass politics.

Il'minskii's ideas and activities were central to this chapter, and not only because of his famous pedagogical system. Although focused on finding the solution to the problem of apostasy, his experience demonstrated the interconnectedness of the problems of the empire with domestic Russian problems, as well as Russians' contested visions of modernization. Il'minskii suggested a solution that reminded many Russians about the ills of their own society and resonated with Slavophile prescriptions for the empire's problems. Seeking to revitalize Russia, those adhering to a Slavophile worldview rejected European forms of enlightenment and instead suggested returning to the order of things in idealized Muscovite Russia. A revitalized form of popular religious life, free from state interference, constituted an important element of the project.

Il'minskii's ideas both appealed to and challenged state and church. The state partially adopted his approach for educating Christian non-Russians, but pressed by the need to integrate Muslims, the government also embarked on a project of secular enlightenment. This government compromise in educational policy dissatisfied Il'minskii and his followers.

Il'minskii's ideas, as well as the Slavophile program in general, resonated within the ruling circles after Alexander II's assassination in 1881. The new government sought ways to stabilize the country along its "native" path, but these ideas were never fully accepted by tsarist officials whose priority was to revitalize state authority rather than society. Il'minskii himself, while emphasizing the private character of his work, nevertheless appealed to the church and civil authorities. Although he eventually gained government support, he compromised some of his own ideas in the process.

His ideas, moreover, came into conflict and competition with the Jadid project of Muslims' enlightenment and integration. For Il'minskii and his followers, Gasprinskii's modernist efforts presented a "complication of the Muslim Question." Muslims now appeared to be consciously alienated, while their domination was reinterpreted as an anti-Russian expansionist nationalist project.

Yet this "complication" of the Muslim Question did not reach the ears of the central secular authorities until the early twentieth century. The Ministry of Internal Affairs continued to treat the question in exclusively confessional terms, seeing it mainly as a problem of apostasy from Orthodoxy. The greatest danger for the governing of the empire, as far as the MVD was concerned, was the "national question"—that is, "ideas about national distinctiveness and the attainment of independence," neither of which, according to some MVD officials, "had yet infected" Russian Muslims.[131] From the MVD officials' perspective, therefore, Islamic subjects could indeed be loyal subjects, and there were as yet no grounds to expect "difficulties of any kind, at least as concerns the majority of Muslims."[132]

This position had changed by the beginning of the twentieth century, as central institutions of the tsarist government began paying increasing attention to the "Muslim awakening." Among the first ones were the officials responsible for censorship at the Main Administration for Press Affairs who noticed the appearance of "new influences" in Tatar literature that "threatened to shatter the centuries-old way of life of the Russian Muslim population." Describing Gasprinskii's newspaper *Terjuman*, N. V. Shakhovskoi, head of the administration, noted the "duplicitous" orientation of the newspaper, which he saw as praising the Russian government while simultaneously praising the Turkish sultan and the European enlightenment of the Tatars.[133] In Shakhovskoi's view, the Muslim movement had evolved into an effort to implant Turkish culture among Russian Muslims.[134] In 1900, the Ministry of Internal Affairs requested information about the new movement from the governors of the Muslim provinces.[135] According to the officials of the Department of Police, these new influences were progressing in stages. They first appeared in the "innocent" form of Gasprinskii's "new method" of instruction. Thereafter, they coalesced into "an intellectual and social movement" that divided Muslims into two camps: "traditionalists" and "progressives." The Department of Police was hard-pressed to predict which of these two parties would emerge the stronger, or how far the "victors" would go. Nonetheless, the department judged both sides as equally "unreliable" from the standpoint of the interests of the Russian governance, as both camps, as the department officials saw them, were equally "alienated from Russia."[136] The broad and rapid politicization of imperial society that culminated in the revolution of 1905 made the changes taking place in the Muslim community more visible to wider circles of the Russian public and the government, and in turn affected the discussion of the Muslim Question.

4 "In Asia We Come as Masters"

The Challenge of the Civilizing Mission in Turkestan

The contentious debate on the premises involved in making Russia a viable imperial power took place at the same time that the country achieved a burst of territorial expansion in the east. Following the occupation of Chimkent in the Kokand khanate in 1864, Russia's conquests in Central Asia significantly enlarged the empire's territory and increased the heterogeneity of its population by forcefully introducing a large number of new Muslim subjects who, in contrast to Crimean and Volga Tatars, had had little previous contact with the Russian empire. This new geopolitical and demographic situation presented Russians with both opportunities and challenges.

The expansion into Central Asia gave Russians an opportunity to claim a "civilizing mission." For the European-minded educated imperial elite, the new Asian territories and subjects held the promise of reestablishing Russia's status as a European Great Power, a status that had recently been challenged by their defeat in the Crimean War. For those educated Russians who hoped for reforms along the "native" path, however, the civilizing mission in Asia promised spiritual revitalization and a cure for Russia's own ills.[1]

The Russians' feeling of moral and cultural superiority was boosted by the seeming ease of their conquest of Central Asia, especially when compared with the difficulties of the Caucasian campaign. What presented a greater challenge was maintaining this domination and connecting the conquered population to the empire. The acquisition of a large number of new Muslim subjects who, together with Muslims of other borderlands, came to constitute the empire's largest non-Christian group made the problem of Muslims' place in a modernizing imperial society especially acute.

A number of recent studies have interpreted Russia's imperial project in Central Asia as a special case that bore more resemblance to colonial Western European overseas empires than to the experience of Russian imperial rule in other borderlands.[2] Among the characteristics of colonial encounter in Central Asia, historians have pointed to Russian imperial arrogance and stereotypical Orientalist views of the new borderlands' Muslim population.[3] Certainly there were significant differences in imperial governance that separated this borderland from others of the empire's Muslim territories, such as the Crimea and Volga regions.

Unlike these regions, which were fairly integrated into the Russian social, administrative, legal, and confessional order, Turkestan was a recent acquisition administered under military rule with Russians constituting the minority among the predominantly Muslim population. Yet, as this chapter suggests, the new borderland was not a world apart. Russia's Central Asia was connected to the rest of the empire not only geographically but also through the transfer of actors, ideas, hopes, and anxieties. One example of such connectivity and interdependence was Russians' thinking about the Muslim Question. The recent conquest expanded the context within which tensions embedded in Russians' thinking about their relations with Muslims—and empire more generally—were revealed and intensified.

This chapter will highlight these tensions by focusing on Russians' responses to the sudden attack upon the Russian garrison in Andijan in 1898. The attack was led by the local Sufi, Muhammad Ali, known as Dukchi ishan, who called for "holy war." With the exception of the cholera riots in Tashkent in 1892, the Andijan uprising presented the most serious challenge to Russian rule in Turkestan in the late nineteenth century and provoked rethinking of Russian–Muslim relations in Turkestan and the empire more generally within the framework of the Muslim Question. When analyzing Russians' reactions to the uprising, historians differentiate between the apocalyptic vision of Islam articulated by the Turkestan governor-general S. M. Dukhovskoi and a more pragmatic and tolerant view of the finance minister S. Iu. Witte. But the range of reactions and meanings attached to them was even wider. One important lesson that some Russians drew from the Andijan uprising was that Islam could not be ignored, as they believed had been the official practice in Turkestan. This chapter explores how Russians came to this conclusion and what meanings they assigned to it. But first, we must overview the system of Russian–Muslim relations in Turkestan that became the subject of such criticism.

"Ignoring" Islam

Since the Middle Ages, eastern Slavs had interacted with the nomads of the steppe as well as with the sedentary Muslims of Asia. The path to Asia was opened after the conquest of the Kazan and Astrakhan khanates (respectively in 1552 and 1556). The expansion into the steppe to the north of the Caspian Sea, to Siberia, and into the southern Urals brought Russia into contact with the nomadic, Turkic-speaking Kazakhs, who swore oaths of allegiance to the tsar during the course of the eighteenth and nineteenth centuries.[4] Orenburg, founded in 1743, became the center of the large new frontier province and the base for Russia's relations with Central Asia.[5] In Central Asia, Russia encountered three polities: the emirate of Bukhara, the khanate of Khiva, and the khanate of Kokand. In the eighteenth and up to the first half of the nineteenth century, Russia undertook several military and diplomatic expeditions to Central Asia, but active military penetration into this region did not begin until 1864.

The expansion was driven by strategic, political, and economic motives. However, St. Petersburg did not have a coherent plan for its expansion in this region, and frontier generals often took the initiative.[6] After Russia's defeat in the Crimean War in 1856, Central Asia became an arena for fierce political and economic competition between Russia and Britain. This competition affected the aspirations of the Russian ruling elite to attain in Central Asia a position equal to that of the European colonial powers.

The Russian military advance into Central Asia took place from bases in Orenburg and Semipalatinsk in western Siberia.[7] In 1864, Colonel M. G. Cherniaev occupied Chimkent in the Kokand khanate. In 1865, he also conquered Tashkent, against direct orders from St. Petersburg. Alexander II approved this arbitrary undertaking and signed a decree formalizing the annexation of Tashkent to Russia in 1866. The newly conquered territories remained under the control of Orenburg's governor-general, N. A. Kryzhanovskii, until 1867, when the governor-generalship of Turkestan with its administrative center in Tashkent was established.

Russia's rapid advance into territories entirely inhabited by Muslims and bordered by Muslim states raised concerns among local imperial authorities about the loyalty of the empire's new subjects. The religiously tinted military resistance of Muslims to imperial rule, combined with many Russians' perspective of Islam as an anti-Christian religion, seemed to offer grounds for Russians in Turkestan to interpret their relations with Muslims as a religious conflict, and to see themselves as a "handful of infidel conquerors."[8] The possible implications of the new geopolitical and demographic situation for the empire were especially felt by General N. A. Kryzhanovskii (1818–1888), who from 1864 to 1881 governed the frontier Orenburg region where Muslims constituted a large portion of the multiconfessional population. The situation seemed to him to be particularly threatening in face of the Muslim uprising against Chinese rule, which by 1864 had spread to the region of Xinjiang, bordering the Russian empire.[9] Kryzhanovskii's report in 1867 to the minister of internal affairs, P. A. Valuev, illustrates his anxieties:

> With the advance into the depths of Central Asia and the annexation of Turkestan to the empire, the entire boundless space from Kazan to the Tian-Shan mountain range has become a territory of uninterrupted Muslim population. . . . The image of such a mass of people confessing a religion according to whose dogmas we, Christians, are regarded as the natural and irreconcilable enemies of all true believers, should automatically draw the government's attention, all the more so since this same Islam has provoked in neighboring China at the present time such a degree of fanatical barbarity that holy war for the faith has been declared, and continues beyond our borders.[10]

These circumstances made the governor-general raise concerns about the Muslim Question in the eastern part of Russia. Valuev regarded the situation less dramatically, hoping that Muslim fanaticism would weaken over time.[11] Such an optimistic view also guided General K. P. von Kaufman (1818–1882), the first governor-general of Turkestan. After the establishment of that governor-generalship in 1867 and von Kaufman's appointment, Kryzhanovskii lost his influence in the affairs of the new borderland.

Von Kaufman enjoyed the special patronage and trust of both Alexander II and war minister D. A. Miliutin. As the emperor's personal agent in a new borderland, von Kaufman was granted unlimited authority. A military engineer by education, he was an experienced borderland officer and administrator. He had served thirteen years in the Caucasian army, fighting mountaineers. From 1860 to 1865, he was the director of the War Ministry's chancellery and a close associate of Miliutin. In 1865, under Miliutin's auspices, von Kaufman was appointed as governor-general of Vilna. Here, he continued the policies of his predecessor M. N. Murav'ev, which were directed toward securing the northwestern borderland within the empire after the 1863 Polish rebellion. In 1866, von Kaufman was removed from this position through the influence of the chief of the secret police, P. A. Shuvalov.[12] In autumn 1867, von Kaufman arrived in the new frontier region of Turkestan, which he administered for fourteen years. Along with his successful military campaigns, which considerably increased the territory of the governor-generalship, he was also remembered by his contemporaries as the organizer (*ustroitel'*) of the new region.[13]

At first comprised of the northern parts of the Kokand khanate and the Kazakh steppe (the Syr-Darya oblast and the Semirech'e oblast),[14] the territory of the Turkestan governor-generalship was enlarged by incorporating parts of the emirate of Bukhara, including Samarkand (1868), the Khiva khanate (1873), the southern part of the Kokand khanate (1876), and the Transcaspian area (conquered by 1884, but added to Turkestan in 1897). The emirate of Bukhara and the Khiva khanate became Russian protectorates. As a result of these acquisitions, the new imperial borders moved south and east to Iran, Afghanistan, and eastern Turkestan, which was then part of the Chinese empire. The newly conquered region was inhabited by various Turkic-speaking and Persian-speaking ethnic groups, and the majority of the new subjects practiced Sunni Islam. Religion and lifestyle (both nomadic and sedentary) played an important role in the self-identification of the local populations.[15] Intensive Russian colonization of Turkestan started in 1890; by the time of the first imperial census, conducted in 1897, the number of Russians had reached 9 percent of the total population.

Russian rule in Turkestan was regulated by the Temporary Statute approved by the Committee of Ministers in 1867. This statute established an administrative system based upon undivided military and civil authority and native self-government. Military rule was justified by considerations of security.[16] The establishment of Russian imperial order in Turkestan was also taking place during the period of Great Reforms. The Turkestan administration thus faced the challenging task of consolidating their control over the conquered population at a time when reform-minded Russians within and outside the government were seeking to transform the empire's core and redefine the principles of borderland policies. In Turkestan, the administrative solution to this problem was found in promoting the integration of the new borderland and people into the modernizing empire under the military leadership.[17]

In Turkestan, von Kaufman attempted to design a confessional order different from that in the rest of the empire. His confessional policy was informed by several assumptions and beliefs. Among these was the belief that "Islam as a dogma is worthless and is not dangerous to our goals; it is only dangerous as a political force and social theory."[18] He also held that the institutionalized hierarchical Islam of the Volga Tatars presented a larger challenge to the Russian government than the less-organized and therefore less fanatical Islam of the settled and nomadic population of Turkestan, and that "the confessional differences are not important, and having a good and honest life is enough in order to get into heaven, for everyone, be one a Jew [Zhid], Muslim [Sart] or Russian Orthodox [Russkii]."[19] Von Kaufman described his policy toward Islam as one of "ignoring" (ignorirovanie). This meant extending religious toleration to Turkestan but, in contrast to Crimea and the Volga region, without offering official patronage (pokrovitel'stvo) to Islam, which meant that no official role was to be assigned to Muslim religious leaders or institutions.

Von Kaufman also tried to weaken the power of the Muslim religious leaders. He abolished the highest religious post in Tashkent (sheikh-ul-Islam) and the chief Muslim judge.[20] Unlike the Muslims in Crimea and the eastern part of European Russia, and later in Transcaucasia, the Turkestan Muslims did not receive an ecclesiastical administration. Von Kaufman also denied the request of the Orenburg Ecclesiastical Assembly to extend its authority over the Muslims in Turkestan.[21] His land reform was similarly intended, among other things, to undermine the power of Muslim religious institutions.[22] The Muslim schools were left outside the government's intervention and regulation. This strategy was based on the assumption that, if left to themselves, they would eventually die out. The reform of Muslim schools by the government was left for the future.[23]

Von Kaufman's approach to "ignoring" Islam extended as far as missionary efforts, which he discouraged. The Orthodox church received limited space in Turkestan. The Turkestan diocese was established in 1871, with its center not in Tashkent but in Vernyi (Semirech'e), which had the largest concentration of Russian settlers.[24] Out of fear of instigating Muslims' discontent, Turkestan's administration did not permit Orthodox missionary activity among the Muslim population; their efforts were limited to Chinese immigrants in Semirech'e.[25]

Von Kaufman's symbolic actions also demonstrated his confessional policy. For example, during his visit to Vernyi, he ignored a mullah who was greeting the governor-general among other representatives of the Russian and native elite. Von Kaufman explained his inattention to the mullah by the fact that the latter was not a state official.[26] At the same time, he also noted that the "Orthodox priest should have met him, not together with other citizens, but near the church with vestments, cross in hand and with bells ringing."[27] He did not come to greet Alexander, the new Orthodox bishop of Turkestan and Tashkent, and noted that the bishop should not be called His Eminence (*vladyka*) outside the church.[28] In other words, von Kaufman presented his public authority as secular and not religious, thus attempting to separate the church from the tasks of governance in this new borderland of a still officially Orthodox imperial state. In contrast to the Muslim provinces of European Russia, at least symbolically, the state ceased to represent itself as either Islamic or Orthodox in Turkestan under von Kaufman.

Von Kaufman planned to conduct the project of integrating Turkestan Muslims into the empire by means of what he termed "Christian Russian civilization without Orthodox belief." In Turkestan, as in the northwestern region where he had struggled with Polish influence, he believed that offering Russian European education was the best way to merge the non-Russians and to turn them into useful Russian citizens.[29] Von Kaufman's greatest hope to educate Kazakhs, whom he believed to be less religiously fanatical and more compliant with Russian influences. However, this assumption also entailed the need to protect Kazakhs from what was perceived to be Muslim propaganda conducted by the Tatars, a process that aimed to secure a smooth integration of nomads into the empire. Von Kaufman paid serious attention to this issue.

In explaining the policy of ignoring Islam, Daniel Brower has suggested that von Kaufman buttressed his positivist faith in social progress with imperial arrogance, reflecting an attitude that also characterized Western European colonial projects.[30] Von Kaufman's belief in the inevitable decline of Islam in a modernizing world was also informed by the political decline of Russia's Muslim rival, the Ottoman empire, viewed as the "sick man of Europe." Alexander Morrison has brought attention to Russia's violent war against the mountaineers, actions that produced a lasting suspicion of Muslims among the Russian officers who served in the Caucasus and later Turkestan, including von Kaufman.[31] Russians' experience with Islam in the Volga region, and especially Il'minskii's perspective on Russian–Muslim relations, also played a role in shaping von Kaufman's confessional policies in Turkestan.

Von Kaufman knew about Il'minskii from the Turkestan School inspector A. L. Kun, a former student of V. V. Grigor'ev, under whom Il'minskii served from 1858 to 1861 in the Orenburg Borderland Commission. Von Kaufman met Il'minskii, and Il'minskii gave him advice on educational policies.[32] Both von Kaufman and Il'minskii suggested that the state ignore Islam. Hence, they both opposed state interference into Muslim religious schools and Muslim religious institutions in general, although for different reasons. Unlike von Kaufman, Il'minskii did not anticipate that Islam would die out; in contrast to von Kaufman's and other imperial officials' dismissive view of Islam, Il'minskii emphasized the religion's strength and vitality. While von Kaufman hoped for the secular enlightenment and integration of both Muslims and the Orthodox, Il'minskii saw the empire's path to renewal in a revitalization of Russian Orthodoxy. But until this goal was to be achieved, it was imperative to ignore, or, when necessary, contain Islam. Although von Kaufman did not share this vision of the empire's future, he agreed with Il'minskii's views about Kazakh education and the need to protect Kazakhs from Islamicization and Tatarization.[33]

Although von Kaufman did not have plans to employ the Orthodox religion as a tool for integrating the peoples of the new Muslim borderland into the empire, he imported experts whose views on Islam and non-Russian affairs had more generally been formed in the environment of Orthodox–Muslim confrontation in the Volga–Ural region. Although Turkestan was under military rule, officials of the Ministry of Public Education and the Ministry of Finance shared responsibility for integrating the new borderland into the modernizing empire. Thus, Tolstoy's system of educating non-Russians in the eastern provinces was, in a modified way, extended to Turkestan. To establish the educational system there, von Kaufman asked the ministry to detach Il'minskii, who refused to come.[34] Alternately, Il'minskii recommended N. P. Ostroumov, who, as we have seen, had arrived in Tashkent in 1877 and was appointed director of the teachers' seminary, founded in 1879.[35] The teachers' seminary accepted Russian and non-Russian students. In accordance with von Kaufman's hope for integrating Kazakhs first, the Kazakh language in the Cyrillic alphabet was among the subjects taught. On Il'minskii's recommendation, other graduates of the Kazan Theological Academy arrived in Tashkent to occupy positions within the domain of the Ministry of Public Education.[36]

Von Kaufman died in 1882, at the time when Alexander III set the program of his reign against the Great Reforms era and declared a new course that reaffirmed autocratic rule and emphasized the dominance of Orthodoxy and Russianness. The new Turkestan governor-general, M. G. Cherniaev, attempted during his short rule (1882–1884) to revise many of von Kaufman's undertakings. On Cherniaev's initiative, in 1882, St. Petersburg sent Senator F. K. Girs to inspect Turkestan to answer questions about the prospects of integrating the new borderland into the empire's administrative structure. Girs's report argued that Turkestan was pacified, had lost its military-political significance, and therefore no longer required any special administrative status based on military rule. One of Girs's arguments in support of this view was his conclusion that the native population was peaceful, not fanatical, and thus less hostile to Russian authorities in comparison to Muslim people elsewhere in the empire.[37] He found evidence for this belief in the ease with which the Russian government was able to introduce reforms that contradicted Sharia law, as well as in criminal statistics that indicated the relatively high "moral" standing of the local population. In 1887, a new Turkestan statute was approved by the emperor, keeping Turkestan under the War Ministry but transferring some branches of its administration to more appropriate ministries. The principle of the division of military and civil administration was introduced at the district (*uezd*) level. Nevertheless, the military–civilian compromise system did not achieve Turkestan's full integration into the empire's administrative structure.

Von Kaufman's successors granted the Orthodox church a more important symbolic role, exemplified by increased participation of clerics in local public ceremonies.[38] Yet the church was not given any significant role in Muslim–Russian relations, and its missionary activity continued to be prohibited. Religious toleration of Islam and the state's commitment to noninterference were largely preserved, even though the latter principle was not consistently carried out. True, no hierarchical structures for Islam similar to those that existed in European Russia and Transcaucasia were created after von Kaufman. Yet, as Robert Crews has demonstrated, local officials, sometime reluctantly, intervened in Muslim communities and were involved in religious controversies.[39] Islam received an additional form of state backing when Tolstoy's system of schools for Muslims was extended to Turkestan. A new type of institution, called Russian-native schools, was introduced under Governor-General N. O. von Rozenbakh (1884–1889).[40] This form of elementary education was designed only for native peoples and presented a hybrid of Russian schools with Muslim confessional schools (*maktabs*). At this point, the question of the language curriculum at the teacher's seminary had to be reconsidered. In the 1880s, given the government's attempt to integrate the settled Muslim population, the Kazakh language taught at the seminary was replaced with the so-called Sart (Uzbek) and Persian languages. The school inspector, A. I. Zabelin, also suggested introducing Arabic into the curriculum. Il'minskii reviewed the proposal for the Ministry of Public Education and opposed Zabelin's idea out of fear of possible Islamicization of the seminary's students were they to learn Arabic. Following his advice, the ministry rejected the proposal.[41] In 1889, governmental inspections were formally introduced to Muslim schools, but the inspections were nominal, and the Muslim confessional schools were mostly still left to themselves.

The Russian administrators' expectations that Islam would weaken and die were soon disappointed. In 1898, an attack on the Russian garrison in the Ferghana Valley forced officials to reevaluate both the tactic of ignoring Islam in Turkestan and the broader strategy for Russian–Muslim relations.

Is Islam a "Hostile Political Force"?

On the night of 17 May 1898, a group of natives, totaling nearly 2,000 people, attacked a camp of sleeping Russian soldiers in the Andijan area of Ferghana. Of the 160 soldiers in the camp during the attack, 22 were killed and 18 were wounded.[42] A member of the Sufi Naqshbandi order, known as Dukchi ishan led the attack, which had been coordinated to occur at the same time as revolts in Osh and Margelan—the latter were prevented by Russian authorities.[43] The leader of the Andijan attack was captured and sentenced to hang by a military court. More than 300 natives were arrested and condemned to hard labor in Siberia, and the *kishlaks* (villages) where the instigators of the conspiracy lived were ordered to be demolished and replaced by Russian settlements. In addition, a fine of 300,000 rubles was levied on the local population.[44] As a result of an investigation that followed the attack, some regional Russian administrators were dismissed from their positions.

The imposition of Russian power in Ferghana Valley was a long process. Although the region was acquired by Russia in 1876, the political struggle in the former Kokand khanate continued even after its incorporation, and revolts and declarations of holy war, usually under the leadership of Sufi sheikhs (known locally as *ishans*) were a frequent phenomenon. Nevertheless, Russian local and central authorities did not see a serious danger in these disorders, considering the population of the region as a whole to be friendly to Russians.[45] In 1896, *Sredne-Aziatskii Vestnik* optimistically declared: "India will eternally remain India hanging on the tip of an English bayonet. . . . Central Asia within one hundred years will be a Russian province. We feel ourselves safe here."[46] The Andijan attack came as a surprise to the Turkestan administration and led to a reassessment of earlier disorders in the Ferghana Valley and of Russian–Muslim relations in general.[47]

Shortly after the Andijan attack, a new governor-general, Lieutenant General S. M. Dukhovskoi (1838–1901), arrived in Tashkent. After his arrival, the high life of Russian Tashkent society continued: the military assembly hosted musical and dancing evenings, bicycle competitions took place at the local velodrome, city garden festivals were arranged, and receptions and dinners were held in the governor-general's palace. On 15 July 1898, the new governor-general organized magnificent celebrations to mark the thirty-third anniversary of the capture of Tashkent; these public activities, including a religious procession, military parade, and a service at a communal grave of fallen soldiers, drew thousands of spectators: representatives of various establishments, military, veteran-participants of the conquest of Turkestan, Russian inhabitants, and natives. At the reception for the representatives of Tashkent in the governor-general's house, Dukhovskoi gave a speech in which he expressed hopes for the rapprochement of the Russian and native parts of the city. Addressing the representatives of the natives, he said:

> Long ago, by the decree of fate I became acquainted with Muslims, whom I got to know well in the Caucasus where I spent almost twenty years governing Erzurum. I had an opportunity to be in Istanbul and eighteen years ago received an order from a sultan. . . . I am telling you about this in order to convince you of my belief that among Muslims there are intelligent and honest people who keep their promises. I am certain that among you there are people of this type and that you will firmly keep your promises that were given thirty-three years ago [when Tashkent was conquered] and now repeated again in your address.[48]

Yet the shadow of the Andijan events loomed over the Russian population. Here is how V. F. Dukhovskaia, the wife of the governor-general, recorded the mood of those days:

> Again we have a time of troubles! Rumors warn us of the possibility of a new revolt. Smoldering unrest, seemingly, grows and becomes more intense. We live here as if on a boiling volcano; one must keep a lookout, a heavy anxiousness, as before a thunderstorm is felt. In Tashkent, the Sart population is 124,000, but the troops only number 15,000, and they are dispersed. Though far from ideal, our posi-

tion in Turkestan is still more secure than the position of the Englishmen in India, where there is only one white soldier for every 3,000 natives! Vigorous measures are undertaken: the troops are concentrated; the Sarts are forbidden to carry weapons. According to reports from the valley of Maly-Alan, many Kirgiz nomads have gathered there, so one hundred Cossacks have been dispatched. My state of mind is very agitated; it is especially terrifying to realize upon hearing the calls of the muezzin in the evening that only one wall separates our garden from the native town. We were informed that in the Ferghana area four natives collected donations among the local residents in favor of a new ishan who, they say, will gather the people for a new *gazavat;* many have been arrested. In the city of Przheval'sk, secret letters sprinkled with blood were delivered to government agencies, warning that the *gazavat* would begin on the night of 30 July; we live in the days of the Huguenots! On further investigation, it turned out that the letters were a hoax, an obscene joke . . . and all our fears proved exaggerated and overblown; soon everything returned to normal, the troubles passed.[49]

Despite these self-calming words, Dukhovskaia's diaries, which she kept during the entire time of her husband's service in Tashkent (1898–1901), offer little evidence of confidence in native attitudes toward Russians. As Dukhovskaia put it, the natives were "superficially kind."[50]

Suspicions also appeared in reports sent by local Russian officials to the governor-general about the mood of the native population in and around Ferghana. A confidential investigation uncovered no evidence of any criminal activity among the natives and concluded that the majority of the population was calm. Despite generally favorable intelligence data, the local administration did not trust this "external calm," however, and viewed the natives as largely hostile.[51] Though there were no "obvious displays of hatred" on the part of the native peoples, Russians in Turkestan assumed that the local population was in a state of "latent unrest" after the Andijan events and that they harbored "concealed contempt" toward Russian power. As the head of the Amu-Darya division wrote in March 1899, "it is never possible to count on Muslim loyalty to Russian authority." He attributed this to "ignorance" of the population, which made it always subject to "harmful propaganda."[52] An official of the Syr-Darya regional administration highlighted another reason for Muslim antipathy: the seizure of land from the nomads for growing Russian settlements. In the official's view, this factor explained what they interpreted as the nomads' sympathy with the Andijan revolt, while the settled population (Sarts) blamed the ishan.[53]

In his reflections on these reports, Dukhovskoi noted, "I find nothing new in this. It is naïve to wish that the Muslims who were subdued by force could have so quickly acquired a fondness for their Christian subjugators. This will only come after centuries. In the meantime, it is imperative to keep the local population from dreaming of something serious, and for this purpose it is necessary to keep a close eye on the ishans, mullahs, and different preachers."[54] For the governor-general it was obvious that resistance to Russian authority in Central Asia was a natural consequence of the region's violent conquest. He interpreted this resistance, however, not only as a conflict between the conquerors and the subjugated, but also as a religious conflict between Christians and Muslims.

A special government commission under Lieutenant General N. I. Korol'kov investigated the Andijan incident. The report produced by the commission was sent out to the ministers, the chief procurator of the Holy Synod, and the governors of the empire's Muslim regions. The report characterized the attack on the Russian garrison as a religious movement and attributed the impetus for the revolt to "Muslim fanaticism."[55] This explanation seemed to be supported by a confession of the head of the rebels, who stated that his goal was to restore a way of life in accordance with Sharia; the officials who compiled the report also made much of the fact that none of the rebels offered any general or specific complaints against the Russian administration.[56] But like contemporary historians, Russian officials offered several explanations for the uprising. The head of the Margelan district pointed out, for example, that no revolt had occurred in neighboring regions (such as Syr-Darya and Samarkand) where the Muslim population was considered equally "fanatical." The peculiarity of the Ferghana situation was explained by the area's complex ethnic composition and the presence of a significant contingent of landless workers, as well as by the region's broader troubled political history.[57]

Local authorities also emphasized the uniqueness of the Andijan incident in comparison to previous disorders in Turkestan.[58] First, the Andijan event was a planned attack on Russian soldiers. Prior to that time, according to local officials, attacks had focused either on other natives or on individual travelers passing through the region, but not on Russian civil officials and especially not on the military.[59] Second, the Andijan attack came as a total surprise to authorities, while in earlier cases officials had been able to use local informants to find out about and prevent attacks before they took place.[60] One explanation for the circumstances in Ferghana, everyone concluded, had to do with the conditions of governance in Turkestan. The basic presumption of the official report on the Andijan revolt was that Turkestan, while conquered, was far from pacified, and therefore was ill-suited for the kind of domestic internal administration anticipated by the statute of 1886.

"The Reform of 1886," the report stated, "stripped the Russian administration of the powers [of rule] that are so necessary in a half-civilized Asian country with a fanatical Muslim population, and has deprived us of loyal subjects among the natives. It is this fact that explains the unprecedented impudence and suddenness of the attack on the Andijan camp."[61] In order to ward off similar revolts in the future, the report suggested a wide-sweeping reform of governance in Turkestan, which included abolishing the division of powers in the regional administration, strengthening the authority of the governor-general, appointing rather than electing native administrators, strengthening the garrisons, increasing the number of regional officials, and raising the regional budget. The report also proposed measures to weaken the alleged religious fanaticism of the natives; these were to be carried out by a new set of special district officials on Muslim affairs.[62]

For Governor-General Dukhovskoi, the Andijan revolt provided a reason to bring the central government's attention to Islam and the empire's relationship with Muslims in general—not just in Turkestan—which, he believed, needed reconsideration. In official reports and publications he emphasized the political role of Islam, a position that reflected his belief in the impossibility of separating the religious and political spheres in Islam, along with his frustration with the Turkestan authorities' long-standing policy of noninterference in Muslim religious matters. For Dukhovskoi, the policy of ignoring Islam mainly reflected a lack of government control over Muslim institutions and practices.

Dukhovskoi's basic thesis was that "Islam is not only a religious teaching but also a political force hostile to us. Ignoring Islam is dangerous." The reason for Muslim hostility, in his opinion, had to be sought in the doctrine embodied in the Koran. Convinced that Islam was irreconcilable with Christian culture and extremely intolerant of other religions, Dukhovskoi dismissed Muslim submissiveness to Russian rule as nothing more than a mirage.[63] The defense of their religious beliefs seemed to Dukhovskoi to be the only stimulus capable of motivating Muslims to wage war. Therefore, Muslim resistance, wherever it occurred, would inevitably be religious in nature.[64] The earlier resistance of the mountaineers in the Caucasus, headed by Shamil, and the "Andijan *gazavat*" of 1898 appeared to confirm this view.[65]

In 1899, Dukhovskoi submitted a report to the tsar in which he raised what he called the Muslim Question as relevant not only to Turkestan but to all the Muslim regions of the Russian empire. Though he acknowledged the peculiarities of individual Muslim regions, Dukhovskoi argued that it was both possible and necessary to approach the Muslim Question, and more specifically, the struggle against Islam, as an empire-wide problem. Dukhovskoi submitted this report shortly after he arrived in Turkestan. By that time, the sixty-year-old governor-general had accumulated significant experience in other borderlands of the empire, having served in the Caucasus in the 1860s and 1870s and in the Amur region earlier in the 1890s. His own principal experience with Muslims involved fighting against them in the east Caucasus and in the Russo-Turkish War of 1877–1878. He had also, however, shown interest in problems related to Islam as they were understood by Russian administrators in other regions of the empire, the Volga–Ural region in particular.[66] With this report, Dukhovskoi asked the tsar for general directions on the Muslim Question as a means of bypassing the existing difference of opinions among the various ministries.[67]

Dukhovskoi identified the Russian state's "wide religious tolerance" as a particular stimulus to borderland separatism.[68] For example, he pointed to the Kazan Tatars, who became "true" Muslims under the liberal policies of Catherine II and consequently developed the "strongest religious and national separatism."[69] The governor-general also criticized the view of those tsarist officials who treated the Muslim Question as a mere religious issue that had no political color. As Dukhovskoi put it, "Russia already finds itself burdened with several borderland questions: the Baltic Question, the Polish, the Finnish, and the Muslim Question may also emerge."[70] Fearing political separatism in the empire's Muslim borderlands, Dukhovskoi considered the Muslim Question to be potentially more dangerous than other borderland issues.[71]

Against the backdrop of the 1900 Boxer Rebellion in neighboring China, the governor-general saw the Muslim Question in even more menacing terms. Regarding the events in China as an anti-European movement, Dukhovskoi considered that Muslims in the Russian empire might pursue a similar course. Consequently, he ordered the governors of Turkestan's provinces to increase their surveillance of nonlocal Muslims and especially of ishans.[72] At Dukhovskoi's request, the diplomatic representative V. P. Nalivkin (1852–1918)[73] prepared a report titled *O vozmozhnykh sootnosheniiakh mezhdu poslednimi sobytiiami v Kitae i usileniem pan-islamistskogo dvizheniia.* (*On the Possible Relationship between Recent Events in China and the Resurgence of pan-Islamism.*) Its basic perspective was the following: anti-European revolts among the Muslims of Asia and Africa (including the Andijan revolt), rising interest in the unification of the Muslim world under the slogan of pan-Islamism, and the popular uprising in China were all the consequence of the awakening of Asia by the Europeans (that is, they were all sparked by the effects of European colonialism). Considering European domination in Asia as the main source of the anti-European movements, Nalivkin warned that, in combination with the Islamic doctrine of holy war, Muslim resistance to European power could emerge as a movement that would be just as powerful as that which had just been witnessed in China. He thus concluded, "One must anticipate *gazavat,* remember it, and prepare for it."[74]

Dukhovskoi forwarded Nalivkin's report to the War Ministry and the Ministry of Internal Affairs, whence it was further forwarded to the Ministry of Foreign Affairs. In a cover letter to the Ministry of War, Dukhovskoi noted the general tranquility prevailing in Turkestan and the fact that most natives in the region were unaware of the events in China. Nevertheless, he cautioned that the strife in the Far East would undoubtedly elicit a response from Muslims and that the Muslim world would be moved to sympathize with China rather than with Europe. "It is not impossible to imagine that the Chinese and the Muslims could unite," he noted. "Therefore, one must begin to consider possible countermeasures."[75]

During and after the investigation of the Andijan revolt, local officials had repeatedly mentioned that one reason for the unexpectedness of the attack was the Russian administration's insufficient attention to and lack of information about the religious life of the Muslim population. As a result of Dukhovskoi's increased interest in Islamic matters, in 1899–1900 the Turkestan administration published *Sbornik materialov po musul'manstvu* (*The Collection of Materials on Muslims*).[76] Its authors, all of them officials, offered readers not so much an analysis of Muslim religious life but rather of what they saw as a religious explanation for the Andijan disorders and Muslim resistance to European colonialism. Both the thesis and its choice of themes were defined by the purpose of the collection: to serve as a manual for regional officials. The image of Islam created by its authors was negative and corresponded in many respects to the views of Russian Orthodox critics of Islam, though with less emphasis on doctrines and more on the political aspect of Islam.[77]

European traditions of explaining Muslim resistance by pointing to the political aspects of Islam were clearly influential. Referring to Western experts on Islam, such as Jules Barthélemy-Saint-Hilaire and Christian Snouck Hurgronje, the author of the article on Muslim pilgrimage emphasized the political danger of the hajj.[78] Likewise, European—and especially French—attention to the role of Sufism in Muslim resistance movements in Africa prompted Russians to similar reflections: "What threat does Sufism pose to Russian possessions in Central Asia?"[79] The Andijan revolt appears to have served as the basis for constructing such parallels. The leader of that revolt had performed the hajj and was a Sufi, which elevated his authority among participants in the attack.

The Andijan attack also gave new relevance to the history of mountaineer resistance in the Caucasus, and provided another "example of a bloody explosion of religious-national fanaticism."[80] The collection underscored the comparison of the Andijan incident with the war in the Caucasus by reprinting translated Islamic views of the holy war that had originally been published in the newspaper *Kavkaz* in 1846.[81] As the authors of the collection saw it, Islam was dangerous, but not all the Muslims in Central Asia were "true Muslims." In much the same way that Caucasian mountaineers prior to their unification by Shamil had been considered "poor Muslims," the authors of the collection pointed out that "Islam was not a characteristic" of the nomadic Kazakhs and Turkmen. Nonetheless, the writers warned that one still had to be cautious because even these poor Muslims could become infected with Islamic religious intolerance, which according to one author was related to their "propensities as steppe predators."[82]

The authors of the collection also referred to Volga Tatars as Muslims who, despite having been in the empire for more than three hundred years, did not appear to have assimilated with the Russians and continued to live in "isolation."[83] These parallels helped create the impression that problems with Muslim resistance and Muslim separateness, seen as arising from Islam's hostility to Christianity, were challenges that faced the Russian administration in all regions where Muslims lived. The Andijan uprising confirmed Muslims' intrinsic alienation and their potential threat to the empire's unity. This is how Dukhovskoi interpreted the Muslim Question. But seen from Turkestan, the problem appeared to be even more acute. Recalling a meeting between Dukhovskoi and the Kazan governor-general in 1899 to discuss the Muslim Question, Dukhovskaia emphasized how Turkestan both highlighted and aggravated the problem of Islam in Russia. She wrote:

> Russians who are acquainted with the Muslim world only through Tatar street hawkers shouting "used clothes for sale, used clothes for sale" or train porters from the Crimea and waiters in restaurants have no idea that Muslims constitute an enormous mass of people—one-ninth of the entire Russian population. Their major places of residence are in Turkestan, Caucasus, Crimea and Kazan province. At first glance,

one might think that Muslims in Kazan have nothing in common with Muslims in Turkestan: they have different pasts, different histories, and completely different conditions of life. But this is actually not the case. All of them are united by the dream of glory and greatness of the "Prophet." And this is also true of the hundreds of millions of faithful Muslims living in India, Turkey, and other Muslim countries. Like the Japanese and the Chinese Questions, the Muslim Question is only temporarily dormant. The Muslims desire nothing less than to have their Crescent imperiously flaunted everywhere.[84]

But neither these local fears nor their views of Islam as a "force hostile to Russian statehood" found support in the official circles of St. Petersburg. Nor did Dukhovskoi succeed in calling a special government committee on the Muslim Question in St. Petersburg. Minister of Finance S. Iu. Witte, responding to Dukhovskoi's policy proposals concerning Islam, acknowledged the existence of the Muslim Question, but unlike Dukhovskoi did not consider the problem to be particularly dangerous to the Russian state. Seen from the perspective of Russia's ambitious economic and imperial goals in the East, the adoption of Dukhovskoi's views, as Witte put it, would have required "a decisive change in policy concerning Muslim subjects. And this, in turn, would have opened Russia to the charge of intolerance toward Islam and would have generated a hostile reaction toward her throughout the Muslim world, with inevitable consequences for Russia's position in the East."[85]

As for Dukhovskoi's apprehensions about the spread of pan-Islamism among Russian Muslims, Witte considered the governor-general's facts to be insufficient for drawing any conclusions. And pan-Islamism itself was, in any case, a new phenomenon that required further study. Witte concluded that the religious–political unification of Russian Muslims would scarcely be possible in practice, given the important ethnic and cultural differences between Muslim groups. Unlike Dukhovskoi, Witte interpreted the Andijan uprising as an accident and viewed Muslims on the whole as acceptably loyal subjects.[86] Dukhovskoi's fears of a looming anti-Russian combination of "China and the Muslims" also failed to find ready support in imperial diplomatic spheres.[87]

The Collection of Materials on Muslims also was not well received in St. Petersburg. In 1900, it was reviewed by Abdul-Aziz Davletshin, a Muslim officer of the General Staff. Davletshin (1861–1920), the son of a Russian army officer, was a noble from Ufa province.[88] As an officer of the Asian department of the General Staff, Davletshin prepared several analytical reports on different questions concerning Islam and Muslims. In his review of the Collection of Materials on Muslims, he criticized what he saw as two important shortcomings of the collection: a one-sided view of Islam influenced by the lingering effects of the Andijan disorder, and an erroneous interpretation of the Koran and its role in the life of Muslims. In his conclusion, Davletshin wrote:

> Introducing readers to Muslims through such materials as this collection hardly
> serves the goals of the government in the borderlands. Using official publications

to disseminate extreme ideas such as the view that Muslims are the most irreconcilable enemies of Christianity, and that Islam teaches its followers to hate all other
religions . . . [and] to kill Christians at any opportunity would provoke enmity and
distrust among the native peoples of Central Asia and would completely undermine
the quality of human decency that our ruling classes display to the natives and that
serves as the main reason for Russia's enormous appeal in the East. Among Muslims,
such views would produce great insult and would lead to even more discord.[89]

In contrast to Witte and Davletshin, N. A. Bobrovnikov, Il'minskii's successor at
the Teachers' Seminary in Kazan, had a different reaction. In his report, *K voprosu
ob oslablenii obosoblennosti magometan* (*On the Question of Weakening the Alienation of Muslims*), forwarded by Pobedonostsev to A. N. Kuropatkin, the Minister of War, Bobrovnikov praised Dukhovskoi's report for "the fullness of the picture and the deep penetration into the secret springs of Muslims' machinations."[90]
When reading about Muslims in Central Asia, Bobrovnikov was inevitably thinking about the Kazan Tatars. He asked "Why is it that our influence on Tatars, before so strong, today equals zero and why are our missionizing efforts powerless?"
And he answered, "Because we, Russians, don't have either [an] integral worldview
or persistent and consistent power in relation to Tatars and other aliens."

Bobrovnikov thus saw a problem in Russians' inability to agree upon and firmly
establish the boundary between religious tolerance and what he called a conniv-
ance (*popustitel'stvo*) toward Islam. He found evidence for the latter in numerous
so-called special "privileges" granted to Muslims, including freedom enjoyed by
Muslim confessional schools and sellers of Muslim religious literature, both of which
were outside state control. Bobrovnikov was especially critical of state-sponsored
Muslim institutions, such as the Kazan Tatar Teachers' Seminary and the Muslim
ecclesiastical administrations. For Bobrovnikov, however, the Muslim Question
was also closely related to the problem of the low cultural and economic standing
of Orthodox Russians and non-Russians living in Muslim borderlands. He wrote:
"Let [the] Russian settler on the Volga, in Central Asia, in the Caucasus, and eastern Siberia come to towns of those borderlands not only as an unskilled employee
of German, Jewish, Belgian, and other entrepreneurs, but also as an independent cultural force. Then Russia's influence will strengthen at home and will spread abroad."[91]

"Are We Well-Suited for Our Mission?"

The Andijan uprising provoked another former close associate of Il'minskii,
N. P. Ostroumov, to reconsider the role of Russians and their cultural mission among
Muslims in Turkestan. In 1877, on recommendation of Il'minskii, his former professor at the Kazan Theological Academy, Ostroumov came to Turkestan, where he
spent the next forty years working for the Ministry of Public Education. He knew
von Kaufman and admired him, but disagreed with his views on confessional issues. Ostroumov agreed with von Kaufman that it was too early to introduce Ortho-

dox missionary activity in Turkestan, but at the same time he did not deny its usefulness in principle. More importantly, Ostroumov disagreed with what he interpreted as von Kaufman's indifferent attitude toward the confessional question.[92]

Ostroumov became acquainted shortly with Dukhovskoi after the new governor-general's arrival in Turkestan. Ostroumov's expertise in local languages and Islam came into demand by the Turkestan administration in connection with the official investigation of the Andijan uprising. He translated and commented on the *ferman* (edict) supposedly issued by the Turkish sultan that had been confiscated from the head of the Andijan rebels, prepared reports on the mood of the native population, edited the governor-general's addresses to that population, drafted official circulars, and participated in a special commission that gathered information on Islam in Turkestan. From Ostroumov's diary, we also know about his frequent private conversations with the governor-general about Islam.

Dukhovskoi appreciated Ostroumov's expertise and proposed that he occupy a position in charge of Muslim affairs in Turkestan. However, Ostroumov declined this opportunity and remained an unofficial advisor to the governor-general.[93] Ostroumov's closeness to Dukhovskoi became a subject of rumors among the Tashkent civil officials and especially the General Staff officers, giving them reason to scoff about his theological educational background.[94] Ostroumov was concerned about these rumors and especially about his official standing, which had never been stable and depended on the favor of the governor-general. In his diary, he presented himself not as an influential advisor but rather as a consultant who provided expertise at the request of the governor-general only because there were no other experts on Islam in the Turkestan administration.[95]

The following scene, as described by Ostroumov, suggests his view of his relationship with Dukhovskoi. While he was at breakfast with the governor-general, an official of the Ministry of Finance, who was also among the invitees, brought the topic of Islam into the conversation. Dukhovskoi asked him if he were an Orientalist and where he had studied Islam. The official answered that he was not an orientalist. Then the governor-general told him, pointing to Ostroumov: "Nikolai Petrovich studied and is familiar with these matters, but is silent."[96] It seems that Ostroumov was influential, inasmuch as his views matched the ideas and beliefs of the governor-general.[97]

In contrast to other officials who served under Dukhovskoi, Ostroumov had a rather positive impression of the new governor-general, describing him as a "sincere, friendly, and impatient" person.[98] What Ostroumov found especially appealing was the special attention Dukhovskoi gave to the "Russian cause" in Turkestan, and the governor-general's devotion to Orthodoxy.[99] He wrote:

> I understood why he [the governor-general] was so excited when he saw the bell arriving from Yaroslavl to the train station for the Sergiev church and said a lot of biting words to Colonel Burmeister, thinking that he was German and Lutheran. The general softened when Burmeister told him that he was a native [*korennoi*] Russian

subject and Orthodox and [had] built a lot of Orthodox churches, including the Sergiev church in Tashkent.[100]

In his diary, Ostroumov also favorably described how Dukhovskoi, unlike other officials, punctually attended church services.

Ostroumov approved and encouraged the governor-general's attention to Islam. He agreed with the Dukhovskoi's report to the Tsar, which characterized Islam as a hostile, militant religion dangerous to European civilization and the Russian state.[101] With Dukhovskoi, he shared the conviction that Islam was a serious spiritual force that could not be "ignored."[102] Ostroumov's attention to Islam, however, had a different meaning and served a different purpose. He expressed his views not only in his conversations with the governor-general, but also in publications.[103] Ostroumov's warnings about Islam were not always appreciated by the local military leadership. Irritated by Ostroumov, Dukhovskoi's aide and, later, the governor-general, General N. A. Ivanov, once asked him, "Why do you intimidate us?"[104] In contrast to many local Russian officers after the Andijan uprising, Ostroumov was not afraid of Muslims and was concerned about the rumors that Dukhovskoi was fearful of Islam. But, unlike progressive Russian empire-builders in Turkestan, Ostroumov believed in the centrality of religion in human life. He explained that Islam deserved distinct attention from Russians because of its militant teachings, but also because, in his opinion, Muslims ascribed a greater meaning and importance to religious practices than Russian Orthodox believers did.[105] Ostroumov's warnings about the strength of Islam were self-reflective and served the purpose of raising the awareness of Russians in the borderlands about their own religious identity and their mission vis-à-vis their non-Russian subjects.

To Ostroumov, the Andijan revolt demonstrated the shortcomings of Russian rule in Turkestan and the empire's borderlands in general. He found these shortcomings primarily in Russians' lack of aspiration, but also in their inability to perform the role of *Kulturträgers*, whose mission was to conquer the non-Russian borderlands not only by arms but also spiritually.[106] In Ostroumov's opinion, Russians' own high moral and religious standing was the key to the success of their civilizing mission in the Muslim borderland.[107] And it was the strength and vitality of Islam, as observed by Ostroumov, that seemed to confirm this conclusion. "Are we well-suited for our mission?" he asked in response in 1909 to the inquiry by Dmitrii, the bishop of Turkestan and Tashkent, about the extent of the danger posed by Islam in Turkestan.[108] And he answered: "We in the Tashkent region are not authoritative representatives of the Orthodox people and the Russian state. The natives, with their seeming lack of culture, see these religiously moral and state shortcomings. We are not ashamed of ourselves in front of the natives and don't pay enough attention to the high cultural task we are called to carry out in this borderland."[109]

Ostroumov admitted that the rapprochement (*sblizhenie*) or even the merger (*sliianie*) of Russians with Muslims should be the main task of the Russian administration in Turkestan. By this, he did not advocate a complete assimilation but the development of consciousness among the natives, with respect to their economic, every-day, and political ties with the core Russian population.[110] But in this project, the cultural transformation of Russians was no less important than the transformation of the natives. When Dukhovskoi proposed in 1899 to send native children on educational trips to European Russia to foster their integration into the empire, Ostroumov argued that such a "privilege" should also be granted to Russian children. "Striving to cultivate the natives, we forget about the Russian students," was his comment on Dukhovskoi's initiative.[111] At the same time, being deeply concerned about preserving the Russianness of Russians living in Muslim borderlands, Ostroumov opposed Dukhovskoi's proposal regarding mixed marriages between Orthodox and Muslims as a means of rapprochement.[112] Similarly concerned about the Russianness of tsarist administrators in Turkestan, Ostroumov, while sympathetic to Dukhovskoi's personal religiosity, criticized his "admiration" of *tamasha* (a form of native entertainment) as inappropriate for a Russian governor-general.[113]

Advocating for the rapprochement of Muslims with Russians, Ostroumov at the same time pointed to Islam as a serious obstacle to such a policy. He stressed that governing Muslims was a difficult task that required Russian administrators to be aware of their cultural mission, as well as to have knowledge of and sensitivity to the cultural peculiarities of the natives.[114] He criticized the Russian administration in Turkestan for what he called a "bureaucratic" (*kantseliarskii*) approach to their responsibilities, pointing to their lack of knowledge of the borderlands, reliance on "external" expressions of loyalty by natives, and the absence of a consistent cultural policy directed toward the "spiritual conquest of the borderlands." Like many other contemporary observers and participants in Russian policy-making in Turkestan at that time, Ostroumov became increasingly concerned about what was often called "the decline of the prestige of the Russian name" among the natives. The Andijan revolt represented one among many other signs of such a decline.[115] But, unlike local military authorities, Ostroumov believed that the reasons for this decline were not the direct result of the 1886 statute, which weakened Russian military power, but were underlying the very nature of Russian borderland policies, especially the military rule in Turkestan.

Ostroumov was not alone in such self-criticism. Similar views were articulated by another Turkestan orientalist and consultant for Dukhovskoi, V. P. Nalivkin. Ostroumov and Nalivkin had different backgrounds, worldviews, and played different roles in shaping Dukhovskoi's stances on matters related to Islam. But they both turned their attention to Russians in Turkestan and relations with the native population. In his book *Tuzemtsy ran'she i teper'* (*Natives Then and Now*), Nalivkin pointed to what he considered the most significant cause of the Andijan uprising: the "terrible and chronic illness of our official life: misappropriation, extortions, fabrication of conspiracy among the local population, and the arbitrariness of the Russian administration in Turkestan."[116] The official corruption associated with the authoritarian style of rule in Turkestan had increasingly become publicly known toward the end of the imperial period. However, what resonated even more for Ostroumov was Nalivkin's criticism of Turkestan officials for a slighting and sometime mocking attitude toward the natives. Both men pointed out on several occasions that Russians should take seriously and learn from the so-called "Asiatics."[117]

For Ostroumov, this meant more than just having respect for the subjugated population. He believed in Russia's civilizing mission in Central Asia, but his understanding of that mission differed from the progressive secular Europe-centered vision of most Russian officials in Turkestan and St. Petersburg. Ostroumov's belief in the Russian civilizing mission was based on his presumption of the superiority of Christianity to Islam. At the same time, he regarded Russia's own state-sponsored modernization project as a rather recent phenomenon that was not entirely beneficial for Russians. While emphasizing the doctrinal differences between Christianity and Islam, Ostroumov also treated Central Asian culture as not totally different from Russian culture, but rather at a different stage of historical development, one that Russians experienced before the radical transformations introduced by Peter the Great.[118] This historical argument allowed Ostroumov to be optimistic about the rapprochement of Central Asia with Russia, but also to point to what he saw as positive aspects of Asian culture that Russian reformers had to take into consideration.

It seems that in Ostroumov's interpretation, the imperial endeavor and its challenges in Central Asia gave Russia a chance to rethink its own path to modernity. For Ostroumov, the encounter with Islam in Central Asia, as it had been for Il'minskii in Kazan, confirmed the premises of Slavophile solutions for Russia's ills, including the focus on revitalized Orthodoxy. Ostroumov's presentation of Islam as a hostile but serious obstacle to the policy of rapprochement had its roots in his confessional worldview, but also was an expression of his concerns about Russians as representatives of a "dominant" nationality on the empire's borderlands. As he wrote in his diary, "We are neither capable of ruling in internal Russia, nor on the borderlands."[119] As in Kazan, Ostroumov's concerns about what he perceived as Russians' weakness vis-à-vis Islam in Central Asia took greater importance when the Russian civilizing mission was challenged by the modernizing efforts of the Tatar intelligentsia, as we saw in the previous chapter.

*   *   *

As in the Volga region, in Turkestan the question of Russian–Muslim relations was embedded in conflicting conceptualizations of Russia's modernization. At the same time, the absorption of a new alien Muslim population into the empire exacerbated tensions that underlined Russian thinking about Muslims in European Russia and the empire's future more generally. This was revealed at the moment of crisis, during the Turkestan natives' attack on the Andijan garrison in 1898 that challenged the perception, widely held among the Russians, that imperial dominance was firmly established in Central Asia.

In less than twenty years, Russia had conquered a large part of Central Asia. Contemporaries noted the ease of the conquest. As Kuropatkin, a participant in the military campaigns and later the minister of war recalled, "the main difficulty was not the enemy but nature."[120] Russia's active military penetration into Central Asia began during the period of Great Reforms and ended when the tsarist government was searching for ways to stabilize the state, which had been shaken by the reforms and the growing revolutionary movement. This was the context for the Andijan uprising. In response to this uprising the new Turkestan governor-general Dukhovskoi brought the issue of Russian–Muslim relations to the attention of the imperial authorities in St. Petersburg conceptualizing this problem as the Muslim Question. Dukhovskoi's formulation of the question as an empire-wide problem, not specific to Turkestan, served, on the one hand, to give greater weight to the urgency of changing the system of governance in Turkestan, a subject of long dispute.[121] On the other hand, the empire-wide politicization of the Muslim Question that Dukhovskoi feared demanded that the state adopt a more coherent and systematic policy—a "state plan"—that would apply to all Muslim regions of the empire. The Muslim Question, as Dukhovskoi saw it, involved not so much the evaluation of an already existing situation, but rather a prognosis for the future in the event that necessary measures would not be undertaken. Fearing the political separatism of alienated Muslims, and having formulated the Muslim Question as one among Russia's many borderland or alien questions, and potentially the most dangerous, Dukhovskoi spoke the language of those reform-minded Russians who insisted on a more proactive role of the government in integrating the non-Russian alien population into the modernizing imperial society. At the same time, similar to many Russians' views of Muslims' alienation discovered during and immediately after the Crimean War, Dukhovskoi explained Muslims' alienation by their faith. While opposed to the missionary activity of the Orthodox church in Turkestan, he placed Muslims into an intrinsic "alien" position, leaving Russian authorities with strong military power and state surveillance as their only option.

Both the confessional underpinning of Dukhovskoi's vision of the Muslim Question and his antagonistic rhetoric went against the perceptions of imperial goals held by such pragmatically thinking St. Petersburg officials as Witte and Davletshin. To them, the view of Andijan as an accident and Muslims as loyal subjects seemed to better serve the goal of successful empire-building. Thus, Dukhovskoi's proposals did not result in a radical shift in imperial policies toward Islam.

Dukhovskoi's view of Islam as both a serious force and an anti-Christian religion were, however, shared by the followers of Il'minskii, Bobrovnikov, and Ostroumov. Like Dukhovskoi and Witte, Bobrovnikov and Ostroumov were concerned about what they perceived as Muslims' alienation, but their thinking about this problem as well as the lessons they drew from the Andijan uprising were different. As we have seen, Il'minskii's and his followers' views echoed some elements of Slavophile vision of the empire's future. The Andijan uprising provided an opportunity to reaffirm some of these views. The attention that both Bobrovnikov and Ostroumov gave to Islam was closely connected to their concerns about Orthodox Russians and their ability to perform their cultural—and spiritual—mission among the supposedly pious Muslims. By calling on Russians to engage with Islam as a serious spiritual force, Ostroumov, unlike Dukhovskoi, drew attention to the weakness of Russian civilizers and the necessity for them to be true Orthodox believers, while at the same time criticizing them for holding a dismissive attitude about Muslim culture. This message was similar to the conclusion of Il'minskii when he "discovered" the strength of Islam while he was searching for ways to solve the apostasy issue in the Volga region. Thus, perceived through the prism of the Orthodox–Muslim encounter, the Muslim Question in Kazan and Tashkent in the interpretation of Il'minskii's followers implied certain concerns about the weakness of Orthodoxy vis-à-vis Islam. The implication of such a vision when applied to the officially Orthodox state-regulated confessional system of a growing and changing empire was that strengthening Orthodoxy made it imperative to contain Islam.

Bobrovnikov regarded Andijan as another opportunity to criticize the official policy of toleration and the institutionalization of Islam in Muslim provinces of European Russia. At the same time, when he compared the current position of Russian Orthodoxy to Islam within the empire, Islam seemed to have certain unjust "privileges," particularly in the seeming freedom of Muslim schools and the circulation of Muslim literature. Thus along with raising the cultural level of the Orthodox population, he argued for tighter state control of Islam. As Muslim modernizers increasingly challenged the Russians' role as civilizers of Central Asia, Il'minskii's followers were forced to rethink their vision of state strategy. Threatened by the "new Tatars," for example, Ostroumov changed his earlier position that supported the state's noninterference in matters related to Islam and came to think that Russians should introduce progressive elements into Muslim schools in order not to lose the initiative in educating non-Russians.[122] But how to control Muslims and even transform them without institutionalizing Islam?

5 Dilemmas of Regulation and Rapprochement

The Problem of Muslim Religious Institutions

As we have seen, the appropriate role of the government in monitoring and regulating Muslim educational institutions formed an integral part of the Russian debate about the place of Muslims in a modernizing empire. This debate was not, however, limited to schools. Since the time of Catherine the Great, the imperial government had recognized Islam as one of several officially tolerated religions in a multiconfessional empire. This official recognition brought with it the state regulation of Muslims' religious life (*religioznyi byt*) and the creation of an official Muslim religious hierarchy. Recent research has tended to emphasize the positive effect of the imperial state's relationship with Islam.[1]

In the second half of the nineteenth century, the tsarist regime's regulation of Islam was challenged by the needs of a modernizing and expanding empire. This chapter examines Russians' deliberations on policies involving organs of Muslim ecclesiastical administration, Muslim clergy, and mosques in this changing context. While the existing confessional order in Muslim regions of European Russia fell victim to criticism, the imperial expansion into the Caucasus and Central Asia forced authorities to rethink the system of the state's relationship with Muslim institutions. These religious institutions consequently became an important element in governmental debate. Caught between conflicting imperatives, Russian policies toward Muslim religious institutions risked exacerbating rather than resolving the tensions that surfaced in Russians' understanding of the Muslim Question.

Defining a Role for Muslim Clergy: "Enemies" or "Servants"?

The state's official recognition of Islam as a tolerated faith, an act that subjected Muslim religious life to regulation and incorporated their spiritual leaders into Russian governmental structures, took place during the reign of Catherine the Great (1762–1796). The tasks of empire-building in the south and the east played an important role in this process. The annexation of Crimea in 1783 posed to the tsarist government the challenging task of gaining the allegiance of the former vassal of the Ottoman sultan to the Russian monarch. Baron O. A. Igel'strom (1737–1818), a Baltic noble and one of the chief architects of Catherine's policy in Crimea, provided a solution to this problem; the result implied incorporation of Islamic spiritual leaders into the imperial bureaucracy and creation of Muslim institutions under the state's control. This strategy formed an essential part of a larger project of integrating Crimea into the empire's social and administrative structures.

Following annexation, the Russian authorities handed over supervision of local religious affairs to the mufti, who then became part of the system of civil administration in the new empire's region.[2] After 1784, Baron Igel'strom was transferred from Crimea to the eastern frontier, where he continued his Islamic policies as governor-general of Simbirsk and Ufa. In 1788, an imperial decree set up the Ecclesiastical Assembly of the Mohammedan Creed (muftiate) (*Ufimskoe dukhovnoe magometanskogo zakona sobranie*), later the Orenburg Mohammedan Ecclesiastical Assembly, in Ufa. Consisting of two or three mullahs from the "Kazan Tatars," the assembly was chaired by a mufti; it supervised the appointment of mullahs as well as examined candidates for religious incumbencies.[3] The creation of an official Islamic institution in the empire's frontier region was motivated not only by the need to establish governmental control over the local Muslim population, but also by the imperial authorities' intention of using Islam and the Muslim Tatars to extend Russia's influence into Central Asia. Indeed, as Daniil Azamatov noted, the first mufti, Mukhamedzhan Khuseinov, played a key role in Russia's diplomatic efforts in the Kazakh steppe.[4] These actions corresponded with Catherine's overall policy, which made room for ideas of religious tolerance but also pursued the state regulation of religious life and religious institutions within the empire.

The structure and responsibilities of the Muslim Ecclesiastical Board in Crimea, as announced in Catherine's 1794 decree to the Senate, were in turn codified in 1831 by the *Polozhenie o Tavricheskom magometanskom dukhovenstve* (Statute on the Tauride Mohammedan Clergy).[5] The laws that regulated the Orenburg Assembly were systematized only in 1857, when volume 11 of the *Svod zakonov* (Compendium of Laws) was published.

Thus, for Muslims in European Russia, Siberia, and Crimea, the state created a hierarchical system of spiritual administration that was generally overseen by the Ministry of Internal Affairs and its Department for Religious Affairs of Foreign Confessions. Russian law recognized both higher and lower Muslim "clergy," with the former staffing the two major agencies of local spiritual administration, the Tauride Mohammedan Ecclesiastical Board (*pravlenie*) in Simferopol and the Orenburg Mohammedan Ecclesiastical Assembly in Ufa.[6] The district of the Simferopol board included Tauride province and the western provinces. The law made the Orenburg Assembly responsible for "all remaining provinces and regions, except the Transcaucasian region, Asian foreigners [*aziatskie inozemtsy*] from Tashkent and Bukhara, and those who live in certain towns in Siberia with no declared allegiance."[7]

The Muslim religious administrative bodies were collegial, comprising two or three individuals under the chairmanship of a mufti. Candidates for the position of mufti were supposed to be elected by the "Mohammedan community" (the Tauride statute defined the electoral process in greater detail) and were subsequently submitted to the MVD for approval by the tsar.[8] On assuming their duties, higher-ranking Muslim officials had to swear an oath of allegiance to the tsar.[9] The law specified salaries and staffing levels. The responsibilities of these Islamic institutions included supervision of mosques, schools, "parish clergy," and the *waqf* lands, along with serving as the Muslim court of appeal for congregations under their jurisdiction.

The lower Muslim clergy were responsible for conducting prayer services and performing religious rituals, including weddings, burials, and divorce, and resolving inheritance questions.[10] They were also required to provide statistical information to the government on the size of their congregations and on births, marriages, and deaths. Parish clergy were elected by local Muslim communities and approved by provincial authorities. In the Tauride district, clerical titles were exclusively hereditary, but in cases where several candidates were vying for a given position, preference was to go to those who spoke Russian.[11] In the Orenburg district, candidates for clerical positions had to be tested at the ecclesiastical assembly on their knowledge of Islamic law.[12]

By creating an official Islamic administrative hierarchy, the government assumed responsibility for managing the Muslim ecclesiastical order. Therefore, questions about the status of Muslim clergy and its relationship both with the Muslim population and the imperial authorities were constantly on the government's agenda. The laws regulating Muslim spiritual affairs were often inadequate to resolve everyday life situations in the growing and changing empire, and thus gave reasons for the government's continuous attempts to improve the system. Although the legitimacy of the state-sponsored Islamic establishment was not universally accepted by Russian Muslims, those who did accept the system and became members of the officially recognized clergy engaged the state in negotiations about their status and the whole empire's official Muslim ecclesiastical order.[13]

From an administrative point of view, the Russian authorities understood Muslim "clergy" to be similar to Orthodox clergy. However, there were significant differences in the organization of the religious hierarchy as well as in the social standing of the clerics. Unlike the centralized order of the Orthodox church, the Muslim spiritual administration was decentralized, and muftis had never achieved a standing within the government comparable to that of chief procurators; they also had less power over the parish clergy.[14] In contrast to Orthodox clergy, Muslim clergy enjoyed fewer privileges and had never formed the rigid hereditary clerical estate (*soslovie*) that in the nineteenth century became to be seen as a burden by the Orthodox church and the state.[15] Unlike their Orthodox counterparts, imams were elected by the members of their congregation. This, though, was only a relative form of autonomy, because the elections had to be approved by provincial authorities. By enlisting the Muslim clergy to serve the state and placing them within a hierarchical confessional order with the Russian Orthodox church at the top, the imperial authorities laid the ground for the Muslim clergy's aspirations to "improve" their status. Thus the state faced the difficult task of managing the Muslim ecclesiastical order while simultaneously guarding the Orthodox church's privileged position. This task became especially challenging when the Great Reforms dismantled the empire's social structure and the state assumed new responsibilities toward its subjects.

During the period of the Great Reforms and the simultaneous territorial expansion into the Muslim East, the issue of Muslim clergy came to be viewed by imperial authorities in light of a new state goal of overcoming the perceived ignorance and alienation of the Muslim population. Believing that the Muslim clergy dominated the minds of the Muslim population and exercised an enormous influence on their spiritual and civil lives, the tsarist officials defined the role of the Muslim clergy through the policy of rapprochement and enlightenment, raising new questions about the clergy's position vis-à-vis Muslim communities as well as the state.

By the early 1860s, some high state officials, like Russia's new minister of interior P. A. Valuev, recognized that the imperfect laws regulating Muslim institutions, the changing demographics of the empire's Muslim population, and the needs of the modernizing state required a general reform of the system of Muslim spiritual administration.[16] But how should the goals of the reform be defined? Enlightened tsarist officials, including Valuev, understood the essential problem primarily to be the cultural ignorance of the majority of the Muslim clerics who supposedly exploited their congregants and kept them in ignorance and isolation, thereby undermining the government's modernizing goals. As Valuev formulated the issue in 1864, unlike the Catholic clergy, the Muslim clergy in Russia "did not have a distinct political orientation," "but could rather be accused of a lack of education, morality, and consciousness."[17] At the same time in which the issue of the Muslim clergy was being discussed within the government, Valuev also raised similar issues with respect to the need for reform of the Orthodox church and the need to turn Orthodox clergy into more effective pastors, a task that appeared to be especially acute in the western provinces.[18]

From the perspective of imperial administrators in the eastern borderlands, however, the problem of Muslim clergy seemed to be more complicated than Valuev defined it. Provincial administrators of the frontier Orenburg province, whose own Muslim population constituted approximately half of all Muslims living within the district of the Orenburg Assembly, were especially anxious about the Muslim clergy's perceived alienation and ignorance.

The governors of Orenburg province had begun discussion of the reform of Muslim spiritual administration as early as the 1850s. The governor at the time, I. M. Potulov, defined the goal of the reform as making the Muslim clergy more useful to the state. To meet this goal, he suggested revising the existing election rules for the parish clergy by administering the exam at the assembly prior to the official approval, and not vice versa, as was currently the practice. He also proposed granting Muslim clergy some "privileges" (exemption from taxes and other duties) in order to "bind this class of people" to the government.[19]

These proposals were forwarded to the Ministry of Internal Affairs. Seeking to revise the existing laws regulating the Muslim ecclesiastical order, the ministry requested responses from the local governors and commissioned its expert on Muslim law, A. K. Kazem-Bek, to design a new project. Kazem-Bek envisioned creating a uniform system of religious administration, based on Sharia and Russian laws, for Muslims living in the districts of the Orenburg Assembly and the Tauride Board.[20] But events such as the emigration of Crimean Tatars to Turkey at the end of the Crimean War, the drafting of a new order in 1863 for governing the Bashkirs, and anxiety that general reforms would "ignite religious fanaticism" forced the ministry to postpone an attempt to transform Muslim religious institutions fundamentally. Instead, it limited itself to gathering materials and soliciting officials' opinions on the subject.

The issue of the Muslim clergy and its position with respect to both the Russian authorities and the Muslim population was raised with particular urgency in 1866–1867 by the Orenburg governor-general N. A. Kryzhanovskii in his personal report to the tsar and in a special report to the Minister of the Internal Affairs. Kryzhanovskii addressed the issue as an aspect of the Muslim Question. As administrator of the Orenburg region (1864–1881), Kryzhanovskii worried that the tremendous confessional diversity of this vast frontier region was "harmful" for its inhabitants' moral and political lives.[21] He was particularly disturbed by Islam, which—in light of Russia's expansion into Central Asia and the current Muslim rebellion in neighboring China—he saw as likely to develop into a serious political problem that he called the "Mohammedan Question."[22] Kryzhanovskii questioned the state's practice of religious tolerance, which in his view developed into "state patronage" of Islam and contributed to a "loss" (*ushcherb*) of Orthodoxy, while still leaving Islam outside state control. As he saw it, the state's goal should have been to contain Islamic influence while also combating Muslims' perceived ignorance and alienation.

He argued that Muslim clergy—an "inward-looking estate"—was using its vast influence over the minds of the Muslim population to economically exploit the population, cultivate ignorance and religious fanaticism in them, and hamper their integration into the structure of the Russian state. He regarded this influence as particularly "harmful" during the time of the Great Reforms. Kryzhanovskii wrote that Muslims' "ignorance" and "religious fanaticism" would present an especially serious problem once Muslims, who constituted the majority of the population in the region, began to participate in the new courts and institutions of self-government. Viewed in light of the eventual introduction of such courts and institutions created by the Great Reforms that aimed to better integrate different social and confessional groups, the very existence of Muslim institutions appeared to Kryzhanovskii as not in tune with the spirit of the times.[23]

To "bring the Muslims closer to Russia," Kryzhanovskii deemed it essential, as had Potulov earlier, to place Muslim clergy in a "more appropriate relationship to the government" by bringing their actions under closer state control while also uplifting their cultural level.[24] However, compared to Potulov's suggestions, his plan was grander in scale and more contradictory. He recommended starting with a reform of the Orenburg Ecclesiastical Assembly, which, in his view, would involve the introduction of a Russian government official into the assembly to monitor its enactments; the appointment of assembly members who could read and write Russian, and, later, had graduated from gymnasiums; the conducting of official correspondence and the maintenance of parish registers in Russian; the replacement of collegial consideration of certain matters by administrative action; the appointment of clergy instead of their election; the conferral of a government stipend on all members of the clergy, with the aim of "prohibiting all extortion" and "rendering the mullahs dependent on the government," its cost to be covered by a direct tax levied on the Bashkirs, which in Kryzhanovskii's opinion could in turn weaken their attachment to the clergy; and finally a prohibition against Bashkir and Tatar mullahs teaching among the Kazakhs.[25] Thus, in order to turn the Muslim clergy from "enemies" to "useful servants" of the government, Kryzhanovskii suggested breaking their dependence on the community and providing them with state salaries and education. These measures were to be connected to the government's attempts to control the Muslim confessional schools and to introduce Russian education in them. In other words, according to Kryzhanovskii, Muslims were to be enlightened and integrated within state-sponsored confessional institutions. At the same time, Kryzhanovskii's plan sought to undermine clergy's power over the Muslim population and prevent the spread of Islam among the nomadic Kazakhs believed not to be historically Muslim. In the newly acquired Turkestan oblast that until 1867 was under the jurisdiction of the Orenburg governor-general, Kryzhanovskii suggested no radical measures in relation to the Muslim clergy, who, as he argued, had less influence on the Muslim masses than their counterparts in internal Russia.[26]

In light of Kryzhanovskii's report, Alexander II recommended further study of this question, a task he entrusted to the Ministry of Internal Affairs. The governor-general's suggestions were reviewed by Valuev and his successor as Minister of Internal Affairs, A. E. Timashev. Valuev thought that demanding a gymnasium education from mullahs could leave Muslim parishes without clergy and he consequently worried that a class of underground mullahs would operate without any official oversight.[27] Timashev, who shared the governor-general's opinion that the chief task of the proposed reforms was to weaken the opposition of Muslim institutions to "Russian civilization," held that Muslims might interpret introducing a Russian official into the assembly and requiring the use of the Russian language in official communications and in parish registers as "restraint of religion." Hence, while acknowledging those steps as desirable, the MVD saw their introduction as fraught with "substantial impediments."[28]

A copy of Kryzhanovskii's suggestions was also forwarded to the governor-general of Novorossiia and Bessarabia. In 1868, the Tauride provincial administration (*gubernskoe pravlenie*) suggested limiting the influence of the Muslim clergy by reducing staffing in the mosques. The governor-general, convinced that these measures fell short, instead favored educating Crimean Tatars to bring them closer to the Russian population, while also transforming the Tauride Ecclesiastical Board into a department of the provincial administration.[29] At the same time, the Ministry of Internal Affairs drafted a questionnaire regarding the proposed reform of Muslim religious institutions for the opinions of the governors-general of Orenburg, Novorossiia, and Bessarabia. In 1870, a special government committee, including the governors of the Ufa, Orenburg, Ural, and Turgai regions and chaired by the governor-general, was set up in the Orenburg region to discuss the reform.

The discussion in Orenburg and Tauride province demonstrated the tremendous diversity of opinions on the proposed reforms. The Orenburg governor-general himself changed his position considerably: in 1867 he had considered reform of the ecclesiastical assembly essential, but by 1870 he viewed the elimination of the assembly as the goal of the reforms, arguing for the separation of matters of religious and civil administration.[30] Both Kryzhanovskii's reports had underlined the need to appoint rather than elect candidates to fill religious vacancies, but the Orenburg committee proposed that mullahs be elected by the community and confirmed by the authorities. Members of the clergy were required to know Russian in 1867, but not in 1870. The governor of Tauride province was against abandoning the collegial nature of the assembly, arguing that such a step could lead to abuses by the muftis, but he favored retaining the hierarchical organization of Muslim government.[31] The clear disparity of these views forced Timashev to recognize the impossibility of formulating common principles for reform. The Ministry of Internal Affairs decided not to undertake general measures, fearing that far-reaching reforms might lead the Muslim population to "suspect infringements on their religion."[32]

The tsarist government took up the issue of organization of the Muslim clergy in Transcaucasia as a special case. Several proposals were drafted following instructions from the local administration, but military operations in the region prevented any of them from becoming law. After the Caucasian War ended in 1864, questions about Muslim clergy again became relevant, along with issues concerning the establishment of administrative and judicial institutions in the region. The viceroy in the Caucasus, Grand Duke Mikhail Nikolaevich, paid special attention to the issue of Muslim clergy. Considering their importance in the spiritual and civil lives of Muslims, he assigned clergy an important role in achieving Muslims' rapprochement with the government. The organization of a Muslim clerical hierarchy that would be dependent on the government was viewed as the key to the successful integration of the new borderland into the empire.[33] In a plan to organize the clergy in Transcaucasia, drawn up in 1869, the viceroy specified the goals of the impending reform:

> Equip the government with the means to monitor Muslims; oppose any strengthening of corporate spirit within the clerical estate; obstruct the entry of foreign clerics from Turkey and Persia; limit, to the extent possible, the clergy's sphere of activity among the Muslim population without encroaching on religious beliefs; make the influential segment of the clergy directly dependent on the government by connect-

ing their material interests with government service; and establish oversight over religious schools and property.[34]

Now that the Caucasian War was over, the viceroy maintained, the government could be "freer in pursuing its goals" than in earlier plans (e.g., the one drawn up in 1849 under orders from Prince M. S. Vorontsov), which contained no provisions for governmental oversight over the clergy.[35]

Two administrative bodies were set up in Tiflis—one for Sunnis, headed by a mufti, and one for Shiites, headed by a sheikh-ul-Islam with responsibility for all parts of Transcaucasia except those that came under the military-communal administration (*voenno-narodnoe upravlenie*).[36] The emperor appointed the mufti and the sheikh-ul-Islam based on recommendations from the Ministry of Internal Affairs.[37] The hierarchy of the Transcaucasian clergy was designed as a three-tier system, with the provincial *majlis*—collegial bodies whose members were appointed by the governor with the consent of the ecclesiastical governing board—serving as intermediaries between the parish clergy and the governing boards.[38] The law regulated the position of the Transcaucasian clergy in detail. The important condition for receipt of an incumbency was that the candidate be a Russian subject who would make a formal declaration disavowing Muridism (a Muslim insurgency movement in North Caucasus led by the Sufi sheikh of the Naqshbandi order).[39] The Transcaucasian clergy was granted special privileges, but their responsibilities were otherwise similar to those in other parts of the empire.

In his comments on the project, Kazem-Bek doubted that the government's plans to prohibit contacts between Muslim clerics in the Caucasus and their counterparts elsewhere, which constituted the main goal of the reform, could be successfully carried out. He argued that since Sharia sometimes prescribed communication with members of the clergy in other countries in order to resolve controversial issues, the unconditional prohibition of such contacts could simply force these relationships underground.[40]

Even so, the project to organize Muslim clergy in Transcaucasia was approved by Timashev. Despite the fact that the Ministry of Internal Affairs had been unsuccessful in designing a general reform of the administration of Muslims' spiritual affairs, under pressure from the viceroy the bill became law on 5 April 1872. The needs of the borderland could not wait. In their opinion on this law, the State Council's combined Legal and State Economy departments maintained clearly that this statute should not subsequently be used as the basis for administering Muslim clergy in the internal provinces. There, the situation was assumed to be quite different because of the distance from foreign Muslim states as well as the different ethnographic composition of these Muslim populations who lived near Christians, recognized Russian power, and did not doubt the religious tolerance of the Russian government. The opinion pointed out that although Muslim clergy in the internal provinces were also aspiring to oppose the rapprochement of Muslims and Russians, these attempts could not be successful without help from abroad. In other words, it was the special conditions of the southern empire's borderland that justified the creation of the Muslim clerical hierarchy in Transcaucasia.[41]

As Russia annexed new Muslim-populated regions to the east and southeast, the state developed yet another style of interaction with Muslim spiritual leaders. In the Steppe region, according to the 1891 statute, the regional tsarist administration oversaw Muslim religious affairs run by mullahs who were elected (among the Kazakhs) by the owners of *kibitkas* (nomad tents) and subsequently approved by the governors.[42] The statute regulated clerical activity in the most general terms. It gave official standing to members of the clergy but limited their numbers. It also left undefined the duties and privileges of mullahs, since, according to the Steppe Statute, mullahs were viewed only as officiates (*verosluzhiteli*) and had to pay taxes and duties like other Kazakhs.[43] They were, moreover, no longer authorized to deal with matters relating to marriage and family, which were to be resolved on the basis of *adat* (local customary law).[44] The Steppe Statute was not extended to Tatars, whose religious affairs were governed by the Orenburg Ecclesiastical Assembly.

Elsewhere in the empire, the spiritual life of Muslims was left unregulated by imperial law. In the North Caucasus, in the Kuban, Terek, and Daghestan regions, and in Stavropol province, the supervision of Muslim religious affairs rested on the practices and precepts of the local administration. Mullahs were elected by Muslim communities and confirmed by local tsarist authorities. In practice, the Kuban and Terek regions were regulated by the Transcaucasian Statute of 1872, but the *kadis* (Islamic law court judges), who also sat on the local courts (*gorskii sud*), could adjudicate only marital questions, while cases involving inheritance or wardship were brought to the local verbal courts (*gorskii slovesnyi sud*). In the Daghestan region, too, customary legal norms coexisted with Islamic law.[45] During the Caucasian War, the Muslim clergy in the North Caucasus was predominantly anti-Russian in its sentiments, while imam Shamil during his rule over the people of Chechnya and Daghestan (1834–1859) asserted Sharia (Islamic divine law). In their efforts to limit Islam's influence, the tsarist administration in the Caucasus endorsed *adat* as a counterweight to Sharia.[46] Nor were there legal regulations of the religious life of Muslims from the Inner Bukeev Horde of Astrakhan province, in the Transcaspian territory, or Turkestan, where von Kaufman did not consider the Muslim spiritual leaders as allies in the state-sponsored modernization project and pursued a policy of ignoring Islam. In 1884, M. G. Cherniaev, Turkestan's governor-general, set up a special commission composed of local *ulamas,* and suggested adopting the regulations for Transcaucasian clergy to Turkestan, but his proposal was not put into practice and the commission was dissolved.

After the Andijan revolt, the issue of Muslim clergy in Turkestan took on more salience. The Turkestan governor-general, S. M. Dukhovskoi, criticized von Kaufman's policy, which he believed left politically dangerous Islam outside state control. In his report to the Ministry of War, he suggested the creation of a special Muslim ecclesiastical board in Turkestan, similar to the one in Transcaucasia, though, headed not by a mufti but by a Russian official with a good knowledge of Sharia, and also skilled in Turkic and Persian languages. The Ministry of Internal Affairs and the Ministry of War, however, considered the organization of the highest Muslim clergy "undesirable" because they believed that such an organization could lead to the "unification" of Muslims.[47]

In 1899, in a report submitted to the emperor, Dukhovskoi recommended a broad program to regulate the state of Islam in Turkestan and elsewhere in the empire, articulated in terms of "the struggle with Islam as a political force." Above all, Dukhovskoi suggested abolishing the existing Muslim religious administrations and transferring their functions to local administrations. He viewed these administrations primarily as bodies that united Muslims in "anti-Russian and anti-Christian propaganda" and felt that they hindered the penetration of Russian culture and ideas of assimilation. He also considered it to be essential to narrow the range of matters that could be resolved by Sharia.[48] Dukhovskoi's radical plan found no support in the higher echelons of government and was never put into practice.

Orthodox clerics and missionaries were particularly vocal in their criticism of state-sponsored Muslim establishments. In their eyes, the muftis were anti-Russian elements who promoted Muslim isolation rather than served as agents of rapprochement. The Orthodox missionary and publicist E. N. Voronets, for example, argued that in matters of state policy, the officially Orthodox Russian government could not trust the "infidel, foreign-born, fanatical, and single-minded specialists, the muftis," and that the government had made a mistake in creating administrative hierarchical bodies to manage the religious affairs of Muslims, institutions which, he claimed, were neither characteristic of Islam nor necessary to the state.[49] Viewed within the framework of their understanding of the Muslim Question, which emphasized the danger of Islamic domination, the existing state-sponsored system of Muslim ecclesiastical administration seemed to strengthen Islam and the unity of Muslim believers.

Il'minskii and his followers in Kazan also criticized the state institutionalization of Islam as a deviation from what they saw as the "traditional" approach of the Muscovite state to Islam, and suggested tolerating Islam but leaving it without state regulation and support. This emphasis on state noninterference into religious life was also characteristic of the Slavophile vision of state–church relations, which they also desired for the Orthodox community. Like other proponents of church reform, Slavophiles sought to rejuvenate Orthodoxy. But in contrast to reformers like Valuev, for example, their vision involved reviving the medieval parish, with clergy close to the congregants in occupation and spirit rather than efficiently serving the institutional church and state.[50] This closeness between the spiritual leader and his congregation, as well as relative autonomy from the state, was something that the Muslim communities seemed to possess, and thus represented a model that Il'minskii and his followers tried to replicate.[51] Il'minskii and his supporters believed that Orthodoxy would eventually triumph, but until that time, Orthodoxy would need the protection of the state, while Islam and its institutions—apparently strong—required government control and containment but not support or modernization. As the Muslin Question became more "complicated," the emphasis on control became stronger.

Despite these criticisms, the state maintained what appeared to be an asymmetrical system of Muslim spiritual administration. In European Russia, Crimea, and Transcaucasia, Muslims had official organs of spiritual administration and their clergy were incorporated into the structures of the government. This system, however, was characterized by a high degree of regional diversity in the social status of the clergy as well as in the laws that regulated the operation of the ecclesiastical organs. Elsewhere in the empire a different principle was in place, whereby Muslim clerics were seen only as fulfilling a liturgical function and, hence, no official Islamic hierarchy was created.

From the latter half of the nineteenth century, the MVD discussed the possibility of creating a uniform system of Muslim religious administration; in practice, however, few substantial changes were made. The continuous expansion of the empire and the inclusion of new territories and peoples, as well as the military conflicts with the Ottoman empire, rendered successful unification objectively difficult. But there were additional obstacles. Government officials themselves could not agree on how best to approach Islam or on how to resolve the tension created by viewing the Muslim clergy both as useful "agents" and as "enemies" of the state. Having inherited a state-sponsored system of Muslim spiritual administration and thus having created a class of religious bureaucrats, the imperial authorities in St. Petersburg were hesitant to make radical changes in the existing order out of fear of provoking popular discontent ("religious fanaticism"). Since there seemed to be neither a perfect moment for fundamental reform nor agreement on what that reform should be, the government instead limited itself to partial modifications of the existing system.

From the 1860s on, many officials within the imperial elite began to think in terms of an enlightenment and integration policy that relied extensively on the use of the Russian language and on the intensification of governmental control over clerical activities—a move well illustrated by the steps taken toward regulating the clergy operating under the Orenburg Ecclesiastical Assembly, where, under the aegis of a program of "enlightenment" and "rapprochement" of Eastern *inorodtsy* with Russians, the government sought to introduce Russian classes into Muslim confessional schools.

Despite the support of S. Tevkelev, appointed Orenburg mufti in 1865, these measures met with opposition from Muslim clergy and Muslim communities alike. Under such circumstances, the government decided to Russify the clergy first; in 1890, knowledge of Russian became a condition for holding a religious post in the Orenburg area. On numerous occasions in later years, tsarist officials discussed the possibility of extending that 1890 statute to other regions inhabited by Muslims, but the idea had to be abandoned because of the Muslim clergy's disinterest in learning Russian as well as concerns that, in the absence of a sufficient number of candidates able to read and write Russian, some Muslim congregations could find themselves left with no officiates at all.

Thus, instead of reforming the clergy, the state attempted to establish tighter control of the Muslim spiritual administration. The government ascribed considerable significance to the personality of anyone who headed the Muslim clergy and its religious administration.[52] This individual, as the governor-general of Orenburg and Samara, A. P. Bezak, expressed it, should exert "a moral influence on his coreligionists" and be "a sponsor of the idea of rapprochement between the Mohammedan population and the Russians."[53] Initially the law envisaged that all Muslim clerics were to be elected by the community, but in relation to the mufti this rule was never put into practice.[54]

The issue about elections came to a head when the mufti G. Suleimanov died in 1862 and the position of the Orenburg mufti remained vacant for some time. The opinions of provincial administrators on the question of elections or appointment, solicited by Valuev, were divided. And so were the opinions of Muslims.[55] In the end, Valuev did not suggest legal modifications to the procedures for electing muftis, but relied instead on the passage of temporary rules. As he explained to the Council of Ministers:

> At present it is easier for the government to offset any unfavorable results of the election of a mufti by reserving to itself, on the basis of existing law, the right to refuse to approve a candidate who does not conform to the government's views and to prefer a more worthy candidate selected by the Mohammedans themselves than to assume all moral responsibility for this choice. When the public participates in the selection of a mufti, the moral responsibility for an unsuccessful choice falls on the public, and the Mohammedans will not be able to blame government arbitrariness for any untoward consequences of its own mistakes.[56]

Valuev also pointed out that "the Mohammedan clergy in Russia had no common and defined political tenor whatsoever that would demand particular vigilance in the selection of members of the higher clergy, such as is the case, for instance, with respect to the Roman Catholic clergy."[57]

Following Valuev's recommendations, the subsequent two muftis were appointed on the basis of government approval of an elected candidate. However, neither of these men—first, S. Tevkelev (in 1865), a landowner and Russian officer, and later, M. Sultanov (in 1886), a noble and peace mediator (*mirovoi posrednik*) in Ufa province, had a religious education and thus did not belong to *ulama*. In the new political climate of the late 1880s, the Ministry of Internal Affairs determined that it was time to move to the direct appointment of muftis and members of the assembly.[58] This procedural change was justified by the important role played by the leader of the Muslim clergy and the limited likelihood that Muslims themselves would ever elect individuals who "conformed to the views" of the government. This recommendation, made in relation to the Orenburg district, was approved by the tsar in 1890 and in 1891 was also extended to the Tauride district.[59]

Another important aspect of relations between the state and Muslim institutions concerned financial support of Muslim clergy. Those officials who viewed Muslim clergy as "servants of the state" suggested that the state had to take responsibility for such support. From the moment the Muslim spiritual administrations came into being, the state had provided part of their funding. The Muslim heads of these religious institutions frequently asked the government to increase their staff and to raise funding levels. The government's position on this issue was ambiguous. On the one hand, officials declared on several occasions that "only the Orthodox church had the right to receive state funds to meet its needs."[60] On the other hand, having found the Muslim clerics' petitions for higher stipends "justified," the Ministry of Internal Affairs—while making no general legislative changes—allocated allowances to individual muftis while also trying to shift the responsibility for financing their religious institutions to the shoulders of Muslims, through pious endowments (*waqf*) in Crimea and Transcaucasia, or by increasing the marriage tax, as in the Orenburg region.

Mosques and the Limits of Religious Tolerance

The tensions revealed in Russians' attitudes and policies toward the organs of Muslim spiritual administration were also characteristic of the government's policies toward another important Muslim institution—the mosques. In accordance with Catherine's approach to Muslim institutions, the government viewed the mosques as places where the state could communicate to its Muslim subjects the ideas of obedience to God, Monarch, and the Fatherland, as well as to explain the government's policies. At the same time, while tolerating Islam, the state protected the dominant position of the Orthodox church.

The tradition of Orthodox proselytism, particularly in the Volga, complicated this twofold task. It was during the time of an aggressive missionary campaign, associated with the Office of New Converts (1730–1762), that the state engaged in regulating the mosques, seeking to protect the newly baptized non-Russian population from "temptation" to Islam while also maintaining a shaken sociopolitical order in a multiconfessional region. Catherine II inherited this problem. She halted aggressive missionary activity in the Volga region by shutting down the Office of New Converts and banned church authorities from interfering with decision-making concerning mosque construction.[61] Her policy of toleration toward Islam initiated a wave of mosque construction. The state itself, driven by commercial and diplomatic interests, became involved in this process at what was then the empire's eastern frontier.[62]

Yet as the state officially remained the protector of Orthodoxy, it implemented measures to limit the spread of Islam, where possible. Thus, previous laws that had established a minimum size for a Muslim parish remained in place. Concerns remained that mosques might "tempt" Christians. For the state, the issue of regulating mosques also had a financial aspect. Since mosques and the clergy who served in them were financially dependent on the local community, the construction of new mosques decreased the income of some mullahs and increased the revenues of others. Either situation affected the financial responsibility of the state's Muslim tax-paying population. This aspect of regulation was not unique to Islam. In an attempt to prevent the proliferation of poor churches and clergy, the state also regulated the size of Orthodox parishes and the numbers of clergy.[63]

The tsarist government recognized mosques as places where Muslims were officially permitted to conduct public prayers. The state viewed the mosques as it did other public buildings, regulating their construction, renovation, and external appearance. As was the case with the organization of the Muslim spiritual administration, in some regions the construction of mosques was regulated by law, while in others it was established by practice. The Construction Statute (*Stroitel'nyi Ustav*) determined the procedure for opening mosques in the districts of the Tauride Ecclesiastical Board and the Orenburg Ecclesiastical Assembly, as well as in the Steppe region. In the Tauride and Orenburg districts, a Muslim community wishing to build a new mosque was required to petition the ecclesiastical board or the assembly before seeking approval from the tsarist administration. Muslim and Russian authorities had to determine a "real need" for the construction of a new mosque, and would evaluate the possibility of its financial support by the population.

According to the law, the question of necessity was determined on the basis of the size of a parish (at least two hundred tax-paying male souls were required), while the promise of financial support was to be guaranteed by the community and recorded in a special *prigovor* (decision).[64] When giving permission for the construction of a new mosque, or, for that matter, any other non-Christian prayer house, the MVD had to make sure that the new mosque would not be located near Orthodox churches.[65]

Orthodox church officials were involved in decisions about constructing mosques, but the nature of this involvement varied in different parts of the empire. In Tauride province, the agreement of diocese authorities was necessary if a mosque was to be built near Orthodox churches. In the district of the Orenburg Assembly, where apostasy from Orthodoxy was a pressing problem, the construction of a mosque was permitted only if it would not "tempt" neighboring Christians and the newly baptized.[66] In the Steppe region, the law only specified the participation of the secular authorities. Until 1905, in the Ural and Turgai oblast, the MVD allowed one mosque per *volost*.[67] In other Muslim regions of the empire, questions concerning such construction were not specified by law and were resolved by administrative practice.

Yet even the existing state regulations concerning mosque construction and the appointment of clergy were not always followed in practice, and their different interpretations by local authorities and Muslims caused numerous conflicts that state officials had to resolve. Throughout the empire, illegal religious institutions and clergy proliferated, and there were so-called "mosques built without official permission" (*samovol'no postroennye mecheti*) and "false mullahs" (*samozvannye mully*) who operated without the state's authorization and thus outside government control. Nor could the law anticipate the multiplicity of situations it was assumed to cover, forcing tsarist officials to make continued attempts to modify the existing system. Finally, the state's policy of mosque regulation faced the challenge of multiple tasks: guaranteeing freedom of religious expression for Muslims while at the same time protecting the economic well-being of the Muslim population and securing the privileged position of the Orthodox church. The policy of regulation faced even a greater challenge as educated Russians became increasingly concerned about the Muslim Question. Thus, mosque regulation became another contentious issue in a broader policy about Muslim institutions.

During the period of the Great Reforms, some Russian authorities and clerics alike formulated the mosque issue as a problem of their "multiplication" (*razmnozhenie*), meaning that there was an excessive number of them. As was the case for other confessions, including Orthodoxy, this issue was viewed as an economic problem, yet it had an additional dimension. Viewed in the context of the Muslim Question, which centered on concerns about Muslims' alienation and their potential to dominate, mosques now came to be seen as institutions that were alien (*chuzhdye*) to Russian culture and posed a threat to Orthodoxy. These anxieties were especially strong in the Volga region among local church figures and missionaries faced with the large wave of apostasy that reached its peak in the late 1860s. In 1867, alarmed by this spread of Islam, the archbishop of Kazan and Sviiazhsk, Antonii, pointed to the "extraordinary multiplicity of mosques" in Kazan province, which for him demonstrated the "domination" (*gospodstvo*) of Islam in the region. He proved his point by statistics, indicating that in 1865 the ratio of believers to prayer houses constituted 1,186,536 to 485 among the Orthodox and 447,476 to 710 among the Muslims. He also provided a list of mosques that, in his view, had been opened in violation of the existing regulations.[68]

Antonii's report provoked a government investigation. In 1869, Vice Governor Rozov reported to the Ministry of Internal Affairs that the mosques listed by Antonii had been built long ago and that the authorities could not reconstruct their documentary history, nor find any evidence of government permission for their construction. Fearing Muslims' discontent should their mosques be closed, Rozov proposed not to shut unauthorized old mosques, but to let time destroy them instead by not allowing their renovation. As for the construction of new mosques, he proposed to follow existing regulations.[69]

In 1868, the Kazan missionary E. Malov published an essay on the mosques in Russia, arguing that "seduction" of baptized Tatars into Islam by the mullahs was an important element of the local politics of mosque construction and the opening of new parishes. Most of Malov's study was a history of mosque construction in Russia. He noted a steady increase in the number of mosques and mullahs and felt that this demonstrated the rising strength of Islam. Calling on the authorities to stop the spread of "unauthorized" mosques, Malov also pointed to what he saw as the "unfairness" of state regulations of Orthodoxy in comparison to those of Islam. He believed that both the law and local practices placed Muslims in more favorable conditions than Orthodox believers in terms of the relationship between parish size and numbers of clergy. Malov thus proposed to increase the minimum requirement for a new mosque from 200 to no less than 1,500 taxpayers, while still allowing only one mullah to serve a Muslim parish. Malov did not view the proposed measures as restrictions on Islam, and he pointed to similar and even harsher government policies toward what it viewed as excessive numbers of Orthodox churches and clergy.[70]

The issue of excessive mosques had been raised by local secular tsarist authorities, but mostly from an economic perspective.[71] In 1867, however, the Orenburg governor-general, N. A. Kryzhnovskii, deployed the mosque issue and emphasized its other aspects to challenge the state's policy of religious tolerance. He pointed to the excessive number of mosques as evidence of what he saw as the state's protection of Islam that helped Muslims dominate Orthodoxy in the Orenburg region. Like Antonii, Kryzhanovskii illustrated his point by comparing the numbers of mosques and Orthodox churches. He called on the government to enforce the existing regulations in relation to mosque construction in order to protect the economic interests of the Muslim population, prevent the development of Muslim religious fanaticism, and safeguard the dominant position of the Orthodox.[72]

The state regulation of mosque construction—however inconsistent—provoked frequent complaints by Muslims to the authorities. Clearly, the existing law failed to address the needs of various Muslim communities who were increasingly affected by the developing imperial economy, mobility, and urbanization. For example, in urban centers Muslims sometimes did not have a sufficient number of the registered census souls to build a new mosque, but the real number of inhabitants, including seasonal workers, women, and Muslims born after the last census exceeded the required norm of two hundred taxpaying souls. There were also cases in the countryside when the number of Muslims did not meet the required norm, yet the nearest mosque was too far away to meet their needs. The Muslims' complaints indicated that in these kinds of situations the existing state regulations failed to guarantee the promised freedom of prayer and religious service and thus failed to satisfy their religious needs.

In the 1860s, the Ministry of Internal Affairs, whose officials reviewed complaints coming from both sides, attempted to modify the existing regulations of mosque construction. The ministry's officials agreed that the excessive construction of mosques had negative economic consequences for the Muslim population, but suggested that the communities themselves should be the best judges of this issue.[73] In 1869, the Department for Religious Affairs of Foreign Confessions in the MVD developed a project that changed the existing provisions regulating the size of Muslim parishes. For populous communities, it suggested that the norm be increased up to five hundred registered souls for the "cathedral" mosques (*sobornye mecheti*), with a minimum of fifty souls required for thinly populated communities. In the latter case, the government was not only guided by considerations of religious tolerance, but also by the interests of governance; the "mosque was to guarantee a more proper keeping of vital records and timely fulfillment of government requirements such as the administration of oaths." In response to the anxieties expressed by the Orthodox clerics, the Ministry of Internal Affairs also pointed out that "it would hardly be in accordance with the dignity of the Orthodox church to suggest that its interests require the persecution of Muslim religious institutions."[74]

In 1875, the ministry submitted to the second department of His Imperial Highness's Chancellery, whose responsibility was to review legislative proposals, a more radical project that allowed every Muslim town and village community to have a mosque regardless of the number of parishioners, as long as they had the means to support it.[75] However, as with other matters concerning Muslim religious institutions discussed by the government during this period, this project was shelved. One reason given for this inaction was a report from the Orenburg governor-general, Kryzhanovskii, who argued that during a time when relations between Russia and the Ottoman empire had worsened, any reforms to Muslim religious institutions would be imprudent (*neostorozhnye*).

The question about mosques' regulation arose again in the 1880s as a result of continuing complaints by Muslims to the Ministry of Internal Affairs about local authorities who either closed ramshackle mosques or did not allow the construction of new mosques if there were not a sufficient number of registered souls. The Orenburg Ecclesiastical Assembly petitioned the MVD to change the existing regulations by eliminating the required norms and allowing Muslims to build mosques as long as they could support them.[76] In addition, the officials of the Department for Religious Affairs of Foreign Confessions recognized that the norms established in 1829 were outdated. On the one hand, according to the department, the required norm of two hundred souls did not prevent construction of mosques in populous urban areas where the mosques could have a certain religiously political significance. But on the other hand, and this constituted the central argument of the department, Muslim communities in underpopulated rural areas were deprived of the ability to satisfy their religious needs.[77]

In the project submitted to His Imperial Highness's Chancellery in 1880, the MVD stressed that the existing norm represented a constraint on religious expression (*religioznoe stesnenie*) in relation to the thinly populated communities in the districts of the Tauride Ecclesiastical Board and the Orenburg Ecclesiastical Assembly and corresponded neither with the principle of religious toleration nor with existing regulations concerning other groups of Muslims or non-Orthodox believers.[78] The report pointed out that this new measure would have a calming effect on a population that already suspected the government of religious proselytism.[79] The officials of the Department for Religious Affairs of Foreign Confessions argued that Muslims' commitment to support the mosques and the clergy would be the best guarantee that mosques would be established where they were "really necessary." Again, as they had before, the department argued for the important role of mosques and clergy in governance. The MVD suggested keeping the same norm of two hundred souls, providing these were actual male parishioners, not registered souls. The main innovation, however, was the suggestion to give the head of the Department for Religious Affairs of Foreign Confessions the right to allow exceptions to this rule under certain circumstances.[80] This project was thus less radical than both the 1875 proposal and the suggestions of the Orenburg Assembly. The solution allowed the MVD to resolve the multiple complaints coming from thinly populated Muslim communities, and to guarantee freedom of religion on an individual-case basis. In 1886, the State Council changed the norm for construction of new mosques for two hundred registered male souls with a requirement for two hundred actual male inhabitants. In the Council's opinion, such a requirement aimed to satisfy the religious needs of the Muslim population while also protecting Orthodoxy in the districts of the Orenburg Ecclesiastical Assembly and the Tauride Ecclesiastical Board.[81]

The state thus continued to be involved in regulating construction of mosques, even though, in practice, the authorities were not always able to enforce their regulations. The perceived problem of excessive mosques and the tensions associated with it remained. In 1891, the Ufa governor reported to the MVD that the rural population of the province had immediately taken advantage of the new regulations, which had resulted in a sharp increase of new mosques. According to the governor, by 1 January 1891 there were 1,452 mosques in Ufa province, some 200 of which were approved after the new law was issued—that is, during the period of 1887–1890.[82] The governor wrote that the new law did not prevent the construction of new mosques, and that this was harmful to the material well-being of the clergy, as well as for imperial governance. He also admitted that, in reality, the authorities had difficulty controlling the emergence of new mosques and asked the MVD for guidance on this matter.[83] The new law did not resolve the conflicting situations associated with the Muslim communities' desire to build mosques, and the state remained involved in the politics of local mosque construction. Finally, to the Orthodox missionaries and clerics, the officially approved mosques, along with those that escaped government regulations entirely, represented most vividly both the presence and what they interpreted as the "strength" of a hostile confession in a way that reminded them of the "weakness" of Orthodoxy.

The Implications of State Policies

The tsarist state's interest in Muslim religious institutions derived mainly from the needs of empire-building. Catherine II and her successors officially recognized Islam, turning it into a tool of imperial governance and expansion. In the second half of the nineteenth century, the modernization of the empire's old order, affecting the Orthodox church, the creation of new secular institutions, along with imperial expansion into Muslim lands, forced authorities to reconsider state policy toward Muslim institutions. The concerns embodied in the Muslim Question played out in Russians' deliberations on the system of Muslim ecclesiastical administration and the regulation of mosque construction.

The main problem, as many educated Russians inside and outside the government saw it, was Muslims' ignorance and alienation; for this, they felt, the Muslim clergy was to blame. One conclusion that tsarist administrators drew was that the solution to this problem should aim to make the clergy more useful to the state by lifting their cultural level and social status. The empire's recent military conflicts with Muslims, however, as well as a widely held perception of Islam as a religion hostile to Christianity, cast doubts about the possibility and necessity of such an approach. Moreover, the question arose about the very compatibility of Islam and its institutions with the goals of a modernizing state. These doubts suggested that the state pursue different strategies of weakening, ignoring, or controlling Muslim institutions rather than improving and relying on them. In addition, Muslim institutions appeared as strong rivals to what was perceived to be a weak Orthodox church, leading to the conclusion that Islam needed to be contained.

What were the implications of government's policies undertaken during the second half of the nineteenth century toward Muslim religious institutions? The government made attempts to Russify and maintain tighter control over clergy in the district of the Orenburg Assembly, but despite the plans prepared within the Ministry of Internal Affairs, nothing was accomplished to bring together the existing systems of Muslim ecclesiastical administration in European Russia, Crimea, and Siberia. Radical proposals to demolish the Muslim hierarchy and separate matters of religious and civil administration were also rejected by the central authorities. An elaborate state-sponsored system of Muslim administration was created in Transcaucasia, while in the newly conquered area of Turkestan, authorities followed the principle of "ignoring" Islam. Despite the recognized need for a unified approach and a general reform of Muslim administration, the government committed to a particularistic system and partial transformations. Regional diversity, ministerial rivalry, governmental fear of popular response, as well as different opinions within tsarist officialdom, could explain this situation. Committed, on the one hand, to guarantee the freedom of religious expression to the Muslim population, and, on the other, to protect the Orthodox church, the tsarist state remained involved in regulating mosques' construction while readjusting its requirements. In other words, the government modified the policy toward Muslim institutions without dismantling the foundations of the confessional system.

This approach did not satisfy various Russian critics of state policy toward Islam. To Il'minskii's followers, the state erroneously continued to play the role of a patron of Islam; Islam also appeared to be "privileged" vis-à-vis the officially "dominant" Orthodoxy. The state's continued reliance on Muslim clergy as its servants created aspirations among members of the official clergy to improve their status by asking for more state funding and privileges. The asymmetrical system of Muslim ecclesiastical administration and government deliberations on this issue provoked Muslims to develop their own proposals on how to improve the existing system and rebuild it. As we will see, these claims presented an even greater challenge to the autocratic state during the era of mass politics, when religious institutions were appropriated by Muslim intelligentsia as institutional symbols of Muslim national identity.

Group of Tatars at work repairing roadway in Balaklava in front of the Store of the 14th Regiment, 1855. Roger Fenton's Crimean War photo series. Library of Congress, Prints & Photographs Division.

Nikolai Ivanovich Il'minskii. Kazan Federal University, N. I. Lobachevskii's Library, Manuscripts and Rare Books Division.

اسماعيل بك غصپرينسكى

Измайлъ бекъ Гаспринскій.

Собственность издат. „Гасръ"

Ismail Bey Gasprinskii. Bakhchisarai Historical and Cultural Museum Complex. The Memorial Museum of Ismail Gasprinskii

128

1898 г. Участники Андижанского восстания в цепях

Participants of the Andijan uprising in chains, 1898. K. Ramzin, *Revoliutsiia v Srednei Azii v obrazakh i kartinakh* Tashkent: Izd-vo. Saku, 1928.

The Teachers' Seminary in Tashkent, 1907. Nikolai Petrovich Ostroumov is in the middle of the second row. TsGARU.

Ali Mardan Topchibashev, the deputy of the First Duma, 1906. TsGAKFFD SPb

Nikolai Alekseevich Bobrovnikov holding the "Materials of the Special
Committee on Education of Eastern *Inorodtsy*." The Kazan Federal University,
N. I. Lobachevskii's Library, Manuscripts and Rare Books Division.

Andrei (Ukhtomskii), Bishop of Mamadysh, 1907. Archive of Anna Gorshkova, Internet Project "Great Russian Album," www.rusalbom.ru

Archival photograph representing participants of a Muslim congress in St. Petersburg (dated 1913). TsGAKFFD SPb.

Muslim soldiers in the mosque before being sent to the front, Petrograd, 1914.
TsGAKFFD SPb,

Part Two
The Muslim Question during
the Era of Mass Politics

6 Challenges of Revolution and Reform

As it had in the Crimean conflict fifty years earlier, the empire's military's failure in the Russo-Japanese War of 1904–1905 discredited the tsarist government, hurt Russians' national pride, and further aggravated the country's already tense political situation. The growing sociopolitical crisis forced the government of Nicholas II to consider changes. The appointment in late August 1904 of P. D. Sviatopolk-Mirskii as the new minister of interior indicated such a transformation. Sviatopolk-Mirskii soon submitted his program of reforms to Nicholas II, which included an expansion of civil liberties and public participation in the government. The resulting "political spring" in relations between state and society, a course initiated by the new minister, stimulated discussions of reform among educated members of the imperial society, just as they had in the late 1850s.

This new push for political liberalization was taking place in a dramatically different context than the Great Reforms of a generation earlier. In the early years of the twentieth century, Russian society faced a complex tangle of unresolved problems. The social changes stimulated by the Great Reforms had led to the rise of new forces, including professional groups and an industrial working class who, along with the peasants, challenged the tsarist regime with liberal, nationalistic, and socialist demands. In the liberal atmosphere of Sviatopolk-Mirskii's ministry, these disaffected groups began to organize into an opposition movement. In January 1905, workers marched toward the Winter Palace with a petition for the tsar, only to be fired upon by government troops. The resulting massacre unleashed a revolution that rapidly spread to the non-Russian borderlands, reaching an especially high degree of intensity in the Baltic provinces, the Kingdom of Poland, Ukraine, and Transcaucasia.

The revolution was not the only stimulus for the next round of reforms, as historians have demonstrated, but it certainly determined their scope, pace, and methods.[1] Under increasing pressure, Nicholas II agreed to further concessions that culminated in the October Manifesto issued on 17 October 1905. The manifesto announced the establishment of the State Duma to perform legislative functions and granted civil liberties, personal inviolability, and freedom of consciousness, speech, assembly, and association. The October Manifesto contributed to the political mobilization of Russian society and catalyzed the growth of national movements. National parties that arose during this time demanded various new rights and different degrees of autonomy for the groups they claimed to represent.

Nicholas viewed the introduction of limited parliamentary government as a temporary concession; he fully intended to preserve autocratic rule in Russia. The government and the Duma leadership were not able to work together, and the meetings of both the First Duma (April–July 1906) and the Second Duma (February–June 1907) were dissolved. Yet the elected Duma presented a new forum for addressing the empire's multiple questions. It also transformed political culture. How did the radical changes enacted during the revolution, the October Manifesto, and subsequent reforms reset the Muslim Question? Did the tsarist government reformulate the Muslim Question?

The Challenge of Muslim Political Awakening

The Revolution of 1905 gave strength to all national movements in the empire.[2] The rights and freedoms granted in the October Manifesto created a favorable environment for the formation of national cultures and political mobilization. The relaxation of censorship promoted the rapid development of publishing and the press in national languages, enabling the non-Russian intelligentsias to raise their own questions as well as to reinterpret the sharp vital issues of the empire's sociopolitical life for a broader circle of the non-Russian and Russian reading public. The aspirations of the Muslim intelligentsia to reach the reading public further stimulated debates on the problem of appropriate literary language for various Turkic Muslim groups and additionally led to the articulation of alternative national projects to Gasprinskii's vision of Russian Muslim community.[3] The growing number of periodicals published by Muslims facilitated contacts between writers and editors and created preconditions for the self-organization and mobilization of the Muslim intelligentsia. In turn, the increasing number of Muslim publications served as an important source of information about the life and aspirations of the empire's Muslims for Russian observers.[4]

Tatar publishing, especially, experienced a boom. New Tatar periodicals were launched in a number of imperial cities, including Kazan, Orenburg, Ufa, Ural'sk, Astrakhan, Bakhchisarai, Baku, St. Petersburg, and Moscow.[5] In Kazan alone, twenty Tatar publishing houses issued 5,154 different book titles and a total number of 38,714,032 copies.[6] For the most part, Tatar-language publications were pro-Jadid. A general characteristic of the printing houses that opened after 1900 was that almost all of them published titles on nonreligious subjects, such as history, geography, zoology, medicine, literature, philosophy, and mathematics, demonstrating a growing interest in secular knowledge among Tatar readers.

Jadidism, having begun primarily as a cultural-pedagogical movement, began to acquire a more political character in this era. From late 1904, Muslim assemblies and public gatherings began to be held in different cities of the empire. Recalling this time, the Orthodox priest S. Bagin wrote: "The liberation movement has stirred up the Tatar-Mohammedans. . . . Everywhere one hears of meetings, assemblies, unions, circles, newer and newer publications and printing houses, magazines and newspapers, etc."[7] Muslims took the opportunities provided by the new civil freedoms and political institutions created by the revolution, and became engaged in politics by submitting petitions to the government, organizing Muslim congresses, founding a political organization, cooperating with Russian parties, creating a Muslim faction in the State Duma, and confronting Russians with new types of claims. The Muslim intelligentsia viewed it as their task to prepare their masses for participation in Russia's rapidly changing political life.[8]

After establishing contacts with Muslims in various regions of the empire, as well as with Russian liberals, representatives of the moderate wing of the Jadid movement organized two All-Russian Muslim congresses. The first was held in Nizhnii Novgorod in August 1905; the second in St. Petersburg in January 1906. They also founded the Union of Muslims of Russia (Ittifak), which claimed to represent the interests of all Russian Muslims regardless of class and sectarian differences. The congress participants were aligned in two groups. The first, led by Tatars A. Ibragimov, I. Bey Gasprinskii, Y. Akchurin, and Azeri A. M. Topchibashev (Topchibashi), appears to have had the greatest support among Muslim delegates at the congresses. In terms of political orientation, this group was closest to the newly formed party of the Russian Constitutional Democrats (Kadets).[9] The second faction, headed by the Volga Tatar A. Iskhakov, adhered to a more radical, socialist-revolutionary program and had less of a following; at the first congress they represented less than 20 percent of the total number of 108 delegates, and their position was not adopted in the platform of the congress.[10]

Muslim political activism, and especially the Muslims' alliance with Russian liberals, came as a surprise to the Russian public, which was at first broadly sympathetic to what it perceived as the Muslim awakening. Reporting on the Second Congress of Muslims, the popular journal *Niva* noted that it was clearly a mistake to dismiss Tatars and Bashkirs as people of "sluggishness and inertia."[11] The missionary journal *Pravoslavnyi blagovestnik* cited a short commentary from A. S. Suvorin's *Novoe vremia* that struck a similar tone:

> A few years [ago] the stagnation, cultural and intellectual isolation, and general distrust of Muslims toward outsiders was striking. . . . But today the mass of Russian Muslims, fifteen million strong, has awakened from its slumber and is seeking new life as a means of combating its discontent. Muslims are aiming to unite themselves without regard to ethnic distinctions. Through pan-Turkism, they are attempting to establish ties—at present merely moral in nature—with the entire Muslim world.[12]

The editors regarded this phenomenon as "deserving of sympathy and highly noteworthy."[13]

The imperial authorities did not share the broader public opinion on the spread of "new trends" among the Muslim masses. In February 1906, the Tauride governor reported to the Ministry of Internal Affairs on the discussion of the results of the Second Muslim Congress at the meeting of the representatives of Crimean Muslims. He characterized the Tauride Muslims as "politically atrophied," with no idea about political parties or their programs. He wrote that, after listening to the report of the delegates to the congress, the majority of Muslims had understood nothing and that the debates had been chaotic. The governor suggested that the decision of local Muslims to support the strategy of the Muslim faction to unite with the Kadets was not so much a conscious one, but the response to the propagandizing of their progressive leaders.[14]

The First and the Second Muslim Congresses did not receive the sanction of the minister of the interior; they were held as unofficial meetings. The authorities feared that Muslims would discuss political issues at their gatherings. The Second Congress appeared to give credence to such fears, as a number of Muslims reported to the government about the apparently revolutionary intentions of the congress.[15] The liberal newspaper *Rech* reported the motivation behind the refusal by the former Minister of the Internal Affairs, P. N. Durnovo (1905–1906), to give official sanction in the following terms: "If we permit the holding of a Muslim congress, we will have no grounds to deny the Jews, the Poles, and other groups."[16]

In August 1906, a group of Muslims (Ibragimov, merchant M. Maksudov, and mullah L. Iskhakov from St. Petersburg) approached the government to officially allow a Muslim congress. The petitioners presented the goal of the future congress as rather conservative, aimed at preventing the spread of teachings of pan-Islamism, anarchism, and socialism, which they felt were undermining religiosity among the Muslim population. The proposed program included questions about the religion and education of Muslims.[17] Later, *Rech* reported that the organizing committee for the congress condemned the petitioners for "not conforming to the aspirations of progressive Muslims."[18] This time, the minister of the interior did approve the holding of a third congress. In connection with the impending meeting, the conservative *Novoe vremia* expressed the hope that "the extreme elements that constitute the minority among the Muslims will not prevent the congress from pursuing the serious work needed to reform religious schools in the Muslim world."[19]

The Third All-Muslim Congress, held in August 1906 in Nizhnii Novgorod, was attended by about eight hundred delegates. Its chair was A. M. Topchibashev (1862–1934), an Azerbaijani lawyer and editor of the liberal Russian language newspaper *Kaspii*, published in Baku.[20] The congress established the Muslim Union (Ittifak) as a political party that would "bring all the Muslims citizens of Russia together in one movement" for the purpose of improving the religious, cultural, socioeconomic, and political conditions facing Muslims within the empire. The party's program combined the political slogans of the Kadets with a call for cultural-religious autonomy for the Muslim community.[21]

Ittifak claimed to represent the interests of all Muslims in Russia. In reality, the liberal core of the party was unable to unite either with more radical groups or with conservatives. Azeris and Tatars of the Volga–Ural region and Crimea constituted the majority of the party, while Muslims from the Kazakh steppe, Siberia, the northern Caucasus, and Central Asia were a distinct minority. Although Ittifak was organized according to regions, the Kazan group appeared to be the best organized and most active within the party.[22]

Having established a political party, Russian Muslims participated in all four of the State Dumas.[23] In the First Duma (27 April–8 July 1906), the twenty-five Muslim deputies registered with the Kadet bloc, thus declaring their liberal orientation, but by the Second Duma (20 February–2 June 1907), a special Muslim faction was formed. This faction was led by Topchibashev, who, though not formally a deputy, was a resident of St. Petersburg at the time. The faction brought together the majority of the Muslim deputies, which ultimately had more than thirty members by the end of the work of the Duma.[24] The Muslim faction adopted the program of Ittifak. Six Muslim delegates (most of them Social Revolutionaries, one from the Caucasus, the others from the Volga–Ural region) organized a separate-bloc under the name Muslim Labor Group, which joined the Labor faction (Trudoviki); their only real activity was the short-term publication of a newspaper and translations into the Tatar language of some brochures published by the Russian Trudoviki.[25] The Trudoviki did not gain broad support among Muslims. Following the dissolution of the Second Duma, Muslims with left-leaning sympathies tended to join either the Social Revolutionaries (SRs) or the Social Democrats (SDs).

From the perspective of the Russian educated elite who were attempting to understand the Muslim Question, the most important aspect of the Muslim political awakening was its explicitly religious character. The Duma's Muslim faction was the only faction to form on the basis of confession. The rest were formed according to party affiliation, nationality, or region. As we have seen, the Muslim movement was not unanimous in its political outlook, but the existence of the Muslim faction nevertheless suggested an aspiration among Russian Muslims, especially Tatars, for a broadly united Muslim front. The Tatar and Azeri delegates in the Duma claimed to represent the interests of all Muslims in Russia, regardless of class or locality. In their opinion, Muslims constituted a single "national" group united by a common religion and culture.[26]

The Central Committee of the Ittifak justified the existence of a special Muslim faction by the fact that Russian Muslims had common interests, which developed in response to the imperial confessional policies. In particular, they stressed the Russian state's "confessional view" of Muslims, which brought with it legal and administrative restrictions on that population. The faction thus focused its energies on the implementation of the freedoms proclaimed by the October Manifesto, the equalization of the rights of Muslims with the native Russian population, and the solution of the "unresolved questions of Muslim life," including reform of the Muslim ecclesiastical administration and Muslim confessional schools.[27] Topchibashev later wrote that the empire's confessional order preconditioned the mobilization of Russian Muslims into the all-Muslim liberation movement. Progressive Muslim intelligentsia used officially tolerated Islam as a mobilizing tool to achieve national (*natsional'nye*) and political goals.[28]

The reforms of 1905 gave Russia's Muslims a chance to act out their own answers to the Muslim Question and, in effect, reformulate it. Among the questions discussed by the Duma, the Muslim faction devoted its greatest attention to issues of schooling, religious tolerance, and peasant colonization in the eastern regions of the empire. Muslim deputies advocated for elementary education in native languages. Viewing the impending introduction of universal elementary education in the empire as a potential way of imposing assimilation, the Muslim deputies sought to reform and secure the autonomy of Muslim primary schools (the *maktabs*), which, together with the ecclesiastical administration, they viewed as national and sociopolitical rather than religious institutions.[29] At the same time, they did not deny the importance of the Russian language as the state language. The Muslim faction did not propose to introduce freedom of consciousness, which meant that they did not call for the liquidation of the empire as a confessional state. Instead, they advocated for the equality of all creeds by calling for the removal of existing restrictions and persecutions on the basis of religion, and generally treated the issue of religious toleration as an essential component of civil equality.[30]

Thus, liberal Muslims reformulated the Russian Muslim Question as one having to do with the intersecting interests of different nationalities of the Russian empire (*natsional'nosti*). They claimed that, after the Great Russians and Ukrainians, Muslims constituted the largest nationality with a distinct consciousness (in different Muslim publications, the numbers ranged from twenty to twenty-five million),[31] which had a right to be recognized as a political element of the state and not simply as a tolerated alien religious group (*terpimaia chuzhdaia religiia*). They also claimed that the assimilation of Muslims into Russians was not only impossible, but also not necessary because Muslims were loyal subjects: they paid taxes, fulfilled state duties, and followed state laws.[32] Topchibashev articulated the problem this way: "Foremost, we want to be Russian citizens with the same political, civil, and religious rights."[33]

During the revolution, the problem of special interests and rights of nationalities—formulated as the Nationality Question—came to the forefront of Russian political life. Understood as an issue about equal rights for different nationalities in the empire, this question was raised both by Russian liberal political figures and liberal elements of the tsarist government. I. I. Tolstoy (1858–1916), a historian, archeologist, numismatist, and the minister of education in Witte's government (October 1905–October 1906), addressed the Nationality Question (or, from a traditional Russian point of view, the Alien Question) in relation to the empire's School Question and supported non-Russians' educational projects during the revolution. Tolstoy was an advocate of equal rights for Jews, seeing this move as a means for solving what he saw as the "most important national–religious problem for Russia—the Jewish Question.[34] He wrote that the goal of the state was to balance the aspirations of different nationalities rather than to force their assimilation, which he regarded as impossible and desirable only in a pragmatic or administrative sense.[35] Along with other famous Russian scholars, publicists, and statesmen, Tolstoy was a member of the Kruzhok Ravnopraviia i Bratstva (Society for Equal Rights and Brotherhood), which propagated ideas of equal rights, religious freedom, and civil emancipation of national minorities.[36] Given the resonance of other nationality questions, and especially of the Jewish Question within Russian educated society, Muslim publicists and politicians followed the path shown by Jews, as well as by Poles and Finns, to make their cause known to the Russian public and the government.[37]

The Muslims' clear intention to participate in the discussion of political issues generated anxiety on the part of tsarist authorities, who were generally suspicious of any political activity. The government officials viewed the Third Muslim Congress quite negatively, accusing the congress's participants of "having deviated" from their program and touching upon questions that were supposedly not subject to public discussion. These (questions) included the criticism of the dissolution of the First Duma and the expression of support for the establishment of a constitutional regime in Persia in 1906.

The official newspaper *Rossiia* denounced the congress for having "violated the government's trust"; the paper stressed the need to be more cautious about allowing such congresses in the future.[38] Based on its interpretation of the Third Congress, the Ministry of the Internal Affairs began to be fearful of Muslim political activity, and especially of ties between local Muslim congresses and the Muslim faction in the Duma, which it considered wholly antigovernment.[39] A new specter of oppositional mobilization based on Islamic belief seemed to be joining the dangerous mobilization of other imperial national groups and industrial workers that had already achieved a profound disordering of autocratic institutions.

Despite this concern and the suspicion engendered by the Muslim congresses, tsarist officials in St. Petersburg refrained from accusing the Muslim population as a whole of anti-state activity because, in comparison with other non-Russians, direct Muslim participation in the revolutionary events of 1905–1907 seemed relatively modest. A rapprochement had occurred between Muslims and some of the revolutionary elements within Russian society. Left-wing parties formed among Muslim workers in the Caucasus, Kazan, and Crimea. As yet, however, these parties were small and seemed to have had little influence on the population.[40] A political organization established by Muslim conservatives, called Sirat-al-Mustakim (The True Way), also seemed to have little impact on political life.[41] Among tsarist officials, the opinion prevailed that the overwhelming mass of Muslim subjects was still "loyal to the throne and Fatherland" and that the activity of the most vocal Russian Muslim political organization, Ittifak, was not yet much to worry about.[42] According to later estimations by the Department of the Police, Ittifak was considered inactive after 1906.[43] In 1906, in a review of the effect of the "liberation movement" on different nationalities of the empire, A. S. Budilovich (1846–1908), a professor of Slavic languages and a member of the Council of the Minister of Education and of government committees in 1905–1906 that dealt with issues related to Islam, noted that in comparison to the political programs of the Armenians,

Georgians, Jews, and Poles, the Muslim demands were mostly of a religious character and were moderate enough to be attainable "within certain limits." Budilovich felt that the most serious issue confronting the government was the "Tatarization" of Russian Muslims.[44]

A Limited Expansion of Religious Tolerance

In the face of political crisis, the tsarist government came to reconsider the state policy of religious toleration. Religious freedom constituted an important component of civil equality. Thus, Sviatopolk-Mirskii's program of reforms included expansion of religious tolerance, especially for one of the empire's most persecuted groups, Old Believers.[45] The imperial decree issued on 12 December 1904, based on some of Sviatopolk-Mirskii's recommendations, promised future reforms in different spheres of Russian life, including the elimination of confession-based constraints for Old Believers, as well as for non-Orthodox and non-Christian subjects.[46] It fell to the Committee of Ministers, chaired by Witte, to develop a plan for the implementation of the decree.[47]

The 1904 Imperial Decree stimulated a petition campaign. Muslim communities in different parts of the empire submitted hundreds of petitions about their needs in the spheres of religion and education, some of which were either written or organized by Jadids. In their petitions, Muslims asked Russian authorities to stop what they saw as "forceful baptism" and denunciations of Islam in the Russian press; they requested that apostates from Orthodoxy be allowed to officially return to Islam. The petitions also raised the question of reform of Muslim institutions, specifically demanding restoration of the principle of muftis' elections and asking that the Russian-language requirement for candidates for ecclesiastical positions in the Orenburg muftiate be abolished. The petitioners also demanded the creation of Muslim ecclesiastical administration units in all Muslim regions of the empire, including northern Caucasus and Central Asia, the equalization of civil rights for Muslim and Orthodox clergy, and the elimination of restrictions on the construction of mosques.[48]

In some petitions, the nature and especially the language of the demands represented claims that went beyond questions concerning the so-called "organization of religious life" (*ustroistvo religioznogo byta*). For example, representatives of the Kazan Muslim community, among whom were "progressive" Muslims, asked for the elimination of "legal isolation" (*pravovoe obosoblenie*) of Muslims by means of restrictive norms for non-Christians articulated by the Town Statute (*Gorodovoe polozhenie*), for an end to the existence of a special procedure (requiring permission from the Ministry of Justice) for the appointment of non-Christians as attorneys (*prisiazhnye poverennye*), to eliminate existing restrictions on Muslims in teaching profession, and for the end of the ban on ownership of immovable property in Turkestan by Muslims from internal provinces. The petitioners also protested against the official categorization of Tatars as *inorodtsy*, although not against the legal category itself.[49]

Although not the sole factor, societal pressure for greater religious tolerance forced the government to pursue the reforms. Based on the Committee of Ministers' decisions, the tsar signed the Decree on Religious Toleration, promulgated on 17 April 1905, well before he agreed to accept the sweeping political reforms outlined in his October Manifesto. This decree marked a significant moment in the transformation of religious life in the empire. It eliminated official discrimination against non-Orthodox confessions and legalized conversion from Orthodoxy to other Christian creeds. The decree also permitted exclusion from Orthodoxy for those individuals who had an official Orthodox status but in reality practiced a non-Christian religion, to which either they or their ancestors had belonged prior to baptism.[50] If they so desired and were able to prove their "real" religious affiliation, baptized Tatars apostates could now be registered as Muslims. Other groups of apostates, such as Estonians and Latvians, as well as former Uniates converted to Orthodoxy, also received the right to return to their original beliefs. By resolving the apostasy problem in this way, the intention of the April 1905 decree was to eliminate confessional and social tension and to ease administrative difficulties in the borderland regions.

Perhaps more significantly, as Paul Werth has noted, the decree represented a shift, although incomplete, in official conceptualization of the essence of confessional affiliation. If earlier the policy directed toward apostates had focused on bringing their religious beliefs into accordance with their formal confessional status (i.e., Il'minskii's approach), the decree of 1905 allowed apostates to do the opposite: they could now change their religious affiliation to suit their actual religious convictions.[51] The decree questioned compulsory affiliation with the Orthodox church of those who were Orthodox only "externally" but did not belong to the church with "heart and consciousness."[52] To justify this fundamental shift in state policy in relation to Tatar apostates, the Committee of Ministers explained that there was no hope of returning them to Orthodoxy. The apostates were considered for all intents and purposes to have been lost to the church.[53]

The 1905 decree represented an important concession that the imperial authorities agreed to make to resolve the persistent apostasy problem. Yet this solution was only partial. The decree confirmed the privileged position of the Russian Orthodox church. Conversion from Orthodoxy to non-Christian creeds was still not permitted; the regulations concerning Tatar apostates were an exception to this rule. The decree explained that open permission for conversion from Orthodoxy to non-Christian creeds went against the recognition of Christianity as the true belief.[54] In its commentary on the Committee of Ministers' position, the Ministry of Internal Affairs made it plain that the newly recognized freedom to convert from Orthodoxy did not amount to legal recognition of apostasy per se.[55]

The Committee of Ministers called the special government commission to bring existing legislation into accord with the 1905 April Law on Tolerance. The committee emphasized that "the Muslim population of the internal provinces was politically loyal and friendly to Russia and that these historically developed relations should be valued and not damaged."[56] This statement provided additional justification for the government concession in relation to the baptized Tatar apostates as well as the promise to eliminate constraints on Muslim religious life. The questions raised in the Muslim petitions provided the basis for the program of the special commission's sessions on Islam. The tsar's October Manifesto, however, announced an elective Duma with legislative powers. This change in existing legislative procedure consequently limited the goals of the commission to gathering materials and establishing the principles for future bills on religious tolerance. Members of the State Council, representatives of the Holy Synod, and the Ministries of Justice, Internal Affairs, and Public Education were among the participants in the commission. Count A. P. Ignat'ev, a former governor-general of Kiev, was the chair.[57] Initially, the government had planned to invite representatives of the Muslim clergy to at least some of the sessions, but after the commission had changed its goals this idea was dropped so as not to "instigate vain expectations among the Muslim population."

The commission addressed issues related to Islam on the basis of a report titled *Po delam very musul'man-sunnitov* (*On the Confessional Matters of Sunni Muslims*) and two supplements, *O sudebnom dele Kirgizov* (*On the Legal Practices of Kirgiz*) and *O polozhenii musul'manskoi zhenshchiny* (*On the Condition of a Muslim Woman*). The report presented a summary and interpretation of the Muslim petitions and opinions by Russian authorities from the Muslim provinces and Russian experts on Islam. Before his appointment in 1898 as a member of the State Council, the author of the report, V. P. Cherevanskii (1836–1914) had served within the Ministry of State Control for a period of about thirty years, including twelve years in Turkestan (1868–1880). He was known to the Russian reading public as the author of novels, plays, and literary sketches, as well as of articles on economic questions. In 1901, he published *Mir islama i ego probuzhdenie* (*The World of Islam and Its Awakening*), a book in which he emphasized the militancy and intolerance of Islam toward Europe and warned that the further spread of Islam presented a danger to world culture. He wrote: "Where a Muslim lives, the Muslim Question takes residence." Admitting the impossibility of religious struggle against Islam, he saw European education as a solution to the problem.[58] Cherevanskii was acquainted with Il'minskii's former student Ostroumov, and was highly appreciative of his recent book *Koran i progress* (*Koran and Progress*).[59] Accordingly, Cherevanskii consulted with him in preparation for the 1905–1906 committee. Later, in 1909–1911, on the basis of materials that he had collected for the commission, Cherevanskii wrote a series of articles about Muslim religious institutions in Russia; these were published by the Kazan missionary journal *Sotrudnik Bratstva Sv. Guriia.*

Cherevanskii and the other commission members had to perform the uneasy task of extending religious tolerance toward Muslims while safeguarding the dominant position of the Orthodox church. This task was even further complicated given Cherevanskii's own views of Islam and the Muslim Question. The tensions that underlined the government's effort at reform were revealed in his report as well as in the commission's deliberations. Cherevanskii's report characterized the majority of Muslim petitions not as a free expression of the petitioners' will but rather as a result of "outside influences." Nevertheless, he suggested eliminating what he viewed as limitations on Muslims' religious freedom. He proposed to ban the involvement of the Orthodox diocese authorities in the process of granting permissions for mosque construction and to abolish the Russian language requirement of 1890 for mosques' personnel (but not for the members of the Orenburg Ecclesiastical Assembly). He also supported the autonomy of Muslim confessional schools.

At the same time, Cherevanskii opposed the idea of equal civil standing for Muslim and Orthodox clergy, justifying this position by pointing to the absence of "clergy" in the Christian sense in the Islamic tradition, as well as to the "unfairness" that would result if the idea of equal status were applied to what he viewed as Muslim "cultural ignorance" and Orthodox "serious academic education." Yet he suggested maintaining the existing diverse systems of state-sponsored Muslim hierarchy, although with some modifications. In Turkestan, following the opinion of the local administration, he supported the policy of "ignoring" Islam.[60] He made an exception, however, for Kazakhs, proposing to establish a special Muslim administration for them on the principle that they had become Muslims as a result of Russian policies in the eighteenth century.[61] At the same time, Cherevanskii considered it to be "the greatest mistake" to replace *adat* with Sharia in the legal practice of the Kazakhs.[62]

In contrast to the Orenburg mufti, who wanted the district of the Orenburg Ecclesiastical Assembly to be enlarged by adding to it the regions of northern Caucasus and Siberia, Cherevanskii proposed instead to divide the existing muftiate according to territorial and ethnic principles in order to prevent what he regarded as the danger of creating a Muslim "state within a state." He did not, however, oppose the idea of extending the system of state-sponsored Muslim administration to the North Caucasus, but suggested placing this region under the jurisdiction of the Transcaucasian Muslim administrations.[63] Without elaborating on this question, he stated that the policy of rapprochement of Muslims with Russians should be continued but should be gradual and not forced.[64]

In this report, Cherevanskii essentially articulated how the Muslim Question was still generally understood within the central government and how the state should respond. According to the Committee of Ministers, Muslims, as loyal subjects of the tsar, deserved to be able to practice their religion, although within certain limits. Following this officially declared position, Cherevanskii's response to Muslims' demands sought to satisfy their "just" religious needs by expanding religious tolerance, while simultaneously preserving the empire's state-regulated hierarchical confessional system. At the same time, Cherevanskii's report brought up concerns, which existed among some Russians within and outside the government, about the possibility of politicization of Islam and the dangers of Tatarization. Cherevanskii's proposal was thus a compromise between contrasting views on the problem of relationship between the state and Muslim institutions. As such, it had some rather contradictory features.

Other members of the commission agreed with the goals of reform as defined by Cherevanskii. Overall, the commission's members desired unification of the diverse system of the empire's Muslim ecclesiastical administration, but also considered it necessary to prevent the possibility of religious unification of Muslims. The commission supported the idea of establishing new Muslim ecclesiastical administrations, although it did not propose how to determine their number and location. Unlike Cherevanskii, the participants refused to consider the Russian-language requirement for Muslim clergy as a constraint on religion. In a special opinion, A. S. Budilovich proposed the creation of a Muslim ecclesiastical administration system on the basis of territory, rather than ethnic criteria. He insisted on government control over Muslim confessional schools and disagreed with the Muslim clergy's complete authority over family and inheritance matters in the Muslim community.[65]

After the commission finished its work, its materials were forwarded to the Ministry of Internal Affairs, which in turn formulated policies with a broader goal than those of the 1905 special government commission, aspiring to address all of the religious issues raised by Muslims and to review imperial legislation concerning Muslim religious affairs.[66]

The questions discussed by the government's special commission were also addressed by the participants in the Third Muslim Congress, who proposed their own project of reform of Muslim ecclesiastical administration. To administer Muslim religious, educational, and charity affairs, the participants suggested the creation of an autonomous system of regional muftiates located in the Volga–Ural region, Crimea, Turkestan, and with two in the Caucasus, each of which would be headed by an elected sheikh-ul-Islam. They also proposed the creation of an elected position of the highest spiritual authority, called ra'is-ul-Islam, who would represent the interests of all Russian Muslims to the tsar. The delegates also demanded that Muslim clergy be accorded equal rights with the Orthodox clergy. This project presented a direct challenge to the 1905 commission's perspective on religious toleration and the goals of state confessional policy.[67]

Competing Visions of Aliens' Education

Along with the religious reform of the early twentieth century, the tsarist authorities also came to reassess the goals and methods of education for non-Russians. To address the "question of the education of eastern aliens," the government again formed a special commission (*Osoboe soveshchanie po voprosam obrazovaniia vostochnykh inorodtsev*) that became active in the spring of 1905. Once again, as it had been in the 1860s, this issue was discussed within the framework of government efforts to introduce universal elementary education and thus turn the emancipated lower classes into "loyal and enlightened subjects." For non-Russians, it was hoped that reforms in education would encourage rapprochement. This time, however, the discussion had to take into account several new factors, including the Decree on Tolerance; the government's experience following the educational reforms of the 1860s–1870s, which had encountered the resistance of the Muslim population; and the counter-projects of Muslim progressive educators themselves.

The specific goal of the commission was to determine the principles for non-Russian education in Crimea, Caucasus, Siberia, Central Asia, and the eastern part of European Russia. In response to the government's plans for educational reforms, I. Gasprinskii came to St. Petersburg to deliver a petition drawn up in Simferopol, which he presented to the Minister of Education, V. G. Glazov (April 1904–October 1905).[68] Unlike the commission on religious tolerance, however, the commission on the education of eastern non-Russians proceeded without formal consideration of Muslims' opinions or projects.

The meetings were chaired by A. S. Budilovich. Originally from Grodno province, Budilovich taught at educational institutions in the empire's borderlands, Warsaw University, and Dorpat (Tartu) University, where he was actively engaged in fighting against Polish and German influences. In 1901, he became a member of the Council of the Minister of Education.[69] Budilovich's personal experiences, professional interests, and state service responsibilities made him especially interested in the alien questions and the related problem of Russian national consciousness. He viewed the destruction of the empire by political non-Russian nationalisms (especially in the western regions) as particularly damaging to the idea of the Russian core. Thus, to preserve the empire, he favored Il'minskii's educational approach for non-Russians (while exempting Ukrainians and Belorussians, whom he did not consider to be aliens in relation to Russians). This approach, in Budilovich's view, seemed to promise a more "organic" (as opposed to "mechanical") connection between the empire's core and the periphery.[70] Along with Budilovich, participants in the special commission included the directors of teachers' seminaries in Turkestan, Transcaucasia, and Kazan; the inspectors of the Simbirsk Chuvash School, the Tatar School in Simferopol, the schools of the Bukeev Horde, and Orthodox parish schools in the Volga region; and Russian orientalists, most of whom were followers of Il'minskii.

A reassessment of Il'minskii's educational ideas was at the center of the commission's discussions. S. V. Chicherina (Bobrovnikova) (1867–1918), a publicist, the author of articles on aliens' education and ethnography, and the wife of N. A. Bobrovnikov, director of the teachers' seminary in Kazan, presented a moving scene of the powerful memory of Il'minskii. During her travels in the Volga region in the summer of 1904, she visited Il'minskii's grave at the cemetery just across from the Kazan School for Baptized Tatars, which he had established. There, Il'minskii's presence created, as Chicherina described it, a "mood for prayer," so that she "unintentionally became influenced by his belief."[71] She noted fresh flowers at the bottom of the cross, "placed by somebody's caring hand." Soon she saw an old man, "dressed in a Tatar robe." When approaching Il'minskii's grave, "he fervently prayed, bowed three times and kissed the earth and the cross." This man was one of the first pupils of Il'minskii and was now a teacher. Chicherina described that when the man recalled Il'minskii, he "spoke with enthusiasm; his face was full of inspiration and his eyes were shining: 'How can we forget him?' he asked with tears, pointing to the grave dear to him."[72] The memory of Il'minskii was also dear to participants on the government commission, many of whom had had personal relations with him, and their emotional connection affected their discussions on the alien question.

Yet as some of the commission's members realized, their reassessment of the Il'minskii's system had to take into consideration the changing social and political circumstances. The commission viewed Muslims' alienation as the main issue. But as Bobrovnikov pointed out, the Russian Muslim world itself had been changing, and the East was not in the "stagnation" (kosnost') that the Russians had encountered forty years earlier. Islam, combined with the national idea, was "in motion," but, as Bobrovnikov noted, it was moving in a "separate direction from Russia." According to Bobrovnikov, Muslim confessional schools played a key role in the Muslim religious-national movement for unification. Therefore, he concluded, the rapprochement of Muslims with Russians could not be postponed.[73] At the same time, as M. A. Miropiev, the director of the Transcaucasian Teachers' Seminary and a writer on the Alien Question, noted, non-Russians were increasingly resistant to the forced spread of the Russian language.[74] The revolutionary situation made particularly "visible" what the commission's participants interpreted as "anti-Russian separatist tendencies" that had first been noted in Poland and the Caucasus but that had recently started to appear on the empire's other borderlands.[75]

The commission thus sought to find a more accommodative approach to rapprochement. It defined the goals of elementary schools for non-Russians as "moral and intellectual development as well as patriotic upbringing, the spread of the Russian language, and rapprochement with Russians on the basis of love for a common Fatherland." Religious instruction was to remain a significant component of schooling for the Orthodox, whether Russian or non-Russian, while religious education of other Christians and non-Christians would be left to families and clergy.[76] The commission also proposed to model schools for non-Russians (Orthodox, Muslims, and animists in the eastern part of the empire, as well as non-Orthodox Christians in the west) on Il'minskii's system.

But what constituted the "Il'minskii system"? What had he actually said about Islam and Russian-Muslim education? Bobrovnikov recalled that Il'minskii felt no animosity toward Muslims; as he put it, Il'minskii "did not like Islam *because of his* love for the Tatars." Ostroumov also recalled that Il'minskii knew Muslims, but avoided religious debates with them and never criticized Islamic teaching in his lectures at the Kazan Theological Academy.[77] But what should a school for Muslims be if it were to offer a path for enlightenment and rapprochement with Russians? The commission could not find an explicit answer in Il'minskii's writings on this question. At the same time, Gasprinskii's answer, which the commission's participants regarded as the antithesis of Il'minskii's system, reminded them that the Russian government now had to play a more active role in relation to Muslim education.

Some of the commission's participants drew attention to two aspects of Il'minskii's system that they thought might be particularly applicable to the education of non-Orthodox, non-Russians: first, the "ideological" component (which could be reinterpreted in terms of "universal" values [*obshchechelovecheskie tsennosti*] and not strictly Orthodox teaching); and second, the use of native languages (*prirodnyi iazyk*) as a tool of instruction. For them, Il'minskii's system seemed to present a "middle ground between the centripetal state school and the centrifugal confessional or national school."[78] While the key elements of "Il'minskii's school," as the commission viewed them—including freedom of personality, respect for the cultural peculiarities of non-Russians, emphasis on conscious belief, pluralism of the educational system, and societal involvement in the matters of education—had taken shape in the environment of the Great Reforms of the 1860s, they were now resonating with the conviction after 1905 that liberalism of this sort was necessary to keep the empire stable. By relying on Il'minskii's system, the commission hoped to achieve the "voluntary rapprochement" (vs. mechanical and forceful Russification) of non-Russians with Russians. At the same time, the commission envisioned this as a two-way movement in which Russians in the borderlands would also learn non-Russian languages, history, and culture.[79] But this rapprochement was planned to be guided by Russian experts on alien affairs who claimed to understand the cultures of various non-Russian ethnic groups and were ready to satisfy their unique but legitimate needs.

On 31 March 1906, on the basis of the commission's recommendations, the Ministry of Public Education issued its Regulations for Elementary Schools for Non-Russians Living in Eastern and South-Eastern Russia. According to these, a non-Russian language could be used as a tool of instruction during the first year (or first two years), depending on the level of familiarity of the students with the Russian language. To ease the process of learning Russian, the regulations recommended using Cyrillic, or both Cyrillic and the national alphabets (called dual transcription). For Orthodox non-Russians, the curriculum included religious instruction, while the merger of non-Christians with Russians was to be conducted by means of Russian classes at the confessional schools, which were to be subject to government inspection.[80]

Russian educators, who in the early twentieth century designed the state schooling system for eastern non-Russians, continued to define the problem as one of Muslims' ignorance and alienation, complicated by what they now saw as the conscious aspiration of the Muslim intelligentsia for the unification of Muslims and their separation from Russia. As in the 1870s, the government education project of 1906 was designed to fit the existing confessional system. This time, however, Russian reformers thought that Il'minskii's educational system, along with the strengthening of religious consciousness among Christian non-Russians, could (if deprived of its missionary component) serve the goals of enlightenment and rapprochement of Muslims with Russians.

In contrast, Gasprinskii and his followers had increasingly come to associate Il'minskii's system with Christianization and cultural assimilation. Moreover, progressive Muslims claimed that Muslims in Russia represented an autonomous spiritual community that possessed a unique educational system and literature grounded in its own historical development. They insisted that the native language should have importance in its own right, rather than just be a tool for learning Russian. For these reasons, the so-called School Question became an important issue raised by Muslims in their petitions to the government as well as in their emerging national press and political programs.

The Third Muslim Congress criticized the ministry's regulations and instead proposed having elementary schools provide instruction in native languages, using the Arabic alphabet. The Russian language would be introduced in middle school as a subject. The Muslim educational project also envisioned the inclusion of the literary Turkish language into the curriculum. The confessional schools were to be administered by the reformed ecclesiastical administration and representatives of the Muslim communities.[81]

Muslims also sent petitions to the Ministry of the Internal Affairs and the Ministry of Public Education, interpreting the 1906 school regulations as a violation of religious freedom. Muslims were especially outraged by the introduction of dual transcription and by the status of the confessional schools, and thus demanded abolition of the regulations. Under the pressure of this opposition, on 14 February 1907, the minister of education ordered that implementation of the regulations that concerned confessional schools be stopped until the system of Muslim ecclesiastical administration was reformed. The introduction of dual transcription was suggested as optional. Confessional schools were left without specific regulations. The special government commission, with the participation of the well-known Muslim cleric from St. Petersburg, A. Baiazitov, and five other Muslims recommended by the Orenburg mufti, reviewed the regulations. The new regulations were issued on 1 November of that year.[82]

A New Context for the Muslim Question

The political mobilization of Russian society and the tsar's concessions in the early twentieth century set the Muslim Question in a new context. The new freedoms of speech and association and the extension of voting rights empowered Muslims and created opportunity for Jadidism to transform into a liberal political movement. In contrast, Slavophile ideas about Russia's future, some of which were shared by Il'minskii's followers, neither transformed into a political platform nor generated an organized political movement. While some of Il'minskii's sympathizers were represented in government reform commissions on religious tolerance and education, Jadids were largely excluded from these deliberations.

Progressive Muslims redefined the Alien Question in relation to Muslims as a problem of intersecting interests of the empire's nationalities, but tsarist reformers continued to view the issue mainly as one of alienation and potential Tatarization. As Bobrovnikov reminded the members of the commission on alien education, the Muslim political movement "complicated" this problem for Russians by making it urgent for the state to pursue the policy of rapprochement.

Under the pressure of the revolution, the government agreed to reforms by introducing a limited type of democracy, expanding religious tolerance without dismantling the hierarchical confessional system, and offering concessions in language policy in hopes of achieving "organic" relations between the Russian core and the eastern non-Russian periphery, thus preserving the empire. Even so, the government's attempts to satisfy what they saw as Muslims' justifiable religious needs and to find a more accommodating educational approach appeared to fall short of the expectations of Muslim liberals, who challenged the official notions of religious tolerance and rapprochement. More importantly, they confronted Russian society and the government with new types of claims, insisting that the Muslim community be viewed as a nation with distinct interests and rights rather than as a tolerated alien confessional group. Russia's new constitutional context thus sharpened tensions between these different visions of Russian–Muslim relations. The Muslim Question, with all its conflicting interpretations, once again came to the forefront of public and government attention.

7   The Muslim Question in the Aftermath of the Revolution

The introduction of elected legislative institution and the promise of civil liberties had set Russia on a new path. The political liberalizations of the 1905 revolution, however, were not to last. Nicholas II regretted losing the power he had ceded and sought to undo the concessions he had made. The government and the Duma could not work together, and on 3 June 1907, Nicholas dissolved the Second Duma. On the same day, Nicholas and P. A. Stolypin, the Minister of Internal Affairs and Prime Minister (1906–1911), radically changed the electoral law. Nicholas called for the Duma to be "Russian in spirit," by which he meant it should cooperate with the government and demonstrate loyalty to the monarch.[1] Delegations of peasants, workers, left-wing parties, and non-Russians were severely reduced, while Muslims of the Steppe region and Turkestan were excluded completely. In the Third Duma (1 November 1907–9 June 1912), the Muslim faction consisted of only nine deputies; of these seven were Tatars from the Volga–Ural region. By the Fourth Duma (15 November 1912–25 February 1917), the Muslim faction declined still further, to a total of only six deputies, with five from the Volga–Ural region.[2]

P. A. Stolypin, the last reformer in the tsarist government, sought to defeat the revolutionaries and liberals while also transforming Russia into a modern and orderly empire whose citizens would maintain strong allegiance to the state and the monarchy. His primary concern was strengthening a state shaken at its autocratic foundations by the revolution.[3] Maintaining loyalty to the regime among the tsar's subjects became the priority for the government. This was to be achieved by suppressing political opposition, restricting antigovernment propaganda, and policing the country. Repressive measures constituted an integral component of Stolypin's policy, but not the only one.

The continuation of limited reforms was another important element of his program. Although Stolypin radically changed Russia's parliamentary system, he did not intend to and probably could not restore the prerevolutionary political order and govern Russia without an elected legislative institution without raising mass protests.[4] Russian peasants were the main focus of Stolypin's efforts to transform discontented subjects into loyal imperial citizens. Along with fundamental agrarian reform, the government also planned to pursue a series of other changes, including the development of a system of universal primary education and an increase in religious freedoms, as was promised during the revolution. These reforms were also to affect the empire's Muslim population.

Stolypin planned to expand religious tolerance while maintaining the existing state-regulated confessional order with the Orthodox church as a predominant confession. While increasingly concerned about the possibility of the politicization of Islam and thus suspicious of Muslim intelligentsia, the Stolypin government, in line with the promises of the 1905 decree, still intended to satisfy the "just" religious needs of its Muslim subjects. In 1906–1907, the MVD continued to review Muslim petitions addressing religious issues.[5] But the prospects for broad religious reform became bleak after 1909 when Stolypin's government started withdrawing its legislative projects under pressure from the right.[6]

It was then that the Muslim Question, formulated in alarmist terms, moved to the forefront of discussions by the church, the government, and public figures. The consequences of the reforms of 1905—the liberalization of conversion and extension of civil freedoms to Muslims—deeply alarmed church figures and missionaries in the Volga region, who pressed the government to consider the Muslim Question afresh in light of these developments. In 1910, Stolypin responded by launching several government initiatives specifically to discuss and study the issue. His government took up the Muslim Question at the same time that it was reassessing borderland policies in Finland and Poland. The government's goal throughout these deliberations was to preserve the empire's political unity and ensure that the state's interests were fully protected in non-Russian outlying regions.[7] Stolypin relied on Russian nationalism as a principle force for stabilizing the regime, but he could not consistently follow this path without the risk of undermining the foundations of the autocratic multiethnic empire. Nor did there exist a single unified program of Russian nationalism. Appeals to Orthodoxy and Russianness thus became common during the Stolypin period, but these concepts had multiple and often contrasting meanings and were utilized for different purposes.

Taken as a whole, Stolypin's postrevolutionary attempts to reconsolidate state power set the Muslim Question on new foundations. This chapter explores how the question was conceptualized at the 1910 special commission and the Kazan missionary congress; we will pay particular attention to the divergent understandings of this problem among state officials and local church figures.

"Muslim Propaganda" and "Muslim Awakening" Reconsidered

The religious reform introduced in the midst of other fundamental political transformations became a highly contested political issue. While the Decree on Religious Tolerance partially resolved the problem of apostasy from Orthodoxy, it raised related questions about changes of confession, non-Orthodox proselytism (i.e., alleged religious "propaganda" and the so-called "seduction" into non-Orthodox confessions), the relation of the state to different confessions and religion in general, and, ultimately, freedom of consciousness, promised by the October Manifesto. In the context of Russia's democratizing political order, these questions were intensely debated and generated extensive literature. They troubled not only church and religious lay circles, but also those who were indifferent to matters of faith; these questions concerned the political future of the country as well as the confessional order. The legislative tolerance projects drafted by the Ministry of Interior Affairs and submitted to the Second and Third Dumas thus became the subject of fierce debates both inside and outside the Russian parliament. The measures were too weak for liberals and too radical for conservatives.[8]

In the opinion of the legal scholar M. A. Reisner, the Decree on Tolerance did not introduce freedom of consciousness but instead only widened the privileges of the non-Orthodox confessions.[9] And as V. A. Maklakov, the deputy from the Constitutional Democrats, warned in his Duma speech in 1909, the government's middle-of-the-road confessional policy might itself cause a larger problem than the introduction of complete freedom of consciousness.[10] From a conservative standpoint, the government's confessional policy represented the "greatest mistake." In 1912, the *Moskovskie vedomosti* wrote that the government's legislative projects put Russia on the path to a separation of church and state, thus undermining the very special foundation of the empire.[11] Although the Orthodox church formally retained its privileged position in the empire, in principle it now had to compete more openly with other confessions.

The promulgation of the 1905 Decree on Tolerance sparked mass transfer of apostates to Catholicism in the western provinces, to Lutheranism in the Baltic provinces, conversions to sectarian faiths in the south and southwestern regions of Russia, and partially in Siberia, and to Buddhism in Irkutsk province.[12] According to information gathered by the Ministry of Internal Affairs, between April 1905 and January 1910, most apostates from Orthodoxy sought formal affiliation with Catholicism.[13] The Tolerance Decree sparked a wave of petitions among baptized Tatars, especially in the Volga–Ural provinces, asking for permission to be registered as Muslims. According to surveys of the Ministry of Internal Affairs, during the same five-year period more than 50,000 people legally left Orthodoxy for Islam. Most of the transfers were registered in the Kazan, Ufa, Simbirsk, and Penza provinces, with nearly four out of five of these occurring in Kazan province alone. Since these numbers did not include "unofficial" transfers, they almost certainly underestimated the total numbers of Muslim converts.[14] Attempts by other baptized non-Russians in the region, including Chuvash, Maris, and Udmurts, to register their conversion to Islam were less successful because, unlike the baptized Tatars, members of these groups often found it difficult to prove that either they or their ancestors had ever been Muslims, which was the essential condition for registering such status.[15] At the same time, the government allowed animists to transfer to Islam de facto.[16]

The high numbers of transfers to Catholicism in the western regions of the empire especially alarmed Bishop Evlogii (Georgievskii), who launched a campaign for the separation of Kholm province from Congress Poland.[17] The potential dangers of religious freedom granted to Islam were articulated by the Ober-Procurator of the Holy Synod, K. P. Pobedonostsev, a severe critic of the Decree on Tolerance within bureaucratic circles. He warned that if the spread of Islam threatened the British and French empires by possible mutinies of the indigenous populations in distant colonies, in Russia the danger of Islam was much closer to home. As Pobedonostsev concluded, "Islam is a tremendous force that never for a moment ceases its struggle . . . no other religion compares to Islam in the intensity of its faith, and its fanaticism [crossed out: and its unity] that binds its followers throughout the Muslim world."[18]

In the Volga region, the liberalization of conversion and its consequences reinforced these fears among local clerics and missionaries, who viewed Islam as a serious enemy of Christianity.[19] Orthodox clerics considered the Tolerance Decree to be the official "equalization of the Koran with the Gospel," and interpreted the government's compromise in religious policy as the state's sanctioning of apostasy and of official toleration of Muslim propaganda. These critics viewed the decree as a step facilitating mass apostasy of both Russians and non-Russians from Orthodoxy, a policy that would lead to the "defeat" of Orthodoxy and the "victory" of Islam. The changes in state religious policy mobilized Orthodox clerics and lay believers. Conversions from Orthodoxy and the new challenges posed by Muslim propaganda became a central theme of Orthodox periodicals and of the missionaries' congresses after 1905.[20] The anxieties of Orthodox writers concerning what they saw as the catastrophic consequences of the new religious legislation were also picked up by secular Russian nationalist publications, which stirred up their readers with similar reports of a general assault on Orthodoxy from non-Orthodox religions.

The liberalization of religious policy, however, inspired optimism as well as anxiety. The director of the Kazan Teachers' Seminary, N. A. Bobrovnikov, argued in 1905 in the journal *Pravoslavnyi sobesednik* that the expansion of religious toleration in fact established favorable conditions for Orthodox missionizing among the Muslims.[21] This optimism was based on his hopes for the success of Il'minskii's system of religious instruction in native languages and the involvement of non-state actors in advancing this missionary program. S. V. Chicherina also interpreted the conversions to Islam as proof of the success of the Il'minskii system. She pointed out that although there were approximately 40,000 apostates among the baptized Tatars and Chuvash, nearly three times that number (110,000 people) remained loyal to Orthodoxy.[22] In the articles that she was now publishing in Russia and abroad, Chicherina voiced strong support for Il'minskii's system, which, though not capable of converting Muslims to Orthodoxy, offered, in her opinion, the best solution to the problem of keeping those non-Russians who had already been baptized within the church.

As during the period of the Great Reforms, the issue of religious tolerance in the early twentieth century was closely connected to the problem of reforms within the officially dominant confession. After 1905, when the government finally enacted religious reforms, this connection became even more explicit. Even as early as the stage of discussion of the issue of religious tolerance at the Committee of Ministers, the metropolitan of St. Petersburg, Antonii (Vadkovskii), brought Chairman Witte's attention to what he saw as the "unfairness" of the emerging situation: the Orthodox church was deprived of freedoms that were planned to be granted to the non-Orthodox confessions, Old Believers, and sectarian communities.[23] Despite the opposition of Pobedonostsev, the Holy Synod appealed to Nicholas II to summon a church council to discuss the problems and to restore the patriarchate. Without formally approving or declining the Holy Synod's appeal, Nicholas postponed the decision-making about the council until "more favorable times." From March to December 1906, the official preconciliar commission was discussing possible ways to introduce changes in church life. The Holy Synod, under the auspices of a special committee, was preparing for an eventual All-Russian Church Council. The months and years that followed, right through to 1917, were marked by intense debates over Orthodox church reform, revealing the unresolved tension between the different visions for the organization of the church and its relations to the state and society.[24]

For our purposes, what is important about the debate over Orthodox church renewal was the way it was so often linked to discussion of the Muslim Question. The Question thus served here chiefly as a rhetorical tool for drawing the attention of Russian society and the government to the problems of the Orthodox church, rather than to the problem of Islam.[25] The seeming successes of Muslim propaganda made Orthodox reform-minded commentators turn their attention to Muslims' religious life, which suggested the need to address the old problem of the Orthodox parish.

This unresolved Parish Question stood at the forefront of the debates on church reform and was linked to the broader issue of the role of laity in church life. In contrast to the often-noted "apathy of the Russian people for their native Orthodoxy," the Muslims' religious ardor made them people to admire and emulate.[26] In 1909, the bishop of Mamadysh and vicar of Kazan diocese, Andrei, wrote in the newspaper *S. Peterburgskie vedomosti*:

Muslims represent one united, and inspired to a degree of fanaticism, religious mass. The Tatar coachman . . . speaks with non-Russians about Islam, the Tatar tradesman carries religious books under his rags, a Tatar inn owner can always eloquently speak about faith . . . that is what the religious community does; it inspires, organizes, and disciplines the masses, which want to be strong. The Muslim parish will defend itself. What about the Russians? How do they feel about their parish life and their internal life? They don't feel anything! It is a screaming, clamoring, and confused crowd, organized by nobody and inspired by nothing. What about the Russian Orthodox parish? It is a shame to say: the clerical leaders in Russia are themselves against the development of parish life; they are afraid of something! . . . It is a sad situation! . . . Within other confessions, all believers are missionaries, all are interested in the life of their spiritual home, their spiritual family; all have this spiritual family—only we don't have it! . . . All are disconnected, small and large, in parish life and in other aspects of life.[27]

Although the anxieties of Orthodox missionaries about Muslim propaganda, the strength of Islam, and the weakness of Orthodoxy were not new, the 1905 revolution and its aftermath clearly created a sense among them that this particular element of the Muslim Question had now taken on new urgency and meaning. Some Kazan missionaries, therefore, felt that it was necessary to "clarify" this question especially for the central government, which, as they believed, was not taking a firm position.

In 1908, at a missionary congress held in Kiev, Andrei emphasized the urgent need to address the Muslim Question in these terms in the Volga region.[28] At the same time, he sent a report to the Holy Synod and to the Kazan governor and the Ministry of Internal Affairs, calling attention to the rise of "Tatar-Mohammedan propaganda in the Volga region."[29] Bishop Andrei contended that it was impossible to expect Islam to weaken and disappear. His main concern, however, was how to stop what he now interpreted dramatically as an "Islamic invasion" and to protect baptized non-Russians from the influence of increased Muslim propaganda. Considering the religious devotedness of Muslim communities as one of the main reasons for their strength, he therefore concluded that the successful "Russification of aliens" would require the strengthening of the Orthodox parish and the development of the "national-patriotic enthusiasm" of the Russian population. Andrei also advocated Il'minskii's system of religious instruction as a way to bring baptized non-Russians closer to Russians, calling upon the government to draw a distinction between trustworthy baptized non-Russians and Muslim Tatars, whom he described as "loyal enemies."[30]

Andrei (Ukhtomskii) (1872–1937) was born into a noble family in Yaroslavl province. After graduating from the cadet corps in Nizhnii Novgorod, he radically changed his path by entering the Moscow Theological Academy; in 1895, he took monastic vows in Kazan. Andrei's biographer, M. L. Zelenogorskii, attributed this turn in his life to the influence of Father Ioann of Kronstadt, a popular priest and spiritual leader whom young Andrei had met during his travel on the Volga River.[31] Andrei ascended to the newly established curia (*kafedra*) in 1907, and, as the bishop of Mamadysh and vicar of the Kazan diocese, oversaw Orthodox missionary institutions in Kazan. He was a talented and prolific publicist and the editor of the missionary journal *Sotrudnik Bratstva sv.Guriia*, published from 1909 to 1911 by the Missionary Brotherhood of St. Gurii in Kazan. Andrei was an advocate of Russia's renewal, which he understood in a Slavophile sense; he was a passionate proponent of church reform and especially of revitalizing Orthodox parish life. During the years of the revolution, Andrei drew closer to the right-wing Russian nationalistic movement in Kazan. However, the Alien Question soon became a point of disagreement between him and local nationalists and monarchists. The nationalistic slogan, "Russia for Russians," was too narrow for Andrei, who was an advocate of Il'minskii's missionary system, which promised "natural" (vs. mechanical) Russification of non-Russians by means of Orthodox instruction in native languages.

In 1908 in *Moskovskie vedomosti,* Andrei was defending baptized non-Russians and the Il'minskii system from attacks by the Kazan chapter of the ultranationalist Union of Russian People, claiming that it was difficult to find among Russians themselves better Christians and better friends of Russian civil society (*grazhdanstvennost'*) than among baptized non-Russians.[32] Andrei's report to the government, also published as a brochure in Kazan, marked another episode in the worsening conflict between the followers of Il'minskii and his Russian nationalist critics. Andrei asked the government: "Why is a foreign faith (Islam) triumphing over Orthodoxy?"[33] Answering this question, he pointed to the ways that Muslim models might be used to strengthen Orthodox communities, while also emphasizing what he saw as Muslims' hostility to Russia.

In 1909, several conservative newspapers took up the issue of increased Muslim propaganda in Kazan province. *Novoe vremia* suggested that this propaganda had not only a religious, but also a political agenda.[34] *S. Peterburgskie vedomosti* and *Kolokol* wrote about the Tatars' aspiration to create an autonomous state.[35] Upon Andrei's request, priest S. A. Bagin prepared a report on the Alien Question in Kazan province. At the same time, Bagin published an article, "O propagande Islama putem pechati" ("On the Propaganda of Islam by Means of the Press") in *Pravoslavnyi sobesednik,* writing about the "exacerbation of the alien question" in Russia, and noting that this problem required elucidation (*osveshchenie*) and study (*izuchenie*).[36] In his report, Bagin discussed the tensions experienced by the confessionally mixed rural communities as a result of the 1905 Tolerance Decree. The decree seemed, to him, to give freedom to apostates at the expense of that of disenfranchised Christian members of village communities. Moreover, Bagin saw the apostasy movement as an essential component of an organized Muslim political movement designed to enlarge their "nationality," all as part of a bid for political separatism.[37] This reconceptualization of the goals of Muslim propaganda and the Muslim awakening led Andrei to call for a missionary congress in Kazan. He intended this congress—modeled after the Muslim congresses—to unify Russian missionaries and formulate the "Russian cause" more clearly.[38]

Around the same time, the Holy Synod and the Department for Religious Affairs of Foreign Confessions requested that local authorities take up measures to suppress Muslim propaganda in their provinces. With the help of the local police, the Kazan governor, M. V. Strizhevskii investigated the state of Muslim propaganda and the "antigovernment Muslim movement toward the creation of a separate Muslim state" but found no visible traces of it.[39] The Kazan governor reported the results of the investigation to the director of the Department of Foreign Confessions, A. N. Kharuzin, noting that, when compared to the years following the 1905 Tolerance Decree, the apostasy movement to Islam had now declined. Although he failed to find any organized Muslim propaganda, he thought that it was risky to conclude that it did not exist. He suspected that the propaganda existed but that it was so well done that the police could not find the "propagandists." Further, he concluded that this propaganda was "undoubtedly" in the hands of progressive

Muslims, whose goals were not purely religious but also political: the unification of all the alien population and creation of an autonomous state.[40] The governor believed in the eventual assimilation of Muslims, which he thought was "natural" and historically "unavoidable," and considered the cultural and religious separatism of any nationality to be dangerous for the state. He feared that Muslim political aspirations were quite "possible" in the current liberal moment, given the example of the "real" demands for full independence from Russia by some Poles and Finns. Thus, despite any firm evidence, the Kazan governor formulated the problem in regard to Muslims as a potential serious threat to the security of the state, and argued that the government should involve itself in a struggle against a "Muslim liberal movement."[41]

Responding to the Danger of Tatar–Muslim Nationalism: The Special Commission of 1910

The local Orthodox concerns about Muslim propaganda and the possibility of a Muslim separatist movement resonated with Stolypin's efforts to reassert Russian state interests in the empire's borderlands. Stolypin was especially concerned about strained relations between official St. Petersburg and Finland. He undertook several steps after 1907 to increase the political influence of imperial authorities in Finland and to redefine the status of Finland within the empire.[42] The government also became sensitive to cases that appeared to assault the Russian cultural presence in the empire's western borderlands, such as, for example, supposed Finnish "insults" to the monasteries in Sortanlakhti and Serdobol, or pan-Finnish propaganda among the Orthodox in Karelia.[43] Stolypin also supported the administrative separation of the Kholm region from Poland, the idea energetically advocated by Bishop Evlogii, who sought through this move to restore the Orthodox church to predominance in the western part of the empire, where it had been shaken by conversions to Catholicism.[44]

In 1909, fearing the politicization of Islam, Stolypin turned his full attention to the eastern borderlands. Writing to the chief procurator of Holy Synod, S. M. Luk'ianov, Stolypin stressed the menace embedded in the Muslim Question, pointing to the political and cultural nature of Russia's collision with Islam and the danger of Muslim separatism.[45] In January 1910, Stolypin formed a special interministerial commission to address this problem, convened under the auspices of the Ministry of the Internal Affairs. The official name of the commission was the Conference for the Elaboration of Measures to Counteract Tatar–Muslim Influence in the Volga Region (*Soveshchanie po vyrabotke mer dlia protivodeistviia tataro-musul'manskomu vliianiiu v Privolzhskom krae*), or the Commission on the Muslim Question, as it was referred to in government papers.

The chair of the commission was A. N. Kharuzin (1864–1932), director of the Department for Religious Affairs of Foreign Confessions. Prior to this appointment, Kharuzin had served in the tsarist administration on the empire's borderlands of

Estonia, Vilna, and Bessarabia.[46] He was also a passionate scholar and an author of books and articles on history, ethnography, and anthropology. One of his major studies was devoted to the Kazakhs of Bukeev Horde.[47] The commission also included Kazan bishops, representatives from the Ministry of Public Education and the Holy Synod, and the governors of Kazan and Viatka.

The commission's organizers saw both the increase in "Muslim propaganda" and the "awakening of Russia's Muslims" as threats to the integrity of the Russian state. The participants linked the exacerbation of the Muslim Question to the democratization of Russia's religious and political order in 1904–1905, as well as to the general increase in pan-Islamic propaganda among the world's Muslims, especially after the Young Turk revolution of 1908.[48] The goal of the commission was to study the Muslim Question and suggest measures for solving it.

As other Russian commentators did earlier, Kharuzin emphasized that contrary to the situation of the Western European overseas empires, the center of the Russian Muslim Question was not in distant colonies but in Russia itself, where a large group of Muslims, belonging to one ethnicity (*narodnost'*) lived close to the Orthodox Russian and non-Russian populations.[49] The commission's discussion thus focused on the situation in the Volga region, where the Muslim Question appeared to be especially acute. As the participants saw it, it was precisely here, over the course of almost a century, that a mass apostasy movement among baptized Muslims had occurred. It was also precisely the Volga Tatars who had successfully propagated Islam among neighboring non-Muslim peoples, who had become especially responsive to the Jadid's ideas of reform, had taken up leading positions in the early twentieth century's Muslim liberal movement, and had presented themselves as the spokespersons for the Muslim nation. Taking into account these developments, the commission's organizers formulated the problem as the "Tatar–Muslim Question."

Aleksii Dorodnitsyn, the bishop of Chistopol, interpreted the modern movement of Russian Muslims as part of a pan-Islamic movement aimed at the political unification of the world's Muslims under the aegis of Turkey. In his view, the other goals that Muslim modernists had officially declared, such as the raising of religious, moral, and cultural levels, and the attainment of religious and political freedoms, were secondary to this pan-Islamic project.[50] The politicization of the Muslim movement and the formation of an opposition party served to prove Aleksii's point. In his interpretation, Islam's "primordial" hostility was now further freighted by the Muslims' political opposition, which had assumed pan-Islamic goals.

Not all participants, however, considered Islam to be a hostile force. For example, the governor of Viatka province, P. K. Kamyshanskii, related the Muslims' participation in the revolutionary movement to the "decomposition" of religion, suggesting that the government's goal should be to uphold the purity of Islam.[51] The commission's chair, Kharuzin, likewise did not consider Islam, by itself, to be a political problem. Although he did not support placing Islam on the same legal footing as Christian religions, he viewed it as a source of morality that should not be shaken. In Kharuzin's opinion, the basic mass of the Muslim population was politically "reliable."[52] In contrast to the view held by Orthodox clerics, the majority of the commission agreed with Kharuzin, considering most Muslims loyal. However, the loyalty of Muslim subjects, as well as that of Baltic Germans and Finns, was described as "formal" or "superficial" (*vneshniaia*). The fact that Muslim intelligentsia developed a nationalistic movement served as evidence of this "formal" loyalty.[53]

The majority of the commission then related the Muslim Question to antigovernment activity of Muslim intelligentsia, primarily Tatars, who instrumentalized religion to achieve their nationalistic goals, tearing Muslims away from Russia and reorienting them toward Turkey.[54] It is not surprising that Muslim religious institutions, confessional schools, and the Orenburg Ecclesiastical Assembly became the focus of the commission's attention.

The commission members were especially concerned about the reformed confessional schools, the so-called new-method schools. As one member of the commission, N. A. Bobrovnikov, had mentioned in his 1908 report on Muslim schools, it was not the new method of instruction by itself but the "harmful ideas" propagated in these schools that presented a danger to the state.[55] Unlike other members of the commission who tended to give greater attention to foreign (mainly Turkish) influences on the Russian Muslim movement, Bobrovnikov viewed the new-method movement as a Russian phenomenon caused by the neglect of Muslim education by the Russian government. As the result, he claimed, during the 1905 revolution Muslim confessional schools became political tools in the hands of Muslim nationalistic intelligentsia.[56]

The commission members feared that under the guise of a confessional school, which was tolerated by the state but operated outside government control, the new-method schools provided general education that introduced nationalistic ideas to Muslim youth. To prevent the possibility of exploiting Muslim confessional schools as instruments of nationalist propaganda, commission members recommended separating confessional and secular education, leaving the former in the hands of the Muslim clergy while subjugating the latter to the state.[57] In the opinion of the commission, the goal of confessional schools was to teach religion; therefore, general subjects and Russian-language classes were to be removed from the curriculum. The regulations of 1870 and 1906 required the opening of Russian classes in Muslim confessional schools as a way to bring them closer to Russian educational institutions. As we have seen, the Ministry of Public Education's regulations of March 1906, which took a more proactive approach toward Muslim confessional schools, met opposition from Muslim intelligentsia. Objections also came from MVD officials who traditionally feared provoking popular discontent while also noting that the state interference into Muslim confessional schools was a violation of the religious toleration decree.[58] The revised regulations of 1907 no longer required Muslim confessional schools to have Russian classes, mullahs to learn Russian, and the ministry to inspect schools.[59] Kharuzin's commission explained its recommendation concerning Russian classes both by their unpopularity among the Muslims themselves and by the fear that under the guise of these classes, confessional schools would introduce secular subjects "taught in Tatar or Turkish and in a specific pan-Turkic light."[60] The goal of the commission's recommendations was to enhance state control over Muslim education. The commission proposed that those Muslim schools that continued teaching general subjects were no longer to be officially considered "confessional" and therefore were to be subjected to inspection by the Ministry of Public Education. The commissions' organizers were committed to toleration of Islam and its institutions but not to nationalistic goals. Despite the objection of Bishop Andrei and Bobrovnikov, who opposed the state's reliance on Muslim clergy, the commission recommended that authority be delegated to the Orenburg Ecclesiastical Assembly to develop a curriculum for confessional schools.[61]

The commission's deliberations on schooling policy in the Volga region were in line with Stolypin's larger initiative to introduce universal elementary education and reassert the state's role in non-Russian education. The secularization of the confessional schools and especially their role in nationalistic politics in the empire's non-Russian, especially western regions were developments that occurred outside the control of the Ministry of Public Education and reached their climax during the 1905 revolution. These increasingly became matters of attention for Stolypin's government. Indeed, Stolypin had called for another special commission to review the state schooling policy among the empire's non-Russians, to meet in parallel with the Kharuzin commission, which was focused on the Muslim Question more generally. This special commission was chaired by the vice minister of public education and met from November 1910 to October 1911. It viewed schools primarily as champions of the idea of state unity and envisioned the ideal state school as universal for all the empire's religious and ethnic communities, with the state language as the language of instruction, and within which both Russians and non-Russians would be taught to love Russia and become consciously aware of its unity and indivisibility. In the end, the special commission made a concession to non-Russian nationalities, but only to those who possessed a written language and a developed literature, by providing them with the opportunity to receive instruction in their religion and native languages.[62] In the eastern part of the empire, however, this exception extended only to Tatar, while the other non-Russian languages of the Volga peoples were not officially recognized as minority languages. On the matter of non-Orthodox confessional schools, the Special Commission on Education concluded that while "undesirable," they should be "tolerated" by the state. The commission agreed with the Kharuzin commission on ways to prevent nationalistic propaganda in Muslim confessional schools.[63]

It is possible, as some historians have suggested, to explain the Kharuzin commission's decision on state schooling policies, and especially the ban on the Russian language, by grasping the commission's "Orientalizing vision" and the "cultural need of the colonizer to maintain the alterity of the colonized."[64] As Robert Geraci concluded, the commission members "became nostalgic for Muslims they could patronize and ridicule rather than respect as equals."[65] The commission's deliberations, however, seem to reveal much deeper tensions embedded into Stolypin's modernization project. Stolypin's government, as had previous generations of state reformers, assumed that integrating non-Russians into the broad cultural life of the Russian state and thus overcoming what they perceived as Muslim cultural ignorance and alienation was an important task of the modernizing state.[66] In the new political climate, however, Kharuzin's commission came to explain the loyalty of the majority of Muslims in 1905 not by their true sense of devotion to the throne and Fatherland, but rather by their "unpreparedness" to accept revolutionary ideas due to what the commission termed as Muslims' "inertia" and "ignorance."[67] This conclusion raised the dilemma: how, then, to overcome popular masses' perceived ignorance and turn them into imperial citizens devoted to the state without undermining the political order? The police measures, rather than reforms, seemed to offer an easier solution to the problem of enhancing the shaken state authority. The Kharuzin committee's deliberations also illustrated a tension between the imperial government's commitment to satisfy what it viewed as the empire's non-Orthodox subjects' "just" religious needs while also preventing the politicization of religion and its exploitation as a tool of nationalistic propaganda. No less a tension-ridden task was ensuring religious tolerance while also protecting the dominant position of the Orthodox church.

The Missionaries' View of the Muslim Question

The Kharuzin commission acknowledged that, from a theoretical standpoint, the Christianization of all Muslims would resolve the Muslim Question. The participants recognized, however, that while Christianization might be desirable, it was not likely to occur, and even attempting it would cause tension between the state and its Muslim subjects. The commission's participants consequently reached the ambiguous conclusion that missionary activity should remain in the hands of the church, not the state. At the same time, the state should not be "indifferent" to the interests of the Orthodox church in relation to Muslim propaganda, which, they believed, worked hand in hand with Tatar nationalism and separatism. The commission, therefore, recommended supporting various Kazan missionary institutions. As we have seen, however, despite collaboration in considering the Muslim Question as a serious political problem, missionaries and government officials had different understandings of this problem. This became even more apparent when the Muslim Question was taken up by the Orthodox All-Russian missionary congress held in Kazan in 1910. The congress was planned to be the first large-scale event dedicated to the missions among non-Christians. While the Kharuzin commission discussed the Muslim Question behind closed doors, taking care to not publicize its intensions, missionaries addressed the Muslim Question in the press in hopes of drawing the Russian public's and the government's attention both to the problem and its interpretation. The missionary press urged that the congress in Kazan be considered not merely a missionary action but an all-Russian matter, complete with the participation of state officials and broader Russian society.[68] But while the missionary press popularized the idea of the congress in Kazan, its organizers were afraid of the Muslim reaction that such publicity might create. In his correspondence with Kharuzin, Bishop Andrei insisted that the congress be a closed event, since he feared that Muslims could counter with their own enterprises and did not want the congress to turn into another example of the Orthodox church exposing its weaknesses to Muslims. In addition, he feared that public discussion of the problems that Kharuzin's committee had already addressed could prematurely expose the government's intentions concerning the Muslim Question and thereby irritate Muslims.[69]

The official chair of the congress, which took place in June 1910, was the Metropolitan of Moscow and the chair of the Orthodox Missionary Society, Vladimir Bogoiavlenskii. In fact, however, the congress was supervised by Nikanor Kamenskii, the Kazan archbishop, and his assistant, Andrei, bishop of Mamadysh. Among the participants were missionaries representing twenty-three dioceses, as well as professors from the missionary department of the Kazan Theological Academy and lay educators. The program concerned the discussion of missionary efforts among baptized non-Russians, Muslims, Buddhists, and animists.[70] The central issue addressed by the special section on Islam was what some speakers explicitly identified as the Muslim Question. At the core of the problem, as the missionaries saw it, was an enduring and dangerous confrontation between Orthodoxy and Islam. For them, apostasy and Muslim propaganda had attained serious political meaning when the Muslim intelligentsia embarked on the Tatar–Muslim nation-building project.

One of the most outspoken proponents of this point of view was Il'minskii's former student N. P. Ostroumov, who was now serving as director of the Tashkent Teachers' Seminary. He emphasized the importance of the Tatar–Muslim Question and warned that it might become even more dangerous than the Polish, Finnish, and Jewish Questions. He argued that contrary to the government's perception, Muslims were not loyal subjects; some Muslims' political activity clearly indicated this. Ostroumov urged the government to take a more clearly defined position with regard to the Muslim Question, one that committed to religious toleration but that would protect and strengthen the dominant position of Russian Orthodox people in the empire.[71] He maintained that the struggle against Islam was a matter of grave concern not only for the church but also for the state and, indeed, all of Russian society. Another speaker, M. A. Mashanov, a professor at the Kazan Theological Academy, emphasized the political nature of Muslim propaganda and the danger coming from the "new Tatars" who, as he argued, took advantage of state religious toleration to pursue an isolationist Tatar–Muslim national project.[72]

The delegates to the congress, however, not only critiqued the expansion of religious tolerance and attacked Muslim progressive intelligentsia and their institutions, but also turned their attention to the seeming failures of Orthodoxy and the need to revitalize church life in Russia. Several delegates addressed this issue by pointing to the poor conditions of the missions and the shortcoming of the Russian Orthodox community.[73] In his opening speech, Bishop Andrei declared that the organization of parish life should be the main resolution of the congress.[74] Thus the arguments about the religious and political danger of Islam as well as the weakness of Orthodoxy served to give greater weight to such measures as revitalizing Orthodox parish life, strengthening the religious component of Christian non-Russians' education (in the spirit of Il'minskii), translating Orthodox literature into non-Russian languages, and publishing polemical anti-Islamic literature.[75] The congress itself turned out to be not only a discussion of how to strengthen Orthodoxy vis-à-vis Islam, but also a public demonstration of the strength of the Russian Orthodox church, demonstrated through such activities as a religious procession to Il'minskii's grave and baptism ceremonies.[76]

Yet it turned out to be a challenging task to mobilize the Russian public and enlist church and government officials in support of the Russian cause as it was understood by the Kazan organizers of the congress. Il'minskii's missionary system, one of the key elements of this project, came under increasing attack, not only by Muslims but also by Russian nationalists and defenders of "true Orthodoxy" who opposed the use of non-Russian languages in the schools. In 1910, P. F. Zalesskii (1861–1922), professor at Kazan University, a publisher, and also a leader of the local right-wing Black Hundred movement, launched a campaign in the *Kazanskii telegraf* against what he viewed as the "erroneous organization of alien education in Kazan province." He also delivered a public speech at the Provincial Assembly of the Nobility, stressing the same points. He claimed that Orthodoxy in non-Russian languages "humiliated" Orthodox teaching and promoted "alien separatism." The multiethnic Kazan Teachers' Seminary became another target of the *Kazanskii telegraf*, which intimidated its readers with words about the danger of "alien domination."[77] Under the influence of this campaign, some local school councils decided to temporarily stop the implementation of Il'minskii's system, thus in fact abolishing the state school regulations. The new school regulations, issued on 5 June 1913, further reduced the use of native languages in elementary education and represented another blow to Il'minskii's system.[78]

In the middle of the battle over Il'minskii's system, Bishop Andrei, a passionate proponent of this system and the advocate of the Russian cause that aimed for the revitalization of the Orthodox church and the protection of baptized non-Russians from what he perceived as hostile Tatar–Muslim influence, was transferred from Kazan to the Sukhumi diocese in the Caucasus. This transfer was a surprise for many, including Andrei himself.

*   *   *

In the period after the 1905 revolution, the discussion of the Muslim Question reached fever pitch, capturing the attention of the church, the government, and the Russian and Muslim publics. The expansion of religious tolerance and the official recognition of a large group of recalcitrants as Muslims, combined with liberal inclinations and nationalistic claims of the Muslim intelligentsia, greatly alarmed church authorities. Particularly for Il'minskii's followers, these trends exacerbated concerns about what they perceived to be the strengthening of Islam vis-à-vis Orthodoxy. In a sense, the "Muslim awakening" in turn awakened Il'minskii's followers among Russian borderland educators and missionaries.

For both tsarist officials and Orthodox figures, the common enemy was the Muslim progressive intelligentsia. Yet this did not produce common ground in terms of what they perceived as the essence of the Muslim Question. Orthodox missionaries considered Islam to be a hostile confession and perceived Muslims as "loyal enemies." For them, the so-called Muslim political awakening only deepened the danger of the Muslim Question, and implied an eternal confrontation between Islam and Christianity. Moreover, the seeming strengths of Islam served to highlight the weaknesses of Orthodoxy. Il'minskii's followers were threatened not only by the consequences of expanded religious tolerance and civil freedoms, but also by increasing Russian ethnic nationalism and the absence of governmental progress in addressing the pressing issues of the church, specifically parish reform. As a result, the followers opposed the immediate expansion of religious tolerance, reinforcing government mistrust toward the Muslim intelligentsia and to Muslims in general. In turn, their actions hindered meaningful discussions of how Muslims might best be integrated into the empire and effectively governed.

Within the government, Stolypin's interest in the Muslim Question was related to his program of stabilizing and modernizing an empire shaken by revolution. Reasserting the state power in the borderlands was an important component of this project. Viewed from the perspective of their loyalty to the regime, the majority of the Muslim population still appeared to be politically reliable. The problem was seen to lie not in Islam itself but in the Muslim liberal intelligentsia, whose activities—however much they reflected a minority view among Russia's Muslims—were still perceived to be antigovernment and dangerous for the state. When viewed in the context of national movements in the empire's western borderlands, the spread of pan-Islamic ideas and the Iranian and Turkish constitutional revolutions, the threat of Muslim nationalism seemed even more dangerous. This view of the problem limited the solutions available to tsarist officials. Stolypin still hoped to strengthen the empire's unity through the state schooling system. Yet by admitting that Muslims' cultural ignorance contributed to their political loyalty, tsarist officials essentially gave away the goal of Muslim enlightenment and rapprochement with Russians in favor of assuring Muslim loyalty to the regime. Even here, Russian officials were not certain that Muslims would remain loyal in the future, nor that Muslim expressions of what was now often called "formal loyalty" were sincere. This mistrust was rooted not so much in what might be called the "orientalist" stance within the state bureaucracy, but in what some tsarist officials expected as a result of the political trajectory followed by the other "more progressive" nationalities of the empire. The Polish example, especially, provided an easy parallel for Muslims to follow when Russian officials imagined the trajectory of what Muslim radicalism and separatism might someday become. This thinking found its expression, for example, in references in Russian nationalistic newspapers to the Muslim faction as the "Muslim Kolo" (after the Polish faction in the State Duma called *Kolo*) and to authorities' anxieties about the "approaching peril" (*griadushchaia opasnost'*), seen as the point when the Muslim Question would become no less dangerous than the Polish and other alien questions.

In essence, the fundamental issue that concerned all of the parties engaged in debating the Muslim Question was how best to govern the empire in circumstances that many participants saw as increasingly threatening to Russian imperial stability. The special commission of 1910, the central government's first attempt to address these issues in the explicit form of the Muslim Question, led not to a resolution of the problem but to recognition of it. The debate on the Muslim Question, as we have seen, revealed different understandings of the nature of this problem. The commissions' participants ultimately concluded their work by suggesting that new interministerial commissions on the Muslim Question be called to serve as government instruments for further discussion of this problem. The next special interministerial commission was planned to meet in 1914. Meanwhile, the commission developed a strategy for the study of the Muslim Question. This time, would consensus be achieved?

8 "Solving" the Muslim Question

As of 1910, the tsar's government found itself with multiple, contested, and contradictory recommendations about the Muslim Question. While many of these initiatives were launched during Stolypin's time, they were carried out in a changing political context. Stolypin himself did not last long; he was assassinated on 14 September 1911. His coalition with the conservative and nationalist elements in the Third Duma had turned out to be precarious, and he managed to alienate both the Right and the Left. His successors had neither his influence within the government nor his determination to implement a program of reforms. Once again, the government faced increasing opposition from members of educated society and mass protest movements. And once again, Russia became involved (this time indirectly) in the conflict with the Ottomans, which intensified during the two Balkan wars of 1912–1913. Along with other important geopolitical consequences, the Balkan wars stimulated pan-Slavist sentiments within Russian society while at the same time positioning Russian Muslims as potential enemies. This chapter explores how the Russian government attempted to implement its program on the Muslim Question under these challenging circumstances.

Program for the Study of the Muslim Question

A main conclusion of the 1910 Kharuzin commission was that the government lacked information on the topics that might help them to formulate solutions to the Muslim Question, or even to articulate it more clearly. Government officials were increasingly aware that they did not know exactly what was going on within Muslim communities. This issue was repeatedly raised by one of the commission's participants, N. A. Bobrovnikov. Similar concerns were expressed by the Turkestan governor-general, who in 1909 held a special meeting in Tashkent to address the superficial knowledge of natives' life among the imperial administration.[1]

The increased political activity of Russian Muslims in the early twentieth century made the changes taking place in the Muslim community more visible, both to the broader circles of the Russian public and to the government. Practical and observable changes in the lives of Muslims unavoidably called into question the existing presumptions that Muslim society was dominated by an unchanging religious doctrine based solely on the Koran. It became obvious to the government that Muslim society was not in a state of stagnation and was in fact changing.[2] It was this realization that led the 1910 commission to develop a program to study the Muslim Question. An important component of the program was a special journal that would collect and analyze information on Muslim life.

Many government officials, however, associated the "study" (*izuchenie*) of the Muslim Question with information-gathering (*osvedomlenie*). Along with intelligence reports and press reviews routinely prepared within the Ministry of Internal Affairs, special reviews of the Muslim press constituted an important source of information as well as the stimulus for further government investigations. Yet despite this increased emphasis on information-gathering on Muslims, some officials of the MVD occasionally complained that they did not actually know what had been published in the Muslim press.[3] As the tsarist officials began to pay more attention to that press, they became increasingly convinced that it was serving as a powerful propagandistic tool for the Muslim intelligentsia, whose activity, as we have seen, was the primary concern for the Stolypin's government. Thus, in the MVD officials' understanding, the "study" of the Muslim Question implied not only systematic information-gathering, but also a struggle against what tsarist officials saw as "antigovernment tendencies" among Russian Muslims.[4]

The practical realization of the goal of learning about the empire's Muslims was delegated to the St. Petersburg Imperial Society for Oriental Studies, headed by Lieutenant-General N. K. Shvedov (1849–1927) and V. V. Bartol'd (1869–1930), a prominent orientalist, professor at St. Petersburg University, and member of the Academy of Sciences, who became the editor of the new journal, *Mir islama*.[5] The collaboration between the Society for Oriental Studies (which itself aimed to re-direct oriental studies toward practical applications), the government, and Bartol'd, who had already publicly expressed doubts about the possibility of successfully combining "narrowly practical" and scholarly goals, laid the foundation for potential tensions.[6]

The program formulated by Bartol'd anticipated the exploration of "all of the cultural, political, and economical factors, which besides the ideal created by religion, determine the actual lives of the Muslim peoples."[7] He saw this scholarly endeavor as a Russian obligation to the empire's own Muslims, as well as to European scholarship on the Muslim world. Bartol'd invited famous Orientalists, including A. E. Shmidt, A. N. Samoilovich, and I. Iu. Krachkovskii, to contribute to the journal. The introduction to its first issue, which came out in March 1912, stated as its goal the study of actual Muslim life, with attention to the rise of national self-consciousness in the Muslim world. The journal promised to provide an objective account of past and present facts of Muslim life, as reconstructed by means of the European scholarly method of historical analysis (rooted in the German philological tradition), free of pro-Muslim or anti-Muslim polemic as well as independent of government views.[8] The journal was distributed free of charge among the governors, church officials, and curators of the educational districts in provinces with a Muslim population. Bartol'd's scholarly approach to Muslim life challenged government officials' perspective on the Muslim Question and the original goals of the study.

Not surprisingly, the journal very soon disappointed the Ministry of Internal Affairs, which considered its articles to be "excessively theoretical."[9] According to a MVD report, the *Mir islama* "chose facts that were of interest to Muslims themselves, but not to the government . . . and thus could not help the government in its difficult task of struggling against the strong Muslim movement."[10] The academic reputation of the journal and the role of Russian scholarship in European studies of Islam did not seem to impress the MVD officials. In his conversation with Bartol'd, the Minister of Internal Affairs, A. A. Makarov, declared that, on scholarly questions, he preferred at least in principle to consult with Western European scholars.[11]

The Russian government's attempts to study the Muslim Question in collaboration with professional orientalists and by means of a specialized periodical reflected the increasing European interest in Islam during the first decade of the twentieth century. This interest was stimulated by European anxieties about growing unrest in the Islamic world, as well as by the aggravated competition between the European powers for their own influence in the East.[12] Although each assumed a different perspective, several new European journals took the contemporary Muslim world as their focus, including the *Revue du monde musulman,* founded in 1906 in France by A. Le Chatelier, a military officer with extensive experience in West Africa, professor at Collège de France, and founder of the Mission scientifique du Maroc; *Der Islam,* founded in 1910 in Germany by C. H. Becker, professor of history and culture of the Orient at the recently established Kolonialinstitut and director of the Seminar for History and Culture of the Orient in Hamburg; *The Moslem World,* inaugurated in 1911 in England by S. M. Zwemer, an influential American Protestant missionary in Muslim countries and the author of works on their culture and religion; and *Die Welt des Islams,* founded in 1913 in Germany by M. Hartmann, a member of the Imperial German diplomatic service and later a teacher of Arabic at the Seminar für Orientalische Sprachen and the founder of the Deutsche Geselschaft für Islamkunde.[13]

From the beginning, the Russian editors of *Mir islama* had envisioned their organ as a contribution to these European efforts to study the Muslim world. The value of European journals on Islam for the formulation of the government's Muslim policy was also noted by some of the Russian officials, who occasionally relied on them for information.[14] However, in comparison to the European endeavors, the MVD's vision of a Russian periodical on the Muslim Question was much narrower in scope. The government's collaboration with academic experts was rather precarious and did not last long.

At the beginning of 1913, on the recommendation of the chair of the Imperial Society for Oriental Studies, N. K. Shvedov, the Ministry of Internal Affairs appointed a new editor, D. M. Pozdneev, a specialist on the Far East, the director of the

Oriental Institute in Vladivostok (1904–1905), professor at the Practical Oriental Academy in St. Petersburg (Prakticheskaia vostochnaia academiia), and a member of the Society for Oriental Studies.[15] The first issue following this change announced a program that focused on contemporary Muslim life and stressed the connection of the journal to the goals of the Society for Oriental Studies. Like his predecessor, the new editor promised to provide an objective interpretation of events.[16] This strategy was reflected in the themes of the journal, which covered Muslim views on what the editors considered to be the "relevant" questions of the day, including the School Question, the question of the reorganization of the Muslim ecclesiastical administration, the Muslim Women's Question, pan-Islamism and pan-Turkism, and the question of reform in Islam. New authors appeared among the contributors to the journal, including the director of the Tashkent Teachers' Seminary, N. P. Ostroumov, and the ethnographer and a new employee of the MVD, S. G. Rybakov.

The new editor, however, debuted in unfavorable circumstances created by the government's conflict with Bartol'd. In January 1913, the liberal newspaper *Russkaia molva* published an article discrediting the reputation of the new journal and its editor, as well as the Imperial Society for Oriental Studies, by concluding that a "useful cultural undertaking [had] perished at the very start."[17] An interview with Bartol'd by a Tatar newspaper published in Tomsk had a similarly negative effect on the public reputation of the new publication.[18]

The journal's aspiration to "study the present [contemporary Islam] from an objective scholarly perspective" presented the editors with several practical issues, such as finding authors who could combine "the talent of a journalist with scholarly expertise" and of creating timely publication dates so that the issues would not lose their relevance.[19] In its first year under the new editor, *Mir islama* discussed Russian Muslim life primarily through the prism of "questions" (*voprosy iz zhizni musul'manstva*) that had been addressed by the Muslim press, the Duma, and Russian public opinion. In their plans for the coming year of 1914, the editors anticipated expanding the range of questions by paying more attention to Muslim life abroad, and also by establishing a network of special correspondents in Muslim regions who would report on issues not covered by the press. Like their predecessors, the new editors hoped that the journal would contribute to European scholarship on Islam. The expansion of their program required an increase in government subsidies.[20]

The last issue of *Mir islama* came out at the beginning of 1914; further attempts of the Ministry of Internal Affairs to obtain financial support for it were not successful.[21] The lack of funding was a serious problem but not the only hurdle. The new agenda of *Mir islama* did not completely satisfy government officials, whose opinions about the purpose of the governmental periodical were divided. The future of the journal was discussed at the 1914 special commission on the Muslim Question. While some of the commission's participants thought that the journal's goals should primarily be informational, the majority believed that the government needed an official organ (*ofitsioz*) that would not only gather information but also shape public opinion in a pro-government direction.[22] In 1916, Bartol'd proposed that the Academy of Sciences publish the journal *Musul'manskii mir*, focusing on the Muslim world, its history, and contemporary cultural life, but without pursuing any political goals. The first and only issue came out after the 1917 revolution.

In Russia, as elsewhere in Europe, new institutions were founded with the purpose of training students to engage directly with the Orient in such practical matters as administration, commerce, and diplomacy. The Oriental Institute in Vladivostok, established in 1899, and the Practical Oriental Academy, set up in St. Petersburg in 1907, were two examples.[23] As part of the 1910 government program for the study of the Muslim Question, the MVD, too, decided to provide training for its officials serving in the Muslim borderlands. In the fall of 1911, the MVD sponsored courses, established at the Imperial Society for Oriental Studies, where officials from the MVD and other ministries could learn Arabic, Tatar, the Koran, Islamic theology, and Muslim law over a twelve-month period. Among the teachers were orientalists and the mullah L. Iskhakov, who taught the Tatar language; no Orthodox missionaries were invited to teach.

The MVD sent out an announcement about the courses to twenty-one provinces and regions with a Muslim population, but of these, only nine provinces and a few central government departments could afford to send officials to the courses. The regional administrations responded that their officials were burdened with too much work and therefore could not attend. The Department of General Affairs and the Main Administration for the Press reported that no one from their institutions was interested in attending. Out of the sixteen students dispatched by the central and provincial administrations and the ecclesiastical academy, only five students graduated in December 1912.[24] Among them was the ethnographer S. G. Rybakov, who in 1913 was hired by the Department for Religious Affairs of Foreign Confessions to administer Muslim affairs.

The Turkestan administration sent no representatives to the MVD courses. Special courses, however, were established in Tashkent for Russian officers who were to occupy administrative positions in the region, and N. P. Ostroumov was invited to teach. In his instructors' manual, Ostroumov summarized his works on Islam and the Muslim Question, emphasizing that the Muslim Question constituted a serious problem for Russians and therefore required serious attention and study.[25] Yet knowledge of local languages and culture did not become a prerequisite for Russian officials in Turkestan, despite several attempts of some governors-general to raise this issue.

The MVD's courses acquired a negative reputation among some Muslim politicians who viewed them as yet another governmental attempt to uncover Muslim conspiracy and a notorious pan-Islamism.[26] The organizers of the courses also confronted several practical difficulties. In 1912, the courses were discontinued, but discussions among central and local officials on how best to prepare government officials to serve in Muslim regions continued until 1916.

At the same time, the MVD supported projects on the Muslim Question launched by Kazan missionaries, whose understanding of this problem differed from the government's. One such project was led by Andrei, the former bishop of Mamadysh and organizer of the Kazan missionary congress, and N. V. Nikol'skii (1878–1961), who taught ethnography at missionary courses in Kazan.[27] In 1912, their collaboration resulted in a publication titled *Naibolee vazhnye statisticheskie svedeniia ob inorodtsakh vostochnoi Rossii i zapadnoi Sibiri, podverzhennykh vlianiiu islama* (*The Most Important Statistical Information on Aliens of Eastern Russia and Western Siberia Exposed to the Influence of Islam*). This study, based on data collected by local church and civil authorities, was a representation of Islamic influence among baptized non-Russians and animists. It was intended by its editors to serve as a "reference not only for missionaries but also for those who had an interest in the fate of the Russian cause among aliens." Copies were distributed among clerical and secular officials of the Volga region.[28] The statistical study presented what the editors viewed as "the sad facts" of the "subversive" (*pagubnye*) influence of Islam among Eastern non-Russians, or in other words, the success of Muslim propaganda. The statistical picture was accompanied by the following conclusion:

> Seventy-five years ago many areas within some districts of the Kazan, Nizhnii Novgorod, and Orenburg provinces had a multiethnic composition in their populations, with the Tatars, Chuvash, Mordovians, and Cheremis living there; now only Tatar Muslims reside here.[29]

The MVD-sponsored missionary publication was reviewed positively in the July issue of the *Zhurnal Ministerstva narodnogo prosveshcheniia*.[30] In *Mir islama*, however, where Bartol'd was still the editor, it received more criticism. The review, written by Bartol'd himself, primarily questioned the reliability and scholarly value of statistical evidence that demonstrated the dominance of Islam. He thought that the issues raised by the authors were important, but he did not share their anxieties concerning the weakness of Russians with respect to Muslims. In contrast to Bishop Andrei, who saw the solution in a simultaneous revitalization of church life and a containment of Islam, Bartol'd approached the problem of Russia's seeming cultural losses from a different angle. He considered the development of scholarly knowledge and literature to be a crucial factor behind successful national progress. He also compared the elites' secular cultural work, arguing that Tatar scholars' achievements were exaggerated and still lagged behind "true European culture," of which Russian high culture was already an essential part. Thus, Bartol'd concluded, "given the superiority of Russian culture [understood as the secular culture of the educated elites], Muslim propaganda should not be considered dangerous." For him, a greater problem was the cultural gap between commoners and educated Russians, a situation he thought needed to be addressed regardless of the existence or absence of a Muslim threat.[31]

Bartol'd's criticism of the missionary publication revealed the different opinions among educated Russians not only about the essence of the Muslim Question, but also on the nature of the Russian Question—how might Russians transform themselves in a modernizing world? In contrast to Andrei's Slavophile vision of Russia's transformation, Bartol'd saw the answer in European enlightenment and progress.

The missionaries had, of course, long been interested in what they referred to as "Tatar Muslim propaganda," but this issue had another important dimension that concerned not so much the perceived weakness of Orthodoxy, but rather the challenge of preserving the non-Russian cultures of small ethnic groups in the face of assimilationist pressure from Muslim Tatars. It was precisely this issue that concerned Andrei's collaborator, N. V. Nikol'skii, the co-organizer of the MVD-sponsored missionary study. Nikol'skii was born into a family of Chuvash peasants, graduated from the Kazan Theological Academy, and taught Chuvash language, history, and ethnography at different missionary and secular educational institutions in Kazan. In 1906, he published *Khypar*, the first newspaper in the Chuvash language. The 1912 publication called for the development of systematic ethnographic studies of various local non-Muslim, non-Russian peoples as another way of exploring and solving the Muslim Question; Nikol'skii invested his efforts in this endeavor. Since 1904, he had been collecting ethnographic materials on non-Russians, and in particular on the Chuvash, with the help of local priests, teachers, and educated non-Russians. In 1915, he published a program for an ethnographic survey of non-Russians in the Volga region. To explore the influence of Christianity, Islam, and animism on non-Russian minorities, and to understand the interethnic and interreligious relations in the Volga region, the program included a questionnaire to record what non-Russians themselves said.[32]

The journal *Inorodcheskoe obozrenie* (1912–1916) was another attempt by the Ministry of Internal Affairs to study the Muslim Question in collaboration with Kazan missionaries and scholars. It was published by the Kazan Theological Academy as a supplement to the missionary journal *Pravoslavnyi sobesednik*. The journal was distributed among civil and church officials as well as at missionary institutions. Its editor was N. F. Katanov (1862–1922), of native Siberian origin (Turkic-speaking people today known as Khakas), a linguist and ethnographer who taught at Kazan University and the Theological Academy.[33] The goal of *Inorodcheskoe obozrenie* was to "report on the everyday life, politics, and religion of Russian aliens."[34] The Kazan governor, P. M. Boiarskii, felt that this journal would be useful as a source of information on the Alien Question (*inorodcheskii vopros*), which he believed was especially acute in Kazan province. He especially emphasized that it was necessary for the government to obtain timely information on the mood of the Muslim population as reflected in the Tatar press, in order to be able to prevent Muslim religious and political propaganda.[35] This view corresponded to the MVD's vision of the study of the Muslim Question. The government thus subsidized the new organ of the Kazan Theological Academy on the "alien question in Eastern Russia."[36] Despite the shortage of funds and the Kazan governor's later complaints about delays in publication (which meant that the information on the moods of the population was outdated), *Inorodcheskoe obozrenie* had a longer life than *Mir islama*.[37]

By 1912, the MVD had dispatched government officials and scholars to collect information on the Muslim Question across the empire. At the same time, however, it attempted to gather information about the potential Muslim threat beyond the empire. The government asked Russian diplomatic representatives to provide information on the administration of Muslim schools and political activities in the Muslim dominions of European empires. The goal was nothing less than to understand Islam from Cairo and Istanbul to Turkestan.[38] Much of this intelligence-gathering was premised on the need to understand what seemed to be a new threat: pan-Islamism.

The Specter of Pan-Islamism

The majority of Kharuzin's 1910 commission regarded Tatar Muslim nationalism—which they assumed to constitute the essence of the Muslim Question— not as a local and isolated phenomenon, but as a manifestation of a new, worldwide Muslim movement marked by the aspiration to revitalize Islam and unite its adherents under the leadership of Turkey, with the aim of reestablishing the fading grandeur of the Ottoman empire and overthrowing the European political domination of Muslims. According to the commission's members, this new trend originated in the second half of the nineteenth century outside the Russian empire, had a profound impact on Crimean and Volga Tatars, and increased the potential threat of cultural and political movements among Russian Muslims to the unity of the Russian state. Thus, the commission perceived Russian Muslims' national project in terms of what it interpreted as their "aspiration to pan-Islamic and pan-Turkic solidarity."[39] Both the "study" of this international trend and the struggle against it constituted essential elements of the government's efforts to find a "solution" to the Muslim Question in Russia. Historians have noted that Russians increasingly developed an unfounded paranoia toward a supposed pan-Islamic conspiracy during this time.[40] It is important, however, to place these new anxieties within the context of the longer evolution of the Muslim Question. The concerns were neither monolithic nor static.

To be sure, the Stolypin's government's anxieties about the mobilizing power of pan-Islamism against tsarist rule were not entirely new. In the second half of the nineteenth century, the idea of religious solidarity resonated with Muslims living in different parts of the world. Given the different intellectual and political trends in these locations, local Muslims adopted this idea about religious solidarity to suit their divergent goals. In the Ottoman empire, Russia's historic rival to the south, the idea of Muslim solidarity was particularly appealing to intellectual and political elites at times when the empire faced the threat of increased pressure from European powers, who were seeking influence in its territories. The uprisings in the Balkans in 1875–1876 and especially the defeat of the Ottoman empire in the Russo-Turkish War of 1877–1878 had a strong psychological effect on Ottoman society, one perhaps comparable to the impact of the Crimean War on the Russian public.[41] The Russo-Turkish War significantly reduced Ottoman power in the Balkans and demonstrated the military and economic weakness of the state. Faced with the real possibility of the collapse of their empire, the Ottoman government and its educated elites were forced to search for what had caused its failure and what could be done to assure its survival. For his part, as Kemal Karpat has noted, the new Ottoman Sultan Abdülhamid II (1876–1909) sought to turn Islamism into a modern religion and political ideology that could to be used to hold together and revitalize the Ottoman state.[42]

The possible impact of this Ottoman appeal for religious solidarity on the Russian Muslims, referred to as pan-Islamism, had become a matter of increasing concern for the Russian imperial authorities. Already in 1875, in a reply to a report from N. P. Ignat'ev, the Russian ambassador in Istanbul, about the popularity of the idea of Muslim political unity within Ottoman official circles, the minister of internal affairs, A. E. Timashev, wrote:

> Taking into consideration the large numbers of the Muslim population, the expansion of our borders in the east, and the acquisition of areas that are exclusively populated by Muslims and border Muslim states, the Muslim Question has for us an important meaning. . . . Ignat'ev's report concerning the adherence of the statesmen in Turkey to pan-Islamism with political ends complicates the Muslim Question.[43]

The threat of pan-Islamism to the stability of the Russian empire especially troubled tsarist officials on the Muslim borderlands at times of crisis, such as during the 1898 Andijan revolt. To the Turkestan administration, pan-Islamism not only "clarified" the intentions of Afghan natives and Turkish subjects whom the local authorities found "without definite purposes and documents" after the Andijan attack in Russian Central Asia, but it also provided an explanation for the attack itself as a display of anti-European Muslim resistance under the slogan of pan-Islamism. However, as we have already seen, this interpretation of the Andijan events—as well as the general alarmist tone of Turkestan governor-general S. M. Dukhovskoi's report—found few adherents in St. Petersburg's official circles. S. Iu. Witte, the minister of finance, commenting on this interpretation of the Andijan uprising, actually suggested that the religious–political unification of Russian Muslims was hardly possible because of the ethnic and cultural differences among them. At the very least, Witte thought that the problem of pan-Islamism required further study.[44]

At the beginning of the twentieth century, however, pan-Islamic anxieties in Russia intensified. They also acquired a new dimension. The combination of the 1905 revolution, the cultural and political "awakening" of Russian Muslims, and constitutional revolutions in Iran and the Ottoman empire added further complexity to the Muslim Question. The idea of Muslim solidarity resonated with educated Russian Muslims, some of whom attempted to form a unified political Muslim liberal movement. A. Ibragimov (1857–1944), also known as Abdurreşid İbrahim, a Tatar from Siberia, a former member of the Orenburg Ecclesiastical Assembly who in

1895 left Russia for Istanbul, was an active propagandist of Muslim unity. Among Russian Muslims, the ideas of religious solidarity were also intertwined with those of pan-Turkism. Building on Gasprinskii's concept of cultural, linguistic, and religious unity of Muslims of Turkic origin, two expatriates from Russia, Y. Akchurin (1876–1935), also known as Yusuf Akçura, a Tatar journalist, and A. Agaev (1869–1939), also known as Ahmet Ağaoğlu, a publicist from Transcaucasia, emerged as important figures in the development of the ideas of political pan-Turkism. All three men were active participants in the political activities of Russian Muslims during the 1905 revolution. After the suppression of the revolution in 1907, all three left for the Ottoman empire, where they became intellectual leaders in their own right and forceful critics of Russian policies toward Muslims.[45]

The Ottoman sultan, Abdülhamid, mistrusted revolutionaries and opposed the ethnic nationalism promoted by Muslim intellectuals from Russia. He also remained ambivalent toward Gasprinskii. He tried to gain Gasprinskii's support of his policies by offering him money and medals, but prohibited the circulation of his *Terjuman* in the Ottoman state from 1896 to 1908. He also did not receive Gasprinskii when the latter was traveling to Cairo to organize a Muslim international congress. Abdülhamid offered asylum to Muslims from Russia, but remained distanced from the younger generation of nationalist modernists, while many Russian Jadids turned against him because of his political conservatism.[46]

When the revolution of 1908 in the Ottoman empire put an end to Hamidian rule and reestablished constitutional order, pan-Turkism became the official ideology of the Young Turk leadership that came to power. Pan-Islamic propaganda and attempts to mobilize Muslims under Russian rule as allies, however, continued under the new government.[47] After 1908, the ideas of Turkism brought from Russia by émigré Muslim intellectuals found appeal among the Ottoman nationalist ruling elite, who sought to create a core Turkish nation to stabilize their empire.[48] The Muslim activists who remained in Russia propagandized the idea of Muslim solidarity as spiritual and cultural unity both to secure progress for Russian Muslims and to press the government for rights and cultural autonomy for Muslim communities.

The 1908 Turkish revolution coincided with the conservative political turn in Russia, when Stolypin's government took up an initiative that would define the Muslim Question as primarily a problem of the Russian Muslim intelligentsia's separatist tendencies, a phenomenon perceived to be of Turkish creation. While Orthodox clerics and some nationalistic Russian commentators sounded the alarm about pan-Turkism and pan-Islamism as "dark forces"—as essentially anti-Christian, anti-European, and anti-Russian movements of an imperialist nature—the government paid more attention to the liberal underpinnings of these ideologies, believing that they might present an even more dangerous threat to Russian political stability.

This increased concern about the international dimension of the Muslim Question made it necessary to supervise closely and, if possible, control the moods and activities of Muslims outside the Russian empire, as well as the movement of people, literature, and ideas between the Russian and Ottoman empires. Reports by Russian diplomats concerning the political tendencies of foreign Muslims caused anxieties among tsarist authorities about the political behavior of Russian Muslims. Conversely, in investigating the origins and character of the Jadid movement, the Ministry of Internal Affairs searched for Turkish influence and potential connections between Russian progressive Muslims and the Young Turks.[49]

The assumptions of the Ministry of Internal Affairs about the foreign sources of the Muslim progressive movement testified not only to the some tsarist officials' fear of Muslim international solidarity, but also to the mentality of the officials and the conditions of political life in late imperial Russia. During the reigns of Alexander III and Nicholas II, as we have seen, representatives of the highest echelons of power believed in a special path for Russia, one based on the historic unity of the tsar with his people, which precluded any internal social and political conflicts. Viewed from such a perspective, social and political movements like socialism and nationalism appeared to have had an "artificial" character imported to Russia from abroad. Following this logic, the development of a national consciousness among Russian Muslims and the spread of the ideas of pan-Islamism and pan-Turkism in Russia after 1905 were characterized by the Ministry of Internal Affairs as "alien" to Russia and borrowed from Turkey (*nanosnye*). At the same time, the absence of conditions for open political activity in Russia after 1907 forced some radical Muslim figures to leave Russia and conduct the propagation of their ideas among their compatriots outside of Russia, intensifying authorities' fears as well as the need for police surveillance within and outside the empire.[50]

The MVD officials' concerns about foreign influence were reinforced by divisions within the Muslim community, with conservative Muslims leveling charges of anti-government activity against their progressive rivals, activities supposedly instigated by their revolutionary coreligionists in Persia and Turkey.[51] During times of political crisis in Russia, the accusation of pan-Islamism became a tool in local politics within these Muslim communities. In 1908, a group of twelve Tatar imams wrote to Stolypin about the "anti-state activity" of *maktab* teachers (*muʿallims*) and the supporters of Ittifak who advocated the teaching according to the Jadid method, read Friday prayers in Tatar instead of Arabic, and agitated for the transfer of Muslim spiritual affairs into the hands of society. The petitioners attributed these activities to the influence of Turkish and Persian revolutionaries and asked the government not to allow proponents of the new methods to hold teaching positions.[52] In response to this petition, the Department of Police requested that governors and heads of police in Kazan, Simbirsk, Saratov, Ufa, and Orenburg provinces investigate the activities of the *maktab* teachers.

Most of the regional officials admitted to the existence of the progressive movement in their provinces, but did not ascribe to it considerable influence among the population. They also regarded complaints of the imams as manifestations of rivalry within the Muslim communities. The officials, however, disagreed about the political significance of the progressive movement. The governor of Ufa, for example, expressed doubts about the preference of the conservative way of teaching over progressive methods. The heads of the police in Kazan and Ufa did not detect wide familiarity with the progressive movement in their provinces, but considered the movement to be dangerous for the state because of its connection with pan-Islamism. The head of police in the Kazan region worried that the hope of progressive Muslims eventually to gain religious and cultural autonomy was leading this group toward isolation from Russian culture and the creation of a Muslim state.[53] Kazan police officials expressed certainty about the danger of "pan-Islamic" or "Young Turk propaganda" even as they had difficulty detecting its traces because, as the head of the gendarmerie explained, "persons who conduct this propaganda are very careful, and the Tatar population is extremely closed." They were still convinced, however, that the chief "breeding ground" for the pan-Islamist propaganda was the *maktab* and demanded close surveillance of these schools with the help of agents who understood the Tatar language.[54] In order to watch the teachers, the local police recruited a trusted Muslim who reported on Russian pan-Islamists, among whom he mentioned the organizers of the All-Muslim Congress in Nizhnii Novgorod, pointing to their aspiration to create a "worldwide nation of Muslims."[55]

In 1908, in response to the government's anxieties about *maktab* teachers and foreign influences in Muslim schools, N. A. Bobrovnikov, at that time curator of the Orenburg educational district, prepared a report on this question. In it, he emphasized that the new-method movement was not a foreign creation, but a Russian phenomenon, a result of specific Russian circumstances, and, in particular, of the government's neglect of elementary education among the Muslim folk.[56] He did not give much weight to the factor of foreign training of Muslim teachers, which was the primary concern of the government, and he noted that the number of Muslim teachers who had received their education in Egypt, Turkey, and Bukhara was insignificant when compared with the number of teachers who had been trained in Russia.[57] According to Bobrovnikov, while that Russian government ignored the Muslim schools, the Muslim intelligentsia transformed them on the basis of the "pan-Turkic idea" while also having broader pan-Islamic goals in mind.

Bobrovnikov was sympathetic neither to this program nor to the united Muslim political movement. However, in contrast to other Russian government observers, he emphasized the significance of specifically Russian circumstances in understanding the Muslim modernist school movement; he did not wish to blame its origins on foreign influences. He pointed out that the new-method movement itself met the vital needs of the Muslim population, but needed to be protected from tendencies harmful to the state and Muslims themselves. Bobrovnikov also warned against the practice of Russian MVD regional administrators, who relied on Muslim informers for information about new-method proponents without understanding the role that their accusations played in local politics. He additionally called for better control over Muslim schools by Russian government inspectors skilled in Eastern languages.[58] Bobrovnikov's message fell on deaf ears. The 1910 commission chaired by Kharuzin, in which Bobrovnikov also participated, considered pan-Islamism, pan-Turkism, and the new-method movement in Russia to be elements of a single phenomenon that was dangerous to the Russian state.

When the Ministry of Internal Affairs became intensively preoccupied with "studying" pan-Islamism in 1910, the Department of Police also began actively searching for places where the movement might be spreading and gaining popular support. In December 1910, the ministry sent a circular to the heads of regional police, urging that the activity of pan-Islamists in Russia be uncovered, and calling for surveillance of the moods of the Muslim population through a secret-service network. In addition to the reports of the police agents, other important sources of the government's information about the goals and displays of pan-Islamism were the Russian and foreign Muslim press, as well as other printed materials that appealed to Muslim solidarity. A year or so later, on the basis of these collected materials, the Department of Police prepared its own report on the history and character of the pan-Islamic movement. According to the department, the main goal of the movement was the political unification of the Muslim world under the aegis of Turkey. The department believed that this idea was being spread by Young Turks and progressive Muslims in Russia through the press and schools.[59]

For the police and hence the Ministry of Internal Affairs, pan-Islamism thus served to explain the actions and ultimate goals of the Russian Muslim progressive movement. This link also provided grounds for characterizing the movement as "Tatar Turkish separatism." This logic was soon applied to many of the ministry's investigative cases against Muslims who were associated with the progressive movement. It also gave reason for the repression of progressive Muslim institutions: new-method schools, publishing houses, bookshops, and public organizations. Fearing the subversive influence of pan-Islamic ideas in Russia, the authorities also tried to limit Russian Muslims' contacts with their foreign coreligionists.

At the same time, the intensified repression made some officials worry that the progressive movement would simply be pushed underground, making it increasingly difficult for the government to obtain reliable information on the moods of the Muslim population and the "true" aspirations of the Muslim intelligentsia. In 1912, for example, an expert on Muslim affairs at the Ministry of Internal Affairs, P. V. Antaki, was concerned enough about this difficulty to criticize the government's decision to close the prayer assembly of the Muslim intelligentsia in St. Petersburg:

> I often visit the Muslim prayer assembly at Demidov Lane, and quite often talk to members of the intelligentsia who provide me with not just interesting information but words of great value, because these conversations keep me informed about Muslim politics and acquaint me with the life of Tatars. It is especially valuable if one considers that Muslim life is rather closed, and it is almost impossible to penetrate into the Tatar environment since they are rather suspicious and mistrustful of the authorities.[60]

Despite this difference of opinion about how best to keep informed, the Department of Police relied on Muslim informers. As might be expected, some of these informants were opportunists. One such was M. Bek Hajetlashe. According to MVD sources, Hajetlashe was from a family of a Circassian noble from Kuban oblast who had immigrated to Turkey.[61] In 1909, he offered to assist the Department of Police in combating pan-Islamism by means of a journal. Since 1908, Hajetlashe had published *Musulmanin* with the support of Turkish Circassians from Kuban oblast. According to Hajetlashe himself, after the revolution in Turkey, the journal lost financial support because of his ideological disagreement with the "circle of Circassians." He hoped to continue publishing his periodical in Paris with the support of the Russian government; to find collaborators, he undertook a trip through the Russian Muslim regions. As a result of his travels, in 1910 he sent the MVD his "Trip Notes" (*Putevye zametki*), in which he reported about the influence of the Young Turks' propaganda in Russia, the agitation of the Muslim intelligentsia, and the threat of political pan-Islamism.[62] In 1911, in a letter to S. M. Syromiatnikov, a journalist and the editor of the official newspaper *Rossiia*, Hajetlashe also confirmed that his goal was to struggle against Muslim modern intelligentsia and the Young Turks.[63] Hajetlashe's declared goal matched that of the Department of Police, who noted the "sincere disposition of Hajetlashe to Russia."[64]

The idea of a special pro-government Muslim periodical such as Hajetlashe's attracted the attention of senior tsarist officials, including Stolypin and Kharuzin. The journal received MVD funding in 1910–1911 and also was exempted from a custom tax.[65] The editors, who declared the journal to be a nonparty organ, published articles in a Russian patriotic tone that lacked any vividly expressed political orientation. Within the MVD, there was significant support for the journal; the main criticisms were about its "academic" character, its primary focus on Caucasian Muslims, and on the fact it was not widely read in Russia.[66] The Orthodox missionaries, however, discovered dangerous pan-Islamist ideas in some of its articles. Liberal Muslims did not trust Hajetlashe, rightly suspecting him of collaborating with the government. After Stolypin's assassination in 1911, *Musulmanin* stopped receiving government financial support and ceased to exist.

Nonetheless, Hajetlashe continued to collaborate with the MVD. In 1911–1912, with its support, he published the weekly newspaper *V mire musul'manstva* in St. Petersburg. Once again, his publication was declared to be a nonparty organ devoted to the interests of Russian Muslims. The MVD hoped this newspaper would not fall into the hands of the Muslim Duma faction, but would rather help create a new faction.[67] Under the MVD's guidance, *V mire musul'manstva* criticized the Muslim deputies of the Third Duma, accusing them of "inactivity," and denounced individual deputies.[68]

These articles, as well as the suspicion that Hajetlashe was collaborating with the government, led to a conflict between the newspaper's editors and some members of the Muslim Duma faction, who called on the electorate not to trust the newspaper.[69] In 1911, the liberal newspaper *Rech* published a letter to the editor that identified Hajetlashe as a provocateur.[70] The article analyzed the opposite ways in which Hajetlashe addressed pan-Islamism in writings submitted to different journals. Whereas in one article, published in 1908 in *Ofitserskaia zhizn,* he condemned pan-Islamism as a "menacing movement" and a threat to Europe, in another version of the same article, published in 1911, he praised the cultural-enlightening movement among Muslims and avoided the very word *pan-Islamism.* To demonstrate Hajetlashe's "duplicity" and "traitorous policy," the authors presented a detailed analysis of both variants of the text and also published a letter that Hajetlashe had sent in 1909 to a member of the Duma Muslim faction, in which he assigned to himself the role of leader of the Muslim movement for unification.[71] These public revelations, however, neither stopped Hajetlashe, who continued to play his provocative role, nor discouraged the government from relying on his assistance in understanding and solving the Muslim Question.

In December 1913, Hajetlashe sent the MVD another report about the anti-Russian mood of Muslims and the pan-Islamic propaganda that he had uncovered during his trip through the Volga region. Again, he pointed to pan-Islamism as the goal of "progressive" Muslims. To fight this trend, he proposed to renew the publication of *Musul'manin,* arguing to tsarist officials that Russia needed a periodical that would combat anti-Russian propaganda in the European press. The idea of a journal was attractive to S. P. Beletskii, the director of the Police Department; however, the bureaucratic correspondence between that department and the new director of the Department for Religious Affairs of Foreign Confessions on this matter continued for several years without further action. Thereafter and throughout World War I, Hajetlashe continued to inform the government about what he presented as the "mysterious world" of Russian Muslims, and, at least in his mind, to help the government in solving the Muslim Question.[72]

The "Hajetlashe affair" revealed new dimensions of the Muslim Question. In hindsight, it is clear that Hajetlashe neither helped the government to understand pan-Islamism nor to resolve the Muslim Question. Instead, his provocative role and his collaboration with the authorities intensified anti-Muslim fears among some Orthodox readers of his journal and helped to further discredit the government in the eyes of the Russian Muslim intelligentsia. The government's enthusiasm in searching for pan-Islamism provoked criticism from Muslim liberals, who argued that the "Muslim awakening" and their "aspiration for civilization" had no relation to pan-Islamism.[73] Considering pan-Islamism to be a "hostile invention of the right," they accused the government of believing in "fantasies" and of "artificially" creating the Muslim Question.[74] A member of the Muslim faction, S. Maksudov, was especially vocal on this matter. In his Duma speech, he said: "Our nationalists . . . earn prestige among a certain public by raising the Polish and the Jewish questions. But these two questions seem to be a little played out, and therefore there is a need to create some sort of a new alien question. Now they are with all energy trying to create the Muslim Question in Russia."[75] Simultaneously, Orthodox missionaries and the right-wing nationalistic press criticized the government for underestimating the dangers of the pan-Islamic movement. The right-wing *Russkoe znamia,* whose articles often led to government investigations, reported about the travels of the leaders of the Muslim "revolutionary" congresses, Gasprinskii, and the deputy of the first Duma, S-G. S-Kh. Dzhanturin, for consultations with foreign leaders of the "revolutionary Muslim movement." Considering pan-Islamism to be especially dangerous to the state, the newspaper asked, "Against whom is this unification directed?"[76]

Meanwhile, the Ministry of Internal Affairs continued its efforts to collect information on Muslim activities abroad. It dispatched its expert on Muslim affairs, Antaki, to Istanbul and Cairo to collect information on confessional schools, with a study of pan-Islamism constituting the secret part of Antaki's program. P. V. Antaki had graduated from the Lazarev Institute of Oriental Languages in Moscow and from 1909 had been employed by the Department for Religious Affairs of Foreign Confessions.[77] The government was particularly interested in his views of foreign Muslims' image of Russia, the moods of Russian Muslims residing in Turkey and Egypt, and the role of pan-Islamic propaganda among Russian hajjis.[78]

Antaki's resulting report noted that the goal of preserving the disintegrating Ottoman empire in the face of increased European pressure lay at the core of political pan-Islamism, at least as it was organized and implemented by Abdülhamid. At the same time, he pointed to the ambivalent attitude of the former sultan and the Young Turk government to the different groups of pan-Islamists. Like the observers in Russia, he viewed pan-Turkism in Russia as closely related to the pan-Islamic program, and he emphasized the role of Russian Muslim émigrés in what he called "Constantinople's pan-Islamism" and their critical attitude toward Russia. "Why do Muslims of Turkey and Egypt hate Russia?" asked Antaki, "if Muslims in Russia have a better life than the Muslim subjects of England, France, Muslim immigrants in Turkey, and even the native population of the Russian empire?" Antaki, as had previous critics, blamed Tatar anti-Russian propaganda.[79] He saw pan-Islamism and especially anti-Russian propaganda as factors that had a much greater destabilizing effect on Russian–Muslim relations than in other European empires with Muslim dominions, in large part because of the continental character of the Russian empire and the close relationship between Russian and Turkish Muslims.[80] Without making it explicit, Antaki's report pointed to the possibility that the Ottoman empire might mobilize Muslim Turkic subjects against the tsar, much as Russia had mobilized Christian and Slavic people against Ottomans, with potentially grave consequences. As tensions in the Balkans continued to intensify, and especially after the outbreak of war in the region in 1912, this problem became especially acute. In this context, Antaki's contention that the government needed to exercise stronger control over channels of subversive propaganda seemed to many within the government to be the only solution.

During the Balkan crisis of 1912–1913, fears of the mobilizing power of pan-Islamism and concerns about Muslims' loyalty were raised by the right-wing Russian press. *Novoe vremia* reported about the "unrest" (*volneniia*) among Caucasian Muslims instigated by pan-Islamic propaganda, while *Russkoe znamia* feared that pan-Islamic propaganda would strengthen the aspiration for separatism among

Russian Muslims.[81] While concerned about the subversive influence of Turkish propaganda, the tsarist authorities also feared that the rising pan-Slavic and anti-Turkish sentiments of the Russian public could provoke pan-Islamic sentiments among Russian Muslims. For example, in 1912 the head of police in Baku reported to the Department of Police that the antagonistic mood of the Muslim population toward Russia was to a certain extent a reaction to the "unrestrained" Russian press coverage of Balkan politics from the openly pro-Slavic position.[82] Yet, except for fundraising campaigns to support their coreligionists, the police organs did not find other serious evidence of anti-Russian activities among the empire's Muslims.

The problems of pan-Islamism and pan-Turkism in Russia, however, were not simple, and some educated Russians within and outside the government raised questions about how these phenomena might best be understood and evaluated. First, some argued that an interpretation of the intentions of progressive Muslims through the lens of political pan-Islamism might be a far too simplified understanding, both of the goals of the progressive movement in Russia and of pan-Islamism in general. Contributors to *Mir islama,* for example, pointed to the complexity of the purposes and consequences of the pan-ideologies that united various contradictory currents of Muslim thought. Even Antaki acknowledged the different goals pursued by pan-Islamists.

No less important was the question concerning the degree of influence the pan-ideologies had on the empire's Muslim population. For MVD officials, the answer to this question had been connected to their estimation of the influence of the Muslim political organization Ittifak and the Muslim Duma faction, both of which they labeled as pan-Islamist. Although after 1907 some of the party's leaders had emigrated, both the party and the faction remained under the government's suspicion. Despite its best efforts, the MVD, however, could find no confirmation of rumors that periodically appeared about active pan-Islamic antigovernment activity of that faction. In 1909, the head of police in Nizhnii Novgorod reported to the MVD about a supposedly secret meeting on the present condition of Muslims in the empire, at which plans were to be made to establish connections with the pan-Islamic movement. The meeting did take place, but according to information provided by the police officials themselves, it was devoted to the Muslim faction's report about its activity and plans to organize a permanently acting bureau to support the faction. The relatively innocuous topics did not, however, prevent the local police from conducting a search of two deputies—an action that provoked criticism by both the Muslim liberal press and the MVD.[83] Nor were searches for a supposed "Muslim bank" any more fruitful.[84]

But despite this anti-Muslim fervor, some officials within the Ministry of Internal Affairs came to recognize the limited appeal of both the Muslim progressive movement and of pan-Islamism to the broader Russian Muslim population. When in 1907 the director of the Department for Religious Affairs of Foreign Confessions sent out a circular addressed to the governors of provinces with Muslim populations, asking them to report on the activities of the "Union of Muslims" and evaluate its popularity among the Muslim population, the majority of the governors claimed that its influence was insignificant. Six years later, after scores of government investigations and repressions, the semiofficial journal *Mir islama* similarly concluded that Russian Muslims were indifferent toward the party as well as to the Duma faction.[85] The Ministry of Internal Affairs apparently concluded that the "Union of Muslims" and the Muslim faction did not receive significant support from the population. The ministry's officials explained, first, that the Muslim masses were "unprepared" to respond to the union's ideas, and second, that there was little chance for political unification of Muslims on the basis of religion.[86] Although this conclusion did not mean that progressive Muslims fell out of government suspicion, it suggested that pan-Islamism was no longer at the center of the Muslim Question by 1913.

Some Russian officials downplayed the risk of pan-Islamism on the theory that it would not be possible for different Islamic groups to overcome their religious tensions. In January 1910, a recent conflict between Shi'a and Sunni groups in Bukhara provided evidence for a report from the acting head of the chancellery of the Turkestan governor-generalship, who noted that pan-Islamic ideas had little influence in preventing discord between Shi'a and Sunni Muslims.[87] That same year, the head of police in Tiflis concluded that it would be difficult to find Caucasian Shi'a Muslims receptive to pan-Islamic ideas.[88] A commentator in *Mir islama* in 1913 notably wrote that political pan-Islamism (except in North Africa) was a utopian project.[89]

Another caveat about the limited power of pan-Islamism and pan-Turkism came from Bobrovnikov. In an article in 1913 on Muslim education in Central Asia, he repeated the view he had expressed earlier: that the new-method movement was a Russian, not a foreign, creation. He openly criticized the government for not understanding the nature of the progressive Muslim movement in Russia. Moreover, he wrote that the movement itself had been transformed during the preceding decade. In his opinion, Muslim public figures no longer viewed schools as a political tool and had lost the anti-Russian ardor that had been characteristic of the revolutionary era. Bobrovnikov also pointed out that the idea of pan-Turkism, and specifically Gasprinskii's attempts to create a common language on the basis of literary Ottoman Turkish (which Bobrovnikov considered to be artificial), had given way to the free development of literature and education in various Turkic dialects—a phenomenon Bobrovnikov considered to be both healthy and vitally important.[90]

As a whole, however, these observations did little to change the nature of government anxieties toward the progressive Muslim elite, whose oppositional political activities now defined the essence of the Muslim Question. Yet despite these existing fears, the Russian government sought to maintain a public view of the majority of Russian Muslims as loyal subjects. The official government newspaper *Rossiia* published articles on pan-Islamism by A. Allaev, who simultaneously recognized the wide reach of the ideals of pan-Islamism and praised Russian Muslims' devotion to the authorities. Only the Muslim intelligentsia, he claimed, "did not understand in whose favor they acted." The *S. Peterburgskie vedomosti*, referring to the opinion of S. Gabiev, the editor of the *Musul'manskaia gazeta*, reported that the declaration of Holy War by Turkey during the Balkan crisis had no effect among Russian Muslims. Gabiev, however, contested this statement by responding that Russian Muslims undoubtedly sympathized with the Turks, which nevertheless did not in any way change their faithful feelings toward Russia.[91] Nevertheless, for some elements of Russian society and government, the supposed dual loyalties of Muslims remained a problem. The phantom of pan-Islamism had not lost its hold on Russians. The thinking of Russian officials on this issue could be characterized by the following conclusion, repeated in many government documents: "The movement has not been observed, but the danger is always there."

Stasis, Frustration, and the Perennial Muslim Question

In 1913, the Ministry of Internal Affairs began assembling members for yet another special interministerial commission on the Muslim Question. While the explicit topic of this commission was to consider the organization of the state administration of Muslim religious affairs in the empire, the actual agenda was much broader and included a reevaluation of the current state of the Muslim Question as redefined in the aftermath of the revolution.[92] As the minister of the interior, N. A. Maklakov, explained to the orientalist A. E. Schmidt in his invitation for Schmidt to participate in the commission, its main task was to provide a "lively exchange of opinions about the contemporary state of Russian Muslims from the standpoint of their religious life and social movements and about the necessary government measures, which would secure state interests but also satisfy the fair [spravedlivye] needs of the Muslim population."[93] In preparation for the commission's meetings, the MVD sent out a circular to the governors, requesting that they provide information on the Muslim Question while also advising them to avoid publicizing this endeavor.[94]

I. M. Zolotarev, the deputy minister of internal affairs, was appointed to be the chair of the future commission. In comparison to the 1910 commission, the composition of the participants in 1914 had changed. Those invited to participate included representatives of the Holy Synod; delegates from the Ministries of Public Education, Internal Affairs, and War; representatives of the administration and the governors of the different regions of the empire inhabited by Muslims; several orientalists, including N. K. Shvedov, the chair of the Imperial Society for Oriental studies; D. M. Pozdneev, the editor of *Mir islama;* and A. E. Schmidt, the head of the MVD's courses on Islam and a professor at St. Petersburg University.[95] The Orenburg mufti M. M. Sultanov, the acting Tauride mufti A. D. Karashaiskii, and M.-S. A. Baiazitov, imam from St. Petersburg, were also invited, although only to those sessions that addressed specific issues related to Muslim clergy's staffing and salaries.[96] Discussion of the Muslim Question took place without the participation of the Muslim clergy. The Kazan Orthodox missionaries were not invited.

Muslim liberals welcomed the convening of this special commission, viewing reform of the administration of Muslim religious affairs as their "national matter."[97] This issue had frequently been raised by the Muslim Duma deputies, who demanded the creation of new ecclesiastical assemblies, state financial support for the Muslim clergy, and parity with regard to the rights of Orthodox clergy. At the same time, S. Maksudov, a member of the Muslim faction, feared that the Muslims who had officially been invited to participate would not be able to defend their interests because of what he called their "oriental shyness" or because they did not know Russian well enough.[98] The liberal Tatar newspaper *Vakyt* wrote that it was the Muslim Duma faction who represented the Muslim population of the empire, and who had to explain the needs of the nation to the government.[99] The liberal *Russkie Vedomosti* and *Utro Rossii* also criticized the government for not collaborating with the Muslim intelligentsia, instead planning what they called a "bureaucratic commission."[100]

The commission began its work in the spring of 1914, just months before the outbreak of war. The first session was devoted to discussion of the current state of the Muslim Question in different regions of the empire. This time, when addressing this issue the commission sought to evaluate the moods of the entire empire's Muslim population; major trends among the Muslim clergy and intelligentsia; relations between conservative and progressive Muslim elements; the activity of Muslims in institutions of local self-government (*zemstvos* and city governments); the Muslims' level of organization; their attitudes toward the government and Russian culture; the status of Islam in confessionally and ethnically diverse regions; interethnic relations within Muslim communities and specifically the role of Tatars; Islamicization of animists and baptized non-Russians; and, finally, pan-Islamism and pan-Turkism.[101]

In discussing the mood of the Muslim population in various parts of the empire, the commission's participants noted that the pan-Islamic and pan-Turkic movements, which the government had feared in 1907–1910, had not, in fact, enjoyed substantial success among Russia's Muslims. In the commission's opinion, individual manifestations of religious solidarity in response to the events in the Balkans, as well as the political activity of the Muslim minority during the revolution of 1905, had not altered the basic loyalty of the mass of the Muslim population. This loyalty, which they thought had also been demonstrated during the recent celebration of the tri-centennial of the Romanov dynasty, served as evidence that allowed MVD officials to question the claims of the Muslim intelligentsia about the oppression of the Muslim masses by the government.[102]

Moreover, commission members found the very idea of a religion-based political unification of Muslims within the Russian Empire to be unrealistic.[103] Far more real and more dangerous for the commission was what they referred to as "pan-Tatarism." By this, they meant the liberal stance in the political orientation of the religious–national movement of Kazan Tatars, who also seemed to aspire to subordinate other Muslim peoples to their cultural, political, and economic influence. At the time of the commission's discussion, this problem had appeared concretely only in the Volga–Ural region. For that reason, as in 1910, members of the 1914 commission understood the Muslim Question to be a Tatar Muslim Question—a problem that for the time being was relevant only to a single region of the empire.

As had the previous commission, the 1914 commission also connected the Muslim Question to the problem of modernization in the empire, but in a more explicit way. The commission emphasized that although Islam separated Muslims from the rest of the empire's population, Muslims in Russia did not constitute a single group united by the consciousness of common interests. The participants came to the conclusion that various Muslim groups' political loyalty was determined by their so-called distance from "nature" (in other words, it was tied to the level of civilization). The majority of the Muslim population, characterized by commission members as "children of nature," thus appeared to be especially obedient to the law and the government, and showed strong devotion to the monarch. By contrast, Kazan and Crimean Tatars, who were engaged in commercial and industrial activities, had achieved a high level of material well-being, adopted the basics of European culture, and thus were committed to political radicalism and nationalism.[104]

Given this thinking, the Muslim Question was once again characterized as a struggle against "Tatar domination." Fearing the "denationalization" of other non-Russian peoples, and their susceptibility to liberal influences, the commission's members at the same time worried about the effect of strengthening non-Russian national consciousness.[105] The government faced a dilemma: How should less populous nationalities be protected from Tatar influence without simultaneously encouraging their ethnic nationalism? This question, in turn, complicated the issue of state–Islam relations. The commission's members inevitably drew comparisons to the government's unsuccessful attempts to stop Polonization in the northwestern region by nationalizing Catholicism.[106] Yet the state's experiences in combating Polish influence did not diminish the commission's hope of stopping Tatarization.[107] Viewing Islam and its institutions, such as the Muslim ecclesiastical administration, confessional schools, as well as the press, as the main channels of Tatar influence, the commission came to the conclusion that to prevent Tatarization the government had to weaken Islam and its institutions.

The original intent of the commission was to discuss the empire's organization of the Muslim religious administration. S. G. Rybakov (1867–1922), an official of the MDV, prepared a report for the commission on the administration of Muslim religious affairs. Rybakov had graduated from St. Petersburg University and had served in the Turgai and Baikal regions. On a commission from the Geographical Society, he traveled to Siberia and Central Asia to collect ethnographic materials about Russian Muslims. He published works on Muslims folklore and on Islam and Orthodoxy in Russia. He was a graduate of the MVD's courses on Islam, and since 1913 had been employed by the Department for Religious Affairs of Foreign Confessions, for which he prepared several analytical reports on Islam in Russia.[108]

Rybakov reiterated views familiar to Il'minskii's followers a generation earlier: by creating the Muslim clergy, he claimed, the government contributed to the emergence of Tatar Muslim propaganda in the Volga–Ural region and Siberia, and to the strengthening of Islam in Russia in general. In his opinion, the system of muftiates served Muslim rather than state interests. He felt that the system of Muslim–state relations established in other regions of the empire, such as Turkestan, the Steppe region, and the Caucasus, conformed more closely with state interests. In these areas, no official Muslim hierarchy had been created, the clergy was not recognized as an estate, and religious life was not regulated by law. Rybakov thus suggested that the existing diverse system of state–Muslim relations be unified to reflect the principle of complete state noninterference into the religious affairs of Muslims.[109]

Although the plans for unifying the system of administering Muslim spiritual affairs had been discussed within the Ministry of Internal Affairs for more than half a century, disagreements about the course of state policies toward Islam and fear of Muslims' resentment continuously impeded efforts at radical governmental reform. Like the previous reformers, the commission's members were torn between the state's commitment to religious tolerance and the fear of religion becoming a tool of political propaganda. It was this fear that explained why the commission had opposed the suggestions of both the 1905 and 1910 government commissions to "decentralize" the Orenburg Ecclesiastical Assembly by creating national muftiates, as well as the demands of Muslim liberals to create a unified system of religious administration for all regions in the empire. Rybakov's proposal appealed to the 1914 commission, but its participants were seized by the traditional concerns about the potential consequences of the government's radical reformism. As a result, the commission only recommended that the existing administrations be weakened by decreasing the scope of matters in their jurisdiction, by strengthening government control, and by not creating new organs in Turkestan, the Steppe region, and the Caucasus.[110] Ultimately, then, the commission proposed no changes to the existing system of administration of Muslim religious affairs in the empire.

The commission's understanding of the Muslim Question also affected the way it addressed another old question pertaining to the Russian language requirement for the Muslim clergy. If, in the second half of the nineteenth century, when this requirement was introduced, the government had viewed knowledge of Russian as a means of "enlightenment" and "rapprochement" of the supposedly ignorant Muslim clergy with Russia, now the authorities feared that the Russian language could become a channel for revolutionary ideas.[111] While also admitting the low level of Russian-language knowledge among the Muslim clergy, the commission recommended that mullahs should be required to only speak Russian, and in certain cases the language requirement should be abolished completely.[112]

Although the commission considered Muslim clergy overall to be politically loyal to the regime, many participants were fearful of the mobilization of this part of the Muslim population, even if they were to be mobilized in support of the government.[113] This position was articulated during discussion of a petition from a group of Muslims who proposed to establish the All-Russian Muslim Union, *Pravyi put'*, with the goal of "uniting loyal Muslims to counteract leftist movements among the

Muslim population." The union's program resembled those of Russian monarchist organizations. Yet the commission decided that, despite its conservative orientation, the union would serve as a "tool for uniting Muslims regardless of their nationality," which, in turn, would strengthen Muslim separatism. The commission also feared that politically "unreliable" elements might penetrate the union while its legalization by the government would create a precedent for other nationalities (Jews in particular) to raise their own claims.[114]

On the constantly contentious School Question, the commission proposed nothing new, but supported the decisions of the 1910 commission chaired by Kharuzin on separation of Muslim secular and confessional education. Nor did the committee formulate any firm guidelines on how the government might best conduct studies of the Muslim population or monitor it. Indeed, the committee issued no new conclusive opinions on any aspect of the Muslim Question. Although the participants had decided to call similar commissions at least once every two years, the 1914 commission was the last attempt by the tsarist government to review state policies toward Islam and find solutions to the Muslim Question within a special government institution.

While the government commissions dithered, Muslim leaders continued to press their case for religious tolerance and freedom. In June 1914, the Muslim Duma faction received official permission to organize the Fourth Muslim Congress, which took place in St. Petersburg. About forty deputies came to the congress to discuss the reform of Muslim religious institutions. The head of the Muslim faction for the Fourth Duma, K.-M. Tevkelev, was the official chair of the congress, while A. M. Topchibashev actually carried out this function. The deputies addressed the problems of administration of Muslim religious affairs, Muslim confessional schools, and other religion-related issues. They petitioned the MVD for permission to prolong the congress for two more days, but received a denial.[115]

In his concluding speech, Topchibashev summed up the government's historical attempts to solve the issues related to Islam in Russia. Among the concrete questions raised by the 1905 program of the Committee of Ministers and discussed in government special commissions, only one issue had been put into law: the exemption of Muslim clergy from military service. Topchibashev condemned the government for not fulfilling the tsar's will with regard to religious tolerance, but also for "consciously ignoring Muslims and their interests." He criticized government officials for not relying on Muslims, by whom he primarily meant the Muslim intelligentsia, when addressing issues related to Islam. He said: "They talk about us, judge us, want to organize our lives, but all without listening to us, or our opinions and our wishes about our matters."[116] He claimed that both the government and the Russian public did not know and did not want to know about Russian Muslims and their needs, noting that the June 1914 congress itself was closed to the Russian press and the Russian public. Topchibashev pointed out that even high-ranking tsarist officials were unaware of the legal constraints put on Muslim subjects and believed that Muslims in Russia enjoyed the benefits of religious tolerance. He also claimed that Muslims in Russia could not fully enjoy the benefits of religious tolerance granted them, not simply because of the still-existing legal constraints, but more importantly because Muslims did not have the tools to exercise their rights.

By this Toptchibashev meant, first of all, the absence of modern Muslim clergy. He claimed that the Muslim clergy remained "ignorant," "backward," and materially deprived, and that the government created obstacles for Muslims' attempts to solve these problems. "But why did the Russians do this?" asked Topchibashev. He answered: "Because they don't trust Muslims and want to assimilate them." Finally, as Gasprinskii and others had been claiming since the end of the nineteenth century, Topchibashev stated: "The hope that Russia might assimilate twenty million Muslims is a chimera, an unrealizable dream." This statement evoked "prolonged applause" among the participants in the congress. He further explained that there was no need to assimilate Muslims, because they were loyal citizens. He condemned what he termed the Russian "confessional view of Muslims, not as citizens and children of the common Fatherland, but just as Muslims, followers of Islam, and stepchildren of the country."[117]

* * *

The government's program of action on the Muslim Question as outlined by the 1910 special commission did not eliminate either the problem itself or its contentious nature. By defining the Muslim Question as a result of anti-state political activity of the Muslim progressive intelligentsia, officials of the Ministry of Internal Affairs formulated their primary goal as one of struggle with the progressive movement and of monitoring the moods of the Muslim population, actions in which the work of the police was instrumental. The danger of pan-Islamist sentiments for imperial governance, which many government officials associated with the aspirations of the progressive movement of Russian Muslims, made this solution seem even more urgent.

Thus, the MVD's own program of studies of the Muslim Question became dominated by the goal of intelligence gathering. The MVD's perspective on the Muslim Question brought government officials into conflict with some prominent academic experts on Islam and discredited government publishing and educational initiatives related to Islam in the eyes of Muslim progressive intelligentsia and the broader Russian liberal public. This distrust grew as the government repressed institutions established by progressive Muslims and continued to rely on dubious informers in its efforts to solve the Muslim Question. While not sharing the Orthodox clerics' view of Islam as a hostile religion, the Ministry of Internal Affairs supported some missionaries' projects that were intended to struggle with Islam and in principle recognized the state's responsibility for protecting the Orthodox church, as the deliberations of the special government commissions demonstrated. Yet the decisions on these issues remained vague, and the problem of strengthening Orthodoxy through reform was not fully addressed.

The imperial government thus found itself on the eve of the war in a state of paralysis concerning its policies toward its Muslim subjects. The Muslim Question, in the eyes of government officials, remained confined to the problem of progressive Tatars and their perceived efforts to influence and unify Russia's Muslims. Neither governance through Muslim institutions nor cultural and political integration seemed viable, and neither course was clearly chosen. Surveillance and repression were the only options. Unsuccessful attempts at reform, and the regime's efforts to collaborate with Orthodox missionaries, outraged members of the Muslim liberal intelligentsia, who saw rather bitterly that the Muslim Question (as it was understood by government and church figures) was an artificial creation. As the result, the demands of the Muslim intelligentsia quickly outgrew the government's earlier concessions and promises. The war sharpened these lines of conflict.

9 World War I

The outbreak of war in July 1914 imposed new pressures on the Russian empire. Military defeats intensified imperial authorities' old misgivings about non-Russians' "separatism." All of the belligerent states raised the issues of nationality and religion to destabilize the enemy, thus making questions about the loyalty and patriotism of Russia's diverse subjects acute. This was especially the case for those residing in border areas or who had become prisoners of "propaganda camps" in Germany and Austria-Hungary.

State authorities' concerns about the loyalty of Muslim subjects increased when Turkey entered the war. As during the Crimean War, tsarist officials found themselves wondering if Muslims would support the imperial cause or side with the enemy. This time, however, Russia also had to deal with the legacy of the unresolved Muslim Question. In 1914, Russia entered the war while having within its borders a much larger Muslim population than sixty years earlier. Significant portions of Muslims resided in the recently conquered region of Turkestan and were not fully integrated into the empire's social and political institutions. At the same time, as we have seen, during those sixty years Russia had witnessed significant social and political transformations that affected Muslims living in the empire's European provinces. Some were soldiers of the imperial army defending Russia against Germany and its allies. Muslim intelligentsia responded to the state's appeal for support of the war effort and used it as an opportunity to assure their own role in the imperial politics while they pressed the government to accept their vision of Muslims' place in a modernizing imperial society.

Wartime demands for more manpower forced the government to extend the obligation for military service to the Muslims of Central Asia who had earlier been exempt. The decree on the military draft, issued on 25 June 1916, sparked a bloody revolt in Central Asia that was directed primarily against the imperial administration, but also included brutal attacks on local Slavic settlers. The revolt discredited the tsarist regime's policies and highlighted the contested nature of the Muslim Question. But now its flipside, the Russian Question, also became a highly pressing issue.

What Are the "True Moods" of Russian Muslims?

The spread of oppositional political movements and nationalist ideas among Russian Muslims in the prewar period, along with Muslims' religious ties with Turkey, provided the primary basis for the increased anxiety felt by the tsarist government concerning Muslims in the world military conflict, especially when Turkey was inclining toward an alliance with Germany. For the government, the most pressing question was whether Muslim subjects would remain loyal to the Russian state and the monarch, or whether they would respond to nationalist and pan-Islamic propaganda. At the beginning of the war, on 28 August 1914, the Department for Religious Affairs of Foreign Confessions requested information from local governors of the Muslim regions about the "moods of the Muslim population."[1] The department was interested not only in Muslims' behavior but also in their feelings toward the state and Russia's position in the war. The department inquired about how

> the Muslim population . . . and the Muslim clergy met the news about the war, whether there were any undesirable incidents during the mobilization, whether and in what form Muslims expressed their patriotic feelings, whether or not they took care of the families of their coreligionists conscripted into the army, provided medical and other help to the wounded soldiers, and to what degree the local mullahs promoted and strengthened the understanding by the population of the significance of the current events and of the duties of all loyal subjects of the empire despite their religion and nationality.[2]

Official reports from the regions in response to this inquiry generally emphasized the high degree of loyalty among Russian Muslims and noted an increase in their patriotism. The telegrams of Muslim spiritual leaders to the tsar, patriotic demonstrations, ceremonial prayers for the health of the emperor and his family and the victory of the Russian forces, and charity toward sick and wounded soldiers and the families of conscripts served as evidence for this conclusion. The Tauride governor reported that "the high degree of the patriotic mood" of Crimean Tatars during the current war significantly contrasted with the Tatars' behavior sixty years earlier during the Crimean War, when "just foreseeing the oncoming war, the Tatars emigrated to Turkey en masse, and those who stayed tried to escape military service by different means and followed the Turkish emissaries after being fanaticized by the local clergy."[3]

Although all of the governors underscored Muslim loyalty and patriotism, not all of them believed that Muslims would remain patriotic in the event that the Ottoman empire would join the war. Some governors also had doubts about the sincerity of the feelings of loyalty expressed by Muslims. The Turkestan governor-general was convinced that although he was unable to detect either signs of animosity toward Russia or open expressions of sympathy toward Turkey, the majority of Turkestan Muslims "had undoubtedly been interested in the future destiny of Turkey."[4] The observed preservation of the traditional lifestyle by the majority of the Turkestan Muslims and the lack of any noticeable aspiration toward Europeanization, as well as the existing ties with the Ottoman empire that were maintained through pilgrimage, made the governor-general doubt the "true" moods of local Muslims.[5]

Doubts about the sincerity of Muslim patriotism were also expressed by the Kazan governor, who had noticed that "since the beginning of the war, and in particular after the declaration of war with Turkey, the Muslim population of Kazan province became especially cautious in revealing feelings about political issues, and were trying to exercise greater precautions in relation to the Russians." The governor, consequently, stated that Muslims "certainly had sympathies for Turkey, which were stirred up by the Tatar press before the war" and that the patriotic feelings expressed by the Muslims in most cases are "not sincere and are fragile."[6]

The governor found proof for "secret sympathies to Turkey among the Muslim people" in the "unpatriotic expressions" of Muslims' letters from the front that had been detected by military censors and in rumors circulated among wounded Tatars. He also pointed to nationalistic sentiments and "unfriendly" views of Muslims about the war in the Tatar press, which revealed to him the "secret, latent political desires of the Muslim intelligentsia." The governor wrote that the Muslim population appeared to be calm and devoted to the tsar only "if one looked at their outward [vneshnii] deeds," while the Muslim intelligentsia and the clergy "dabbled in politics," had been compelled to constrain their nationalist propaganda out of fear of repression, and were trying to appear loyal in the eyes of the government. Nevertheless, he concluded his report on an optimistic note, trusting that the rise of patriotic sentiment among the Russian people in the provinces, together with the supervision of suspicious elements, could not only prevent undesirable disturbances among the Muslims, but also would impart to them the awareness of the "necessity to fulfill their civic duty and devotion to the fatherland."[7]

Based on the governors' reports, the Ministry of Internal Affairs evaluated the "mood" of the empire's Muslim subjects, both of the broad masses and of the intelligentsia, as reflecting loyalty. This, in the MVD's opinion, created unfavorable conditions for pan-Islamic and pan-Turkic propaganda.[8] Yet, such a conclusion did not eliminate tsarist officials' doubts about Muslim loyalty, which became particularly aggravated when Turkey joined the war against Russia and the holy war was announced in Istanbul.

Immediately after news reached St. Petersburg of the 18 October 1914 attack by the Turkish fleet on the coast of the Black Sea in Russia, N. A. Maklakov, the minister of internal affairs, sent a circular to the governors of the Muslim provinces to discuss preventive measures against possible pro-Turkish propaganda in the Russian empire. The circular specified that "although Russian Muslims on the whole are quite loyal, it is difficult to guarantee that the propaganda of the pan-Turkists and pan-Islamists would not meet a response from some individuals and groups, which, in turn, could stimulate unrest among Muslims in general."[9] A day later, after receiving additional information from the Russian diplomatic agency in Istanbul, the Ministry of Internal Affairs sent out a new circular informing the governors about a proclamation of jihad. The circular requested that the governors prevent the distribution of this proclamation within the empire. The MVD also suggested that the Tauride and Ufa governors ask the muftis to issue a proclamation that would explain the obligations of Muslims as loyal subjects from a religious standpoint, and also to warn them not to follow the disloyal agitators.[10] About a month later, on 12 November, Maklakov reported to S. D. Sazonov, the minister of foreign affairs, that up to that point he had not received any adverse information about the behavior of the Muslim population.[11]

The tsarist government faced its first actual challenge in the border provinces of Kars and Batumi, populated by Muslim Turks and Ajarians, when the Ottomans invaded this region in November and December 1914. Local tsarist authorities in the Caucasus accused the Muslims there of collaborating with the enemy. To clear the war theater of what they characterized as an "unreliable and dangerous element," the Russian authorities deported them deeper into the Russian provinces.[12] In April 1915, on the initiative of the viceroy of the Caucasus, the Council of Ministers discussed further punitive measures for the "Muslim traitors": the deprivation of Russian subjecthood and property.[13] Yet tsarist officials abstained from accusing the empire's entire Muslim population of treason. Maintaining the public image of Russian Muslims as loyal subjects was important not only for the empire's internal stability, but also for Russia's success in the propaganda war when the nationality question took on special international meaning.

Nationalist propaganda, with its destructive consequences for multinational dynastic empires, was soon taken up by all the belligerent parties.[14] Germany attempted to use centrifugal tendencies long in place in Russian society to weaken the Russian state.[15] Aspiring "to reach all of the elements hostile to the Russian state idea,"[16] German propagandists considered Russian Muslims to be a special object of their propaganda. Having declared itself a patron of Islam, Germany had, already before the war, monitored the moods of Russian Muslims, and propagandized the image of Russia as hostile to Muslims. To develop pro-German sympathies in Turkey, beginning in 1908, the German embassy had sponsored the publication of the newspaper *Osmanischer Lloyd* in Istanbul.[17] Its articles and reports devoted to Russia had a generally anti-Russian character. After the beginning of the war, German propaganda was further extended to Muslims fighting on the side of Russia and other countries of the Entente.

Prisoners of war held in the territory of Germany and Austria-Hungary also became both objects and instruments of German anti-Russian propaganda among Russian Muslims, and indeed among Asian and African colonial subjects of all the Entente countries. Special camps were created with the goal of spreading nationalist propaganda among Russian subjects of different nationalities, including Ukrainians, Poles, Finns, Georgians, and Muslims. The center for propaganda among the Muslim prisoners of war from Russia was a special camp near Berlin called *Weinberglager*, in Zossen.[18] Starting in June 1915, a systematic program of propaganda was instigated among these prisoners, carried out in close cooperation with so-called "native propagandists."[19] Among the native propagandists were former active participants in Muslim political movements in Russia during 1905–1907 who later immigrated to Turkey, including the journalists A. Ibragimov, A. Agaev, and Y. Akchurin.[20]

The rhetoric of liberation and pan-Islamic slogans constituted the essence of the propaganda material developed within Germany's Ministry of Foreign Affairs for Russian, British, and French Muslims. By calling the Muslims to jihad and to struggle for the "German–Islamic cause," German propagandists were counting on the mobilization of the Muslim people against Russia, France, and England, who were presented as the "enemies of Islam." They additionally hoped to establish Muslims' economic cooperation with Germany in the long run, fashioning the German nation as "the patron of Islam."[21] Initially, the chief task of German propaganda was to form voluntary divisions from prisoners of war, which were to participate on the side of Turkey. But already by the early months of 1916, and especially after the February revolution of 1917 in Russia, the emphasis in German propaganda changed. Military purposes were replaced with propaganda focusing on developing sympathy with Turkey and Germany.[22] The joyful reaction of Russian prisoners of war to the news of the February revolution, and Germany's hopes for a separate peace treaty with the new Russian government, led to the elimination of anti-Russian content from German propaganda.[23]

Some 1,100 people from the *Weinberglager*, or approximately 9 percent of the prisoners of war held there, responded to the call for jihad and were sent to the Ottoman empire.[24] The proposal to resettle other prisoners of war to Turkey was well received. By May 1916, the number of those who had expressed a desire to move to Turkey reached 9,000.[25] In their official reports, German propagandists expressed hopes for the success of their propaganda among the imprisoned Russian Muslims, especially Tatars, who supposedly had "friendly feelings toward the Turks and Germans" and were "intensively reading newspapers."[26]

However, the German reports also pointed to difficulties associated with propaganda among Muslim prisoners of war from Russia. The calls for jihad ran against Muslims' concerns about the fate of their families and their land allotments at home should they be seen as collaborating with Germany and Turkey against Russia.[27] The Germans could not easily rely on what they had assumed to be Muslim religious solidarity; instead, they had to find ways to foster such feelings.[28] To achieve this, the propagandists separated Muslims from non-Muslims. In the case of the Russian Muslims, this was not an easy task, owing to the absence, aside from a few exceptions, of separate Muslim divisions within the imperial army, and also because the prisoners of war consciously manipulated their confessional affiliations to achieve their own goals.[29] The directors of propaganda in the Muslim camp, H. von Cosack and Ibragimov, reported about the large "Russian party" that created obstacles for their propaganda.[30] Also, as had happened in other special national camps, German propaganda provoked conflicts among the propagandists and Muslims, as well as among the prisoners of war themselves.[31] Finally, the German hosts were not successful in providing especially good conditions for Muslim prisoners in the camps. Reports on the success of the propaganda often mentioned that the conditions created for the French and Russian prisoners of war were better than those for Muslims, which in turn prevented the success of the propaganda.[32]

Within the countries of the Entente, reactions to German propaganda among the Muslims had a double character. On the one hand, they prophesied the fiasco of the Germans' strategy of propagating jihad. On the other hand, the governments of the Entente countries not only kept a close watch on German propaganda, but also began massive counter-propaganda efforts.[33] Russian newspapers of differing political orientations, as well as the Russian Muslim newspapers, wrote about the unpopularity of the idea of jihad, as well as about the loyalty of Russian Muslims to the Fatherland and the throne.[34] Such statements in the press also served as propagandistic efforts against Germany, at least to some extent.

Even before the war began, the Russian government had taken German propaganda seriously. During the war, the Ministry of Internal Affairs' increased attention to this issue testified to its fears concerning "possible fluctuations and German sympathies among Russian Muslims."[35] In 1916, once again offering the MVD his services as a propagandist of pro-government ideas among Russian Muslims, M. Bek Hajetlashe warned the Russian government about new complications of the Muslim Question raised by German anti-Russian propaganda. As before, Hajetlashe's goal was to receive government subsidies for the publication of his journal, intended for Russian Muslims. In convincing the MVD of the urgent need for counter-propaganda, Hajetlashe did not provide concrete examples of the effect of German propaganda on Muslims, but rather forecast its success and the serious consequences it posed for the future. He warned the government that the "subtle [neulovimaia] work of the political reeducation of Russian Muslims was already underway. Still devoted to the throne and the Fatherland, the Muslim population, left to itself, could unwittingly be subjected to the fatal consequences of such propaganda."[36] Hajetlashe predicted that, after the defeat of Turkey, Afghanistan would play the leading role in the Muslim movement. Therefore, in the reports he now submitted to the MVD, Hajetlashe paid special attention to the Central Asians who lived close to the border with Afghanistan, rather than the Volga Tatars.[37]

The Ministry of War was also concerned about German–Turkish propaganda in Afghanistan. Russian intelligence, however, found no proof of the rumors about Afghanistan's preparations for entering the war against Russia under the leadership of Turkish–German agents. The attaché to the staff of the Turkestan military district concluded on the basis of intelligence information gathered in 1915–1916 that "if on the surface the Afghans are ready to help their coreligionists, in their souls they are against the agents." He added, "neutrality is beneficial for Afghanistan."[38]

Still, Hajetlashe continued to inform the government about the danger of war propaganda, and some of these warnings resonated with the concerns of some MVD officials about Muslim loyalty. The MVD's files on German propaganda pointed not only to the "facts" of German propaganda, but also to the "facts" demonstrating the "gravitation of Muslims toward Germany and its ideals." Among these "facts" were rumors circulating among Muslims about the conversion of the German emperor Wilhelm II to Islam and pro-German sympathies spread by Muslim prisoners of war returning from Austria and Germany, who told their compatriots about the good living conditions in Germany and opportunities for obtaining highly paid jobs and free education.[39]

Again, the Ministry of Internal Affairs was especially suspicious of the Muslim intelligentsia. In the view of tsarist officials, both the appeals by Muslim journalists for Muslim solidarity and the shades of pan-Islamism in German propaganda seemed to offer evidence for the assumption that both parties had a common goal. The MVD officials, for example, detected pro-German sympathies among Russian Muslims in a speech by G. Kh. Enikeev, a member of the state Duma, to the Muslim congress in Petrograd in June 1914. Enikeev spoke about the need to organize the Muslim "parish," referring to the success of Germans in this matter.[40] But perhaps the most incontestable evidence for the MVD's assertion of the Muslim intelligentsia's pro-German orientation was the fact that Russian Muslim political emigrants had cooperated with the German government, even though the liberal Muslim press in Russia criticized their claim to speak on behalf of Russian Muslims. Yet even while government officials considered the activity of Muslim emigrants from Russia to be aimed at "shaking the state," they were not inclined to see in it a reflection of the "moods" of all the Muslim subjects of Russia.[41]

In 1915, P. V. Antaki, the MVD's expert on Islam, reported that "the present war has demonstrated that Russian Muslim soldiers are devoted to their oath. Hundreds of thousands of Russian Muslims bravely defended their Fatherland-Russia."[42] The same year, V. O. Klemm, advisor to the Third Political Department of the Ministry of Foreign Affairs, reported to the Russian council in India that the stance of Russian Muslims was highly loyal, as demonstrated by their prayers for Russian success, their participation in military campaigns, and their military service awards for bravery.[43] The Russian government paid serious attention to German propaganda, but German pan-Islamic provocations did not change their general view of the Muslim population as loyal to the tsar. A report prepared in 1916 for the Ministry of Internal Affairs by S. G. Rybakov, for example, pointed to the "high level of patriotic enthusiasm among Russian Muslims," and warned against casting suspicion on the entire "Tatar nationality."[44] He concluded that the government might expect individual disturbances among the Muslim population, but not mass complications.

Imperial Patriotism and "Alien Separatism"

The idea that the empire's subjects should be united in a common struggle against the enemy received heightened value in official wartime rhetoric.[45] The government presented the war as an "all-Russian cause" and expected its subjects to support the Fatherland regardless of their nationality or religion. The circumstances of the war forced the tsarist officialdom to rely on public initiative. The appeal to patriotism inevitably led to the mobilization of society as a whole.

About a half a million Russian Muslims fought at the front. Both private individuals and Muslim institutions (for example, the Ecclesiastical Assembly in Ufa) provided the means and premises for infirmaries. Muslims worked as volunteers and hospital attendants, collected donations for supporting wounded men and families of soldiers, and more. The appeal to Muslim charity for the needs of the war also led to the creation of new institutions. In December 1914, with the active support of the members of the Muslim Duma faction and other public figures led by the Russian Muslim officer A.-A. Davletshin, the All-Russian Congress of representatives of Muslim public organizations was held in Petrograd at a local benevolent society. A member of the State Duma, I. A. Akhtiamov, presided over the congress. The participants in the congress decided to unite the efforts of Muslim public organizations to render assistance to wounded men, soldiers, and their families.

For this purpose, they proposed the creation of a network of committees of Muslim public organizations, with a central committee in Petrograd. The role of these committees was to collect donations, mainly to provide medical aid to Muslims on the Caucasian front.[46] Although the MVD supported this initiative, it edited the statute of the committee by adding a clause that specified that "the activity of the committee and its local branches would stop after the end of the war." With this condition, the Temporary Muslim Committee on Rendering Assistance to Soldiers and their Families, with its network of local chapters, was created in Petrograd on 5 February 1915.[47]

Both Russian newspapers generally and private sources acquired by the MVD officials regarded the 1914 congress as an important patriotic event. The congress opened with expressions of loyalty (*vernopoddanicheskikh chuvstv*), prayers for the health and well-being of the emperor and the ruling house, as well as with the composition of telegrams to the emperor and the chief commander of the Russian army. It closed with a children's concert, a theatrical performance, and the singing of the national anthem and patriotic songs. Both during and after the congress, the delegates stressed the allegiance of Russian Muslims to their Fatherland rather than to Turkey. Russian newspapers wrote that the congress's participants, presenting the "collective opinion" of their people (as Muslims of the British Empire had done earlier), not only demonstrated the loyalty of Russian Muslims, but also the failure of German and Turkish plans to mobilize Russian Muslims to a holy war.[48]

For the participants in the congress, its patriotic character served as an argument for, and public demonstration of, Muslim loyalty and patriotism. Following the example of publicizing expressions of loyalty by British Muslims, the Russian press used the patriotism displayed by Russian Muslims at the congress to counteract the German propagandists' reports about unrest in the Muslim regions of the countries of the Entente. For propagandistic purposes, the Russian government sent the resolutions of the congress to French authorities in Algeria.

Both the participants at the congress and the majority of its observers in the government and the Russian press characterized as patriotism the enthusiasm of Muslim public organizations in the cause of providing support to soldiers and their families. Even so, behind this seemingly unanimous evaluation were different interpretations of patriotism. On the occasion of the opening of the congress in Petrograd, the newspaper *Kaspii* (published in Baku by A. M. Topchibashev) quoted the following paragraph from the newspaper *Yulduz:* "The moment had come when Muslims, coming out as a nation, would show how they love and appreciate their Fatherland, how they respond together during hard times for the Fatherland."[49] The newspaper *Baku* explained the Muslims' initiative to create special all-Russian Muslim infirmaries by citing Muslims' aspiration, "along with the other nationalities of Russia . . . to demonstrate their patriotic feelings separately from the others [*v otdel'nosti*]."[50] For the participants in the Petrograd Congress and their sympathizers, the ideas of loyalty to the Fatherland and to their nation were not contradictory.

In contrast, the Russian authorities viewed any expressions of non-Russian nationalism during the war as isolationism. The Kazan governor, in his report of 19 November 1914 on the "moods" of the Muslim population, mentioned above, pointed to the "insincerity of patriotic feelings" among Tatars, and also noted that "all of the comments of the progressive Tatars concern their national questions." In the opinion of the governor, wartime was not the right moment for upholding national interests.[51] For the same reason, the central authorities had also been suspicious of the public prayer in memory of Gasprinskii at the last session of the Petrograd congress, viewing it as an expression of national sentiment.[52]

Differences in views of patriotism by Muslim public figures and tsarist state officials were also revealed in the conflict around selecting a symbol for the Provisional Committee on Rendering Assistance to Soldiers and their Families. In the spring of 1915, the Ministry of Internal Affairs had reviewed the petition of the committee to adopt a distinctive sign for the committee that would correspond with the religious views of Muslims. For this sign, the petitioners proposed a five-pointed red star. Z. Sh. Shamil, a member of the committee, but also an employee of the MVD, asked the Department for Religious Affairs of Foreign Confessions to support the petition. In his opinion, a special symbol of this kind was very important for a successful fundraising campaign among the ordinary people. Nor did Shamil insist exclusively on a five-pointed star. As he said, the committee was ready to submit another symbol for approval if the ministry so instructed—for example, a red hexagon. In an attempt to convince the MVD of the necessity of a special sign, Shamil highlighted Russian Muslims' loyalty, while also warning that the refusal to approve a symbol could be interpreted by the Muslims as oppression.

Even so, the Department for Religious Affairs of Foreign Confessions recommended rejecting the committee's petition. In his report on this matter, G. N. Taranovskii, the department's director, justified the refusal on the basis of several political considerations. According to him, the committee was not a religious organization, but represented a non-Christian charitable organization created to assist the needy, regardless of their confession. Therefore, acceptance by the committee of a religious emblem would, in his opinion, "once again emphasize in public and state life a religious discord, isolation, and intolerance, especially in relation to Christianity." Moreover, Taranovskii saw in the committee's choice of a star, which was the most popular emblem, alongside a crescent among the Muslims of the Volga provinces, an expression not only of an association with the enemy—Turkey—but also with the "systematic aspiration of Tatars in every possible way to maintain their prestige and domination among their coreligionists of other nationalities."[53] Taranovskii also feared that the appearance of the Muslim symbol alongside the already existing emblem of the Red Cross could be wrongly interpreted as an official recognition of equality for both emblems and, by implication, of both religions, Islam and Christianity. In the "eyes of the ignorant masses," he feared, such a symbol might indicate that the committee was being given the status of an official establishment. Nor did he consider it impossible for a non-Christian charitable organization to accept the Red Cross, noting that a Japanese medical–sanitary group had already accepted it, "not as a religious symbol, but as a commonly accepted emblem of mercy and compassion to suffering neighbors."[54] On the basis of these arguments, the Minister of Internal Affairs thus denied the petition, arguing that a special symbol had "as its final goal the maintenance among the Russian Muslims of a known isolation on religious–national grounds, even in the case of the noble cause of rendering assistance to the defenders of the Fatherland and their relatives."[55]

During the war, the imperial government expected its subjects to provide assistance to Russia's war effort with no distinction of religion or nationality. Thus Muslims, along with other Russian subjects, made donations to the Committee of Her Imperial Highness the Great Duchess Tat'iana Nikolaevna, and also for the Russian Organization of the Red Cross.[56] The government also allowed the creation of nationality- and confession-based public organizations for rendering assistance to refugees and wounded men.[57] At the same time, certain limits were placed on this "nationalization" of social activity. While the government allowed Muslims to help their coreligionists, it was suspicious of any attempts by Muslim intelligentsia to use the rhetoric of nation and present their patriotic deeds as a distinct Muslim cause. Tsarist officials viewed such attempts as a display of separatism, a challenge to the dominant position of Orthodoxy, and an assertion of the domination of the Tatars among other nationalities. None of this, in the eyes of MVD officials, corresponded with "essential state interests."

The "Muslim Cause" versus the "Russian Cause"

During the summer of 1915, the imperial regime confronted profound challenges. Military defeat and evacuation severely undermined the reputation of the tsarist generals and ministers. The government faced both the problem of economic disruption and a fresh outbreak of labor protests. Within the Duma, the Progressive Bloc pressed the government for reforms and demanded a "united government" that would enjoy public "trust." Although some ministers were willing to seek agreement with the educated elements of society, Prime Minister I. L. Goremykin convinced Nicholas II to call off further discussions. Nicholas reaffirmed his control over ministerial appointments and put himself in charge of the armed forces.[58]

In this context, the Nationality Question became a highly pressing issue. The war had internationalized the empire's nationality questions and mobilized non-Russian and Russian nationalists. The Muslim intelligentsia justified their claims for equal rights and cultural autonomy for Muslims by pointing to their loyalty and patriotism, displayed in the past as well as during the ongoing war. Some Muslim publicists bitterly complained that, when compared to other non-Russians—Jews and Poles in particular—the special needs of Muslims had not received much support from the Russian progressive public.[59]

Yet the claims of the Muslim intelligentsia did have some defenders among educated Russians. In September 1915, A. N. Samoilovich (1880–1938), a specialist on Turkic languages, Orientalist, and former contributor to *Mir islama,* wrote to the MVD on the occasion of the appointment of M.-S. Baiazitov, who was unpopular among the Muslim intelligentsia, as the Orenburg mufti. Samoilovich called on the government not to forget about the "true needs" of Russian Muslims, "loyal Russian citizens," and not to antagonize Muslim society by applying what he termed a divisive policy (*politika raz"edineniia*) in relation to Muslims.[60] During the war, however, the ethnic identity and political orientation of the academic experts on Islam themselves, including Samoilovich and Bartol'd, had come under the suspicion of the Ministry of Internal Affairs.[61]

The tsarist authorities continued to rely on the official Muslim clergy, who also served as official spokespersons for the Russian Muslims. In 1915, Baiazaitov, officially responding to an inquiry from the British Muslim Society in Cairo about the conditions under which Russian Muslims lived, wrote that Muslims in Russia enjoyed freedom of religion, full rights, and had a better standing in society than other non-Christians. According to Baiazitov, Muslims were thriving and lived in peace with Russians.[62]

In February 1916, Duma deputies intensified their critique of the government for not fulfilling its promises of religious tolerance. The deputies demanded the complete elimination of all restrictions based on religion and nationality.[63] The ministers' position was that the current moment was not suitable for resolving this issue and they postponed its solution until after the war, when "it would become clear to what extent these measures were timely and corresponded to the domestic political situation."[64] This decision also affected the resolution of the demands that had been raised by Muslims during the prewar period. The government's strategy on these questions was articulated in a note prepared in 1916 upon the order of the Minister of Internal Affairs, A. N. Khvostov (appointed in September 1915), in connection with the impending discussion of budget issues in the Duma.

The note pointed to the complexity of the Muslim Question because of both the heterogeneity of Russian Muslims and the wartime situation, which made the "possible positions of Muslims unclear and dependent on the results of the war." These circumstances made the revision of imperial laws on Islam "untimely." Khvostov's recommendation to the Ministry of Internal Affairs was to "abstain from giving clearly formulated promises in one or another direction, and to limit itself to a statement that the government realized the urgency of the question and when resolving it would take Muslims' needs into consideration."[65]

In contrast, the government felt that the Polish Question could not be postponed. Having already foreseen that Poland would be a potential war zone, S. D. Sazonov, the minister of foreign affairs, had suggested that the government meet "the reasonable wishes" of Polish society in the sphere of self-government, language, school, and church-related matters. After the war began, Grand Duke Nikolai Nikolaevich made political promises to the Poles. The rapidly changing situation on the western front forced the tsarist government to formulate its vision of Poland's political future. In the fall of 1916, Germany and Austria-Hungary declared the creation of the independent Kingdom of Poland. The new head of the tsarist government, A. F. Trepov, publicly declared in the Duma the intent to "recreate a free Poland," but in an "inseparable unity with Russia." Nevertheless, tsarist officials, fearing the subversive influence of an autonomous and independent Poland on the rest of the Russian empire, could not come to an agreement on this issue.[66]

In 1916, the tsarist rule faced a serious challenge in Turkestan, where the government's decision to extend military conscription to local Muslims caused a dramatic social explosion. The introduction of universal military service in 1874 was one of the Great Reforms aimed at modernizing the empire's social order. By the end of 1915, however, according to the minister of war, seven million people, including 114,000 Russians, were exempted from military service for cultural, economic, and political reasons.[67] With the exception of special native regiments, the majority of the Muslim population of Central Asia and the Caucasus was also exempt from conscription into the army. This exemption was part of an imperial bargain offered in exchange for their loyalty to the tsar. While Muslims viewed this as a "privilege," the exemption became a thorn in the side of the tsarist administration and the Russian public. The question about extending military conscription to the empire's subjects who had until then been exempt from the draft had been raised before World War I, but was shelved by the government. In 1911, a special government commission in Turkestan objected to the conscription of the native population, whom it considered to be "unreliable."[68] Instead, at the beginning of the war, the government introduced a military tax. Soon, though, the increased wartime demands for new sources of manpower for construction work forced the government to extend the mobilization to the native populations of Siberia, the Caucasus, and Central Asia.

On 25 June 1916, the tsar signed a mobilization order that called upon the "alien" male population of the empire aged eighteen to forty-three to register for work in the rear of the front lines. Even before the imperial decree had been publicized, rumors about the impending conscription caused panic among these populations: rumors were circulating saying that natives were being sent to dig trenches between the fighting armies or that natives would be actually conscripted not as workers but as soldiers in order to free their lands for Russian settlers.[69] In the Caucasus, there were rumors that Russia considered Muslims their enemies and had plans to kill them through the exhausting military service.[70] In July 1916, grand Duke Nikolai Nikolaevich, the viceroy of the Caucasus, sought to change the conscription orders as applied to the Caucasus, arguing that "any policies affecting the Muslim population require for their fulfillment a series of preparatory measures that in turn need a considerable amount of time."[71] In Turkestan, the conscription decree was announced to the population in the local press on 7 July 1916, without advance notice or preparatory measures, thus causing further rumors and confusion among the population. Moreover, the government's announcement coincided with the labor-intensive cotton harvest and the Muslim fasting period.

The native population responded almost immediately. They refused to register for service; attacked local native and Russian officials and Russian settlers; destroyed bridges, telegraph lines, and railroads; and fled to Persia, China, and Afghanistan. In the Dzhizak district, Holy War against Russians was declared. The disorder began in the Samarkand oblast and spread to Syr-Darya, Ferghana, Semirech'e, the Trans-Caspian area, and the Steppe oblast. In August, a bloody conflict erupted between nomads and Russians in the region of Semirech'e, in the southern part of Turkestan (the main area of Russian colonization). Thousands of Slavic settlers and tens of thousands of nomadic Kyrgyz and Kazakhs died.[72]

To resolve the crisis, the government dispatched General A. N. Kuropatkin (1848–1925), who had recently been appointed to the post of Turkestan's governor-general.[73] Kuropatkin had extensive military and administrative experience in Central Asia and was a prolific writer. In his book *The Tasks of the Russian Army* [*Zadachi russkoi armii*], published in 1910, he described the imperial order that he established during his tenure as governor of the Trans-Caspian region in 1890–1898. In this order, Russians were placed symbolically on the top, followed by natives, who were the former masters of the region, then other Russian subjects starting with the Christians, and finally the foreigners. He emphasized, however, that this hierarchy did not apply to legal matters; these were resolved on the basis of the idea of justice rather than nationality.[74] The key element of this order was the strong state as protector of both its Russian and non-Russian subjects. It was this kind of paternalistic style of rule that Kuropatkin sought to reestablish to resolve the crisis in Turkestan.[75] He arrived in Tashkent in August 1916. In a speech delivered to the local military and civil authorities, he promised to punish the rebels and protect Russians' status as the "elder brother."[76] According to N. P. Ostroumov's recollections, Kuropatkin also blamed Russians, especially Cossacks, for giving the natives reasons for their discontent. According to Ostroumov, Kuropatkin's negative comments about Russians and especially Cossacks supposedly offended some

Russians and made them suspect that the general sympathized with the natives.[77] To restore order in a borderland driven by violent interethnic conflict was a challenging task and Kuropatkin contemplated the need to separate Russians and native nomadic peoples.[78]

In their analysis of the revolt's causes, different Russian Turkestan officials emphasized diverse factors. The head of the Turkestan secret police pointed to the role of rumors surrounding the imperial decree, and unsuccessfully tried to find an Afghan connection to the revolt.[79] The military governor of Ferghana, A. I. Gippius, in his report to Kuropatkin blamed tsarist authorities for provoking the revolt. To calm the population agitated by the draft, Gippius issued appeals in which he reinterpreted the content of the imperial decree by allowing recruitment to be conducted on a voluntary basis. To convince the local population to fulfill the government order, Gippius relied on traditional Russian appeals to Muslim religious authority. In the yard of a mosque in Namaghan, he dressed in a robe and turban to read extracts from the Koran to convince the population to submit the authorities.[80] The unauthorized reinterpretation of the tsar's will by Gippius and his actions in Namaghan upset his superiors. Gippius was dismissed from his position, replaced by Colonel P. P. Ivanov, and called to Tashkent and then to St. Petersburg. To justify his actions, Gippius explained that his decision to read the Koran came out of fear that native resistance to the draft could acquire a religious character, as well as out of his disappointment with the local Muslim clergy. Thus, to establish order, Gippius concluded: "Knowing Arabic, I could arrange everything myself." He then wrote: "Everything went very calmly and seriously, dead silence reigned, and some elders even cried from tender emotions."[81] He also pointed out that it was possible to rely on the native population's patriotism, and warned that Ivanov would "uncover political conspiracy, write about political ferment in Ferghana, about secret intrigues and connections with Afghanistan, about Ferghana *ishans,* bandits, Muridism, pan-Islamism, etc."[82]

His expectations proved to be correct, at least to a certain extent. On 8 August, in his report to the governor-general, P. P. Ivanov, now the acting military governor of Ferghana, articulated what he saw to be the reasons for the revolt and provided an evaluation of the current moods of the population in that region. A central idea of the report was what he viewed as the unpreparedness of Asians, whom he characterized as corrupted and only submissive to strong power, for the institutions of self-governance and rule of law established in Turkestan as the result of the Great Reforms. In his opinion, it was Russian military power that prevented the native population from rising against the "infidels." Once this power appeared to be weak in the eyes of the natives, they rebelled. According to Ivanov, the anti-Russian propaganda of the militant Muslim spiritual leaders had played a decisive role in this turn of events. Ivanov thus concluded that the imperial decree was just a pretext for and not the cause of the revolt. He discovered only "superficial tranquility" in the local population and did not trust their manifestations of patriotism.[83]

The Department for Religious Affairs of Foreign Confessions, in St. Petersburg, was especially interested in the role played by religious factors in the revolt, and by the Muslim clergy in particular. According to its information, both mullahs and *kadis* had played an important role in the disturbances in Ferghana and the Syr-Darya and Samarkand regions. For the Steppe region, the MVD officials had suspicions rather than evidence. To resolve the question, the vice governor of the Ural oblast, who was the acting military governor, responded that he could not definitely determine the role of the Muslim clergy in the revolt of the nomadic tribes, although he concluded that the "disturbances undoubtedly happened not without the influence of mullahs, most of whom were ignorant, fanatical, and hostile to the Russian state, but this influence was very subtle."[84]

In his final report to the tsar on the 1916 events, Kuropatkin recognized the government's responsibility for the revolt and pointed to the hurried implementation of the imperial decree. Kuropatkin also emphasized the significance of that revolt by comparing the casualty figures—ninety-seven killed, eighty-six wounded, and seventy-six missing—with the low number of total losses of the Russian army during the conquest of Turkestan. Kuropatkin reminded the tsar about the severe punishment of the rebels in Andijan in 1898 and reported that the natives' punishment for "spilling Russian blood" had been no less severe in 1916.[85]

In 1898, as we have seen, the official explanation of the Andijan revolt pointed to the religious "fanaticism" of the natives and the "liberalism" of Russian rule in Turkestan, identifying the Muslim Question in these terms. In present revolt, however, the religious factor was not given the same prominence. In fact, Kuropatkin thought that loyalty to Islam was weakening among the new generation of nomadic population. His report only briefly mentioned the role of Muslim clerics, some of whom supported the rebels. At the same time, he, too, criticized the 1886 Turkestan Statute, which in his view weakened Russian rule in Turkestan.

The official investigators of the 1898 Andijan revolt claimed that they did not hear any specific complaints against Russian rule, other than about the decline of morals, and pointed to the "advantages of Russian rule" for the natives. In 1916, by contrast, Kuropatkin found evidence to conclude that the local population was justified in its dissatisfaction with the Russian order in Turkestan. He pointed to the role of the cotton industry in the destruction of the local way of life, government policies of resettlement and dispossession of the indigenous nomad population, and harmful practices of the tsarist secret police. As S. M. Dukhovskoi had in 1898, Kuropatkin emphasized the need for government control of the native administration and religious institutions. But unlike Dukhovskoi, he had a more optimistic view of the integration of the "hardworking sedentary people" and the nomadic tribes; he thought they could be "called to a new life."[86]

In Kuropatkin's view, the government's "firmness of power" (*tverdost' vlasti*) and "paternalistic care" (*otecheskaia zabota*) constituted the two most important principles in the relationship between the Russian administration and the native population. As he wrote to the minister of the Internal Affairs, A. D. Protopopov:

"We should aspire that they fear and respect us. They will love us later."[87] Kuropat-kin severely punished the rebels and carried out the tsarist project of conscription into labor battalions. He also then took steps to develop a new statute for Turkes-tan, one of the important aspects of which was to strengthen the tsarist adminis-tration and supervise the native population in the region.

In contrast to the Andijan uprising, the 1916 revolt took place in a context of representative politics, which meant that investigations were not limited to the tsar's personal agents. The circumstances of the revolt and the horrors experienced by the native population were investigated by Duma deputies A. F. Kerensky (a member of the labor faction) and K.-M. Tevkelev (the chair of the Muslim faction). They felt that the revolt took place as a result of the misinterpretation of the decree by the native population, who had "fantastic notions" about the provisions of the draft. The deputies blamed local authorities for not explaining the decree, for the rude implementation of the draft, and for not considering local customs and religious beliefs.[88] In December, the Duma discussed the interpellations to the government from the Social-Democrats, the Labor faction, the Muslim faction, the Kadets, and the Progressists about the circumstances of the revolt. Some of the deputies drew parallels between the revolt of 1898 in Andijan and the events of 1916, accused the central authorities of criminal activity and treason, and questioned the legiti-macy of the unlimited autocracy in Russia.[89]

The draft in Turkestan and the revolt presented an opportunity for progressive Muslim intelligentsia to assert their voice in imperial politics. As Adeeb Khalid noted, local Jadids saw Turkestan's exemption from military service as a practice of exclusion and assisted the authorities in recruitment. He interpreted this posi-tion as Jadid political strategy "aimed at the creation of a Muslim voice in Turke-stan and of Muslim participation in the imperial mainstream."[90] Muslims of Turke-stan were not represented in the Fourth Duma, but local members of Muslim and Russian communities traveled to Petrograd to invite the Duma delegation to in-vestigate the circumstances of the revolt.[91] Muslim Duma deputies thus became the spokespersons for the Turkestan Muslims and associated the latter's interests with the Muslim cause.

Tsarist authorities could not ignore the Duma. Kuropatkin read the minutes of the Duma's meetings concerning the 1916 revolt, and the Ministry of War pre-pared to respond to the Duma's interpellations. At the same time, the government remained suspicious of Muslim progressive intelligentsia and ambivalent about the degree to which the Muslim faction represented the moods of the Muslim popu-lation. Within the Department of Police, there was a belief that the Muslim fac-tion's position did not reflect Muslims' interests, and the Ministry of Internal Af-fairs continued to seek ways to combat the influence of liberal Muslim intelligentsia on the masses.[92]

Over the summer of 1916 and through February 1917, the officials of Department for Religious Affairs of Foreign Confessions discussed two projects intended to counteract the influence of the progressive Muslims. Each of these came from Muslims who had already established relations with the department: M. Bek Hajetlashe and M.-S. Baiazitov. Hajetlashe—ever the publisher—was seeking government support for founding a press in St. Petersburg that would specialize in popular literature for the Muslim masses, while Baiazitov, now the new mufti, suggested opening a press at the Orenburg Ecclesiastical Assembly in Ufa to publish the Koran, Muslim religious literature, and a newspaper in the Tatar language, to foster Muslim loyalty to the regime.

Both Hajetlashe's and Baiazitov's proposals were supported by the director of the Department for Religious of Foreign Confessions. The objection to Baiazitov's plans for a Muslim religious press came from Russians who were sympathetic to Il'minskii's understanding of the Muslim Question. One of them was the department's own official, Rybakov. He argued that, first, the state should not support Islam or the muftis' attempts to monopolize the publishing of religious literature. Second, he stated that while Islam was not the enemy of the state, it represented a threat to Russian culture. Rybakov feared that the government's support of the assembly's publishing endeavors would strengthen Tatarization and hence the Muslim cause. Therefore, he encouraged the government not to repeat its "mistakes" of the eighteenth century, when the state supported and institutionalized Islam. Instead, he called to satisfy "the just needs" of the Muslim population and to strengthen Russian culture.[93] To achieve the second goal, Rybakov urged the government to support another publishing project that was brought up at about the same time by Andrei, now the bishop of Ufa and Menzelinsk. Andrei's idea was to publish a newspaper in Ufa for baptized Tatars, in the Tatar language in Cyrillic script.

The Department for Religious Affairs of Foreign Confessions also consulted Andrei about Baiazitov's proposal. Andrei knew Baiazitov personally, and as he mentioned in his report to the department, he "trusted" him. But he was convinced that Baiazitov would not be able to compete with the progressive Muslim press that, he believed, was guiding the moods and lives of the Muslim masses and turning them into an anti-Russian force. Andrei saw the recent example of this influence in the attempts by Muslim Tatar deputies to use the investigation of the 1916 revolt and the drafting of the new statute for Turkestan as an opportunity to advance the Muslim national cause. He wrote: "That is what Messrs. Tevkelevs, Akhtiamovs, and other members of the Muslim Duma faction do while Kuropatkin and the Russian administration, with some minor exceptions, although not consciously, help them."[94] While attacking the Muslim faction promoting the Muslim national cause more than once elsewhere, Andrei regrettably noted that there was no faction within the Duma that would support Russian Orthodoxy and the Russian cause, understood in a Slavophile sense.[95]

Andrei concluded that Baiazitov's project would not serve the Russian cause and that the government should not support Islam. Instead, he suggested opening teachers' seminaries for baptized non-Russians. Baiazitov's idea, however, was supported by the Ufa governor and the Minister of Internal Affairs, but the correspondence on this matter was interrupted by the revolution and the proposal was not put into practice. Andrei's newspaper received a one-year subsidy of 5,000 rubles. Yet despite this achievement, Andrei's cooperation with the tsarist authorities in promoting what he considered the Russian cause turned out not to be very successful.

The developments provoked by the war made the Russian cause seem urgent and forced Andrei to act on his own. By the end of 1915, the eastern borderlands became home to many refugees who had fled the occupied western provinces. To assist the refugees, nationality-based committees were established in Ufa. Andrei noticed that while Poles, Jews, and Latvians received help from their national committees, no organized public support was given to the Russians. Andrei complained: "It is a pity that all nationalities in Russia are organized . . . and together defend their interests, but only Russians represent the disorganized masses."[96] In May 1916, Andrei proposed the establishment of the *Vostochno-russkoe kul'turno-prosvetitel'skoe obshchestvo* (Eastern Russian Society for Culture and Enlightenment) with the goal of developing the "material and spiritual forces of Russian nationality and the defense of Russian culture." Andrei emphasized that while in the western borderlands Russian culture struggled with Catholicism, in the east, Russian culture needed to be strengthened in the face of the Tatar–Muslim world. The essential result of such strengthening would be the revitalization of Orthodox parish life, through elections of clergy and transformation of the parish into a self-governing community with the rights of a legal entity.

The German and Austrian occupation of Russian Poland, much of the Baltic provinces, and the western borderlands, along with the government's promises to Poland, gave new urgency to the concerns felt by Andrei and his sympathizers about the future of the eastern borderlands, Russian–Muslim relations, and ultimately about the unresolved Russian Question. The possibility of the political resurrection of Poland, and thus a strengthened Polish element in the northwestern provinces, reinforced their anxieties about the perceived weakness of the Russian Orthodox church and the fate of the Russian cause in the empire's east. Once again, Andrei's calls to reform the Orthodox parish reminded the government about the Russian side of the Muslim Question.

Before the war, the central authorities had become interested in the Muslim parish boards (*prikhodskie popechitel'stva*) that, according to government information, had become established in the 1900s with the aim of supporting mosques, Muslim clergy, schools, and charity organizations. In 1914, the issue of Muslim parish boards was discussed both at the special government commission on the Muslim Question and at the Fourth Muslim Congress in St. Petersburg. The 1914 commission recommended establishing such boards for the purpose of managing the economic matters of the Muslim parishes.[97] Based on the explanations of some Muslim clerics, the commission also assigned a political role to these boards, one of protecting Muslim believers from antireligious ideas and the destructive influence of the Muslim intelligentsia.[98] At the same time, the Muslim congress that met in St. Petersburg in 1914 took up the parish issue as an essential element in the reform of the Muslim religious administration, thus promoting the Muslim cause.

Both of the government's special commissions on the Muslim Question, in 1910 and 1914, mentioned the need to strengthen Orthodoxy and Russian culture, but both overlooked the issue of Orthodox parish reform. Although the state protected the status of the Orthodox church as the "dominant confession" in the Russian empire, the government shelved all plans for reforms in the sphere of church renewal. During the war, the proponents of church reform, both inside and outside the government, insisted that parish reform could not be postponed until after the war (as measures concerning Islam had been) unless the government was willing to be accused of a "conscious violation of the essential interests of the Orthodox church and the Motherland."[99] In July 1916, without official sanction, Andrei introduced elections of parish priests into the Ufa diocese. This initiative, as well as Andrei's public speeches and publications, dissatisfied the Holy Synod, while his criticism of the notorious G. Rasputin, confidant of the tsaritsa, whose interference in state affairs appalled even the tsar's strongest supporters, irritated A. A. Vyrubova, who was influential at the court, and Pitirim, metropolitan of Petrograd and Ladoga. According to the later testimony of S. P. Beletskii, the former director of the Police Department, the Holy Synod was considering removing Andrei from his position as the head of the Ufa diocese, but was fearful of public reaction.[100]

*   *   *

Recent studies have paid new attention to World War I in terms of the radical shift to "modern" policies of mass mobilization and nationalization.[101] Although the tsarist regime initiated these policies, it also attempted to preserve the old order. It was impossible, however, to do both. Deliberations about the Muslim Question demonstrated this dynamic. The pressures of the war did not change but rather reinforced the official understanding of and concerns about the Muslim Question, while simultaneously exacerbating a conflict between the major actors involved in the discussion of this issue. The war strengthened Russians' anxieties about Muslims' political loyalty. Although some local governors and police frequently expressed doubts about the "true moods" of the Muslim population, throughout the war the imperial authorities maintained the opinion that on the whole the Muslim population was loyal and patriotic. This position served both to maintain order within the multiconfessional empire and to counter German propaganda. As it had done before the war in its Muslim policies, the tsarist government primarily concerned itself with the liberal Muslim intelligentsia's supposed aspiration for separatism and domination.

To support the war effort, the government had to rely on public initiative, which in turn mobilized the empire's population along national and confessional lines. Muslim liberals attempted to use loyalty and patriotism as an argument to advance their claims for official recognition of the Muslim nationality. They challenged the official understanding of the Muslim Question by interpreting it as the nationality issue related to ideas of national rights and citizenship. MVD officials, by contrast, continued to view the Muslim intelligentsia's nationalistic claims and sentiments as significant threats to the stability of the state. The central government's belief in Muslims' loyalty allowed the government to postpone answering the questions raised by the progressive Muslim intelligentsia. While tsarist officialdom refused to further modernize the empire's confessional and sociopolitical order, it extended universal military service, which was associated with modern citizenship, to those Muslims who were heretofore exempt from conscription. A bloody conflict in Central Asia caused by the imperial decree announcing the draft caught these administrators by surprise and reinforced some doubts about Muslims' ability to be part of a modern imperial society.

Authorities were able to suppress the rebellion, but not its echoes across Russian society. The investigation of the circumstances of the revolt by Duma deputies only resulted in the further discrediting of the autocratic regime. The war also mobilized Il'minskii's followers, whose alternative understanding of the Muslim Question remained closely related to their anxieties about the perceived weakness of Orthodoxy. Andrei, the Bishop of Ufa and Menzelinsk, passionately advanced the Russian cause, understood in a Slavophile sense, which he saw in competition with the Muslims' own national cause. While seeking state support for his initiatives, Andrei criticized the government's cooperation with both the Muslim progressive intelligentsia and the official Muslim clergy.

Again the government had no definite answer to the Russian Question raised by Andrei and his supporters. As the war mobilized the Russian population on the eastern borderlands, he and his allies tried to take the issue of church reform into their own hands. By February 1917, the monarchy appeared to be oppressive to the champions of both the Muslim and the Russian cause.

Conclusion
Could the Muslim Question Have Been Solved?

This book has examined the creation, development, and internal contradictions of a set of perceptions about Muslims, bundled under the construct of the Muslim Question. The conception of a "question" about Muslims—in Russian, *vopros*—served for educated Russians as a way of articulating their anxieties about the place and roles of Muslims in an Orthodox Russian imperial state. The Muslim Question was thus a set of changing and contending ideas, a concept whose various meanings emerged as imperial Russia embarked after the Crimean War on the project of modernizing its empire. The Question continued to produce a vital and highly contested set of issues until the end of the tsarist regime. Could the challenges it involved have been solved?

Russian imperial development and expansion throughout the nineteenth and early twentieth centuries were part of a broader pattern of European expansion that occurred more generally in the Muslim world. Imperialism required Europeans to design policies that would assure their control over Muslim dominions and solidify their empires' statuses as great powers.

Russians addressed these issues through the prism of the Muslim Question. As we have seen, the concept became a familiar one in Russian political discourse after the Crimean War, though its meaning was inconsistent and contentious. The Muslim Question emerged in Russia during that part of the nineteenth century when conquests in Central Asia significantly enlarged the empire's Muslim population and when Russian imperial elites could thus compare their new imperial "problem" to the experiences of the British, French, and Dutch empires. However, in the same way that other European imperial powers conceptualized and addressed the challenges presented by Muslims within their particular sociopolitical situations, Russia, too, produced its own set of understandings.

Above all, the emergence of the Muslim Question in imperial Russia was related to contentious Russian visions of how their unique land-based and multiconfessional empire should be developed and governed in the modern imperial age, and when intensified pressure from Britain, Germany, and other European powers seemed to threaten Russia's very viability as a world power. The Muslim Question was thus something of a shorthand term for determining how to transform Russia's social and political order internally to enable it to prosper in the imperial age. Once the Great Reforms put forward the agenda of enlightenment and social rapprochement, a reformist Russian state had to play a more active role in transforming the empire's diverse subjects into imperial citizens within its expanding territory. From the beginning, however, modernization and reform themselves in Russia were contested issues, especially after the assassination of Tsar Emancipator Alexander II in 1881, an event that further complicated the issues involved in making Muslims within the empire into "Russians."

Unlike Western European overseas empires, Russia's land-based empire evolved over centuries as a socially and culturally diverse political system. Many educated Russians were consequently encouraged to believe that a reforming and modernizing imperial state might reduce these differences. Some even hoped that non-Russians might eventually merge socially and culturally with Russians, something that would have made the Russian empire unique within the world imperial system. The possibility of such a merger, however, was also a source of Russian anxieties, especially when the empire was shaken by the attitudes of some Crimean and Volga Tatars during the Crimean War, and as imperial Russia extended its rule into Central Asia, forcefully bringing into its boundaries a large group of new and culturally alien Muslims. The Polish rebellion of 1863, in particular, helped to crystallize the problem of imperial diversity and spawned other "alien questions" beyond those concerned with Muslims.

Perceptions of the challenges posed by Muslims were only intensified by the ways Russian public, church, and state figures understood other alien questions—particularly the Polish one. In the eastern borderlands, the Polish rebellion of 1863 and its lingering aftermath of resentment and hostility stimulated Russian nationalism and sharpened Russians' awareness of their multicultural environment. As we have seen, the transfers from the west to the east of such imperial agents as Kazan archbishop Antonii and state officials and publicists B. M. Iuzefovich and A. S. Budilovich contributed to this process. For the imperial authorities, the Polish rebellion demonstrated how a similar threat to the integrity of the imperial state could develop and gain followers among other non-Russians. Viewed from this perspective, the Muslim Question developed into what was considered a potentially very dangerous threat to the very stability of the empire.

Moreover, as we have described, all alien questions—whether Polish or Muslim—were closely intertwined with the domestic problems Russia faced in modernizing its empire. This was especially the case in terms of Russian concerns about the role and authority of Orthodox clerics and the central place of the Orthodox parish, and hence directly touched upon the contentious question of Orthodox church reform itself and its relationship to competing conceptualizations of Russia's modern transformation.

Until its demise in 1917, tsarist Russia officially remained an officially Orthodox state governed by an autocratic ruler, notwithstanding the limited powers granted to the State Duma in the early twentieth century. Confession was an important component of identity for the tsar's subjects and served as an instrument of governance. Since the eighteenth century, limited religious tolerance had been one of the key principles of building a multiconfessional empire. Moreover, the state went further than just tolerating different non-Orthodox confessions; it presented itself as a defender of officially tolerated faiths and institutionalized confession by creating special organs of religious administration and cooperating with religious elites.

Well before Russia's expansion into Central Asia, the Muslims of European Russia, Crimea, and later Transcaucasia thus received official recognition of their Islamic faith and a hierarchical system of spiritual administration along with the officially recognized clerical estate. The imperial confessional system was hierarchical, with the Orthodox church subjugated to the state but officially occupying a "dominant" position. One of its privileges was the exclusive right to proselytize within the empire. As the result of its state-supported missionizing efforts from the second half of the sixteenth to the first half of the eighteenth century, a problematic category of apostates from Orthodoxy to Islam emerged, especially in the Volga region. As we discussed, the apostasy issue was the Orthodox church's "internal" confessional problem, but it had an imperial dimension as well. It was this dimension that, in fact, became especially pronounced in the second half of the nineteenth and early twentieth centuries. Governing the empire by means of the confessional system in which the state attempted to be both the guarantor of Orthodoxy's dominant position and the protector of Islam, while also playing the role of supreme interpreter and arbitrator of conflicting interests, turned out to be a formidable task, especially in the face of the multiple challenges of cultural, social, and political modernization after 1861.

Both in the wake of the Crimean defeat and as a result of the Polish rebellion, Russian public and state figures alike became increasingly concerned about what they perceived as the alienation and ignorance of Muslim population. The identification of the particular Muslim Question during the course of the Great Reforms meant that much of the perception about Muslim reluctance to assimilate, addressed in terms of rapprochement and enlightenment, paralleled debates about how to civilize and integrate Russia's peasants. Additionally, some Russian commentators raised questions about the very compatibility of Islam with the values of the officially Orthodox imperial state. The problem of Muslims' integration and enlightenment inevitably became even more acute as the empire extended its rule in the Caucasus and Central Asia.

The Great Reforms also redefined the long-standing issue of apostasy among baptized non-Russians from Orthodoxy to Islam in the Volga–Ural region. In the eyes of contemporary observers, the liberal reforms of the 1860s stimulated apostasy. At the same time, the era of Great Reforms created favorable conditions for a group of lay missionaries and their sympathizers within the church to emerge. With N. I. Il'minskii as a central figure, this group suggested new perspectives on— and solutions to—the problem of apostasy. As we have seen, Il'minskii came to a conclusion about the relative strength of Islam and weakness of Orthodoxy. He reformulated the immediate task of the church as one of stopping apostasy by instilling conscious religiosity among the already baptized, rather than Christianizing Muslims (although without abandoning such as strategy as a long-term goal). Il'minskii thus brought into the discussion of apostasy a new view of Islam as a vital force, along with an informed understanding of multicultural localities, a perspective he combined with a strong adherence to Orthodox belief and animosity toward traditional Islamic teaching.

While Il'minskii's approach to apostasy was developed within the existing official confessional system, it also presented a strong challenge to the state-sponsored Orthodox church. It redefined the nature of the Orthodox community in Russia by raising a series of questions about the role of lay people in church life, about the relationship between a priest and his parish, and about the nature of religious belief itself. Il'minskii discovered that Muslims in Russia seemed to possess what the Orthodox church was missing—a vibrant religious community. Intensifying during the aftermath of the Great Reforms, Il'minskii's missionary project, which grew out of his understanding of local Orthodox–Muslim rivalries, offered a continual reminder of the urgent need to transform one of Russia's foundational institutions if it was to continue to play an effective and influential role in a modernizing multiconfessional society.

Il'minskii's ideas were clearly reformist in spirit, but they also suggested a Russian alternative to the Western European idea of progress, a unique "Russian path" to the modern age. What united Il'minskii and many of his sympathizers within church, government, and public circles was the emphasis they all placed on the centrality of religion in the life of society, and their views of the nature of religious belief and church life in Russia. As one of Il'minskii's best-known supporters, Bishop Andrei, argued at the beginning of the twentieth century, Il'minskii essentially put into practice the program of the Russian Slavophiles, for whom Russia's transformation had to begin from the bottom, with a critical role played by a renewed "popular" Orthodoxy rather than the traditional hierarchy alone.

From the perspective of Il'minskii and some of his followers, the very necessity of Russia becoming a modern empire was harmful for Orthodoxy and beneficial for Islam. Like many Slavophile thinkers, Il'minskii called for a return to something resembling pre-Petrine times, when—as he believed—the state had neither subjugated the Orthodox church nor patronized Islam. Il'minskii was sympathetic to *narod* and suspicious of the intelligentsia, both Russian and non-Russian, and of their nationalistic projects. He was critical of the state's efforts to govern Muslims through official religious institutions and to promote secular enlightenment. Il'minskii and his local associates, including N. A. Bobrovnikov, N. P. Ostroumov, and later Bishop Andrei, were employed by state institutions. They actively sought state support for their views, had sympathizers within the central government, and exercised influence, although limited, on the state's policies toward Islam. At the same time, relying on the state while trying to build a vibrant local Orthodox community of believers without state interference was a challenging—if not intrinsically impossible—task. Their alliance with the state thus remained precarious.

When the Muslim Question was raised and discussed in public circles and within the government after the Great Reforms, it was largely formulated as a problem of Muslims' alienation. At the same time, however, these discussions revealed a constant fear of Muslim, and particularly Tatar, domination. Some in the government saw the solution to this problem through educational measures that also preserved the existing confessional and political order. The regime's response was contradictory. It supported Il'minskii's schools for baptized non-Russians but also encouraged secular education among officially recognized Muslims, thus simultaneously accepting and contesting Muslim religious identity. Given this, it is not surprising that the results were unsatisfactory. The apostasy problem was not resolved. Muslim masses resisted the introduction of Russian-language classes and the imposition of state control over confessional schools. Moreover, as Russian politics turned to the right after 1881, the compromise in schooling Muslims came to be increasingly seen within ruling circles as a potentially dangerous path, since the schools were also producing a new Muslim intelligentsia.

The state's project of enlightenment and rapprochement was also constrained by a lack of capable personnel and insufficient financial resources. In addition, the pressure of a continually tense international environment, along with tsarist officials' traditional fears of popular revolt in response to government reforms, made security considerations and concerns about Muslims' loyalty a priority for the imperial authorities. Yet the traditional expressions of Muslims' loyalty seemed no longer to be enough, and uncertainty about the "true moods" of the Muslim population and their perceived alienation increasingly disturbed the tsarist authorities. Finally, those government officials who took seriously the official Orthodox character of the state were faced with the difficult issue of articulating an appropriate relationship between the Orthodox state and Muslim religious institutions. Il'minskii's advice was to allow Islam and its institutions to operate without state interference, and instead to support and concentrate on the problems of apostasy and Muslim propaganda, which in his eyes constituted the essence of the Muslim Question.

Within bureaucratic circles, the conviction grew that establishing official Islamic administrations was the wrong policy, one that did not correspond to the spirit of the Great Reforms and might in fact help Islam to "dominate" Orthodoxy in the eastern borderlands. The authorities were thus faced with a dilemma: How could Islam be controlled without institutionalizing it and, consequently, as they feared, strengthening it? As a result, plans for the unification of the existing system were shelved, while no ecclesiastical administration was created for Muslims in the North Caucasus and Central Asia. In Simferopol, Ufa, and Tiflis, however, the state-sponsored Islamic establishments were preserved, and the state there continued to rely on Islamic religious authority in its interactions with its imperial Muslim subjects, but the Russian state never openly claimed for itself the status of a simultaneous Russian and Muslim power. This approach appeared to be inconsistent and did not please Il'minskii and his supporters. At the same time, the state policy toward Islam laid the foundations for claims by Muslims who appropriated state religious institutions and pressed the government to widen the limits of religious tolerance. The state also failed to solve the problems of the Orthodox church raised by the Great Reforms, while Il'minskii and especially his followers increasingly had to defend their views against both Russian and non-Russian opponents, as well as compete for state support with Muslims.

The debate on reform and how to govern Muslims thus became a focal point for those living in Russia's multicultural regions who sought to find their own ways to meet the new challenges they faced. In effect, the empire itself was seen as an arena in which various projects as well as claims for leadership and inclusion into imperial politics came into contact and competition. As we have seen, Il'minskii's vision of reform and empire was challenged by the reformist project of I. Bey Gasprinskii, the leader of the Jadids, a group of Muslim intellectuals that emerged in the second half of the nineteenth century. The Jadids saw themselves as the reformers of their society and claimed leadership within their community. They reimagined the nature and boundaries of the Russian Muslim community they claimed to represent, and articulated a program of Muslim confessional nationalism. It is not surprising that Il'minskii and his followers were among the first who became threatened by this emerging sociopolitical force and worried about what they perceived as the "complication" of the Muslim Question. Conceived within the imperial setting, the projects and claims of the Jadids and Il'minskii's followers fell into competition. While Il'minskii and his supporters warned the government about the political implications of apostasy and Jadid educational reform, officials of the Ministry of Internal Affairs did not assign serious political significance to the Muslim Question but viewed it primarily as a confessional issue. The central government's attitude only changed when the country entered the era of mass politics and the Jadid movement itself became politicized.

The revolution of 1905 brought the competition between Il'minskii's followers and the Jadids into the open, especially about the role and nature of the imperial Russian state. Jadids made use of the new freedoms and political institutions to pursue their liberal and nationalist goals. They presented Russians with new types of claims, demanding the recognition of Muslims as a nation rather than as the followers of an alien confession. In effect, they reformulated the Muslim Question as the problem of the intersecting interests of the empire's various nationalities. The Jadids' ideas constituted the platform for a Muslim Duma faction, and that faction allied with Russian liberals such as the Constitutional Democrats. Meanwhile, as Bishop Andrei and his supporters complained, no faction within the Duma defended the Orthodox community's interests (understood in a Slavophile way). To Russian reform-minded Orthodox observers, Muslims seemed to be more successful in mobilizing as a religious community as compared to their Orthodox counterparts. The Muslim political "awakening," however, did mobilize Il'minskii's followers. As we have seen, they responded to the Muslim congresses by holding a missionary congress in Kazan.

Il'minskii's followers viewed Gasprinskii's nationalism as an "artificial" project that forcefully drew into its orbit neighboring non-Russian and non-Muslim communities while also representing Muslims' "conscious" alienation from Russia. From their point of view, the situation only deteriorated as the twentieth century began. Yet, in the aftermath of the 1905 revolution, Il'minskii's sympathizers still hoped to preserve the empire by transforming it into one that they perceived would allow an "organic" relationship between Russians and non-Russians.

The arguments for this conception of empire were clearly articulated by Il'minskii's supporter A. S. Budilovich, a specialist in Slavic philology and a prolific publicist. Budilovich explained the rise of non-Russian nationalism as a result of mistaken state policies that maintained and in certain cases institutionalized the cultural peculiarities of the borderlands. In Budilovich's view, non-Russian nationalism was especially dangerous for the Russian people who had been enserfed by the state, separated from their Westernized elite, and deprived of a clearly designated national territory. He warned that introducing the principle of national self-determination as the solution to the nationality questions would leave the Great Russians without their own autonomy and thus, in effect, without a national existence while also provoking interethnic conflict. Budilovich thus argued that just as Russians needed the empire to preserve the unity of what he viewed as the Russian core, so did the different groups of non-Russians need Russians as the mediators. Instead of remaking the empire into a federation, he suggested introducing decentralization, local self-government, and the establishing of "organic" relations between the non-Russian borderlands and the Russian center. He conceived of the Russian empire, as he put it, as a ship with many non-Russian cabins and a Russian keel.[1] The "amicable delimitation of local and state interests" that Budilovich hoped for was not achieved during the late tsarist regime. His solution was no longer enough for the non-Russian nationalists, who increasingly associated Russianness (and Orthodoxy) with assimilation and cultural, religious, and political oppression.

The demands of Muslim liberals for participation in politics as well as for equal rights and cultural autonomy for what they imagined as the Muslim nation also went against the government's concept of its leading role in determining and satisfying the "just" religious needs of its Muslim subjects in limited cooperation with their official representatives, the Muslim clergy. Despite the changing sociopolitical circumstances, the tsarist government continued to address the Muslim Question through the prism of the existing confessional system, as a problem of Muslim (especially Tatar) alienation and domination. However, the confessional system was no longer sufficient either to accommodate the new claims of the Muslim intelligentsia or to manage the intensified Orthodox–Muslim rivalry. Moreover, as the country went through the turbulence of the 1905 revolution, government officials came to redefine the issues of Muslim alienation and ignorance.

By the time of the conservative turn in 1907, the Muslim masses appeared to be loyal to a government whose primary concern now was internal security, especially when compared with the revolutionary Poles, Armenians, and Jews. It was the suspected subversive activity of the Muslim progressive intelligentsia that presented the problem, and which thus became the essence of the Muslim Question as reconstituted by officials of the MVD. The attention paid by both the MVD officials and Il'minskii's followers to the Muslim intelligentsia resulted in a joint discussion of the Muslim Question within a special government commission of 1910, which revealed different understandings of this problem. Central government officials neither accepted the missionaries' view of Islam as a hostile anti-Christian force, nor were they responsive to the message about the reverse side of the Muslim Question—the Parish Question, or the Russian Question, as it was clearly articulated by Bishop Andrei.

Tsarist officials' belief in the loyalty of the majority of the Muslim population was, however, largely based on a perception of Muslims' cultural ignorance. The vast majority of Muslims, they thought, were simply unprepared for mass mobilization under the modern slogans of liberalism, socialism, or nationalism. In the officials' view, it was only a small group of successfully modernized Muslims, mostly Tatars, who posed a threat to the security of the regime and the stability of the empire. Formulating the problems related to Muslims from this perspective, tsarist authorities after 1905 came to view the Muslim Question as less dangerous than other alien questions, particularly the Jewish and Polish Questions. Still, the examples of nationalistic movements and political radicalism among other non-Russian subjects, combined with officials' concern about Muslim cultural alienation, made Russian officials uncertain about the future and the reality that might lie behind what they perceived as Muslim loyalty. As a result of this perspective, in the aftermath of 1905 and subsequent constitutional revolutions in Persia and Turkey, MVD officials concentrated their efforts on struggling with the Muslim intelligentsia.

At the same time, the theme of "protecting Orthodoxy" was appropriated by many tsarist officials when addressing the Muslim Question. It became especially pronounced in the official discourse at a time when the government became increasingly suspicious of its non-Russian subjects, whose loyalty had been "tested" by the revolution of 1905. Yet relying on Orthodoxy and Russians to preserve the empire was a response to the growing threat of non-Russian and Russian nationalisms, rather than a consistent policy. No real steps were made in response to proposals to strengthen the Russian core by reforming one of its main institutions—the Orthodox church. The expansion of religious tolerance in 1905, especially in relation to the issue of apostasy from Orthodoxy, threatened the church. But unlike, for example, the chief procurator of the Holy Synod, K. P. Pobedonostsev, who was a fierce opponent of both church reform and the expansion of religious tolerance, Il'minskii's followers connected the two and opposed not the expansion of religious tolerance as such, but the timing of the reform. As Andrei pointed out in 1908,

> police prohibition of religious propaganda and protection of the Orthodox church is . . . an abnormality which is offensive for the Orthodoxy, but unfortunately is necessary for five–seven years until the life of Orthodoxy could normalize: the church council would be summoned and the ways for animating spirituality among the Orthodox clergy and their parish would be found.[2]

For Andrei, as for Il'minskii earlier, the Muslim community represented both the "enemy" and a model for the reform of Russian Orthodoxy. At the same time, the pressure of the Muslim intelligentsia for the reform of their own religious institutions constantly appeared to be in competition with similar efforts of their Orthodox opponents. Faced with a welter of conflicting views, the regime responded by shelving both the tolerance projects and church reform. Before 1917, no change was consequently made in the confessional system. World War I itself only sharpened the Russian–Muslim rivalry and strengthened the alienation of both the Muslim intelligentsia and Il'minskii's followers from the tsarist state, which now was seen as an oppressive regime.

As a set of conflicting views ideas and about the very modernization of the Russian imperial state, the Muslim Question was thus not a problem that could be "solved." Instead, its contours and contradictions revealed the fundamental dilemma of transforming an imperial, autocratic, and Orthodox state while also keeping its structures intact. Central here were the tensions embedded into the empire's unique confessional system. One was the conflict between the regime's commitment to privileging Orthodoxy and the limited tolerance toward Islam. A no less formidable problem was the state's need to satisfy Muslims' religious needs while preventing Islam and its official religious institutions from becoming the tools of nationalistic and political propaganda. As the state itself increasingly adopted nationalistic rhetoric, it became even more difficult to pursue both agendas.

The story of the Muslim Question also reminds us that Russian perceptions of and policies toward Islam should be studied in relation to other confessions and especially the Orthodox church. As critically thinking Russians understood, the question of "what we need from Muslims" was closely connected to the path taken by Russians themselves. The contentious nature of reform in the late tsarist period contributed to the fact that although educated Russians shared a sense of cultural superiority with Western Europeans vis-à-vis Islam, not all those engaged with the Muslim Question were self-confident civilizers. As we have seen, some even saw Orthodox Russians as "disadvantaged" when compared with Muslims, and with Tatars in particular. To Il'minskii and his sympathizers, mullahs and Muslim religious schools appeared to be closer to the people, while Muslim communities seemed to enjoy more freedom in their religious life than native Orthodoxy, and appeared to be more successful in mobilizing collective efforts to press for their needs. And at least in the view of some, the less Russians themselves succeeded in reforming their society (or perceived reform efforts as successful), the more threatening Muslims appeared to be to the integrity of the state and its culture. Moreover, while the Muslim Question was a part of a larger debate on Russia's development, Il'minskii, Ostroumov, and others who engaged its issues not only related their visions of reform to Islam, but also developed them in a process of interaction and rivalry with Islam.

The story of the Muslim Question also shows that Russian perceptions and fears of Islam were not static but were conditioned by historical circumstances and the political situation. Not surprisingly, the short period of liberal constitutionalism promised by the Provisional government gave Il'minskii's supporters hope that they might advance their vision of reforms, but also compelled them to adapt their strategies to the new political situation. A remarkable change in rhetoric about Muslims especially marked the publications of Bishop Andrei, who gave up the Slavophile idea of an idealized monarchy after the February revolution in favor of a broad renewal of Russian life. Quickly disillusioned with the revolution and Bolshevism, which to him represented violence, coercion, and godlessness (*bezbozhie*), he was soon expressing his gratitude to the Muslim community itself for "protecting the Orthodox churches in Ufa province from plundering by local thieves and robbers."[3]

Here, indeed, was a fitting coda to the question of Muslim loyalty in Russia that had centered debates about Islam throughout the final decades of the imperial regime and exemplified the difficult problems imperial Russia faced in modernizing its multiconfessional empire.

Notes

Introduction

1. Aksakov, "O bratstvakh v Zapadnom krae," *Den,* 14 March 1864, in *Pol'skii vopros i zapadno-russkoe delo,* 333–334. Aksakov lived from 1823 to 1886.

2. Witte, *Vospominaniia,* 522. Witte lived from 1849 to 1915 and was in power or close to those in power during the most important decades of Russia's modernization. Important books about Witte include von Laue, *Sergei Witte;* Anan'ich and Ganelin, *Sergei Iul'evich Witte;* Wcislo, *Tales of Imperial Russia.*

3. Anan'ich et al., *Vlast' i reformy,* 304.

4. The important studies of the peasantry, emancipation, and reform in the countryside remain Zaionchkovskii, *Otmena krepostnogo prava v Rossii;* Emmons, *The Emancipation of the Russian Serfs;* Field, *The End of Serfdom;* Zakharova, *Samoderzhavie i otmena krepostnogo prava v Rossii;* Eklof, *Russian Peasant Schools;* Wcislo, *Reforming Rural Russia.*

5. On the public and government discussion of the Clerical Question, see Freeze, *The Parish Clergy.*

6. On some of the empire's confessional questions, see, for example, Polunov, "The Religious Department and the Uniate Question" and "The Orthodox Church in the Baltic Region." Among the many other vital "questions" that emerged during this time was also the Labor Question. On the public and government discussion of this issue, see Zelnik, *Labor and Society.*

7. The problem of religious freedom in tsarist Russia is the focus of a special forum in *Kritika: Explorations in Russian and Eurasian History* 13, no. 3 (2012): 509–634.

8. For a few examples of studies that address the issue of citizenship in imperial Russia, see Jersild, "From Savagery to Citizenship"; Kotsonis, "Face-to-Face"; Burbank, "An Imperial Rights Regime"; Lohr, "The Ideal Citizen and Real Subject"; Morrison, "Metropole, Colony, and Imperial Citizenship."

9. The cooperation with loyal non-Russian elites and the respect for the status quo as basic elements of the early Russian cautious policy of incorporating the conquered territories and peoples into the imperial state are explored by Andreas Kappeler in *The Russian Empire,* 52–56. On the simultaneous and interconnected development of imperial and national imagination in Western Europe, see Cooper, *Colonialism in Question,* 171–172.

10. The now-classic work on nation as an imagined community is Anderson, *Imagined Communities.*

11. On the connection between the Great Reforms and nationalism in the consciousness of Russian bureaucracy in the northwestern region, see Dolbilov, "Prevratnosti kirillizatsii."

12. As N. Kh. Bunge, minister of finance and then chair of the Committee of Ministers put it: "The Poles opened the eyes of Russian society and the government." Bunge, *Zapiska, naidennaia v bumagakh N. Kh. Bunge*, 47.

13. Nol'de, *Iurii Samarin i ego vremia;* Iosifova, "Iu. Samarin i ego 'Pis'ma iz Rigi,'" 3–14.

14. On Katkov, see Tvardovskaia, *Ideologiia poreformennogo samoderzhaviia.* On Aksakov, see Tsimbaev, *I. S. Aksakov.*

15. *Moskovskie vedomosti*, no. 196 (9 September 1863), in *Sobranie peredovykh statei Moskovskikh vedomostei* (1897): 524–525.

16. Polvinen, *Derzhava i okraina*, 31. On the Russian debate of the Jewish Question during the reign of Alexander II, see Klier, *Imperial Russia's Jewish Question.*

17. Isakov, "Ostzeiskii vopros," 25–26. On Russian polemic on the Baltic Question (*Ostzeiskii vopros*), also see Andreeva, *Pribaltiiskie nemtsy.*

18. "Eshche ob 'Okrainakh' Ju.F. Samarina," *Rus* (21 September 1885), in Vol. 6, *Sochineniia I. S. Aksakova*, 160.

19. Iuzefovich, "Khristianstvo, magometanstvo," 29. For an analysis of Aksakov's and Katkov's discussion of the Polish and Baltic Questions and their conceptions of the Russian nation during the period of the Great Reforms, see Renner, *Russischer Nationalismus.* For a general discussion of the "alien questions," see Campbell, "Edinaia i nedelimaia."

20. This excluded Ukrainians and Belorussians, who were considered by Russian nationalists as a part of the Russian nation. On the category of aliens, see Slocum, "Who, and When, Were the *Inorodtsy?*

21. See Steinwedel, "To Make a Difference," 67.

22. On the emergence of new ideas and practices of territory in the eighteenth century as well as their implications for Russian governance and the formation of national consciousness, see Sunderland, "Imperial Space." Also see Sunderland's insightful commentary on an increasing differentiation between the center and the peripheries during the late imperial era, which he has called colonialization, "The Ministry of Asiatic Russia," 123. On the spatial imagination of the Russian empire, see Bassin, "Geographies of Imperial Identity" and Gorizontov, "The 'Great Circle' of Interior Russia"; on the spatial approach to Russian history, see Matsuzato, "General-gubernatorstva."

23. See, for example, "Zapiska stats-sekretaria barona [A. P.] Nikolai po voprosu o preobrazovanii tsentral'nogo upravleniia na Kavkaze," October 1882, in Biblioteka RGIA, pechatnaia zapiska, papka 263, p. 3; Semenov, ed., *Okrainy Rossii*, 1–2; Slavinskii, "Natsional'naia struktura," 282–283.

24. On the history of the integration of this region and its people into the empire, see Kappeler, *Russlands Erste Nationalitäten;* Romaniello, *The Elusive Empire.*

25. Wortman, *Scenarios of Power*, 246.

26. Anan'ich et. al., *Vlast' i reformy*, 393.

27. For important studies that analyze enlightenment, nationalism, and political movement among the Russian Muslims, see Khalid, *The Politics of Muslim Cultural Reform;* Noack, *Muslimischer Nationalismus;* Usmanova, *Musul'manskie predstaviteli;* Iskhakov, *Pervaia russkaia revoliutsiia.*

28. During the period 1810–1817 it was the Main Administration for Religious Affairs of Foreign Confessions; in 1817 it was a part of the Department for Religious Affairs at the newly created Ministry of Religious Affairs and Enlightenment that oversaw all of the

confessions and the educational system of the empire; it was again restructured to be the Main Administration in 1824–1832.

29. After 1897, it was the First Department of the Ministry of Foreign Affairs, and in 1914 four political departments (*politicheskie otdely*) were created.

30. Among major studies that have come to this conclusion, see Miller, "*Ukrainskii vopros*"; Geraci, *Window on the East;* Brower, *Turkestan.*

31. For example, this question was addressed in Weeks, *Nation and State;* Staliūnas, *Making Russians;* Dolbilov, *Russkii Krai.*

32. Miller, "Rusifikatsii"; Weeks, "Russification: Word and Practice"; Dolbilov, "Russification and the Bureaucratic Mind"; Staliūnas, "Did the Government Seek to Russify."

33. The pejorative aspects of Orientalism, forcefully introduced to the literature by Edward Said in his *Orientalism,* have been a source of much contention and debate. On the applicability of Said's perspective to the Russian case, see Khalid, "Russian History and the Debate over Orientalism." On the interpretation of Russian relations with the eastern and southern borderlands through the prism of colonial discourse, see Khalid, *The Politics of Muslim Cultural Reform;* Jersild, *Orientalism and Empire;* Sahadeo, *Russian Colonial Society.*

34. Morrison, *Russian Rule in Samarkand.* See also his analysis of the impact of Russian Orientalist attitudes on colonial governance in Turkestan, in "Applied Orientalism."

35. Geraci, *Window on the East,* 350; see also his "Russian Orientalism at an Impasse."

36. Knight, "Grigor'ev in Orenburg"; and his "On Russian Orientalism: A Response to Adeeb Khalid"; Schimmelpenninck van der Oye, *Russian Orientalism.*

37. Tolz, *Russia's Own Orient.*

38. The study of the Great Reforms in Russia is a well-developed field of historiography. Some works that represent this rich body of literature include Eklof et al., *Russia's Great Reforms;* Taranovski and McInerny, eds., *Reform in Modern Russian History;* Anan'ich et al., eds., *Vlast' i reformy.*

39. Alexei Miller has suggested differentiating between different versions of Russian nationalism that did not necessarily contradict the empire. Another idea useful for this study is to view different Russian and non-Russian nationalistic projects in interaction. This approach was developed in relation to Ukrainian nationalism in Miller's "*Ukrainskii vopros.*"

40. Crews, *For Prophet and Tsar.*

41. Major works analyzing non-Orthodox confessions and the regime's confessional policy in imperial borderlands include Charles Steinwedel, *Invisible Threads of Empire;* Werth, *At the Margins of Orthodoxy;* his many insightful articles that explore the religious issue within the imperial context were recently translated into Russian and published in *Pravoslavie, inoslavie, inoverie;* Crews, *For Prophet and Tsar;* Breyfogle, *Heretics and Colonizers;* Dolbilov, *Russkii krai;* Gerasimov et al., *Konfessiia, imperiia, natsiia.* For a more detailed analysis of recent scholarship on the history of Russian Orthodoxy and imperial confessional diversity, see Werth, "Lived Orthodoxy and Confessional Diversity." Also, see his *The Tsar's Foreign Faiths* that appeared only when my manuscript was being readied for publication.

42. Nicholas Breyfogle has recently reminded us about this important factor in his "Enduring Imperium." On the argument about the interconnectedness between the metropole and periphery in other European colonial contexts, see Cooper and Stoler, *Tensions of Empire.*

1. The Crimean War and Its Aftermath

1. Anan'ich et. al., *Vlast' i reformy,* 305; Chernukha and Anan'ich, "Russia Falls Back, Russia Catches Up," 60–61; Figes, *The Crimean War,* 442–444.

2. Olga Maiorova has analyzed how the war affected the vision of Russianness as articulated by Russian intellectuals; see her *From the Shadow of Empire.* Mara Kozelsky has emphasized the role of the war in the development of Russian Orthodox nationalism and Christian renewal in Crimea; see her *Christianizing Crimea.* For the recent reinterpretation of the Crimean war as a major turning point in the history of Russia, Europe, and the Middle East, see Figes, *The Crimean War.*

3. For the account of the Crimean War, see Tarle, *Krymskaia voina;* Curtiss, *Russia's Crimean War;* Goldfrank, *The Origins of the Crimean War;* Figes, *The Crimean War.*

4. Markevich, *Tavricheskaia guberniia,* 4.

5. Fisher, *The Russian Annexation of the Crimea,* 139, 149–150. On the incorporation of Crimea into the Russian empire, see O'Neill, *Between Subversion and Submission.*

6. Dubrovin, ed., *Materialy dlia istorii Krymskoi voiny,* Vol. 1, 130. On the religious aspects of the Crimean War, see Goldfrank, "The Holy Sepulcher and the Origin of the Crimean War." On Russian patriotism and its identification with Orthodoxy in popular representations of the Crimean War, see Norris, *A War of Images,* 54–79. On the importance of the religious factor for understanding the Crimean War, see Figes, *The Crimean War,* xxiii.

7. Pogodin, "Nastoiashchaia voina v otnoshenii k russkoi istorii, July, 1854," in *Istoriko-politicheskie pis'ma,* 141–144. About Pogodin, see Umbrashko, *M. P. Pogodin.*

8. On the role of Innokentii in holy war propaganda, see Kozelsky, *Christianizing Crimea,* 127–140.

9. "Vozzvanie Tavricheskogo muftiia Seid-Dzhalil-Efendi vsemu musl'manskomu dukhovenstvu i narodu v Tavricheskoi gubernii obitaiushchem," in Dubrovin, *Materialy dlia istorii Krymskoi voiny,* Vol. 1, 250–252. In his report to the governor-general of Novorosiia and Bessarabia concerning the speech given by chief mullah Seid-Ibrahim-Efendi in October 1853 at the Khan mosque of Evpatoriia, the governor of Tauride province expressed hope that the "feeling of loyalty to the government expressed by the Tatars in Evpatoriia were also characteristic of the majority of the Tatar population of Crimea." GAARK, f. 26, op. 4, d. 1396, ll. 1–2.

10. GAARK, f. 26, op. 4, d. 1393, ll. 9–10 ob.

11. GARF, f. 109, op. 28 (1853), d. 101. Part 1. ll. 2–18. Part 2. ll. 1–7 ob.

12. GAARK f. 26, op. 4, d. 1393, ll. 9 ob.–10, l. 12 ob.

13. GAARK f. 26, op. 4, d. 1393, ll. 9 ob.–10. See his report from 31 March1854, l. 13 ob.

14. Markevich, *Tavricheskaia guberniia,* 12–13.

15. Tarle, *Krymskaia voina,* Vol. 2, 106–125.

16. Mikhno, "Iz zapisok chinovnika o Krymskoi voine," 6–37; GAARK, f. 26, op. 1, d. 20004, l. 27 ob.

17. Markevich, *Tavricheskaia guberniia,* 13–31.

18. The reports can be found in GAARK, f. 26, op. 1, d. 19999, 20034 and f. 26, op. 4, d. 1408, 1493. On cases of collaboration between Crimean Tatars and the allies, see Kirimli, "Emigration from the Crimea to the Ottoman Empire," 753–756.

19. Markevich, *Tavricheskaia guberniia,* 32–33, 94–103, 110–112. Markevich men-

tions a case reported by a local head of the police from the occupied Baydar Valley about a Tatar who helped a Christian merchant's wife to escape captivity by dressing her in a Tatar dress. See his *Tavricheskaia guberniia*, 25.

20. GAARK, f. 26, op. 2, d. 34, l. 1; Markevich, *Tavricheskaia guberniia*, 31–32; Mufi-izade, *Ocherk voennoi sluzhby krymskikh tatar,*17.

21. Markevich, *Tavricheskaia guberniia*, 31, 236, 223.

22. *Materialy po istorii Tatarii*, 156–164.

23. Ibid., 161.

24. Ibid., 162.

25. The Russian policies toward Muslim religious institutions will be discussed in more detail in chapter 5.

26. This theme has been emphasized by several authors, among them Kozelsky, "Casualties of Conflict" and Kirimli, "Emigration from the Crimea."

27. For example, see the 1854 report of the head of Sevastopol's gendarmerie to the Tauride governor Pestel about the accusations against the mayor of Backchisarai, in GAARK, f. 26, op. 4, d. 1393, ll. 87–88 ob.

28. Markevich, *Tavricheskaia guberniia*, 30. For example, the head of the Tauride Chamber of State Property argued against the expropriation of weapons from Tatars in 1854 and opposed the order of Chief Commander Men'shikov about relocating Tatars from the coastal villages; GAARK, f. 26, op. 4, d. 1393, l. 12; f. 26, op. 1, d. 2004, l. 1820 ob. The records of authorities' concerns about robberies by Armenians, Russians, and Greeks of property left by Tatars who had fled from the Evpatoriia district to the allies are in GAARK, f. 26, op. 1, d. 20024, ll. 1–8.

29. Cited in Markevich, *Tavricheskaia guberniia*, 246–248.

30. The emigration of Crimean Tatars to the Ottoman empire had already begun during the war. On the refugee issue, see Hakan Kirimli, "Emigration from the Crimea," 757.

31. GAARK, f. 26, op. 4, d. 1605, ll. 1–1 ob.

32. Fisher, "Emigration of Muslims from the Russian Empire," 359; Kozelsky, *Christianizing Crimea*, 149; Figes, *The Crimean War*, 422.

33. On the Murid movement and its leader Shamil, see Gammer, *Muslim Resistance to the Tsar.*

34. Fisher, *Emigration of Muslims,* 356.

35. Kozelsky, *Christianizing Crimea,*150–151.

36. See "K voprosu ob ustroistve uchilishch dlia inorodcheskikh detei Kazanskogo uchebnogo okruga," and "K voprosu ob obrazovanii inorodtsev," in *Materialy po istorii Tatarii*, 2, 159. Kazan Tatars were eligible for military conscription, while Crimean Tatars were freed of this obligation. Instead, they had to maintain a special Tatar squadron and pay dues, including a special Tatar city fee. The question concerning the conscription of Crimean Tatars was discussed by the government but a decision was postponed.

37. *Russkii vestnik, Sovremennik, Morskoi sbornik, Severnaia pchela, Vestnik Evropy* were among the contemporary journals that discussed this issue.

38. "Obshchii obzor pereseleniia Krymskikh Tatar," 1860, in Chernyshev, "Prichina emigratsii Krymskikh Tatar v Turtsiiu," 125–126. In 1860–1863, according to official statistics, 192,360 Tatars had emigrated and fewer than 100,000 remained in Crimea. See Martianov, "Posledniaia emigratsiia," 699–700.

39. Levitskii, "Pereselenie Tatar iz Kryma v Turtsiiu," 637. "Obshchii obzor pere-

seleniia Krymskikh Tatar," 1860, in Chernyshev, "Prichina emigratsii Krymskikh Tatar," 125–128.

40. "Antonii (Amfiteatrov) to the Ober-Procurator of the Holy Synod, 1867," in *Materialy po istorii Tatarii*, 451.

41. Kozelsky emphasized the development of patriotic discourse with Orthodox themes in Crimea during and after the Crimean War; see her *Christianizing Crimea*, 133–149. However, as we will see, this was not the only trend that developed during this time.

42. "Vnutrennee obozrenie," 811–812.

43. Ibid., 810.

44. Totleben, "O vyselenii Tatar iz Kryma," 532; See also Ushakov, "Zapiski ochevidtsa o voine Rossii protiv Turtsii," 0179–0181.

45. The report was published by *Vestnik Evropy* in 1882. According to the editors, it was written at the beginning of the 1860s.

46. Levitskii, "Pereselenie Tatar," 623.

47. Ibid., 624.

48. Cited from Martianov, "Posledniaia emigratsiia tatar iz Kryma," 701.

49. Ibid., 706.

50. "Materialy komissii dlia izyskaniia sposobov uderzhat' tatarskoe naselenie v Krymu," in GARF, f. 730. op. 1, d. 1859, l. 2.

51. Ibid., ll. 2 ob.–111.

52. *Materialy po istorii Tatarii*, 213–216.

53. "N. P. Ignat'ev to A. N. Gorchakov, 18 May 1865," in *Materialy po istorii Tatarii*, 215–216.

54. The question of Russia's relations with the Slavs was articulated in his *Opinion on the Eastern Question*, published in *Birzhevye vedomosti* in 1869 and as a book in 1870. On Fadeev's views, see Thaden, *Conservative Nationalism*, 146–163; and Kuznetsov, *R. A. Fadeev*.

55. Fadeev, "Shest'desiat let Kavkazskoi voiny," in Vol. 1, Part I, *Sobranie sochinenii*, 3–10; and "Pis'ma s Kazkaza," ibid., 100.

56. On Katkov, see Tvardovskaia, *Ideologiia porerformennogo samoderzhaviia*; on Katkov's definition of nation, see Renner, "Defining a Russian Nation."

57. Katkov, *Sobranie peredovykh statei Moskovskikh vedomostei za 1864 g.*, 318.

58. Ibid., 318–319.

59. Ibid., 320. On Russian imperial imagination in relation to the North Caucasus, see Jersild, *Orientalism and Empire*.

60. Arapov et al., *Severnyi Kavkaz v sostave Rossiiskoi imperii*, 163–181.

61. Fadeev, "Pis'ma s Kavkaza," in Vol. 1, Part 1, *Sobranie sochinenii*, 149.

62. On the Russian government's changing policies concerning Muslims' immigration to the Ottoman empire as well as return immigration in the late nineteenth and early twentieth centuries, see Meyer, "Immigration, Return, and the Politics of Citizenship."

63. Gugov et al., *Tragicheskie posledstviia Kavkazskoi voiny*, 102, 100, 106.

64. Ivanov, "O sblizhenii gortsev s russkimi na Kavkaze."

65. "N. A. Kryzhanovskii to A. E. Timashev, 6 December 1876"; and "Acting Head of the Main Administration for the Press, V. V. Grigor'ev to the Chair of the Moscow Censorship Committee, 15 January 1877," in *Materialy po istorii Tatarii*, 347–348.

66. *Materialy po istorii Tatarii*, 346.

67. Cited in Larionov, *Nachal'noe obrazovanie inorodtsev*, 5.

2. The Challenges of Apostasy to Islam

1. See, for example, Kefeli-Clay, "L'islam populaire chez les Tatars chrétiens orthodoxes"; idem, "Constructing an Islamic Identity"; Werth, *At the Margins of Orthodoxy*. On the concept of "apostasy" in law and administrative practice, see idem, "The Limits of Religious Ascription." On the place of Christianization in the state's policy toward Islam, see Vorob'eva, *Christianizatsiia musul'man*.

2. Werth, *At the Margins of Orthodoxy*, 176; Geraci, *Window to the East*, 108–109.

3. SZRI (1896), Vol. 11, Part 1, Article 4.

4. On the integration of non-Russian people of the Volga region into the empire, see Kappeler, *Russlands erste Nationalitäten*. On the incorporation of Kazan into the Muscovite state, see Romaniello, *The Elusive Empire*.

5. On the Orthodox missionary activity in this region, see Mozharovskii, *Izlozhenie khoda missionerskogo dela*.

6. On other events that demarcated periods of tolerance and oppression toward Tatars as reflected in Russian laws, see Nogmanov, *Tatary Srednego Povolzh'ia*.

7. On Catherine's approach to Islam, see Fisher, "Enlightened Despotism and Islam."

8. The Russian policies toward Muslim religious institutions will be addressed in chapter 5.

9. *Kratkii istoricheskii ocherk Kazanskoi eparkhii*, 14; Mozharovskii, *Izlozhenie khoda missionerskogo dela*, 24–25.

10. *Kratkii istoricheskii ocherk Kazanskoi eparkhii*, 15; Mozharovskii, *Izlozhenie khoda missionerskogo dela*, 45–46, 51–52, 107.

11. "Pis'mo N. I. Il'minskogo ober-prokuroru Sv. Sinoda D. Tolstomu. Iz neizdannykh pisem Il'minskogo," 26.

12. *Kratkii istoricheskii ocherk Kazanskoi eparkhii*, 32; Mozharovskii, *Izlozhenie khoda missionerskogo dela*, 116.

13. RGIA, f. 821, op. 133, d. 545, l. 1 ob.

14. RGIA, f. 797, op. 3, d. 12644, ll. 50–53.

15. Werth, *At the Margins of Orthodoxy*, 178–182.

16. RGIA, f. 797, op. 3, d. 12644, l. 11 ob.–12.

17. Znamenskii, *Na pamiat' o Nikolae Ivanoviche Il'minskom*, 30. For more details on this missionary activity, see Mozharovskii, *Izlozhenie khoda missionerskogo dela*, 177–208.

18. RGIA, f. 821, op. 133, d. 454. ll. 298 ob.–299.

19. PSZ II. (1841), Vol. 16, No. 14409, Article 17.

20. RGIA, f. 796, op. 125, d. 1518, ll. 14 ob.–15.

21. The Kazan Theological Academy was founded in 1798 and was to serve as the center of theological education for the eastern part of the empire. In 1818, the academy was converted back into a seminary, while its educational district was transferred to the control of the Moscow Theological Academy. The difficulty of administering an enlarged district from Moscow, as well as the "special missionary needs" of the eastern part of the empire, served as reasons for reestablishing the Kazan Theological Academy in 1842. The academy's district included Kazan, Simbirsk, Penza, Tambov, Saratov, Astrakhan, Orenburg, Viatka, Perm, Tobol'sk, Tomsk, Eniseisk, and Irkutsk provinces, and the Yakut region. See Znamenskii, *Istoriia Kazanskoi dukhovnoi akademii za pervyi (doreformennyi) period ee sushchestvovaniia (1842–1870 gody)*, 3, 5.

22. The Tatar language was taught at the "old" academy in 1810. See Blagoveshchenskii, *Istoriia staroi Kazanskoi dukhovnoi Akademii,* 115.

23. "O vvedenii prepodavaniia v Kazanskoi Akademii iazykov, upotrebliaemykh nekhristianskimi narodami po Kazanskomu dukhovno-uchebnomu okrugu, 1844–45," in NART, f. 10, op 1, d. 243, ll. 1–1 ob., 4.

24. Muhammad Ali Kazem-Bek (1802–1870), a celebrated Orientalist, philologist, and historian, was born at Resht in Persia; his family soon moved to the Caucasian port city of Derbent. In 1823, under the influence of Scottish missionaries, Kazem-Bek converted from Islam to Christianity, assuming the name Alexander. He began his academic career at Kazan University in 1826, where he taught until 1849, when he transferred to St. Petersburg. In addition to his academic research, Kazem-Bek served as a consultant on Muslim affairs for the Russian government. See Kazem-Bek's academic biography in Rzaev, *Mukhammed Ali M. Kazem-Bek.* On Kazem-Bek and the Kazan school of Orientalism, see Schimmelpenninck van der Oye, *Russian Orientalism,* 93–121.

25. Znamenskiii, *Istoriia Kazanskoi dukhovnoi Akademii,* 349.

26. Ibid., 350.

27. Znamenskii, *Na pamiat' o Nikolae Ivanoviche Il'minskom,* 48.

28. Ibid., 42.

29. Ibid., 70, 72.

30. Il'minskii, "Izvlecheniia iz proekta 1849 goda o tatarskoi missii," in Znamenskii, *Na pamiat' o Nikolae Ivanoviche Il'minskom.* Prilozhenie 1, 327–329.

31. Ibid., 327, 333.

32. *Kazanskie vesti* 66 (1891), cited from Znamenskii, *Na pamiat',* 15–16.

33. Znamenskii, *Na pamiat',* 23–25.

34. Ibid., 45–46.

35. "Instruktsiia bakkalavru Kazanskoi Dukhovnoi Akademii Il'minskomu dlia puteshestviia na Vostok," in NART, f. 10, op. 1, d. 994, ll. 4–7.

36. Znamenskii, *Na pamiat',* "Prilozhenie" 2, 338–356, "Prilozhenie" 3, 357–386.

37. The anti-animist division was closed after only two years. Znamenskii, *Istoriia Kazanskoi Dukhovnoi Akademii,* Vol. 2, p. 11.

38. In addition to Kazan, theological academies existed in Moscow, Kiev, and St. Petersburg.

39. According to the academy's historian Znamenskii, the struggle against the Church schism was the "innermost cause" (*zadushevnoe delo*) of the Kazan Archbishop Grigorii (Postnikov). While in St. Petersburg, where he also served as a member of the Holy Synod, Grigorii taught courses against the schism to priests from various Russian dioceses. The new rector of the Kazan Theological Academy, Agafanagel (Solov'ev) (1854–1857), was the principal instructor at the academy's anti-schism division, and his passionate efforts helped the academy build an extensive collection of manuscripts and books related to the schism. The transfer of the Solovetskii monastery's library to the Kazan Academy in 1855 created favorable conditions for the study of old Russian literature and the history of the Church schism, and these became the predominant interests of the academy's students, while *Pravoslavnyi sobesednik,* published by the academy from 1855, was conceived as a journal having its primary focus on the Old Belief. Znamenskii, *Istoriia Kazanskoi dukhovnoi akademii,* Vol. 2, pp. 371, 378–380. At the same time, the Holy Synod directed the editors of the existing religious journals to publish articles that could help to convert Schismatics to Orthodoxy. See Krasnosel'tsev, *Kratkaia istoriia zhurnala "Pravoslavnyi sobesednik,"* 4.

40. Znamenskii, *Istoriia Kazanskoi dukhovnoi Akademii*, 11, 374.

41. Ibid., 411–413.

42. Ibid. According to the academy's information, by August 1866, among the thirty-six students who had graduated, only two were employed by the academy, while six taught Tatar at the seminaries. Ibid., 449.

43. Ibid., 438–439.

44. According to Znamenskii, the report was written by Il'minskii; see his *Istoriia Kazanskoi Dukhovnoi Akademii*, 117.

45. "Otzyv professorov Kazanskoi dukhovnoi akademii N. I. Il'minskogo i G. S. Sablukova v Akademicheskoe pravlenie o prichinakh otpadeniia kreshchenykh tatar iz pravoslaviia v magometanstvo i o sredstvakh k bolee prochnoi russifikatsii tatar, 9 fevralia 1858," in *Materialy po istorii Tatarii*, 223.

46. Ibid., 226–227.

47. Ibid., 232.

48. Ibid.

49. Cited from Znamenskii, *Istoriia Kazanskoi dukhovnoi Akademii*, 415.

50. Ibid., 413.

51. Znamenskii, *Na pamiat',* 109.

52. On Russian "sectarians" and popular religion, see Klibanov, *Istoriia religioznogo sektantstva;* and Freeze, "Institutionalizing Piety: The Church and Popular Religion." For a discussion of Russian "sectarians" within the context of empire, see Breyfogle, *Heretics and Colonizers.*

53. RGIA, f. 821, op. 133, d. 454, ll. 299–299 ob.

54. On the legal status of Schismatics in the Russian empire, see Iasevich-Borodaevskaia, *Bor'ba za veru;* Papkov, *Tserkovno-obshchestvennye voprosy;* Waldron, "Religious Toleration in Late Imperial Russia."

55. Valuev, *Dnevnik,* 29, 275, 305.

56. The Holy Synod considered that the academy's divisions had failed in their main purpose—the training of missionaries to propagate Orthodoxy among Muslims and Buddhists. Therefore, according to a new statute issued in 1870, the Kazan Academy lost its exclusive status as a missionary training school. Missionary subjects remained in the curriculum, but the statute did not make provision for incentives for students to choose these subjects, and thus the status of the professors remained uncertain. Znamenskii, *Na pamiat',* 270–272; Znamenskii, *Istoriia Kazanskoi dukhovnoi akademii,* 476, 500. Despite all of these setbacks, however, the teaching of Islam at the academy continued. N. P. Ostroumov (1846–1930), a student of Il'minskii, taught anti-Muslim subjects during most of the 1870s, and after he left in 1877 for Turkestan, he was replaced by his student, M. A. Mashanov (1852–1924).

57. Werth, "The Limits of Religious Ascription," 495, 500–501.

58. "Proshenie kupecheskogo plemiannika Mukhammed-Rakhim Iagudina Aleksandru II o razreshenii kreshchenym tataram g. Buinska ispovedovat' magometanskuiu veru, 3 sentiabria 1866," in *Materialy po istorii Tatarii,* 271; "Proshenie krest'ian 5-ti dereven' Buinskogo uezda ministru vnutrennikh del A. E. Timashevu s zhaloboi na pritesneniia so storony mestnogo pravoslavnogo dukhovenstva, 23 dekabria 1868," in ibid., 277; and "Prosheniia krest'ian Kazanskoi gubernii Tetiushskogo uezda," in NART, f. 2, op. 2, d. 1712, ll. 1 ob–15.

59. Typically, in accordance with the 1854 decree that was intended to protect ani-

mists from Muslim propaganda, animists' petitions about their conversion to Islam were also rejected. However, more than once the MVD satisfied individual petitions. RGIA, f. 821, op. 133, d. 433, ll. 2–2 ob.

60. "Vypiska iz dela ob otpadenii krest'ian vtorogo stana Kazanskogo uezda i o soprotivlenii ikh mestnym vlastiam" (dated not earlier than 26 July 1866), in *Materialy po istorii Tatarii,* 239.

61. NART, f. 968, op. 1, d. 20, l. 10.

62. NART, f. 1, op. 2, d. 231, l. 138.

63. Il'minskii's ideas about preventing apostasy were outlined in an 1858 report written upon the request of the Holy Synod, "Otzyv professorov Kazanskoi dukhovnoi akademii N. I. Il'minskogo i G. S. Sablukova v Akademicheskoe pravlenie o prichinakh otpadeniia kreshchenykh tatar iz pravoslaviia v magometanstvo i o sredstvakh k bolee prochnoi russifikatsii tatar," in *Materialy po istorii Tatarii,* 223. Il'minskii's system is outlined in Il'minskii, "Ob obrazovanii inorodtsev posredstvom knig, perevedennykh na ikh rodnoi iazyk"; idem, *Sistema narodnago i v chastnosti inorodcheskago obrazovaniia;* idem, *Kazanskaia Tsentral'naia kreshcheno-tatarskaia shkola.*

64. For an analysis of these efforts, see Freeze, *The Parish Clergy in Nineteenth-Century Russia,* 208.

65. Werth, *On the Margins of Orthodoxy.*

66. "Pis'mo professora N. I. Il'minskogo i.d. ober-prokurora D. A. Tolstomu o poezdke sovmestno s vitse-gubernatorom E. A. Rozovym po Kazanskoi gubernii dlia ob"iavleniia tataram tsarskogo otkaza na ikh domogatel'stva ob otstuplenii ot pravoslaviia, 11 iiulia 1866," in *Materialy po istorii Tatarii,* 241.

67. Znamenskii, *Na pamiat',* 199–201.

68. The Brotherhood was named after *sviatitel' Gurii,* who was a canonized Kazan diocese's first archbishop.

69. Il'minskii, *Iz perepiski po voprosu o primenenii russkogo alfavita,* 18–24, 37–46.

70. Il'minskii, "Prakticheskie zamechaniia o perevodakh," 163, 175; and "Zapiska prepodavatelia universiteta N. Il'minskogo, 9 dekabria 1866," in Il'minskii, *Iz perepiski ob udostoenii inorodtsev sviashchennosluzhitel'skikh dolzhnostei,* 9.

71. "Vypiska iz opredeleniia Synoda," in Il'minskii, *Iz perepiski ob udostoenii inorodtsev sviashchennosluzhitel'skikh dolzhnostei,* 5–7.

72. For example, Il'minskii, "Oproverzhenie islamisma kak neobkhodimoe uslovie k tverdomu priniatiiu tatarami khristianskoi very," in Znamenskii, *Na pamiat',* prilozhenie, 388; Il'in, "Znachenie religii Mukhammeda v istorii," 51; Voronets, "Kharakter mokhammedanstva po Pal'grevu," 237; Volkov, "Islam i ego vliianie na zhizn' ispoveduiushchikh ego," 361.

73. "Pis'mo N. I. Il'minskogo k rektoru Kazanskoi dukhovnoi Akademii arkhimandritu Nikanoru, 8 September 1870," 144; and also RGIA, f. 821, op. 133, d. 433, l. 6.

74. Sergii (Vasilevskii), *Vysokopreosviashchennyi Antonii (Amfiteatrov),* Vol. 1, 98, 264.

75. Ibid., 279.

76. Letter No. 25, dated 30 April 1867, in *Pis'ma Vysokopreosviashchennogo Antoniia,* 37.

77. Letter No. 26, dated 25 August 1867, in *Pis'ma Vysokopreosviachennogo Antoniia,* 38.

78. RGIA, f. 821, op. 8, d. 743, ll. 31–31 ob.

79. Ibid., l. 47 ob.

80. Ibid, l. 62 ob.

81. *Moskovskie vedomosti*, no. 101, 8 May 1867.

82. Katkov developed this idea mainly in relation to Russian Catholics. For example, later S. Bagin in his missionary report to the head of the Kazan mission, Bishop Andrei, used Katkov's metaphor. NART, f. 1, op. 6, d. 607, l. 43.

83. Tarasova, *Vysshaia dukhovnaia shkola v Rossii*, 26–27.

84. Ternovskii, *Istoricheskaia zapiska*, 60.

85. For the content of the articles, see Khabibulin, *Iz istorii Kazanskogo islamovedeniia*, 170–176.

86. An earlier attempt by the Rector Ioann to change the content of the journal, by addressing the relevant social questions, was stopped by the Holy Synod in 1859: the editor and the censor received a warning and censorship was moved to Moscow. Krasnosel'tsev, *Kratkaiia istoriia zhurnala "Pravoslavnyi sobesednik,"* 31.

87. RGIA, f. 821, op. 133, d. 454, l. 271 ob.

88. Polunov, *Pod vlast'iu ober-prokurora*, 99.

89. Iuzefovich, *Politicheskie pis'ma*, 1–2.

90. Iuzefovich, "Khristianstvo, magometanstvo i iazychestvo," 28–29.

91. Ibid., 40.

92. Ibid., 37.

93. Werth, "The Limits of Religious Ascription," 502.

94. RGIA, f. 821, op. 8, d. 743, ll. 104–106 ob.

95. Ibid., ll. 124 ob.–128.

96. Ibid., ll. 181–89.

97. Ibid., l. 142. Il'minskii's report to Pobedonostsev on these issues, is on ll. 81–98. ob.

98. RGIA, f. 821, op. 133, d. 454, l. 302.

99. *Otchet Obshchestva vosstanovleniia pravoslavnogo khristianstva na Kavkaze,*152.

100. On the Russian Orthodox church during the late imperial period, see Freeze, *The Parish Clergy in Nineteenth-Century Russia;* Polunov, *Pod vlast'iu ober-prokurora;* idem, "Church, Regime, and Society in Russia (1880–1895)"; Shevzov, *Russian Orthodoxy on the Eve of Revolution.*

101. See, for example, "Pol'skii vopros i zapadno-russkoe delo. Evreiskii vopros, 1860–1886," Vol. 3, in *Sochineniia I. S. Aksakova*, 109, 248, 337–338, 506. The newspaper *Den* was published from 1861 through 1865. Also see Papkov, *Tserkovno-obshchestvennye voprosy*, 42, 84.

102. Tsimbaev, *I. S. Aksakov*, 124. In 1862, the newspaper was temporary closed. The formal pretext was Aksakov's refusal to name the author of an anonymous article about the state of Orthodox clergy in Vilna province. Aksakov refused to reveal the author because he knew that the church authorities would punish him. See Tsimbaev, *I. S. Aksakov*, 117.

103. N. S. "Tserkovno-prikhodskie bratstva v Pribaltiiskom krae," 437–439.

104. Grigor'ev, "Neskol'ko slov o prichinakh uspeshnogo rasprostraneniia magometanstva sredi inorodtsev-iazychnikov," 86–87.

105. Mashanov, *Religiozno-nravstvennoe sostoianie kreshchenykh tatar*, 41–45; Il'minskii, *Sistema narodnogo i v chastnosti inorodcheskogo obrazovaniia*, 7–8.

106. "Otchet Ufimskogo eparkhial'nogo komiteta Pravoslavnogo missionerskogo obshchestva," 104–105.

107. Mashanov, *Religiozno-nravstvennoe sostoianie kreshchenykh tatar*, 39, 44, 51.

108. Ibid., 45.

109. Rybakov, *Islam i prosveshchenie inorodtsev,* 15. This argument was also used by proponents of Il'minskii's system, who considered baptized non-Russians as better agents of Christianity in non-Russian environments than ethnic Russians.

110. I. Kh., "Vpechatleniia poezdki po inorodcheskim mestnostiam Orenburgskogo kraia v 1900 godu," in *Pravoslavnyi blagovestnik* 6 (March 1905): 255–256.

111. Iznoskov, "Materialy dlia istorii khristianskogo prosveshcheniia inorodtsev Kazanskogo kraia," 224.

112. I. Kh., "Vpechatleniia poezdki po inorodcheskim mestnostiam Orenburgsogo kraia v 1900 godu," *Pravoslavnyi blagovestnik* 6 (March 1905): 255–258; and 7 (April 1905): 312.

113. Iuzefovich, "Khristianstvo, magometanstvo i iazychestvo," 61.

114. Ibid., 60.

115. *Materialy po istorii Tatarii,* 242; NART, f. 1, op. 2, d. 231, l 39 ob–40; RGIA, f. 821, op. 8, d. 743, l. 106.

116. RGIA, f. 821, op. 8, d. 743, ll. 45–45 ob.

117. Il'minskii's 1858 report, in *Materialy po istorii Tatarii,* 222 and NART, f. 1, op. 6, d. 607, l. 179.

118. Il'minskii, "Ex oriente lux," 50–51. Il'minskii also expressed similar thoughts in the report about his studies abroad that he submitted to the Kazan Theological Academy; see his 1858 report in *Materialy po istorii Tatarii.*

119. For example, see Kazanets, "Novoe tatarskoe izdanie po geografii," 186. Later, S. Bobrovnikova also mentioned that "the missions find small sympathy and interest in Russian society," while "the Muslims are an energetic, organized force, and work with an untiring solidarity to undo the work of the followers of Ilminskii"; Bobrovnikoff, "Moslems in Russia," 31.

120. Freeze, *The Parish Clergy in Nineteenth-Century Russia,* 398, 466.

121. RGIA, f. 821, op. 133, d. 454, l. 302.

122. Werth, "The Limits of Religious Ascription," 504–506.

3. "What Do We Need from Muslims?"

1. Smirnov, "Po voprosu o shkol'nom obrazovanii inorodtsev-musul'man," 17.

2. Dowler, *Classroom and Empire,* 18–20, 240; Geraci, *Window on the East,* 150–151, 156.

3. Eklof, *Russian Peasant Schools,* 64–68. On government educational policies and especially the Tolstoy system, see Alston, *Education and the State in Tsarist Russia,* 87–104 and Sinel, *Classroom and the Chancellery.*

4. On Tolstoy's church reform, the impetus for which came from the western provinces, see Freeze, *The Parish Clergy,* 298–347.

5. "Zhurnal Soveta ministra narodnogo prosveshcheniia po voprosu o prosveshchenii inorodtsev, 2 fevralia 1870 g.," in *Materialy po istorii Tatarii,* 281–285; "Ofitsyail'nye dokumenty," in *Sbornik dokumentov i statei,* 157–159.

6. "Zhurnal Soveta ministra," *Materialy po istorii Tatarii,* 282.

7. Dolbilov, *Prevratnosti kirillizatsii,* 6.

8. On educated Russians' views of peasants, see Eklof, *Russian Peasant Schools.*

9. See Kareev, "Ideia progressa."

10. For example, these issues constituted the essence of what Christian Snouck Hurgronje (1857–1936), a Dutch orientalist and advisor on native affairs to the colonial government of the Netherlands East Indies, whose works were also known to Russian academic and government experts on Islam, later conceptualized as the "problem of Islam" in his *Mohammedanism*, 146, 149, 178. On the development of Western views of Islam and the Muslim world, see Rodinson, *Europe and the Mystique of Islam*.

11. Religious "fanaticism" was identified by some educated Russians as present not only in Islam but also in Judaism, Catholicism, and Russian sectarianism. However, for state reformers like Tolstoy and especially for later reactionaries like the Ober-Procurator of the Holy Synod Pobedonostsev, "political fanaticism" was the real danger that represented an especially grave problem; such "fanaticism" was apparent as early as the 1860s–1870s. See Pobedonostsev's reference to what he called "political and tribal fanaticism" in his letter to N. I. Il'minskii (24 April 1885), in RGIA, f. 1574, op. 1, d. 146, l. 31.

12. "Iz obshchestvennoi khroniki," 421.

13. Il'in, "Znachenie religii Mohammeda v istorii," 49; Zarinskii, "Apologiia islamizma," 285–286; Solov'ev, *Magomet*, 78.

14. In 1922, the Russian Orientalist V. Bartol'd challenged this view by pointing out that it is circumstances of life that influence religion, rather than vice versa. Bartol'd, "Musul'manskii mir," 230.

15. "Zhurnal Soveta ministra," in *Materialy po istorii Tatarii*, 284.

16. *Sbornik dokumentov i statei*, 14–17, 186.

17. "Zapiska ordinarnogo professora S. Petersburgskogo universiteta V. V. Grigor'eva," in *Sbornik dokumentov i statei*, 204.

18. "Materialy po voprosu ob obrazovanii Krymskikh Tatar, izvlechennye iz del Tavricheskoi direktsii uchilishch i drugikh mestnykh istochnikov direktorom Tavricheskikh uchilishch Markovym," in *Sbornik dokumentov i statei*, 102–103.

19. On Markov as an "enlightener" (*prosveshchennyi pedagog*), see *Izvestiia Tavricheskoi ucheonoi arkhivnoi komissii*, Vol. 35 (Simferopol, 1903), 44–46; Also see Rozanov, "Pamiati E. L. Markova," 3.

20. "Materialy po voprosu ob obrazovanii Krymskikh Tatar, izvlechennye iz del Tavricheskoi direktsii uchilishch i drugikh mestnykh istochnikov direktorom Tavricheskikh uchilishch Markovym," in *Sbornik dokumentov i statei*, 98–99.

21. Ibid., 108.

22. Ibid., 98–99.

23. Ibid., 110.

24. Il'minskii, "Ex oriente lux," 48–51.

25. See his 1870 report to the curator of the Kazan educational district, P. D. Shestakov, in *Materialy po istorii Tatarii*, 293.

26. "Dokladnaia zapiska professora N. I. Il'minskogo popechiteliu Kazanskogo uchebnogo okruga P. D. Shestakovu," in *Materialy po istorii Tatarii*, 294.

27. RGIA, f. 1149, op. 9, d. 77, l. 12 ob. 16.

28. For a detailed description of schools created by the 1870 Regulations, see Dowler, *Classroom and Empire*, and Geraci, *Window on the East*.

29. *Materialy po istorii Tatarii*, 313.

30. *Sbornik zakonov o musul'manskom dukhovenstve*, 26, 44.

31. NART, f. 968, op. 1, d. 78, ll. 5–6; Znamenskii, *Uchastie N. I. Il'minskogo*, 102.

32. RGIA, f. 821, op. 8, d. 814, ll. 9–9 ob. Also, *Sbornik zakonov o musul'manskom dukhovenstve,* 44–45.

33. RGIA, f. 821, op. 8, d. 809, l. 80.

34. Anan'ich et. al., *Vlast' i reformy,* 374.

35. RGIA, f. 821, op. 133, d. 467, ll. 477 ob.–478.

36. Ibid., l. 479 ob.

37. Znamenskii, *Uchastie Il'minskogo,* 1, 4, 106.

38. *Sbornik zakonov o musul'manskom dukhovenstve,* 50–51.

39. On Russian educational policies in the Caucasus, see Gatagova, *Pravitel'stvennaia politika.* On educational policies in Turkestan, see Dowler, *Classroom and Empire.*

40. Sorenson, "Pobedonostsev's Parish Schools," 191.

41. Ibid., 194.

42. Freeze, *The Parish Clergy,* 448.

43. On Russification as a concept and practice, see Miller, "Rusifikatsii: Klassifitsirovat' i poniat'"; Weeks, "Russification: Word and Practice 1863–1914"; Dolbilov, "Russification and the Bureaucratic Mind"; Geraci, *Window on the East;* Staliūnas," Did the Government Seek to Russify Lithuanians and Poles," idem, *Making Russians.*

44. Wayne Dowler has also noted that Il'minskii's thinking about nationality was colored by Slavophilism. See his *Classroom and Empire,* 44. On Slavophilism, see Gleason, *European and Muscovite;* Christoff, *An Introduction to Nineteenth-Century Russian Slavophilism;* Walicki, *The Slavophile Controversy.* On Slavophilism in the context of Romanticism, see Riasanovsky, *Russia and the West* and Rabow-Edling, *Slavophile Thought.*

45. Znamenskii, *Na pamiat',* 129. Russian documents from the nineteenth to the early twentieth century referred to Kazakhs as "Kirgiz," while the Kyrgyz peoples of present-day Kyrgyzstan were called "Kara-Kirgiz."

46. Il'minskii, "Mnenie po voprosu o merakh dlia obrazovaniia kirgiz," 1870, in Il'minskii, *Vospominaniia ob I. A. Altynsarine,* 160.

47. Il'minskii, *Vospominaniia ob I.A. Altynsarine,* 14–15.

48. Znamenskii, *Na pamiat',* 148. Also, NART, f. 968, op. 1, d. 8, ll. 73, 79.

49. Il'minskii, "Mnenie ob uchitel'skoi shkole dlia inorodtsev Orenburgskogo kraia," in *Vospominaniia ob Altynsarine,* 167.

50. Ibid., 166–167.

51. On the Kazakhs in the Russian empire, see Martin, *Law and Custom in the Steppe;* Geraci, "Going Abroad or Going to Russia?" and Sabol, *Russian Colonization.*

52. Lazzerini, "Volga Tatars in Central Asia," 84–85, 88–90.

53. Valikhanov, "Sledy shamastva u kirgizov," and "O musul'manstve v stepi."

54. Il'minskii, *Vospominaniia ob I. A. Altynsarine,* 4.

55. "Letter to Il'minskii, 12 September 1882," in *Vospominaniia ob I. A. Altynsarine,* 250.

56. "Pis'ma uchitelei ob Altynsarine: Arsenii Mozokhin, 28 sentiabria 1889 g.," in Il'minskii, *Vospominaniia ob I. A. Altynsarine,* 375.

57. "Pis'ma uchitelei: Iz pis'ma F. D. Sokolova, 9 avgusta 1889 goda k N. I.," in Il'minskii, *Vospominaniia, ob I. A. Altynsarine,* 385.

58. Znamenskii, *Na pamiat',* 143.

59. Mashanov, *Obzor deiatel'nosti,* 176–177.

60. Il'minskii, "Chernovik stat'i o rasprostranenii magometanstva sredi Kazanskikh tatar, posle 1878," RGB, f. 424, karton 1, d. 11, l. 1.

61. Bobrovnikov, "Zametki k zapiske po inorodcheskomu voprosu, 1903," RGB, f. 424, karton 4, d. 2, l. 43.

62. *Sbornik dokumentov i statei,* 326–327.

63. Cited in Larionov, *Nachal'noe obrazovanie inorodtsev,* 90.

64. *Zapiska, naidennaia v bumagakh N. Kh. Bunge,* 16.

65. See, for example, Gradovskii, *Natsional'nyi vopros,* 23; *Zapiska naidennaia v bumagakh N. Kh. Bunge,* 17. Later these ideas were expressed by Bishop Andrei, "O merakh k okhraneniiu Kazanskogo kraia ot postepennogo zavoevaniia ego tatarami, 14 ianvaria 1908," RGIA. f. 1276, op. 4, d. 815, ll. 1–4.

66. Reisner, *Gosudarstvo i veruiushchaia lichnost',* 196–198, 406.

67. *Vsepoddanneishii otchet ober-prokurora Sv. Sinoda,* 125–126. Such an identification of religion with nationality was criticized by M. N. Katkov. See Katkov, *Sobranie peredovykh statei,* 373.

68. Iznoskov, "Inorodcheskie prikhody Kazanskogo uezda," 225.

69. Rybakov, *Islam i prosveshchenie inorodtsev,* 14.

70. On the process of "Russians going native," see Sunderland, "Russians into Iakuts?" 806–825.

71. Chicherin, *Kurs gosudarstvennoi nauki,* 188.

72. Aksakov, "Pol'skii vopros i zapadno-russkoe delo," 443.

73. Mashanov, *Religiozno-nravstvennoe sostoianie,* 37–41.

74. Larionov, *Nachal'noe obrazovanie,* 96.

75. Leont'ev, *Sobranie sochenienii,* Vol. 7 (St. Petersburg, 1913), 374.

76. Andrei, "Ob obrusenii," 58–61.

77. Ostroumov, *Islamovedenie,* 3.

78. Ostroumov, "Kolebaniia vo vzgliadakh," 148–149.

79. On Gasprinskii's life and ideas, see Gubaidullin, "K voprosu ob ideologii Gasprinskogo"; Klimovich, "Na sluzhbe prosveshcheniia"; Lazzerini, "Ismail Bey Gasprinskii and Muslim Modernism in Russia"; idem, "Ğadidism at the Turn of the Twentieth Century"; idem, "From Bakhchisarai to Bukhara," Bennigsen, *Ismail Bey Gasprinskii i proiskhozhdenie dzhadidskogo dvizheniia;* Chervonnaia, *Ismail Gasprinskii—prosvetitel' narodov Vostoka. Materialy mezhdunarodnoi nauchnoi konferentsii;* Gankevich, *Na sluzhbe pravde i prosveshcheniiu;* Gankevich and Shendrikova, *Ismail Gasprinskiii i vozniknovenie liberal'no-musul'manskogo politicheskogo dvizheniia.*

80. Bennigsen, "Ismail Bey Gasprinskii i proiskhozhdenie dzhadidskogo dvizheniia, 84.

81. Lazzerini mentions that during that time Gasprinskii had plans to emigrate to Turkey. Lazzerini, "Ismail Bey Gasprinskii and Muslim Modernism in Russia," 4.

82. Gasprinskii, *Russkoe musul'manstvo,* 20–21.

83. Ibid., 19.

84. Ibid., 20.

85. Ibid., 19, 20.

86. Ibid., 45–46. On the need for and role of intelligentsia in popular enlightenment, see Gasprinskii, "Nasha intelligentsiia."

87. Gasprinskii, *Russkoe musul'manstvo,* 38–39.

88. Ibid., 26, 36.

89. Ibid., 46.

90. Until 1905, the newspaper had two sections: one in the Russian language and the second in a simplified version of the literary Ottoman Turkish language, in Arabic script. The school in Bakhchisarai was not the first attempt to reform a Muslim school in Russia, but it had the most significant consequences.

91. Khalid, *The Politics of Muslim Cultural Reform*, 13, 173–175.

92. Ibid., 5, 13, 114–115, 135.

93. On different "styles" of Jadidism, see Khalid, *Politics of Muslim Cultural Reform*, 90–93. On the development of the movement as well as its intellectual origins, see Iskhakov, *Phenomen Tatarskogo dzhadidizma*. On the religious aspect of the reformist movement among the Tatars, see Kanlidere, *Reform within Islam*. For the evaluation of the success of the reformist intellectuals in modernizing the Muslim communities in the Volga–Ural regions, see Tuna, "Imperial Russia's Muslims: Inroads of Modernity."

94. On the role of Marjani, see Schamiloglu, "The Formation of the Tatar Historical Consciousness."

95. GAARK, f. 26, op. 2, d. 1595, 23–23 ob.

96. Devlet-Kil'deev, *Magomet kak prorok;* Murza Alim, "Islam i magometanstvo"; Baiazitov, *Vozrazheniia na rech' Ernesta Renana: Islam i nauka; Otnoshenie islama k nauke i inovertsam;* idem, *Islam i progress.*

97. See Miropiev, "Kakie nachala," 26–30, 39; and his *O polozhenii russkikh inorodtsev.*

98. LOIV RAN, f. 50, op. 1, d. 158.

99. Ibid., l. 42 ob.

100. Gordlevskii, "Pamiati V. D. Smirnova," 413.

101. Ibid., 408.

102. "Letter of Il'minskii to Ostroumov, 20 April 1890," NART, f. 968, op. 1, d. 78, l. 78 ob.

103. NART, f. 968, op. 1, d. 78, l. 79 ob. Il'minskii probably referred to Zahir Bigiev, who was also a prominent Tatar writer. On Bigiev, see Akhunov, "Izvestnyi i neizvestnyi Zahir Bigiev."

104. See, for example, Ostroumov, *Chto takoe Koran? Po povodu statei gg. Gasprinskogo, Devlet-Kil'deeva, i Murzy Alima;* idem, *Araviia i Koran;* idem, *Koran i progress;* idem, "Magometanskii vopros v Rossii."

105. "Letter of Il'minskii to Ostroumov" (3 February 1888), in NART, f. 968, op. 1, d. 78, l. 69 ob.

106. Gasprinskii met Ostroumov during the former's trip to Central Asia in 1893. See Lazzerini, *Ismail Bey Gasprinskii and Muslim Modernism*, 37.

107. Copies of letters signed by Murza Alim to Ostroumov (14 April 1883) are in NART, f. 968, op. 1, d. 72, ll. 5, 5 ob., 7.

108. Ibid. (May 1883), in NART, f. 968, op. 1, d. 72, l. 10.

109. A copy of Gasprinskii's letter to Ostroumov is in NART, f. 968, op. 1, d. 72, ll. 16–16 ob.

110. Letters from 11 February 1882 and 10 February 1884, in *Pis'ma N. I. Il'minskogo K. P. Pobedonostsevu*, 2, 64–65.

111. Letter of 29 February 1884, ibid., 74; letter of 18 February 1885, ibid., 175.

112. Letters of 10 February1884, and 1 February 1890, in ibid., 61, 338.

113. Bobrovnikov, *Inorodcheskoe naselenie*, 1–2.

114. Ibid., 2; idem, *Russko-tuzemnye uchilishcha*, 43, 70.

115. *Vvedenie v kurs islamovedeniia*, 77–78. For the analysis of Gasprinskii's and Il'minskii's ideas as two identity projects; see Tuna, "Gaspirali v. Il'minskii."

116. Ostroumov, *Vvedenie v kurs islamovedeniia*, 77–78.

117. On the development of Jajidism in Central Asia in the context of modernist movements within a larger Muslim world, see Khalid, *The Politics of Muslim Cultural Reform;* Baldauf, *Jadidism in Central Asia.* On the role of Gasprinskii and especially of his concept of a "Muslim nation" in the development of modernist movement in Turkestan, see Abdirashidov, *Ismail Gasprinskii i Turkestan.*

118. The newspaper began publishing in 1870, first as a supplement to the official *Turkestanskie vedomosti.*

119. Ostroumov, "6-i Turkestanskii general-gubernator, general-leitenant Sergei Mikhailovich Dukhovskoi. Dnevnik," TsGARU, f. 1009, op. 1, d. 73. ll. 41–41 ob.; Ostroumov, *Vvedenie v kurs islamovedeniia,* 79.

120. A copy of his proposal is in TsGARU, f. I-1, Op. 11, d. 806, ll. 2–3.

121. TsGARU, f. I-1, op. 11, d. 806, l. 67 ob.

122. NART, f. 986, op. 1, d. 43, ll. 14 ob–15.

123. Ibid., 2; Bobrovnikov, *Russko-tuzemnye uchilishcha,* 43, 70.

124. Among them were S. Maksudov, F. Tukhtarov, and G. Iskhakov. Dzh. Validi (1887–1932), a linguist and publicist, has emphasized the prominent role of the Kazan Teachers' School in the history of Tatar cultural and political movement. See his *Ocherki istorii obrazovannosti i literatury tatar,* 67–68.

125. NART, f. 93, op. 1, d. 516, l. 8.

126. Ibid. Zagidullin has suggested that the errors in translation of the brochure played a certain role in provoking Tatars' misunderstanding of the government's intentions and hence the resistance to the census; see Zagidullin, *Perepis' 1897 goda,* 113.

127. See, for example, Gasprinskii's article in which he defines the Muslim progressives: "Tatarskaia progressivnaia partiia."

128. Gasprinskii, "First Steps toward Civilizing the Russian Muslims," 250–257.

129. For an interpretation of Slavophilism as illiberal engagement with modernity, see Engelstein, *Slavophile Empire.* On the efforts of early Slavophiles to reconfigure Eastern Christianity as a modern religion, see Michelson, "Slavophile Religious Thought."

130. For example, restrictive norms for non-Christians concerned their participation in city governance. Muslim teachers were allowed to instruct only their coreligionists but, unlike their Christian peers, were deprived of state-provided privileges associated with the teaching profession. To become attorneys (*prisiazhnye poverennye*), Muslims had to receive special permission from the Ministry of Justice.

131. RGIA, f. 821, op. 150, d. 406, ll. 1 ob.–2.

132. Ibid.

133. RGIA, f. 821, op. 8, d. 1194, ll. 8 ob.–9.

134. Ibid., l. 18.

135. RGVIA, f. 400, op. 4, d. 14, l. 1.

136. Ibid., ll. 2–3 ob.

4. "In Asia We Come As Masters"

1. Dostoevsky, whose famous words: "In Europe we were dependents [*prizhival'shchiki*] and slaves, in Asia we come as masters" of 1881 are often cited to illustrate Russians' aspiration to dominate the Orient, also connected imperial penetration to Asia with hope for Russia's spiritual revitalization. He wrote: "The turn to Asia and our new view of her might

lead to something like what happened to Europe, when America was discovered . . . the aspiration to Asia will revive our spirit and regenerate us." In Dostoevsky, *Dnevnik pisatelia za 1881 god*, Vol. 3, 609.

2. See Kappeler, *The Russian Empire*; Khalid, *The Politics of Muslim Cultural Reform*; Brower, *Turkestan and the Fate of the Russian Empire*; Sahadeo, *Russian Colonial Society*; Morrison, *Russian Rule in Samarkand*.

3. Brower, *Turkestan and the Fate of the Russian Empire*, 7.

4. For a survey of Russian expansion in this region, see Bekmanov, *Prisoedinenie Kazakhstana k Rossii*; Kappeler, *The Russian Empire*, 33–48, 185–200; Abashin et al., *Tsentral'naia Aziia*, 32–61.

5. Orenburg province was created in 1744. In 1850 and 1865, the vast territories of the province were divided for administrative purposes between the Perm province in the north, Ufa province in the northwest, and Samara province in the west. The southern territories constituted the Turgai and Ural areas (*oblast*). Orenburg province retained the central territories. The Orenburg and Ufa provinces and the Turgai and Ural areas constituted the Orenburg governor-generalship, which existed until 1881.

6. The Ministry of Foreign Affairs and the Ministry of Finance were especially cautious in regard to Russia's expansionism in this region. For the arguments of both ministries, see Abashin et al., *Tsenral'naia Aziia*, 66–67.

7. On Russia's military campaign in Central Asia, see Terent'ev, *Istoriiia zavoevaniia*; Khalfin, *Prisoedinenie Srednei Azii*.

8. RGVIA, f. 400, op. 1, d. 3772, l. 3 ob.

9. Abashin et al., *Tsentral'naia Aziia*, 79.

10. *Materialy po istorii Tatarii*, 190–191.

11. RGIA, f. 821, op. 8, d. 594, l. 62 ob.

12. On von Kaufman's background, see Semenov, "Pokoritel' i ustroitel' Turkestanskogo kraia," in *Kaufmanskii sbornik*, and Glushchenko, *Stroiteli imperii*, 31–176.

13. For an examination of Kaufman's regime in Turkestan, see Mackenzie, "Kaufman of Turkestan."

14. The Turkestan governor-generalship was enlarged by territories taken from the Orenburg and western Siberian governor-generalships.

15. Kappeler, *The Russian Empire*, 191.

16. On the organization of the Russian administration in this area, see *Proekt vsepoddanneishego otcheta K. P. von Kaufmana*.

17. The conflict between the reformist and authoritarian methods of rule in Turkestan is analyzed by Brower, in *Turkestan and the Fate of the Russian Empire*.

18. *Proekt vsepoddanneishego otcheta*, 440. According to the memoirist Evald, Kaufman viewed the connection of Catholicism with politics, and especially the political role of the Catholic clergy, as a serious obstacle to the integration of Poles into the empire. Evald, "Vospominaniia o K. P. von Kaufmane," 189.

19. *Proekt vsepoddanneishego otcheta*, 145 and Ostroumov, *K istorii narodnogo obrazovaniia v Turkestanskom krae*, 43.

20. On Russian policies in relation to indigenous law and especially local legal practices in Central Asia under Russian rule, see Sartori, "The Birth of a Custom," 299–301.

21. *Proekt vsepoddanneishego otcheta*, 207.

22. Glushchenko sees in von Kaufman's land reform a pattern similar to his policies in the northwestern region. Glushchenko, *Stroiteli imperii*, 112–118.

23. *Proekt vsepoddanneishego otcheta,* 437–440.

24. This was the area with the highest concentration of the Russian population.

25. See Ostroumov, "Kitaiskie emigranty."

26. Ostroumov, *K istorii narodnogo obrazovaniia v Turkestanskom krae,* 43.

27. Maksheev, "Prebyvanie v Vernom i vstrecha Kaufmana," 647.

28. Ostroumov, *K istorii narodnogo obrazovaniia v Turkestanskom krae,* 51.

29. Ostroumov recalled how Kaufman spoke with him about his educational policies in Vilna. Ostroumov, *K istorii narodnogo obrazovaniia,* 54.

30. Brower, *Turkestan and the Fate of the Russian Empire,* 14.

31. Morrison, *Russian Rule in Samarkand,* 51–53.

32. Znamenskii, *Uchastie N. I. Il'minskogo,* 13.

33. Von Kaufman practiced similar policies (use of the Lithuanian language with the Cyrillic alphabet) in his struggle with Polish influence in Vilna. Znamenskii, *Uchastie N. I. Il'minskogo,* 11. On Russian language policies in the Vilna general-governorship in 1864–1882, see Dolbilov, "Prevratnosti kirillizatsii."

34. Znamenskii, *Uchastie Il'minskogo,* 27–28.

35. He served as the director until 1883.

36. N. A. Voskresenskii, M. A. Miropiev, I. M. Sofiiskii, and P. A. Perovskii. See Znamenskii, *Uchastie Il'minskogo,* 57–63.

37. *Otchet revizuiushchego,* 454.

38. Sahadeo, *Russian Colonial Society,* 49.

39. Crews, *For Prophet and Tsar,* 241–293.

40. On Russian educational institutions in Turkestan, see Gramenitskii, "Ocherk razvitiia narodnogo obrazovaniia v Turkestanskom krae."

41. Znamenskii, *Uchastie Il'minskogo,* 94–98.

42. "Otchet general-leitenanta Korol'kova," in *Otchet po rassledovaniiu,* 14.

43. Ibid.

44. TsGARU, f. 1, op. 31, d. 1197, ll. 10–10 ob.

45. Manz, "Central Asian Uprisings in the Nineteenth Century: Ferghana under the Russians," 275–276.

46. "Mestnoe obozrenie," *Sredne-Aziatskii vestnik* (March 1896), 62–65.

47. On the Andijan revolt as well as its leader, see Babadžanov, "Dukchi Ishan und der Aufstand von Andizan 1898"; Bobozhonov and Kügelgen, *Manakib-i Dukchi Ishan;* Babadzhanov, "Andizhanskoe vosstanie 1898 goda i 'musul'manskii vopros v Turkestane." On the responses of Muslim society to the revolt, see Komatsu, "Dar Al-Islam under Russian Rule"; idem, "The Andijan Uprising Reconsidered"; and Erkinov, *The Andijan Uprising of 1898 and Its Leader Dukchi Ishan Described by Contemporary Poets.*

48. Ostroumov, "6-i Turkestanskii general-gubernator, general-leitenant Sergei Mikhailovich Dukhovskoi," TsGARU, f. 1009, Op. 1, d. 73, ll. 11–11 ob.

49. Dukhovskaia, *Turkestanskie vospominaniia,* 33–36.

50. Ibid., 44. Dukhovskaia paid several visits to Tashkent. During her stay in St. Petersburg, Dukhovskoi wrote letters to his wife that she partially recounts in her memoirs. The memoirs, written in the form of a diary, give grounds to suppose that Dukhovskaia was well-informed about her husband's views concerning the governance of Turkestan.

51. RGVIA, f. 1396, op. 2, d. 1740, ll. 47–48 ob.

52. Ibid., ll. 45–47 ob.

53. Ibid., ll. 49–50.

54. Ibid., l. 44.

55. "Otchet general-leitenanta Korol'kova," in *Otchet po rassledovaniiu*, 3.

56. Dukchi ishan mentioned the decline of morals among the population and blamed the authorities for the restrictions placed on the pilgrimage to Mecca, certain religious endowments, and abolition of the traditional taxes; see *Otchet po rassledovaniiu*, 9, 21. On the interpretation of religious motivation of the uprising, see Babadžanov, "Dukchi Ishan und der Aufstand von Andizan 1898" and Bobozhonov and Kügelgen, *Manakib-i Dukchi Ishan*, 15.

57. "Zapiski: Margelanskogo uezdnogo nachal'nika polkovnika Brianova, nachal'nika Andizhanskogo uezda podpolkovnika Koishevskogo, nachal'nika Namaganskogo uezda Arvanitaki," in *Otchet po rassledovaniiu*, 44, 50–51, 58. Beatrice Manz also developed an argument that the Andijan uprising had its origins in the politics of the Kokand khanate that had controlled the area earlier. Manz, "Central Asian Uprisings in the Nineteenth Century," 279–281.

58. One of the aims of the investigation was to determine guilt among the officials of the Russian and native administrations who had allowed the attack on the Russian garrison. This circumstance may have also affected the interpretation of the Andijan incident as unprecedented, and therefore unexpected. Such an interpretation would to some extent have justified the inability of the local administration to prevent the attack.

59. "Zapiska nachal'nika Andizhanskogo uezda podpolkovnika Koishevskogo," in *Otchet po rassledovaniiu*, 56.

60. "Zapiska nachal'nika Namaganskogo uezda Arvanitaki," 58; "Zapiska Margelanskogo uezdnogo nachal'nika polkovnika Brianova," in *Otchet po rassledovaniiu* 44–46.

61. "Otchet general-leitenanta Korol'kova," *Otchet po rassledovaniiu*, 25. Korol'kov particularly criticized the principles of separating judicial power from administrative authority, the introduction of the principle of elections for positions in the *volost* administration, and the reduction of the staff in the Turkestan administration.

62. *Otchet po rassledovaniiu*, 28–31.

63. *Vsepoddanneishii doklad Turkestanskogo general-gubernatora Dukhovskogo "Islam v Turkestane,"* 3, 5.

64. "Kratkii obzor sovremennogo sostoianiia i deiatel'nosti musul'manskogo dukhovenstva," 71.

65. That is how the Andijan uprising was interpreted in *Mysli russkogo cheloveka*, reprinted from *Turkestanskie Vedomosti*, nos. 1, 3, 5 (1898), in RGVIA, f. 1396, op. 2, d. 1536, l. 3.

66. For example, V. Dukhovskaia mentioned that Dukhovskoi visited the governor of Kazan province to discuss the Muslim Question. See Dukhovskaia, *Turkestanskie vospominaniia*, 57–59.

67. TsGARU, f. 1, op. 11, d. 1725, l. 207 ob.

68. Ibid.

69. Ibid., ll. 227, 228.

70. *Vsepoddanneishii doklad Dukhovskogo "Islam v Turkestane,"* 18.

71. TsGARU, f. 1, op. 11, d. 1725, l. 223 ob.

72. RGVIA, f. 1396, op. 2, d. 570, l. 13.

73. Nalivkin was a participant in the military campaigns in Central Asia in 1873–1875. He left the service in 1878 and settled with his wife in the Nanai village of the Na-

maghan district, where he studied the life of the natives. In 1884 he became a teacher at the first Russian–native school in Tashkent. He also taught Uzbek and Tajik at the Tashkent Teachers' Seminary. In 1890–1895, he was the school inspector of Syr-Darya, Ferghana, and Samarkand provinces. He prepared several reports on Islam for Dukhovskoi, including the report to the tsar. At the turn of the century, he served as a chief official for special tasks (*dlia osobykh poruchenii*) for the Turkestan governor-general, and then as an aide to the military governor of Ferghana. Unlike Ostroumov, Nalivkin's political views were close to those of the Russian Social Democrats. In 1907, he was elected as a deputy of the Second Duma. He was the author of several books on the languages and life of Central Asian societies. In 1918, he committed suicide. On Nalivkin, see Arapov, "Vladimir Petrovich Nalivkin." For an insightful analysis of Nalivkin's views and of Russian Orientalism, see Abashin, "V. P. Nalivkin."

74. GARF, f. 586, op. 1, d. 208, ll. 2–8.

75. S. M. Dukhovskoi to A. N. Kuropatkin, 29 July 1900, in RGVIA, f. 1396, op. 2, d. 570, ll. 10–12.

76. In relation to this project, a program was developed according to which local officials were asked to gather statistical information on Islam. TsGARU, f. I-36, op. 3, d. 3808, ll. 40, 43–44 ob.

77. Missionaries' writings (for example, some articles from *Protivomusl'manskii sbornik*) were among the sources of the articles in the collection, and one of the authors, N. Ostroumov, widely published his work in missionary journals. Ostroumov claimed in his diary that the collection was put together under his guidance. TsGARU, f. 1009, op. 1, d. 73, l.

78. Iarovoi-Ravskii, "Palomnichestvo (hajj) v Mekku i Medinu."

79. "Kratkii obzor sovremennogo sostoianiia i deiatel'nosti musul'manskogo dukhovenstva, raznogo roda dukhovnykh uchrezhdenii i uchebnykh zavedenii tuzemnogo naseleniia Samarkandskoi oblasti, s nekotorymi ukazaniiami na ikh istoricheskoe proshloe," *Sbornik materialov po musul'manstvu*, Vol. 1, p. 28. On Sufism as explanation of Muslim resistance in the Caucasus and Central Asia, see Knysh, "Sufism as an Explanatory Paradigm." On French anxieties about the role of Sufi brotherhoods in Algeria, see Harrison, *France and Islam,* 19–23. On similarities in the Russian administration of the Caucasus and French rule in Algeria, and especially on the transfer of colonial models, see Bobrovnikov, "Russkii Kavkaz i Frantsuzskii Alzhir."

80. Smirnov, "Dervishism v Turkestane," 55.

81. "Dzhikhad ili gazavat."

82. Mikhailov, "Religioznye vozzreniia turkmen Zakaspiiskoi oblasti," 88; and Artemenko, "Bata. Ocherk kirgizskikh nravov," 107.

83. Smirnov, "Dervishizm v Turkestane," 55, and Artemenko, "Bata. Ocherk kirgizskikh nravov," 109.

84. Dukhovskaia, *Turkestanskie vospominaniia,* 58–59.

85. RGIA, f. 821, op. 150, d. 409, ll. 13–15.

86. Ibid., l. 11 ob.

87. AVPR, f. 147, op. 485, d. 1256, l. 15 ob, l. 33.

88. "Posluzhnoi spisok Davletshina, Sentiabr', 1890," in RGVIA, f. 400, op. 21, d. 1609, ll. 163–265 ob.

89. LOIV RAN, f. 70, op. 1, d. 47, ll. 7–9.

90. RGVIA, f. 165, op.1, d. 565, l. 96.

91. Ibid., l. 97.

92. Ostroumov, *K istorii narodnogo obrazovaniia v Turkestanskom krae*, 44; Znamenskii, *Uchastie Il'minskogo*, 21–22.

93. He explained his decision by stating the impossibility of combining the new position with his service in the Ministry of Public Education, due both to the complexity of Muslim affairs and to the disagreement between different ministries in their views of Islam; see TsGARU, f. 1009, op. 1, d. 73, l. 18.

94. Ibid., ll. 15 ob, 16 ob, 37 ob, 39.

95. Ibid., 37.

96. Ostroumov, "6-i Turkestanskii general-gubernator," in TsGARU, f. 1009, op. 1, d. 73, l. 22.

97. On the question of the status and especially the degree and nature of influence of Russian scholars on policies in Asia, see Knight, "Grigor'ev in Orenburg"; Khalid, "Russian History and the Debate over Orientalism"; Morrison, "Applied Orientalism."

98. TsGARU, f. 1009, op. 1, d. 73, l. 9 ob. In his memoirs, Ostroumov mentioned that many of Dukhovskoi's subordinates did not like the governor-general.

99. At the same time, he was critical of von Kaufman's indifference to the religious question. See Ostroumov, *K istorii narodnogo obrazovaniia v Turkestanskom krae*, 44.

100. TsGARU, f. 1009, op. 1, d. 73, l. 21 ob.

101. Ostroumov mentioned in his diary that he had read, commented on, and overall agreed with the content of the report to the tsar before Dukhovskoi delivered it to St. Petersburg; see TsGARU, f. 1009, op. 1, d. 73, l. 65. Also, Ostroumov, *Istoricheskii ocherk*, 50.

102. Ostroumov, *K istroii narodnogo obrazovaniia*, 46.

103. TsGARU, f. 1009, op. 1, d. 73, l. 10 ob.

104. Ibid., l. 35.

105. TsGARU, f. 1009, op. 1, d. 73, l. 42 ob.

106. Ostroumov, "Kolebaniia vo vzgliadakh na obrazovanie tuzemtsev v Turkestanskom krae," 59.

107. More than once, Ostroumov mentioned that the decline of religiosity and morals among Russians and Europeans in general was their shortcoming with respect to Muslims; see Ostroumov, *Istoricheskii ocherk vzaimnykh otnoshenii*, 45, and idem, *Sarty*. Part 1 (Tashkent, 1896), 82.

108. TsGARU, f. 1009, op. 1, d. 175, l. 118.

109. Ibid.

110. "Obshchii vzgliad na zadachu russkoi administratsii Turkestanskogo kraia v otnoshenii k musul'manskomu ego naseleniiu. Mnenie chlena komissii direktora muzhskoi gimnazii N. Ostroumova, 5 sentiabria 1884"; NART, f. 968, op. 1, d. 43, l. 7. For his most optimistic prognosis of this policy, see *Sarty*, Part 1 (Tashkent, 1890), and the second edition (Tashkent, 1896).

111. TsGARU, f. 1009, op. 1, d. 73, l. 58.

112. Ibid., l. 10 ob.

113. Ibid., ll. 63, 68.

114. On Russia's cultural mission in Asia, see Ostroumov, *Istoricheskii ocherk*, 58.

115. Among these signs, many observers mentioned the 1892 cholera riots in Tashkent that were accompanied by the assault on the Tashkent's governor S. R. Putintsev by the rebels. They also pointed to the symbolic expressions of this decline as exemplified in

ceremonial encounters between the Russian administration and the native elite, as well as in everyday life encounters (such as natives spitting after a Russian had passed by).

116. Nalivkin, *Tuzenmtsy ran'she i teper,*'131–139.

117. For instance, see his positive description of the Afghan ambassadors, in Ostroumov, *K istorii narodnogo obrazovaniia,* 79. See also his description of the Sarts and Muslim spiritual leaders in ibid., 205–206; for an ethnographic description of Sarts, see Ostroumov, *Sarty.* Nalivkin also pointed to the erroneous perception of the so-called "wild Asiatics" "who, as he thought, in many respects were more cultured than Russians." See Nalivkin, *Tumzemtsy ran'she in teper,*' 95.

118. See, for example, his comparison of the Afghan ambassadors to the Russian ambassadors of the fifteenth and sixteenth centuries; in Ostroumov, *K istorii narodnogo obrazovaniia,* 79. Especially see his comparison of the life of contemporary Sarts with Russians of the seventeenth to early eighteenth centuries, in *Sarty,* Part 1 (Tashkent, 1890), 132; and the second edition (Tashkent, 1896), 188.

119. TsGARU, f. 1009, op. 1, d. 73, 1.81.

120. Kuropatkin, *Zadachi Russkoi Armii,* 142.

121. These measures included reinforcing the authority of the local administration, increasing administrative personnel and budgets, completing a rail connection between Orenburg and Tashkent, and providing stronger regulation of Muslim religious affairs.

122. Ostroumov, *Vvedenie v kurs islamovedeniia,* 212.

5. Dilemmas of Regulation and Rapprochement

1. On the basis of his analysis of court records and Muslims' petitions submitted to the Orenburg Ecclesiastical Assembly, Robert Crews argues that "the tsarist understanding of toleration promoted peace—between rulers and ruled and among the faithful" and that the tsarist state lay at the heart of Islam for most communities of the empire; see his *For the Prophet and the Tsar,* 356, 349. Allen Frank's study of Russia's rural Muslim religious institutions in the southern Ural region, on the basis of local histories written by Muslims, also comes to the conclusion that the relationship between Islam and empire was cooperative. However, in contrast to Crews he points to the autonomous character of local Muslim religious institutions; see his *Muslim Religious Institutions in Imperial Russia,* 314. Dmitrii Arapov's reconstruction of state policies toward Islam led him to conclude that "although not ideal," the system of state regulation of Islam "satisfied basic religious needs of Muslims" and was "steady"; see his *Sistema gosudarsvennogo regulirovaniia islama,* 177 and *Imperatorskaia Rossiia i musul'manskii mir,* 11.

2. On Russia's strategy of incorporating Crimea and on Catherine's policies toward Islam see Fisher, "Enlightened Despotism and Islam under Catherine II"; idem, *The Crimean Tatars.*

3. PSZ I, Vol. 22, no. 16710. On the history of the Assembly, see Azamatov, *Orenburgskoe magometanskoe dukhovnoe sobranie.* On the assembly within the regional context, see Steinwedel, *Invisible Threads of Empire.*

4. Azamatov, *Orenburgskoe,* 23, 47.

5. PSZ II, Vol. 6, no. 5033.

6. SZRI, (1857), Vol. 11, part. 1, articles 1140, 1141.

7. Ibid., art. 1142.

8. Ibid., articles 1236, 1159–1170.

9. SZRI (1896), Vol. 11, part I, articles 1371, 1469, 1584.

10. SZRI (1857), Vol. 11, part I, articles 1143–1146, 1156, 1196–1206, 1211, 1230, 1238.

11. Ibid., Articles 1178 and 1207.

12. Ibid., Article 1238.

13. On the relationship between the mufti and the local Muslim religious figures, see Kemper, *Sufis und Gelehrte,* 53–79, and Frank, *Muslim Religious Institutions,* 104–106.

14. Azamatov, *Orenburgskoe magometanskoe sobranie,*189.

15. On the Orthodox clerical estate, see Freeze, *The Parish Clergy,* 145–187; on Muslim clergy, see Frank, *Muslim Religious Institutions,* 100–102.

16. "Proekt predstavleniia ministra vnutrennikh del P. A. Valueva v Komitet ministrov, 1864," in *Materialy po istorii Tatarii,* 179.

17. Ibid., 176.

18. On Valuev's approach to the church reform, see Freeze, *The Parish Clergy,* 238–247.

19. RGIA, f. 821, op. 8. 594, ll. 1–4, 16 ob.

20. Ibid., 57 ob–58.

21. "Izvlechenie iz otcheta Kryzhanovskogo," in RGIA, f. 821, op, 8, d. 594, l. 28 ob.

22. "Dokladnaia zpiska Orenburgskogo general-gubernatora N. A. Kryzhanovskogo ministru vnutrennikh del P. A. Valuevu o merakh bor'by s rasprostraneniem magometanstva v vostochnoi polovine Rossii, 1867," in *Materialy po istorii Tatarii,*191.

23. Ibid., 197–198.

24. Ibid., 198.

25. Ibid., 200.

26. "Dokladnaia zpiska Kryzhanovskogo, 1867," in *Materialy po istorii Tatarii,* 205.

27. RGIA, f. 821, op. 8, d. 594, l. 62 ob.

28. Ibid., ll. 94–97.

29. RGIA, f. 821, op. 8, d. 605, ll. 35 ob.–42 ob.

30. RGIA, f. 821, op. 8, d. 616, l. 27.

31. Ibid., ll. 28 ob.–31.

32. Ibid., ll. 46 ob.–47.

33. Ibid., l. 4.

34. RGIA, f. 821, op. 8, d. 610, ll. 4 ob.–6.

35. Ibid., ll. 43–44.

36. The areas that fell under the military-communal administration were the Batumi, Kars, and Daghestan regions, Chernomor'e province, and the Zakatal and Sukhumi districts (*okrug*).

37. SZRI (1896), Vol. 11, part. 1, articles 1576, 1461.

38. Ibid., articles 1451, 1463, 1511–1525, 1537, 1561, 1566, 1578.

39. Ibid., articles 1454, 1458, 1459, 1569, 1573, 1574.

40. RGIA, f. 821, op. 8, d. 610, ll. 92–111 ob.

41. Ibid., ll. 149 ob.–50.

42. AVPRI, f. 147, op. 485, d. 1258, l. 448.

43. Ibid. RGIA, f. 821, op. 133, d. 567, l. b.

44. On the legal history of the Kazakh steppe, see Martin, *Law and Custom in the Steppe.*

45. RGIA, f. 821, op. 133, d. 567, l. 6 ob. On the North Caucasus legal culture, see Bobrovnikov, *Musul'mane Severnogo Kavkaza;* idem (ed.), *Obychai i zakon.*

46. Unable to rely on local clergy to exert ideological influence on Muslims, the au-

thorities on occasion had to rely on Muslim clerics from the empire's internal provinces, which was the practice under Prince M. Vorontsov. See Avksent'ev, *Islam na Severnom Kavkaze*, 38.

47. AVPRI, f. 147, op. 485, d. 1267, l. 3 ob.

48. *Vsepoddanneishii doklad Turkestanskogo general-gubernatora Dukhovskogo "Islam v Turkestane,"* 18, 7. "Obshchii svod rabot Komissii po voprosu ob ustroistve musul'manskogo upravleniia v Turkestanskom krae," in AVPRI, f. 147, op. 485, d. 1267, ll. 15 ob.–16.

49. Voronets, *Nuzhny li dlia Rossii muftii*, 5.

50. Freeze, *The Parish Clergy*, 234.

51. See, for example a description of mullahs and their relationship with their congregation in Koblov, *O magometanskikh mullakh*.

52. See Azamatov, "The Muftis of the Orenburg Spiritual Assembly."

53. "Donesenie orenburgskogo i samarskogo general-gubernatora A. P. Bezaka ministru vnutrennikh del P. A. Valuevu o kandidatakh dlia vremennogo zameshcheniia dolzhnosti muftiia, 25 avgusta1863 g.," in *Materialy po istorii Tatarii*, 167–168.

54. SZRI (1857), Vol. 11, part. 1, articles 1161, 1178, 1236, 1237, 1245.

55. Azamatov, *Orenburgskoe magometanskoe dukhovnoe sobranie*, 57–58.

56. "Proekt predstavleniia P. A. Valueva v Komitet ministrov. 1864 g., ne pozdnee 5 noiabria," *Materialy po istorii Tatarii*, 178–179.

57. Ibid.

58. RGIA, f. 821, op. 150, d. 406, ll. 5–5 ob.

59. Ibid., ll. 5–5 ob; f. 821, op. 133, d. 567, l. 9.

60. RGIA, f. 821, op. 133, d. 536, ll. 152 ob. –55 ob.

61. For an overview of Russian legislation regulating the mosques, see Zagidullin, *Islamskie instituty*, 42–97.

62. For a discussion of three particular cases of state-funded mosque construction, see Frank, *Muslim Religious Institutions*, 176–179.

63. On state regulation of Orthodox clergy, see Freeze, *The Parish Clergy*, 52–56.

64. PSZ I, Vol. 12, no. 8978, SZRI (1857), Vol. 12, article 261.

65. The MVD was guided in this respect by article 150 of *Stroitel'nyi Ustav*, which determined the distance between synagogues and Orthodox churches. RGIA, f. 821, op. 150, d. 412, l. 2.

66. SZRI (1857), Vol. 12, part I, articles 262, 263.

67. RGIA, f. 821, op. 150, d. 412, l. 5. This measure had as its goal to weaken Islam among the steppe nomadic population.

68. RGIA, f. 821, op. 8, d. 666, ll. 1–4.

69. Ibid., l. 9.

70. Malov, *O Tatarskikh mechetiakh*, 77, 69–71, 79.

71. For example, the 1856 report of the Orenburg governor Potulov, who suggested ways to decrease the number of mosques. RGIA, 821, op. 8, d. 594, ll. 1–17.

72. *Materialy po istorii Tatarii*, 193; RGIA, f. 821, op. 8, d. 616, l. 14 ob.

73. RGIA, f. 821, op. 8, d. 616, ll. 15–15 ob.

74. Ibid., l. 16 ob.

75. RGIA, f. 821, op. 8, d. 666, l. 25.

76. Ibid., l. 26.

77. Ibid., l. 27.

78. This requirement was not extended to Transcaucasia. By other non-Orthodox, the MVD meant Jews outside the Pale of Settlement.

79. RGIA. f. 821, op. 8, d. 666, l. 28 ob.

80. The project submitted by the MVD to the State Council suggested giving this right to the Minister of Internal Affairs, RGIA, f. 821, op. 8, d. 616, l. 82 ob.; also: RGIA, 821, op. 8, d. 666, ll. 29–29 ob.

81. RGIA, f. 821, op. 8, d. 666, ll. 111–111 ob.

82. RGIA, f. 821, op. 8, d. 616, ll. 119 ob.–120.

83. Ibid., ll. 112–123 ob.

6. Challenges of Revolution and Reform

1. Anan'ich et. al., *Vlast' i reformy,* 457.

2. Ivanov, Pankratova, and Sidorov, *Revoliutsiia 1905–1907 gg. v natsional'nykh raion- akh Rossii;* Kappeler, *The Russian Empire,* 244.

3. On the implications of political liberalization for the development of the Tatar national project that was predominantly focused on cultural and religious issues, see Yemelianova, "The National Identity of the Volga Tatars." On the development of Muslim nationalism, see Noack, *Muslimischer Nationalismus.* For discussion of the political impact of the revolution of 1905 on Russian Muslim communities and especially on the formation of Muslim political movement, see Iskhakov, "Revoliutsiia 1905–1907 gg."; idem, *Pervaia russkaia revoliutsiia.*

4. Ashmarin, "Neskol'ko slov o sovremennoi literature Kazanskikh tatar," 2–6.

5. On Tatar press, see Bennigsen and Chantal Lemercier-Quelquejay, *La presse et le Mouvement National;* Gainullin, *Tatarskaia literatura in publitsistika.*

6. Rorlich, *The Volga Tatars,* 71.

7. Bagin, "O propagande islama putem pechati, 248.

8. "Musul'manskie s"ezdy v Rossii. Vospominaniia Topchibasheva," EHESS, CERCEC, Archives de Toptchibachy, Valise no. 1, p. 7, 12.

9. On the rapprochement of Muslim liberals with the Kadets, see Iskhakov, *Pervaia russkaia revoliutsiia,* 203–206. On the Constitutional Democrats, see Rosenberg, *Liberals in the Russian Revolution.* On the political parties during this time period, see Emmons, *The Formation of Political Parties.*

10. Rorlich, *The Volga Tatars,* 111.

11. *Niva* 7 (1906): 112.

12. "Izvestiia i zametki: Musul'manskii s"ezd," 336.

13. Ibid.

14. "V. V. Novitskii to P. N. Durnovo, 20 March 1906," in RGIA, f. 821, op. 8, d. 1198, ll. 78–79.

15. "Zapiska Departamenta politsii o vtorom musul'manskom S"ezde v sviazi s tret'im, Avgust 1906," in *Natsional'nye dvizheniia v period pervoi russkoi revoliutsii,* 229–230.

16. *Rech,* 137 (13 August 1906), in RGIA, f. 821, op. 8, d. 1198, l. 21.

17. RGIA, f. 821, op. 8, d. 1198, ll. 8–18.

18. *Rech,* 143 (20 August 1906), in RGIA, f. 821, op. 8, d. 1198, l. 21 ob.

19. *Novoe vremia,* no. 10924 (12 August 1906); in RGIA, f. 821, op. 8, d. 1198, l. 20.

20. For characteristics of the political orientation of the newspaper and on Azerbaijani liberalism, see Swietochowski, *Russian Azerbaijan.*

21. "Tretii vserossiiskii musul'manskii s'ezd. Postanovleniia i rezoliutsii," in *Politicheskaia zhizn' russkikh musul'man,* 32, 34.

22. Rorlich, *The Volga Tatars,* 112–117. Tatars (seven of them were from the Kazan province) held eleven of fifteen seats on the party's central committee. See Iskhakov, *Pervaia russkaia revoliutsiia,* 257–258.

23. On the Duma as an imperial forum, see Tsiunchuk, *Dumskaia model' parlamentarisma;* Semyonov, "The Real and Live Ethnographic Map of Russia."

24. Usmanova, *Musul'manskaia fraktsiia,* 38. Also, see her *Musul'manskie predstaviteli.*

25. Usmanova, *Musul'manskaia fraktsiia,* 38–39.

26. Zenkovsky, "A Century of Tatar Revival," 317.

27. "Pis'mo Tsentral'nogo komiteta musul'manskoi partii o neobkhodimosti obrazovaniia musul'manskoi fraktsii v 3-ei Gosudarstvennoi Dume, 17 noiabria 1907," NART, f. 186, op. 1, d. 73, ll. 1–5.

28. "Musul'manskie s'ezdy v Rossii." Vospominaniia Topchibasheva. EHESS, CERCEC, Archives de Toptchibachy Valise no. 1, pp. 3–4. This document was also published in Iskhakov (ed.), *Iz istorii azerbaidzhanskoi emigratsii,* 108–138.

29. Topchibashev, "Zapiska o vseobshchem obuchenii." EHESS, CERCEC, Archives de Toptchibachy, Valise 3, cart no. 9, 1; "Musul'manskie s'ezdy v Rossii. Vospominaniia," ibid., Valise no. 1, p. 22.

30. Usmanova, *Musul'manskaia fraktsiia,* 111.

31. Alisov, "Musul'manskii vopros v Rossii," 29–30.

32. "Rech, proiznesennaia A. M. Topchibashevym 25 iiunia 1914 g. na 4-m Musul'manskom s'ezde," in EHESS, CERCEC, Archives de Toptchibachy, Valise no. 8, l. 3 ob.

33. "Zapiska o polozhenii musul'man v Rossiiskoi imperii, Baku, 1905. Dokumenty iz Rossii." Ibid., Valise no. 3, cart no. 27, p. 27.

34. *Memuary grafa I. I. Tolstogo,* 158.

35. Tolstoy and Gessen, *Fakty i mysli,* 141, 217–219.

36. On the Society for equal rights and brotherhood," see Anan'ich and Tolstaya, "I. I. Tolstoy i "kruzhok ravnopraviia i bratstva."

37. Alisov, "Musul'manskii vopros v Rossii," 29–30.

38. *Rossiia,* no. 238 (14 September 1906); in RGIA, f. 821, op. 8, d. 1198, l. 46.

39. RGIA, f. 821, op. 8, d. 1198, ll. 81 ob–82.

40. Iskhakov, "Revoliutsiia 1905–1907 gg. i rossiiskie musul'mane," 200–201.

41. Fakhrutdinov, *Tatarskoe liberal'no-demokraticheskoe dvizhenie,* 14.

42. RGIA, f. 821, op. 8, d. 1198, l. 68 ob.

43. RGIA. f. 821, op. 150, d. 419, l. 26.

44. Budilovich, "Dobavlenie," in Alektorov, *Inorodtsy v Rossi,* 132; Budilovich, *Mozhet li Rossiia otdat' inorodtsam svoi okrainy,* 26.

45. *Vlast' i reformy,* 470–471.

46. The decree, however, omitted any mention of public participation, which was the most important aspect of Sviatopolk-Mirskii's program.

47. For the discussion of the legislative process of the religious reform, see Waldron, "Religious Reform after 1905"; Dorskaia, *Svoboda sovesti v Rossii.*

48. "Zapiski i prosheniia, podannye gospodinu Predsedateliu Komiteta Ministrov

po inorodcheskim voprosam," in Biblioteka RGIA, Kollektsiia pechatnykh zapisok, papka, 255.

49. "Pamiatnaia zapiska upolnimochennykh musul'manskogo obshchestva g. Kazani prisiazhnogo poveremmogo S. Sh. Alkina, mully G. G. Apanaeva, kuptsa A. Ia. Saidasheva, potomstvennogo pochetnogo grazhdanina Iu. Kh. Akchurina," 12 March 1905, in Biblioteka RGIA, kollektsiia pechatnykh zapisok, papka 255, pp. 57–61.

50. RGIA, f. 821, op. 133, d. 455, l. 303 ob., and f. 821, op. 133, d. 454, ll. 54–53 ob.

51. Werth, *At the Margins,* 224.

52. "Osobyi zhurnal Komiteta Ministrov 25 ianvaria, 1 i 8 fevralia i 15 marta 1905 g. o poriadke vypolneniia punkta shestogo imennogo ukaza 12 dekabria 1904 g.," in *Za pervyi god veroispovednoi svobody v Rossii,*13.

53. RGIA, f. 821, op. 150, d. 7, ll. 262, 266.

54. "Osobyi zhurnal komiteta Ministrov,"in *Za pervy god veroispovednoi svobody,* 17.

55. RGIA, f. 821, op. 150, d. 7, l. 191 ob., 240 ob.

56. RGIA, f. 821, op. 150, d. 7, l, 256 ob.

57. Ignat'ev was also the chair of the special government commission on state police. See Witte, *Vospominaniia,* 362. As Witte later noted, the chair as well as other members were selected to prevent the implementation of the Tolerance Decree.

58. Cherevanskii, *Mir islama i ego probuzhdenie,* Part II, 253.

59. Ostroumov, *Koran i progress.* Some of Cherevanskii's letters to Ostroumov are in TsGARU, f. 1009, op.1, d. 54, ll. 12–13.

60. See his "Zapiska po delam very musul'man-sunnitov," in Bibiloteka RGIA, kollektsiia pechatnykh zapisok, papka 747, pp. 68–69, 31–33.

61. In opposition to the Russian view of recent conversion of Kazakhs to Islam, representatives from the Turgai oblast claimed in their petition that Kazakhs deserved to have a special organ of ecclesiastical administration, on the basis that they had been "true Muslims" since the thirteenth century; in RGIA, f. 821, op. 10, d. 29, ll. 4–9 ob., 13 ob, l. 20 ob. For Cherevanskii's opinion on this question, see his "Zapiska po delam very," 34, 37.

62. He proposed to keep Sharia only among those Kazakhs who already used it in their legal practice. See "Sudebnoe delo kirgizskogo naroda s religioznoi tochki zreniia," in Biblioteka RGIA, kollektsiia pechatnykh zapisok, papka 747, pp. 7–11.

63. "Zapiska po delam very," 38–42.

64. Cherevanskii, "O polozhenii musul'manskoi zhenshchiny," in RGIA, f. 821, op. 10, d. 27, l. 369 ob.

65. See "Zhurnaly Osobogo soveshchaniia po delam very. Zhurnal no. 6," in RGIA, f. 821, op. 10, d. 35, ll. 56 ob, 59, 60, 64–66 ob.

66. RGIA, f. 821, op. 8, d. 633, l. 16.

67. On how the problem of freedom of consciousness was addressed by the Muslim Duma faction, see Usmanova, *Musul´manskaia fraktsiia.*

68. Lazzerini, *Ismail Bey Gasprinskii and Muslim modernism,* 59; and Ostroumov, *Vvedenie v kurs islamovedeniia,* 82.

69. Budilovich's publications on the Alien Question included *Po voprosu ob okrainakh Rossii; Mozhet li Rossiia otdat' inorodtsam svoi okrainy? Neskol'ko dannykh i soobrazhenii ob uspekhakh russkogo iazyka.* On Budilovich, see Grot, "Pamiati Antona Semenovicha Budilovicha."

70. These ideas were articulated in his *Kholmskaia Rus' i poliaki;* and *Noveishii fazes samoopredeleniia narodnostei.*

71. "Soobshchenie S. V. Chicherinoi ob osmotrennykh eiu inorodcheskikh shkolakh," in *Trudy Osobogo soveshchaniia,* 211.

72. Ibid., 211–212.

73. Bobrovnikov, "Poekt shkoly dlia prakticheskogo izucheniia vostochnykh iazykov v Kazani," in *Trudy Osobogo soveshchaniia,* 313.

74. Miropiev, "O primenenii shkol sistemy Il'minskogo na Kavkaze," *Trudy Osobogo soveshchaniia,* 229.

75. Ibid., 224.

76. "Pravila o merakh k obrazovaniiu inorodtsev, zhivushchikh v vostochnoi i iugo-vostochnoi Rossii," *Trudy osobogo soveshchaniia,* 346.

77. "Zhurnal zasedanii Osobogo soveshchaniia po voprosam obrazovaniia vostoch-nykh inorodtsev," *Trudy Osobogo soveshchaniia,* 10, 13.

78. "Doklad predsedatelia Osobogo soveshchaniia po voprosam obrazovaniia vostoch-nykh inorodtsev A.S. Budilovicha," in *Trudy Osobogo soveshchaniia,* IX.

79. "Proekt shkoly dlia prakticheskogo izucheniia vostochnykh iazykov v Kazani," in *Trudy Osobogo soveshchaniia,* 313–317.

80. *Pravila o nachal'nykh uchilishchakh dlia inorodtsev, zhivushchikh v vostochnoi i iugo-vostochoi Rossii, utverzhdennye Ministerstvom narodnogo prosveshcheniia 31 marta 1906 g. i 2 ianvaria 1907 g.* Orenburg, 1907. Also, see Prilozhenie II, in: "Rasporiazheniia i deistviia pravitel'stva i zakonopolozheniia, otnosiashchiesia do musul'man," 269–272.

81. *Tretii Vserossiiskii musul'manskii s"ezd,* 2–10.

82. *Pravila o nachal'nykh uchilishchakh dlia inorodtsev, utverzhdennye ministrom narodnogo prosveshcheniia 1 noiabria 1907 g.* (Kazan, 1907). Also see, Prilozhenie III in: "Rasporiazheniia i deistviia pravitel'stva i zakonopolozheniia, otnosiashchiesia do musul'man," 273–277.

7. The Muslim Question in the Aftermath of the Revolution

1. Ascher, *The Revolution of 1905,* 351.

2. Rorlich, *The Volga Tatars,* 119–120.

3. On Stolypin and his reforms, see Avrech, *P. A. Stolypin i sud'by reform;* Waldron, *Between Two Revolutions;* Ascher, *P. A. Stolypin: The Search for Stability.*

4. Anan'ich et. al., *Vlast' i reformy,* 556.

5. RGIA, f. 821, op. 8, d. 633, l. 16.

6. Waldron, *Religious Toleration in Late Imperial Russia,* 117.

7. On Stolypin's nationalism and borderland policies, see Avrech, *P. A. Stolypin i sud'by reform v Rossii,* 130–179; on state policies in Poland and the western provinces during this period, see Weeks, *Nation and State in Late Imperial Russia;* on state policies in the Baltic provinces, see Andreeva, *Pribaltiiskie nemtsy.*

8. For more details on Stolypin government's legislative tolerance projects and their discussion in the Duma, see Rozhkov, *Tserkovnye voprosy.* On religious reform, and espe-cially the problem of freedom of consciousness during Stolypin's tenure, see Waldron, *Religious Reform after 1905;* Dorskaia, *Svoboda sovesti v Rossii;* Werth, "Arbiters of the Free Conscience."

9. See his analysis of the Decree on Tolerance, in *Gosudarstvo i veruiushchaia lichnost'*, 416–418.

10. Cited in Rozhkov, *Tserkovnye voprosy,* 106.

11. Ibid., 123–124.

12. RGIA, f. 821, op. 10, d. 283, l. 70.

13. Ibid., l. 235.

14. RGIA, f. 821, op. 133, d. 545, ll. 1 ob–2.

15. Werth, *At the Margins,* 252–253.

16. Circular of the MVD from 12 November 1907, in RGIA, f. 821, op. 133, d. 433, ll. 171–171 ob. Cases of conversion of animists to Islam were registered in Ufa (601 people), Samara (85 families), and Kazan (47 people) provinces, RGIA, f. 821, op. 133, d. 545, l. 2 ob.

17. Avrekh, *P. A. Stolypin i sud'by reform,* 180–181.

18. Pobedonostsev, "Chernovik vsepoddanneishego doklada K. P. Pobedonostseva," 204–205.

19. Elisvanov, *Trudnosti i nuzhdy Kazanskoi inorodcheskoi missii,* 4.

20. From 1905 on, *Pravoslavnyi sobesednik* had a special section devoted to the "Eastern *inorodtsy*" and the development of missionary activity among them. Attention to these issues was also given in periodicals that appeared after the revolution, including *Sotrudnik Bratstva sv. Guriia* (published from 1909 by the brotherhood of St. Gurii under the editorship of Bishop Andrei), and *Tserkovno-Obshchestvennaia zhisn'* (published from 1905 at the Kazan Theological Academy).

21. Bobrovnikov, "Nuzhny li tak nazyvaemye protivomusul'manskie i protivoiazycheskie eparkhial'nye missionery," 311.

22. Bobrovnikoff, "Moslems in Russia," 11.

23. Witte, *Vospominaniia,* vol. 2, 362–363.

24. On the Orthodox church and the reformist debate during this period, see Firsov, *Pravoslavnaia Tserkov' i gosudarstvo v poslednee desiatiletie;* Shevzov, *Russian Orthodoxy on the Eve of Revolution.*

25. For example, as the first issue of *Tserkovno-obshchestvennaia zhizn'* from 16 December 1905 pointed out, the goal of the periodical was to clarify "socio-religious understanding of the question of church reform" as well as to provide objective coverage of obscure facts of the church's relation to society. As it also stated, the special goal of the journal was to discuss the questions concerning the religious and daily conditions of Russian *inorodtsy* living in the eastern borderlands of Russia.

26. "O vospitanii budushchikh pastyrei," 238.

27. "Likholet'e v zhizni pravoslaviia sredi privolzhskikh inorodtsev," in *S. Petersburgskie vedomosti,* 128 (11 June 1909), in NART, f. 10, op. 6, d. 607, l. 26. Andrei addressed this subject in his many other publications and reports submitted to the government. Similar to Andrei, A. A. Papkov (1868–1920), a prominent public figure, an official, and governor of one of Finland's provinces and the author of numerous articles on the renewal of Orthodox parish life, pointed to Protestant parishes as objects for comparison. See Papkov, *Pravoslavnye prikhody v Finliandii;* and *O blagoustroistve pravoslavnogo prikhoda.* On the parish life of Old Believers as a model for the Orthodox church, see Iasevitch-Borodaevskaia, *Bor'ba za veru.*

28. RGIA, f. 81, op. 8, d. 801, l. 73.

29. Andrei, "O merakh k okhraneniiu Kazanskogo kraia ot postepennogo zavoevaniia ego tatarami" (14 January 1908), in RGIA, f. 1276, op. 4, d. 815, ll. 1–4.

30. Ibid., 3, 8.

31. Zelenogorskii, *Zhizn' i deiatel'nost' arhiepiskopa Andreia*, 7. On Father Ioann and the formation of his cult in late imperial Russia, see Kizenko, *A Prodigal Saint*.

32. "Pravoslavnye inorodtsy i Soiuz Russkogo naroda," 9 July 1908, no. 108, in NART, f. 10, op. 6, d. 607, l. 116.

33. NART, f. 1, op. 6, d. 607, l. 55.

34. "Magometanskaia agitatsiia," 3 June 1909, no. 11933.

35. Andrei, "Likholet'e v zhizni pravoslaviia sredi privolzhskikh inorodtsev," in *S. Petersburgskie vedomosti* 122 (4 June 1909); "Po Rossii," in *Kolokol* 976 (19 June 1909) in NART, f. 10, op.1, d. 607, ll. 25–27.

36. Bagin, "O propagande islama putem pechati," 247.

37. NART, f. 1, op. 6, d. 607, l. 37.

38. Andrei, *Likholet'e v zhizni pravolaviia*, 10.

39. NART, f. 1, op. 6, d. 607, ll. 1–2; 29–30 ob.

40. Ibid., ll. 88–88a.

41. Ibid., ll. 138–139 ob.

42. Avrech, *P. A. Stolypin i sud'by reform*, 136–158; *Vlast' i reformy*, 566.

43. Ascher, *P. A. Stolypin: The Search for Stability*, 314.

44. On the Kholm Question, see Avrech, *P. A. Stolypin i sud'by reform*, 159–178; Weeks, *Nation and State*, 172–192.

45. Shpitsberg, "Tserkov' i rusifikatsiia buriato-mongol pri tsarizme," 102.

46. Kharuzin's personal file is in RGIA, f. 821, op. 12, d. 558. On Kharuzin, see Kerimova and Naumova, "Aleksei Nikolaevich Kharuzin."

47. Kharuzin, *Kirgizy Bukeevskoi Ordy*.

48. "Predstavlenie A. N. Kharuzina v Sovet Ministrov 'O merakh dlia protivodeistviia panislamistskomu i panturanskomu (pantiurkskomu) vliianiiu sredi musul'manskogo naseleniia," (15 January 1911), in Biblioteka RGIA, kollektsiia pechatnykh zapisok, papka 747, 1.

49. RGIA, f. 821, op.8, d.801, l. 169.

50. Aleksii, *Sovremennoe dvizhenie*, 6–8. See also his *Voinstvuiushchii islam*.

51. RGIA, f. 821, op. 8, d. 801, l. 152.

52. Ibid., ll. 154–154 ob.

53. RGIA, f. 821, op. 8, d. 801, l. 167.

54. "Predstavlenie A. N. Kharuzina," in Biblioteka RGIA, kollektsiia pechatnykh zapisok, papka 747, p. 14.

55. Boborovnikov, "K voprosu o mugallimakh, poluchivshikh obrazovanie za granitsei," 1908, in LOIV RAN, f. 44, op. 1, d. 281, l. 38 ob.

56. Ibid., ll. 3–5, 15 ob., 30 ob.

57. RGIA, f. 821, op. 8, d. 801, l. 172 ob.

58. Dowler, *Classroom and Empire*, 185–186.

59. Gorokhova and Ibragimov, eds., *Medrese g. Kazani*, 153.

60. "Predstavlenie Kharuzina," in Biblioteka RGIA, kollektsiia pechatnykh zapisok, papka 747, p. 5.

61. RGIA, f. 821, op. 8, d. 801, ll.151–154, 180.

62. RGIA, f. 1022, op. 1, d. 28, l. 2, 31, 171.

63. Ibid., 74, 117. The discussion on how Muslim communities in Ufa province responded to the state's project of universal primary education; see Naganawa, "Maktab or School?"

64. Dowler, *Classroom and Empire*, 220. Dowler, however, also mentions the importance of the larger Russian debate on the role of religion in schooling.

65. Geraci, *Window on the East*, 292, 294. See also Geraci, "Russian Orientalism at an Impasse."

66. "Predstavlenie v Komitet Ministrov," 15 ianvaria 1911, Biblioteka RGIA, Pechatnaia zapiska 747, p. 5.

67. RGIA, f. 821, op. 8, d. 801, l. 167.

68. Bashinskii, "Nash s''ezd," 4.

69. RGIA, f. 821, op. 8, d. 801, ll. 73 ob–75 ob.

70. "Missionerskii s''ezd v Kazani 13–26 iunia 1910 goda," 5–8. On the major issues addressed by the congress, see McCarthy, "The Kazan' Missionary Congress."

71. Ostroumov, "Kolebaniia russkogo pravitel'stva vo vzgliadakh na missionerskuiu deiatel'nost," in *Sotrudnik Bratstva sv. Guriia* 43 (1910): 678–679; and also his *Kolebaniia russkogo pravitel'stva vo vzgliadakh na missionerskuiu deiatel'nost'*, 8–11.

72. Doklad Mashanova missionerskomu s''ezdu 1910 goda "Sovremennoe sostoianie tatar-mukhammedan," 71, 74, 103.

73. This self-reflective character of the congress with its emphasis on church renewal is emphasized by Robert Geraci, in *Window on the East*, 306–308.

74. "Pozhelaniia missionerskomu s''ezdu," *Sotrudnik Bratstva sv. Guriia* 33 (1910): 523.

75. Numerov, "Kazanskii missionerskii s''ezd," 1816. For discussion of the congress's provisions on schooling policies, see Dowler, *Classroom and Empire*, 221–223.

76. Pisarev, *Kazanskii missionerskii s''ezd*, 709.

77. For example, *Kazanskii telegraf* no. 5015 (1909) and no. 5092 (1910), in NART, f. 1, op. 6, d. 607, l. 215, 240. Also see, Il'minskii, *O sisteme prosveshcheniia inorodtsev i o Kazanskoi tsentral'noi kreshcheno-tatarskoi shkole*, XXVII. In his letter to S. F. Platonov, dated May 1911, Bobrovnikov explained that by demonstrating his "loyalty" to the Orthodox church, Zalesskii aspired to obtain the position of the curator of the educational district in Vilna. RNB OR, St. Petersburg, f. 585, d. 2306.

78. Il'minskii, *O sisteme prosveshcheniia inorodtsev i Kazanskoi Tsentral'noi kreshchenotatarskoi shkole*, 22.

8. "Solving" the Muslim Question

1. RGVIA, f. 400, op. 1, d. 3772, l. 1.

2. RGIA, f. 1276, op. 7, d. 6, l. 46 ob.

3. RGIA, f. 821, op. 8, d. 835, l 1. 3–4.

4. AVPRI, f. 147, op. 485, d. 1258, l. 50; and RGIA, f. 821, op. 133, d. 511, ll. 27–28, 30 ob.

5. The Society for Oriental Studies was created in St. Petersburg in 1900 with the support of the Ministry of Finance. The official goal of the society was to "spread true information about Russia among the Oriental people, as well as to familiarize Russian society with the material needs and spiritual life of the Orient; to promote rapprochement of Russia with the Oriental countries, and to serve as a champion of Russian culture and

productivity among Oriental nationalities within and outside Russia." See *Imperatorskoe Obshchestvo*, 1. The goal of promoting Russian economic interests in the East played an especially important role in the establishment of the society and its activities. Beginning in 1907, the society was under the jurisdiction of the Ministry of Trade and Industry. See Vigasin et al. *Istoriia otechestvennogo vostokovedeniia*, 112–114. On the history of the journal, see Hairutdinov, "'Mir islama.'"

6. For Bartold's criticism of the Oriental Institute in Vladivostok in 1902, see Vigasin et al., *Istoriia otechestvennogo vostokovedeniia*, 73–74.

7. Bartol'd, "Ot redaktsii," 1.

8. Ibid., 3, 14.

9. RGIA, f. 821, op. 133, d. 563, l. 24 ob.

10. RGIA, f. 821, op. 133, d. 511, l. 30 ob.

11. Vigasin et al., *Istoriia otechestvennogo vostokovedeniia*, 261.

12. On French anxieties about Islam, see Harrison, *France and Islam*, 29–57.

13. On the role of "Islamic" expertise in French colonial rule and especially Le Chatelier's views of Islam within the context of the evolution of French Muslim policy in West Africa, see Harrison, *France and Islam*, 31–33, and also Robinson, *Paths of Accommodation*, 86. The Colonial Institute was established in 1908 in Hamburg; its purpose was to train businessmen and officials for future careers overseas. See Spidle, "Colonial Studies." For a survey of the development of German-language Oriental studies and especially a discussion of the ambiguous role that academic Orientalists played in serving German imperial ambitions during World War I, see Hagen, "German Heralds of Holy War." For a survey of scholarly literature on European perceptions and governance of Muslims during the imperial age, see Motadel, "Islam and the European Empires."

14. In 1913, the official of the Department for Religious Affairs of Foreign Confessions S. Rybakov asked his department to acquire the *Revue* and *Die Welt des Islams*. RGIA, f. 821, op. 133, d. 635, l. 1.

15. The institute was established in 1899 as a result of Witte's initiative. Its task was to train specialists for "practical" activities in the Far East in the diplomatic, commercial, religious, and military spheres. Its first director was the brother of D. M. Pozdneev, A. M. Pozdneev.

16. "Ot redaktsii," I–II. Also, "Ob izdanii zhurnala *Mir islama*," in RGIA, f. 821, op. 133, d. 563, l. 26.

17. *Russkaia molva*, 45 (25 January 1913) and Bartol'd's response to the MVD's criticism are in RGIA, f. 821, op. 133, d. 511, l. 35.

18. RGIA, f. 821, op. 133, d. 563, l. 26.

19. Ibid., l. 27 ob.

20. RGIA, f. 821, op. 133, d. 449, ll. 505–505 ob.

21. Ibid.

22. RGIA, f. 821, op. 133, d. 577, l. 377 ob., 380–382 ob.

23. Vigasin et al., *Istoriia otechestvennogo vostokovedeniia*, 113.

24. RGIA, f. 821, op. 133, d. 636, ll. 109–110; f. 821, op. 133, d. 576, l. 367 ob.

25. Ostroumov, *Islamovedenie*, 3; and *Vvedenie v kurs islamovedeniia*, 55.

26. RGIA, f. 821, op. 133, d. 620, l. 17.

27. In 1911, Andrei was transferred to the Sukhumi dioceses in the Caucasus where he was the bishop until 1913.

28. RGIA, f. 821, op. 133, d. 545, l. 49 ob.

29. Andrei and Nikol'skii, *Naibolee vazhnye statisticheskie svedeniia,* 312; Nikol'skii, *Neskol'ko poiasnenii,* 3, 6.

30. *Zhurnal Ministerstva narodnogo prosveshcheniia,* 50 (July 1912): 83.

31. Bartol'd, [retsenziia na]: Naibolee vazhnye statisticheskie svedeniia, 587–596. On Bartol'd's sense of superiority of European scholarship to "native" forms of knowledge and on Russian Orientalists' thinking about empire within a large pan-European context, see Tolz, "Rossiiskie vostokovedy," 273.

32. Nikol'skii, *Programma,* 1.

33. Katanov also collaborated with the new editors of *Mir islama by* providing reviews of the Muslim press. For the insightful analysis of Katanov's biography within a context of a larger discussion of the definitions of Russianness in the late imperial period, see Geraci, *Window to the East,* 309–341.

34. NART, f. 1, op. 4, d. 5609, ll. 6–7, 11–11 ob.

35. Ibid., ll. 6 ob–12.

36. RGIA, f. 821, op. 133, d. 545, ll. 106–108.

37. NART, f. 1, op. 4, d. 5609, ll. 11 ob–12.

38. RGIA, f. 821, op. 133, d. 470, ll. 167–168.

39. RGIA, f. 821, op. 133, d. 563, ll. 1, 2, 3 ob.

40. Klimovich, *Islam v tsarskoi Rossii,* 221, 231, 244; Arsharuni and Gabidullin, *Ocherki panislamisma,* 3–6; Zenkovsky, *Pan-Turkism and Islam,* 116–117; Geraci, *Window on the East,* 277; Khalid, "Pan-Islamism in Practice," 201; Reynolds, *Shattering Empires,* 91.

41. Karpat has pointed to the war as a "turning point" in the history of the Ottoman empire, pan-Islamism, and the Ottoman middle class. See *The Politicization of Islam,* 148.

42. Karpat, *The Politicization of Islam,* 174. On pan-Islamism, see also Landau, *The Politics of Pan-Islam.*

43. RGIA. f. 821. op. 8. d. 1174. ll. 18–22.

44. RGIA, f. 821. op. 150. d. 409. l. 11 ob.

45. Zenkovsky, *Pan-Turkism and Islam in Russia,* 37–54. On Russian Muslim émigré publicists in the Ottoman empire, see Adam, *Russlandmuslime in Istanbul.* On Agaev, see Shissler, *Between Two Empires.*

46. Karpat, *Politicization of Islam,* 238, 297, 303.

47. Fadeeva, *Ofitsialnye doktriny,* 197, 207. Michael Reynolds has emphasized that preserving the empire's unity was the primary goal of the revolutionaries. This argument and the discussion of Ottoman attempts to mobilize Russian Muslims within a broader context of the geopolitical struggle between the Ottoman and the Russian empires from 1908 to 1914, see his *Shattering Empires.*

48. Karpat, *Politicization of Islam,* 305.

49. The Department of Police considered the Young Turks to be pan-Islamists.

50. GARF, f. 529c, op. 1, d. 27, ll. 47–48 ob.

51. On different aspects of internal politics within Muslim communities and the competition over state support, see Dudoignon, "Kadimism" and Naganawa, *Maktab or School.*

52. *Natsional'nye dvizheniia,* 245–251.

53. Ibid., 252, 261–269.

54. "Nachal'nik Kazanskogo gubernskogo zhandarmskogo upravleniia—Kazanskomu gubernatoru" (8 ianvaria 1909), in NART, f. 1, op. 6, d. 636, ll. 1–2.

55. Ibid., ll. 44–45.

56. K voprosu o muggalimakh, poluchivshikh obrazovanie za granitsei," 1908, in LOIV RAN, f. 44, op. 1, d. 281, ll. 3–4, 15 ob.

57. Ibid., 18.

58. Ibid., 38 ob, 42 ob–43.

59. GARF, f. 102, op. 242 (1912), d. 74, ll. 49–50, 54–62.

60. RGIA, f. 821, op. 133, d. 554, l. 41 ob.

61. Ibid., d. 449, l. 28. On Hajetlashe's publishing activity, see Klimovich, *Islam v tsarskoi Rossii*, 233–264; and Bessmertnaia, "Russkaia kul'tura v svete musul'manstva" and "Musul'manskii Azef."

62. RGIA, f. 821, op. 8, d. 1203, l. 16.

63. BDIC, Archives de M. Hadjetlaché, F delta rés 914 (10) (6) (2).

64. RGIA, f. 821, op. 133, d. 471, l. 243 ob.

65. Ibid., ll. 19–56 ob.; RGIA, f. 821, op. 133, d. 449, ll. 43–45.

66. RGIA, f. 821, op. 133, d. 471, l. 37. The journal had, on average, no more than 750 subscribers in Russia. See GARF, f. 102.00, op. 243 (1913), d. 194, l. 29.

67. RGIA, f. 821, op. 8, d. 1203, ll. 76a–76 b ob.

68. *V mire musul'manstva*, nos. 3, 6, 9, 25, 27, 31 (1911) and no. 3 (1912).

69. GARF, f. 102.00, op. 243 (1913), d. 74, vol. 3, l. 10 ob.

70. Among those who signed the letter were Ibragim Bek Gaidarov, Shakir Mukhamed'iarov, and Dzhamo Bek Gadzhinskii.

71. RGIA, f. 821, op. 133, d. 470, ll. 32–33.

72. RGIA, f. 821, op. 133, d. 471, ll. 233.

73. *Vakyt* (12 December 1912), translation in *Inorodcheskoe obozrenie*, 1 (2), (1913): 123.

74. *Yulduz* (5 December 1910); *Vakyt* (1 January 1913); translation in *Inorodcheskoe obozrenie*, 1(2), (1913): 128.

75. *Gosudarstvennaia Duma. Tretii sozyv. Stenograficheskie otchety*. Sessiia chetvertaia. Zasedanie 67 (26 February1911), Part 2 (St. Petersburg, 1911), 2936.

76. RGIA, f. 821, op. 133, d. 470, l. 51, 60.

77. "Delo o sluzhbe P.V. Antaki," in RGIA, f. 821, op. 12, d. 218.

78. RGIA, f. 821, op. 133, d. 629, l. 1.

79. Ibid., l. 32 ob.

80. Ibid., l. 25.

81. *Novoe vremia* 13165 (1912) and *Russkoe znamia*, 97 (1912), in RGIA, f. 821, op. 133, d. 654.

82. GARF, f. 102, op. 241 (1912), d. 74. ll. 142–142 ob.

83. GARF, f. 102, op. 239 (1909), l. 291, ll. 5–7 ob., 11.

84. RGIA, f. 821, op. 8, d. 1199, l. 58.

85. *Mir islama*, 2 (2) (1913): 109.

86. RGIA, f. 821, op. 150, d. 419, l. 22 ob., 26.

87. RGIA, f. 821, op. 8, d. 1199, ll. 37–41 ob.

88. GARF, f. 102, op. 240 (1910), d. 74, l. 137 ob.

89. "K voprosu o pan-islamisme," 12.

90. Bobrovnikov, *Russko-tuzemnye uchilishcha*, 42, 69–71.

91. *Rossiia* nos. 2011 and 2112 (1912) and *S. Petersburgskie vedomosti*, no. 248 (1912), in RGIA, f. 821, op. 133, d. 646; *Musul'manskaia gazeta*, no. 1 (1912), 2, 3; also, S. Gabiev, "Moi otvet. K stat'e "Gazavat i musul'mane Rossii," ibid., no. 3 (1912), 2.

92. RGIA, f. 821, op. 133, d. 573, l. 3, 6 ob-7.

93. RGIA, f. 832, op. 133, d. 573, l. 6 ob.

94. RGIA, f. 821, op. 133, d. 573, ll. 11–11 ob.

95. In October, Bobrovnikov suggested establishing a "Scholarly Committee" to study the state and the mood of Russian and foreign Eastern peoples in connection with the war, especially focusing on the reasons for the disassociation of Muslims with Russians and their gravitation to Turkey and Persia. The list included many famous scholars and Orientalists, such as Samoilovich and Bartol'd among others, most of whom were labeled by G. N. Taranovskii (the director of the Department for Religious Affairs of Foreign Confessions) as not "truly Russian, separatists, and cadets." Ibid., RGIA f. 821, op. 133, d. 573, ll. 102–108 ob.

96. Because of illness, Sultanov did not come and was replaced by G. Kapkaev from the Orenburg Ecclesiastical Assembly. Instead of Karashaiskii, the acting Simferopol kadi came. There were no Muslim representatives from the Caucasus. The tsarist envoy in the Caucasus reported to Maklakov that mufti G.-E. Gaibov was deaf and that the acting sheikh-ul-Islam did not speak Russian. See RGIA, f. 821, op. 133, d. 573, l. 71.

97. "Reforma dukhovnykh musul'manskikh pravlenii," 754.

98. Ibid., 750.

99. *Vakyt,* 1456 (1914), in RGIA, f. 821, op. 133, d. 573, l. 4 ob.

100. *Utro Rossii,* 100 (1 May 1914); *Russkie Vedomosti* 98 (29 April 1914), in RGIA, f. 821, op. 133, d. 573, ll. 81, 86.

101. RGIA, f. 821, op. 133, d. 573, ll. 97–97 ob.

102. RGIA, f. 821, op. 133, d. 620, l. 19–19 ob.

103. RGIA, f. 821, op. 133, d. 576, ll. 120 ob.-122.

104. RGIA, f. 821, op. 133, d. 577, l. 8 ob, 310–312 ob.

105. RGIA, f. 821, op. 133, d. 576, l. 254–254 ob.

106. Ibid., ll. 251–253 ob.

107. RGIA, f. 821, op. 133, d. 577, ll. 152 ob–158.

108. RGIA, f. 821, op. 12, d. 488, l. 2.

109. AVPRI, f. 147, op. 485, d. 1258, ll. 448–450 ob.

110. Ibid., l. 306, 142 ob–147 ob, 154 ob-160 ob.

111. Ibid., l. 309.

112. Ibid., l. 311 ob.

113. RGIA, f. 821, op. 133, d. 577, l. 11 ob.

114. Ibid., ll. 384–386.

115. "Musul'manskie s"ezdy v Rossii," in EHESS, CERCEC, Archives de Toptchibachy, valise 1, p. 24–26.

116. "Rech, proiznesennaia Topchibashevym 25 iunia 1914 goda na chetvertom musul'manskom s"ezde," EHESS, CERCEC, Archives de Toptchibachy, valise 8, l. 1 ob.

117. Ibid.

9. World War I

1. RGIA, f. 821, op. 133, d. 603, ll. 22–23 ob.

2. Ibid., l. 23.

3. Ibid., ll. 29 ob.–30.

4. Ibid., l. 74 ob.

5. Ibid.

6. Ibid., l. 90.

7. Ibid.

8. Ibid., l. 127.

9. Ibid., l. 127 ob.

10. Ibid., ll. 164–164 ob.

11. Ibid., l. 164.

12. On this case of deportation and other examples of Russian campaigns against enemy aliens, see Lohr, *Nationalizing the Russian Empire*.

13. AVPR, f. 151, op. 484, d. 4326, ll. 1 ob–14.

14. On the liberation rhetoric, see Buldakov, "Pervaia mirovaia voina i imperstvo," 21–25. On the internationalization of the Nationality Question during World War I, see von Hagen, *The Great War*. On Ottoman attempts to mobilize Russian Muslims, as well as Ukrainians and Georgians, see Reynolds, *Shattering Empires*, 107–139.

15. On the German policy of "revolutionizing" the Russian empire, see Zetterberg, *Die Liga der Fremdvölker;* Kolonitskii, "Emigratsiia"; Grekov, *Natsional'nyi aspect";* Hagen, *The Great War;* Novikova, *Finliandskaia karta.*

16. PAAA. R. 20867.

17. The tasks of the Osmanischer Lloyd are described in PAAA. R.123072. On German propaganda in the Ottoman empire on the eve of and during the war, see Farah, *Die Deutsche Pressepolitik.*

18. Another center of German propaganda among French and British Muslim prisoners of war was *Halbmondlager* in the area of Wünsdorf. On the organization of camps and on propaganda, see Höpp, *Muslime in der Mark.*

19. PAAA. R: 21247. The propaganda was coordinated by the News Agency for the Orient (Nachrichtenstelle für den Orient—NfO) supervised by the Orientalist Maks von Oppenheim (1860–1946), in close collaboration with the Political Office of the German General Staff (Sektion Politik), headed by diplomat Rudolf Nadolny (1873–1953); see Höpp, *Muslime in der Mark,* 22. The list of Tatar propagandists in *Weinberglager* is in PAAA. R: 21246.

20. See Höpp, *Muslime in der Mark,* 71, 74, 93.

21. The recommendations of Maks von Oppenheim 27 February 1915 are in PAAA. R: 21245; the directions for the native propagandists of *Halbmondlager* in 1915 are in PAAA. R: 21247.

22. Höpp, *Muslime in der Mark,* 85–86.

23. Ibid., 88.

24. Ibid., 83–84. See also Höpp's discussion of the fate of the "jihadists."

25. Höpp *Muslime in der Mark,* 87.

26. The report of the commandant of the camp from April 1915 is in PAAA. R: 21246; the reports of H. von Cosack from summer 1915 are in PAAA. R: 21247, 21249.

27. PAAA. R: 21246.

28. In addition, to create effective propaganda, the Germans had to take into account the cultural and ethnic differences among Muslims.

29. The commandant of the *Weinberglager* reported on 11 April 1915 that 187 Marianimists had posed as Muslims in order to be in the same camp as their Tatar fellow countrymen, PAAA. R: 21246.

30. PAAA. R: 21247.

31. On conflicts in the Ukrainian camps, see Mark von Hagen, *Velikaia voina,* 390. About the conflicts among Georgian and Tatar prisoners of war, see reports by H. Cosack from 8 June 1915 and 10 June 1915, in PAAA. R: 21247.

32. Later, Germans recognized the ineffectiveness of the propaganda of Jihad during the war. See PAAA. R: 14533, as well as the confession of one of the leaders of the German propaganda, Rudolf Nadolny, in his *Mein Beitrag,* 87.

33. Höpp, *Muslime in der Mark,* 21.

34. For example, the December 1914 issues of *Birzhevye Vedomosti, Sovremennoe slovo, Kolokol,* and *Pravitel'stvennyi Vestnik,* in RGIA, f. 821, op. 133, d. 598, ll. 59–72 ob.

35. RGIA, f. 821, op. 133, d. 634, l. 233.

36. RGIA, f. 821, op. 133, d. 471, l. 234.

37. Ibid., ll. 233, 235.

38. RGVIA, f. 1396, op. 2, d. 1897, l. 32, 9.

39. RGIA, f. 821, op. 133, d. 174, l. 21; RGVIA, f. 1396, op. 2, d. 1897, l. 72. RGIA, f. 821, op. 133, d. 471, ll. 247–250.

40. RGIA, f. 821, op. 133, d. 471, l. 20.

41. RGIA, f. 821, op. 133, d. 634, ll. 234–235 ob., 241–246; AVPRI, f. 151, op. 482, d. 4323, 19–27.

42. RGIA, f. 821, op. 133, d. 614, l. 21 ob.

43. AVPRI, f. 151, op. 482, d. 4323, l. 1.

44. RGIA, f. 821, op. 133, d. 634, l. 233, 235 ob., 255, 260 ob.

45. On the analysis of Russian patriotism through popular entertainment and cultural production, see Jahn, *Patriotic Culture.*

46. RGIA, f. 821, op. 133, d. 598, ll. 45–45 ob.

47. Ibid., ll. 46–47.

48. Ibid., l. 64.

49. "Musul'mane i voina," *Kaspii* 274 (6 December1914), in RGIA, f. 821, op. 133, d. 598, l. 72.

50. Ibid.

51. RGIA, f. 821, op. 133, d.603, ll. 87 ob.–88.

52. *Novoe vremia* (11 December 1914), in RGIA, f. 821, op. 133, d. 598, l. 71.

53. He pointed to the star and crescent as symbols on the coat of arms of Turkey.

54. RGIA, f. 821, op. 133, d. 598, ll. 149–150 ob.

55. Ibid., l. 152 ob.

56. RGIA, f. 821, op. 133, d. 598, ll. 90–90 ob.

57. On refugees during the war, see Gatrell, *A Whole Empire Walking.*

58. *Vlast' i reformy,* 615–641.

59. *Baku,* 44 (25 February 1916), in RGIA, f. 821, op. 133, d. 467, l. 224.

60. *Sovremennoe slovo,* no. 2768 (1915), 2. RGIA, f. 821, op. 8, d. 829, l. 113.

61. The archive of the Department for Religious Affairs of Foreign Confessions has a list of potential participants in a special academic committee at the MVD for the "Investigation of a State of Russian and Foreign Oriental Nationalities and Tribes." The goal of the committee was to provide the government with "objective" information about the contemporary trends and moods of Russian and foreign Muslims. Samoilovich and Bartol'd were listed among other scholars who were to be invited to participate on the committee. The department, however, characterized Samoilovich as a "kadet," and Bartol'd as a "protector of Germans" and "kadet-separatism." The director of the department, G. N.

Taranovskii, concluded that the majority of the scholars were not truly Russian and sympathetic to non-Russian separatism. In RGIA, f. 821, op. 8, d. 829, ll. 108–109; RGIA, f. 821, op. 133, d. 576, ll. 102–109. On academic Orientalists as the advocates of interests of non-Russian minorities, see Tolz, *Russia's Own Orient.*

62. AVPRI, d. 131, op. 482, d. 4323, l. 3.

63. RGIA, f. 1276, op. 12, d. 3, ll. 7 ob–9; *Gosudarstvennaia Duma: Sozyv 4-i, sessiia 4-ia. Prilozheniia k stenograficheskim otchetam.* Vol. 2, no. 64. Petrograd, 1916.

64. "V. B. Frederiks to B. V. Shtriumer" (25 February 1916), in RGIA, f. 1276, op. 12, d. 3, l. 1 ob.

65. RGIA, f. 821, op. 133, d. 638, ll. 11–11 ob, 15 ob.

66. Anan'ich et. al., *Vlast' i reformy,* 630–634.

67. RGIA, f. 1276, op. 11, d. 89, ll. 2–13. On military conscription in relation to nation-building, see Sanborn, *Drafting the Russian Nation.*

68. Tursunov, *Vosstanie 1916 goda,* 81, 182.

69. TsGARU, f. 1, op. 31, d. 1194, l. 29 ob; Kuropatkin's report, in TsGARU, f. I-1, op. 31, d. 1197, l. 5.

70. RGIA, f. 821, op. 133, d. 598, l. 345.

71. Chuloshnikov, *K istorii vosstania kirgiz v 1916 godu,* 53.

72. For an account of the revolt, see Sokol, *The Revolt of 1916;* Tursunov, *Vosstanie 1916 goda.* For an analysis of the revolt through the perspective of the individual experience of both Russians and natives, see Happel, *Nomadische Lebenswelten.*

73. Kuropatkin had participated in major Russian military campaigns in Central Asia from the 1860s to the 1880s; in 1875–1876 he went with the Russian diplomatic mission to Kashgariia; and during 1890–1898 he was governor of the Transcaspian oblast. Kuropatkin was the Minister of War in 1898–1904, when the 1898 Andijan uprising took place, and he was Supreme Commander during the Russo-Japanese War of 1904–1905.

74. Kuropatkin, *Zadachi Russkoi Armii,* Vol. 1, 124–125.

75. The conflict between the tradition of authoritarian rule and the reformist approach is the main theme in the discussion of the 1916 revolt by Daniel Brower, in *Turkestan and the Fate of the Russian Empire,* 160.

76. "Rech Turkestanskogo general-gubernatora," *Turkestanskie vedomosti,* 188 (28 August 1916), 3.

77. TsGARU, f. 1009, op. 1, d. 80, l. 4.

78. Kuropatkin, "Izvlecheniia iz dnevnika gen. A. N. Kuropatkina," 60.

79. TsGARU, f. I-1, op. 31, d. 1194, ll. 29–32.

80. Kuropatkin, " Izvlecheniia iz dnevnika,"53; Gippius, "Zapiska voennogo gubernatora," 190.

81. Gippius, "Zapiska," 190–191.

82. TsGARU, f. 1, op. 31, d. 1194, l. 14 ob., 13, 16.

83. Ibid., ll. 21–27 ob.

84. RGIA, f. 821, op. 133, d. 598, ll. 504–504 ob.

85. TsGARU, f. 1, op. 31, d. 1197, ll. 1–14 ob. The report was publsihed in "Izvlecheniia iz dnevnika gen. A. N. Kuropatkina i rapport ego v fevrale 1917 g." in Galuzo I., ed. "Vosstanie v Srednei Azii." *Krasnyi Arkhiv* 3 (34) 1929): 67–94.

86. Kuropatkin, "Izvlecheniia iz dnevnika," 64–66.

87. Ibid., 57.

88. TsGARU, f. 1, op. 31, d. 1194, ll. 34–36.

89. Bozhko et al., *Vosstanie 1916 goda v Srednei Azii: sbornik dokumentov,* 106–160.

90. Khalid, *The Politics of Muslim Cultural Reform,* 241–243.

91. Ibid., 242.

92. RGIA, f. 821, op. 133, d. 620, l. 44

93. RGIA, f. 821, op. 133, d. 449, l. 485.

94. Ibid., l. 487 ob.–488; Also, *Zavolzhskii letopisets* 3 (1 February1917): 63–69.

95. Andrei, "Rech Ufimskogo Preosviashchennogo Andreia, proiznesennaia v Ufim-skom zemskom sobranii 19 oktiabria 1915 g.," 414–415. On a similar topic, see also Kreshchenyi Tatarin [R. D.] (possibly Roman Daulei), "Gde zhe khristianskaia fraktsiia?" *Sotrudnik Bratstva sv. Guriia* 22–23 (1910): 361–363.

96. "Otchet o zhizni i deiatel'nosti Vostochno-russkogo kul'turno- prosvetitel'skogo obshchestva v g. Ufe za 1916 god," *Zavolzhskii letopisets* 6 (15 March 1917): 171. Also, probably written by Andrei, "K chitateliam "Zavolzhskogo letopistsa," *Zavolzhskii letopisets* 1 (15 December, 1916): 3–4.

97. RGIA, f. 821, op. 133, d. 577, ll. 448–454.

98. Ibid., l. 245.

99. "Mery k ukrepleniiu pravoslaviia i russkoi kul'tury na nashem musul'manskom vostoke i k uporiadocheniiu polozheniia russkogo musul'manstva voobshche," in RGIA, f. 821, op. 133, d. 471, l. 48, ob. 53.

100. "Pokazaniia S. P. Beletskogo," in Shchegolev, ed. *Padenie Tsarskogo rezhima,* Vol. IV, p. 288.

101. Lohr, *Nationalizing the Russian Empire;* Sanborn, *Drafting the Nation.*

Conclusion

1. Budilovich, *O edinstve russkogo naroda,* 37–38; *Vopros ob okrainakh Rossii v sviazi s teoriei samoopredelenia narodnostei,* 9, 17–18.

2. Andrei, "O svobode religioznoi propagandy," in RGB OR, f. 40, karton 13, d. 8, l. 1 ob.

3. Andrei, "Blagodarnost' musul'manskomu obshchestvu," 703. Also see his other articles, in which he treated Muslims as true patriots and allies: "Ishchite zemli i voli," 492–493; "Rech Preosviashchennogo episkopa Andreia o vzaimootnosheniiakh tserkvi i gosudarstva," 432–436.Writing after the February revolution and approaching the question about Muslims from a different perspective, Bobrovnikov, one of most sensitive observers, had argued about the political loyalty of Muslims and the development of ethnic self-consciousness among different groups of Muslims as a "healthy" phenomenon. Bobrovnikov, *Sovremennoe polozhenie uchebonogo dela,*15, 33. On Rybakov's reassessment of the tsarist policy toward Islam and his new project for the empire's Muslim ecclesiastical administration, see RGIA, f. 821, op. 133, d. 567, ll. 2, 25 ob., 13–14.

Bibliography

I. Archival Sources

1. *Rossiiskii gosudarstvennyi istoricheskii arkhiv* (RGIA), St. Petersburg

f. 797 Kantseliariia Ober-Prokurora Sinoda
f. 796 Kantseliariia Sviateishego Sinoda
f. 821 Ministerstvo vnutrennikh del: Departament dukhovnykh del inostrannykh
    ispovedanii
f. 1022 A. V. Petrov
f. 1276 Sovet Ministrov
f. 1574 K. P. Pobedonostsev
Biblioteka RGIA, Kollektsiia pechatnykh zapisok
Papka 747 Materialy po voprosam very musul'man i o primenenii musul'manskogo prava
    v Rossii
Papka 255 Materialy po voprosu peresmotra zakonopolozheniia o nerusskikh narodakh
    soglasno ukazu 12 dekabria 1904 goda
Papka 263 Materialy ob upravlenii Kavkazskim kraem

2. *Leningradskoe otdelenie Instituta vostokovedeniia. Arkhiv vostokovedov* (LOIV, RAN),
St. Petersburg

f. 50 V. D. Smirnov
f. 70 A.-A. Davletshin
f. 44 A. M. Pozdneev

3. *Rossiiskaia natsional'naia biblioteka. Otdel rukopisei* (RNB, OR), St. Petersburg

f. 585 S. F. Platonov

4. *Tsentral'nyi gosudarstvennyi arkhiv kinofotofonodokumentov Sankt-Peterburga*
(TsGAKFFD Spb), St. Petersburg

5. *Gosudarstvennyi arkhiv Rossiiskoi Federatsii* (GARF), Moscow

f. 102 Ministerstvo vnutrennikh del: Departament politsii. Osobyi otdel
f. 109 3-e otdelenie s.e. i. v. Kantseliarii
f. 529c Biuro zaveduiushchego zagranichnoi agenturoi Departamenta politsii v Konstan-
    tinopole
f. 730 N. P. Ignat'ev

6. *Rossiiskaia gosudarstvennaia biblioteka. Otdel rukopisei* (RGB, OR), Moscow

f. 424 N. I. Il'minskii
f. 40 A. S. Budilovich

7. *Rossiiskii voenno-istoricheskii arkhiv* (RGVIA), Moscow

f. 165 A. N. Kuropatkin
f. 400 Glavnyi Shtab. Aziatskaia chast
f. 1396 Shtab Turkestanskogo voennogo okruga

8. *Arkhiv vneshnei politiki Rossiiskoi imperii* (AVPRI), Moscow

f. 147 Sredneaziatskii stol
f. 151 Politarkhiv

9. *Gosudarstvennyi arkhiv v Avtonomnoi Respublike Krym* (GAARK), Simferopol

f. 26 Kantseliariia Tavricheskogo gubernatora

10. *Natsionalnyi arkhiv Respubliki Tatarstan* (NART), Kazan

f. 1 Kantseliariia Kazanskogo gubernatora
f. 2 Kazanskoe gubernskoe pravlenie
f. 10 Kazanskaia dukhovnaia akademiia
f. 93 Kazanskaia uchitel'skaia seminariia
f. 968 N. I. Il'minskii

11. *Tsentral'nyi gosudarstvennyi arkhiv Respubliki Uzbekistan* (TSGARU), Tashkent

f. I–1 Kantseliariia Turkestanskogo general-gubernatora
f. I–1009 N. P. Ostroumov

12. *Das Politische Archiv des Auswärtigen Amts* (PAAA), Berlin.

R: 20867 Der Weltkrieg. Propaganda unter den russischen Kriegsgefangenen durch Inter-
asugabe von Zeitungen.
R: 123070 Osmanischer Lloyd, Bd. 1.
R: 123072, Bd. 3.
R: 123073, Bd. 4.
R: 21246 Der Weltkrieg. Tätigkeit in den Gefangenenlagern Deutschlands, Bd. 3.
R: 21247 Bd. 4.
R: 21249 Bd. 5.
R: 14533 Orientalia Generalia. Der Muhamedanismus.

13. *La bibliothèque de documentation internationale contemporaine* (BDIC), Paris.

Archives de M. Hadjetlaché

14. *La bibliothèque du Centre d'études des mondes russe, caucasien et centre-européen. Ecole des hautes etudes en sciences sociales* (CERCEC, EHESS), Paris.

Archives de Toptchibachy

II. Contemporary Periodicals

Den
Istoricheskii vestnik
Kaspii
Khristianskoe chtenie
Kolokol
Mir islama
Moskovskie vedomosti
The Moslem World
Musul'manin
Musul'manskaia gazeta
Niva
Novoe vremia
Otechestvennye zapiski
Pravoslavnoe obozrenie
Pravoslavnyi blagovestnik
Pravoslavnyi sobesednik
Rech
Rossiia
Rus
Russkaia molva
Russkaia mysl
Russkaia starina
Russkie vedomosti
Russkii vestnik
Sotrudnik Bratstva sv. Guria
Sredne-Aziatsii vestnik
S. Petersburgskie vedomosti
Terjuman-Perevodchik
Tserkovno-obshchestvennaia zhizn'
Tserkovnye vedomosti s pribavleniiami
Turkestanskie vedomosti
Utro Rossii
V mire musul'manstva
Vestnik Evropy
Voennyi sbornik
Zavolzhskii letopisets
Zhurnal Ministerstva narodnogo prosveshcheniia

III. Published Primary Sources

Aksakov, I. S. *Pol'skii vopros i zapadno-russkoe delo. Evreiskii vopros 1860–1886.* Stat'i iz "Dnia," "Moskvy," "Moskvicha," i "Rusi." *Sochineniia I.S. Aksakova.*Vol. 3. Moscow: Tip. M. G. Volchaninova, 1886.

———. "Pribaltiiskii vopros." *Sochineniia I. S. Aksakova. Vol. 6.* Moscow: Tip. M. G. Volchaninova, 1887.

Aleksii, ep. *Sovremennoe dvizhenie v srede russkikh musul'man.* Kazan: Tsenral'naia tip., 1910.

———. *Voinstvuiushchii islam.* Moscow: Tip. A. I. Snegirevoi, 1914.

Alektorov, A. E. *Inorodtsy v Rossii. Sovremennye voprosy. Finliandtsy, Poliaki, Latyshi, Evrei, Nemtsy, Armiane, Tatary.* St. Petersburg: Izd. Ob-va revnitelei russkago istoricheskago prosveshcheniia, 1906.

Alisov, G. "Musul'manskii vopros v Rossii." *Russkaia mysl'* (July 1909): 28–61.

Anderi. ep. *Likholet'e v zhizni pravoslaviia sredi privolzhskikh inorodtsev (stat'i iz S. Petersburgskikh vedomostei, 1909, mai).* Kazan: Tip-lit. imp. Universiteta, 1909.

———. "Ob Obrusenii." *Sotrudnik Bratstva sv. Guriia* 4 (1909): 58–61.

———. "Vozmozhny li dal'neishie otpadeniia inorodtsev ot tserkvi." *Sotrudnik Bratstva sv. Guriia* 17 (1910): 265–267.

———. "O vospitanii budushchikh pastyrei," *Sotrudnik Bratstva sv. Guriia* 15–16 (1911): 238–240.

———. "Rech Ufimskogo Preosviashchennogo Andreia, proiznesennaia v Ufimskom zemskom sobranii 19 oktiabria 1915 g." *Zavolzhskii letopisets* 15 (1 August 1917): 407–415.

———. "Rech Preosviashchennogo Episkopa Andreia o vzaimootnoshenii Tserkvi i Gosudarstva, proiznesennaia 6 avgusta 1917 goda na sobranii dukhovenstva i mirian v zdanii Eparkhial'nogo uchilishcha v g. Ufe." *Zavolzhskii letopisets* 16 (15 August 1917): 428–436.

———. "Ishchite zemli i voli," *Zavolzhskii letopisets* 18 (15 September 1917): 491–494.

———. "Blagodarnost' musul'manskomu obshchestvu." *Zavolzhskii letopisets* 24 (15 December 1917): 703.

———, and Nikol'skii, N. V., eds. *Naibolee vazhnye statisticheskie svedeniia ob inorodtsakh vostochnoi Rossii i zapadnoi Sibiri, podverzhennykh vlianiiu islama. Pod redaktsiei episkopa Andreia byvshego Mamadyshskogo, nyne Sukhumskogo i prepodavatelia etnografii N. V. Nikol'skogo.* Kazan: Tipografiia gubernskogo pravleniia, 1912.

Antonii (Amfiteatrov Ia. G.). *Pis'ma Vysokopreosviashchennogo Antoniia, arkhiepiskopa Kazanskogo (1866–1879).* Kazan: Tsentr. tip., 1912.

Artemenko, S. K. "Bata. Ocherk kirgizskikh nravov." In *Sbornik materialov po musul'manstvu. Sostavlen po rasporiazheniiu i ukazaniiam Turkestanskogo general-gubernatora generala ot infanterii S. M. Dukhovskogo.* Vol. 2, edited by V. P. Nalivkin, 105–127. Tashkent, 1900.

Ashmarin, N. I. "Neskol'ko slov o sovremennoi literature Kazanskikh tatar." *Zhurnal Ministerstva narodnogo prosveshcheniia.* Vol. CCCLXI (September–October 1905): 1–33

Bagin, S. "O propagande islama putem pechati." *Pravoslavnyi sobesednik* (July–August 1909): 245–264, and (September 1909): 385–393.

Baiazitov, A. *Vozrazhenie na rech' "Islam i nauka" Ernesta Renana.* St. Petersburg: Tip. A. S. Suvorina, 1883.

———. *Otnoshenie islama k nauke i inovertsam.* St. Petersburg: Tip. A. S. Suvorina, 1887.

———. *Islam i progress.* St. Petersburg: Tip. A. S. Suvorina, 1898.

Bartol'd, V. V. "Ot redaktsii," *Mir islama* 1, no. 1 (1912): 1–15.

———. [retsenziia na]: *Naibolee vazhnye statisticheskie svedeniia ob inorodtsakh vostochnoi Rossii i zapadnoi Sibiri, podverzhennykh vlianiiu islama. Pod redaktsiei epis-*

kopa Andreia byvshego Mamadyshskogo, nyne Sukhumskogo i prepodavatelia etnografii N. V. Nikol'skogo. Kazan: Tipografiia gubernskogo pravleniia, 1912. In *Mir islama* 1, no. 4 (1912): 587–596.

———. "Musul'manskii mir." In *Sochineniia*. Vol. 6, 207–297. Moscow: Izd-vo vostochnoi lit-ry, 1966.

Bashinskii, B. "Nash s"ezd." *Sotrudnik Bratstva sv. Guriia* 1 (1909): 2–5.

"Bez very." Izvlechenie iz stat'i, napechatannoi v no. 6365 gazety *Novoe vremia* (ot 16 noiabria 1893 g): "Bez very. Iz zapisok sudebnogo sledovatelia E. N. Matrosova." *Pravoslvnyi blagovestnik* 23 (December 1893): 42–49.

Blagoveshchenskii, A. A. *Istoriia staroi Kazanskoi dukhovnoi akademii, 1797–1818*. Kazan: Universitetskaia tip., 1875.

Bobrovnikoff, S. (Bobrovnikova, also Chicherina). "Moslems in Russia." *The Moslem World* 1, no. 1 (1911): 5–31.

Bobrovnikov, N. A. *Inorodcheskoe naselenie Kazanskoi gubernii*. Vol. 1. *Tatary, votiaki, mordva*. Kazan: P. V. Shchetinkin, 1899.

———. "Nuzhny li tak nazyvaemye protivomusul'manskie i protivoiazycheskie eparkhial'nye missionery v guberniiakh Evropeiskoi Rossii?" *Pravoslavnyi sobesednik* (February 1905): 301–316.

———. *Russko-tuzemnye uchilishcha, mekteby i medresy Srednei Azii. Putevye zametki*. St. Petersburg: Senatskaia tip., 1913.

———. *Sovremennoe polozhenie uchebnogo dela u inorodcheskikh plemen Vostochnoi Rossii*. Petrograd: Senatskaia tip., 1917.

Bogoslovskii, G. K. *Kratkii istoricheskii ocherk Kazanskoi eparkhii s prilozheniem biograficheskikh svedenii o Kazanskikh arkhipastyriakh*. Kazan: Tipo-lit. M. A. Chirkovoi, 1892.

Bozhko, F., S. L. Volin, and P. G. Galuzo. *Vosstanie 1916 goda v Srednei Azii: sbornik dokumentov*. Tashkent: Gosizdat UzSSR, 1932.

Budilovich, A. S. *Neskol'ko dannykh i soobrazhenii ob uspekhakh russkogo iazyka v Iur'evskom (b. Derptskom) universitete*. Iur'ev: Tip. K. Mattisena, 1899.

———, ed. *Trudy Osobogo soveshchaniia po voprosam obrazovaniia vostochnykh inorodtsev*. St. Petersburg: Izdanie Ministerstva narodnogo prosveshcheniia, 1905.

———. *Noveishii fazes samoopredeleniia narodnostei, rech 21 dekabria 1905 goda*. St. Petersburg: Tip. V. D. Smirnova, 1906.

———. *Vopros ob okrainakh Rossii v sviazi s teoriei samoopredeleniia narodnostei i trebovaniem gosudarstvennogo edinstva*. St. Petersburg: Tip. Voeikova, 1906.

———. *Kholmskaia Rus' i Poliaki*. St. Petersburg: Tip. "Rossiia," 1907.

———. *Mozhet li Rossiia otdat' inorodtsam svoi okrainy?* St. Petersburg: Tip. A. S. Suvorina, 1907.

———. *O edinstve russkogo naroda. Rech, proiznesennaia v torzhestvennom sobranii S. Petersburgskogo slavianskogo blagotvoritel'nogo obshchestva 14 fevralia 1907 goda*. St. Petersburg: Slavianskoe blagotvoritel'noe obshchestvo, 1907.

Bunge, N. Kh. *1881–1894. Zapiska, naidennaia v bumagakh N. Kh. Bunge*. St. Petersburg, 1896.

———. "Zagrobnye zametki." In *Reka vremen*, edited by V. L. Stepanov. Vol. 1, 198–254. Moscow: Ellis lak, 1995.

Cherevanskii, V. P. *Mir islama i ego probuzhdenie. Istoricheskaia monografiia*. Parts I–II. St. Petersburg: Gos. tip., 1901.

Chicherin, B. N. *Kurs gosudarstvennoi nauki. Part I: Obshchee gosudarstvennoe pravo.* Moscow: Tipo-lit t-va I. N. Kushnerev i K, 1894.

Chicherina S. V. (Bobrovnikova, also Bobrovnikoff). *U privolzhskikh inorodtsev: Putevye zametki.* St. Petersburg: Tip. V. Ia. Mil'steina, 1905.

Chuloshnikov, A. "K istorii vosstaniia Kirgiz v 1916 godu." *Krasnyi arkhiv* 3, no. 16 (1926): 53–75.

Devlet-Kil'deev, A. A. *Magomet kak prorok.* St. Petersburg: Tip. A. S. Suvorina, 1881.

Dostoevsky, F. M. *Dnevnik pisatelia za 1881 god.* Vol. 3. Paris: YMCA-Press, 1951.

Dubrovin, N. F., ed. *Materialy dlia istorii Krymskoi voiny i oborony Sevastopolia. Sbornik izdavaemyi Komitetom po ustroistvu Sevastopol'skogo muzeia.* Vol. 1–5, St. Petersburg: Tip. Departamenta udelov, 1871–1874.

Dukhovskaia, V. F. *Turkestanskie vospominaniia.* St. Petersburg: R. Golike i A. Vil'borg, 1913.

Dukhovskoi, S. M. *Vsepoddanneishii doklad Turkestanskogo general-gubernatora generala ot infanterii Dukhovskogo "Islam v Turkestane."* Tashkent, 1899.

"Dzhikhad ili gazavat, t.e. sviashchennaia voina musul'man s nevernymi." In *Sbornik materialov po musul'manstvu. Sostavlen po rasporiazheniiu i ukazaniiam Turkestanskogo general-gubernatora generala ot infanterii S.M. Dukhovskogo,* edited by V. I. Iarovoi-Ravskii. Vol. 1, 101–128. St. Petersburg, tipo-lit. M. Rosenoer, 1899.

Elisvanov, V. N., *Trudnosti i nuzhdy Kazanskoi inorodcheskoi missii. Rech, proiznesennaia v Obshchem sobranii Bratstva Sv. Guriia 26 aprelia 1915 goda eparkhial'nym inorodcheskim missionerom V. N. Eslivanovym.* Kazan: Tsentral'naia tip., 1915.

Eval'd, A. V. "Vospominaniia o K. P. von Kaufmane." *Istoricheskii vestnik* LXX, no. 10 (1897): 184–199.

Fadeev, R. A. *Sobranie sochinenii R. A. Fadeeva.* Vol. 1. St. Petersburg: Izdanie V. V. Komarova, 1889. Reprint of the original edition. Ann Arbor: University of Michigan Press, 1964.

Gasprinskii, I. "Nasha intelligentsiia." *Terjuman-Perevodchik* 15 (23 April 1892): 29–30.

———. "Tatarskaia progressivnaia partiia." *Terjuman-Perevodchik* 52 (5 July 1905): 1.

———. "First Steps toward Civilizing the Russian Muslims." In "*Ğadidism* at the Turn of the Twentieth Century: A View from Within," edited by Edward Lazzerini, *Cahiers du monde russe et soviétique* 16, no. 2 (April–June 1975): 245–277.

———. "Russkoe musul'manstvo: mysli, zametki i nabliudeniia musul'manina." Originally published in Simferopol in 1881. Reprint in *Rossiia i Vostok,* 17–58. Kazan: Fond Zhien: Tatarskoe knizhnoe izd-vo, 1993.

Gippius, A. I. "Zapiska voennogo gubernatora Ferganskoi oblasti Gippiusa," in P. Rusin, "Gubernator v roli propovednika." *Krasnyi arkhiv* 2 (75), 1936: 188–191.

Girs, F. K. *Otchet revizuiushchego po vysochaishemu poveleniiu Turkestanskii krai tainogo sovetnika Girsa.* [n.p.], 1884.

Gordlevskii, V. A. "Pamiati V. D. Smirnova." In V. A. Gordlevskii, *Izbrannye sochineniia,* Vol. IV, 408–414. Moscow: Izdatel'stvo vostochnoi literatury, 1968.

Gorokhova L. V., ed. *Kazanskaia tatarskaia uchitel'skaia shkola 1876–1917 gg.: sbornik dokumentov i materialov.* Kazan: Izd-vo "Gasyr," 2005.

———, and D. I. Ibragimov, eds. *Medrese g. Kazani XIX–nachala XX vv.: sbornik dokumentov i materialov.* Kazan: Izdatel'stvo Gasyr, 2007.

Gosudarstvennaia Duma. Sozyv 3-i, sessiia 4-ia. Stenograficheskie otchety. Zasedanie 67-e, 26 fevralia, 1911. Vol. 2. St. Petersburg; Gos. tip, 1911.

———. *Sozyv 4-i, sessiia 4-ia. Prilozheniia k stenograficheskim otchetam.* Vol. 2, no. 64. Petrograd, 1916.

Gradovskii, A. D. *Natsional'nyi vopros v istorii i v literature.* St. Petersburg: D. E. Kozhanchikov, 1873.

Gramenitskii, S. M. "Ocherk razvitiia narodnogo obrazovaniia v Turkestanskom krae." Tashkent: tipo-lit. torg. d. "F. i G. br. Kamenskie, 1896.

Grigor'ev, D. "Neskol'ko slov o prichinakh uspeshnogo rasprostraneniia magometanstva sredi inorodtsev-iazychnikov." *Pravoslavnyi blagovestnik* 1, no. 2 (January 1905): 85–89.

Grot, K. Ia. "Pamiati Antona Semenovicha Budilovicha." *Istoricheskii vestnik* 105 (1909): 1097–1122.

Gugov, Rashad Kh., Kh. A. Kasumov, and D. V. Shabaev, eds., *Tragicheskie posledstviia Kavkazskoi voiny dlia Adygov. Vtoraia polovina XIX–nachalo XX veka. Sbornik dokumentov.* Nal'chik: Ėl'-Fa 2000.

I. Kh. "Vpechatleniia poezdki po inorodcheskim mestnostiam Orenburgskogo kraia v 1900 godu." *Pravoslavnyi blagovestnik* 6 (March 1905): 254–258, and 7 (April 1905): 312–315.

Iarovoi-Ravskii. V. I. "Palomnichestvo (hajj) v Mekku i Medinu," *Sbornik materialov po musul'manstvu. Sostavlen po rasporiazheniiu i ukazaniiam Turkestanskogo general-gubernatora generala ot infanterii S. M. Dukhovskogo.* Vol. 1, 129–156. St. Petersburg, tipo-lit. M. Rosenoer, 1899.

Iasevich-Borodaevskaia, V. I. *Bor'ba za veru. Istoriko-bytovye ocherki i obzor zakonodatel'stva po staroobriadchestvu i sektantsvu v ego posledovatel'nom razvitii.* St. Petersburg: Gos. tip, 1912.

Il'in, N. "Znachenie religii Mukhameta v istorii." *Pravoslavnyi sobesednik* 3 (1876): 47–61.

Il'minskii, N. I. "Ob obrazovanii inorodtsev posredstvom knig, perevedennykh na ikh rodnoi iazyk." *Pravoslavnoe obozrenie* 10, no. 3 (1863): 136–141.

———. "Prakticheskie zamechaniia o perevodakh i sochineniiakh na inorodcheskikh iazykakh." *Pravoslavnyi sobesednik* 1 (1871): 160–183.

———. *Iz perepiski po voprosu o primenenii russkogo alfavita k inorodcheskim iazykam.* Kazan: Tip. Imp. Universiteta, 1883.

———. *Iz perepiski ob udostoenii inorodtsev sviashchennosluzhitel'skikh dolzhnostei.* Kazan: Tip. V. M. Kliuchnikova, 1885.

———. *Sistema narodnogo i v chastnosti inorodcheskogo obrazovaniia v Kazanskom krae.* St. Petersburg: Sinod. tip., 1886.

———. *Kazanskaia Tsentral'naia kreshcheno-tatarskaia shkola. Materialy dlia istorii khristianskogo prosveshcheniia tatar.* Kazan: Tip. V. M. Kliuchnikova, 1887.

———. *Vospominaniia ob I. A. Altynsarine.* Kazan: Tipo-lit. V. M. Kliuchnikova, 1891.

———. *Pis'ma Nikolaia Ivanovicha Il'minskogo k ober-prokuroru Sviateishego Sinoda Konstantinu Petrovichu Pobedonostsevu.* Kazan: Redaktsiia Pravoslavnogo sobesednika, 1895.

———. "Ex oriente lux. Odna iz neizdannykh zapisok N. I. Il'minskogo po voprosu ob ustroistve uchebnykh zavedenii." *Pravoslavnyi sobesednik* (January 1901): 40–53.

———. "Pis'mo N. I. Il'minskogo ober-prokuroru Sviateishego Sinoda D. Tolstomu." In "Iz neizdannykh pisem Il'minskogo." *Sotrudnik Bratstva sv. Guria* 2 (1909): 24–32.

———. "Pis'mo N. I. Il'minskogo k rektoru Kazanskoi akademii arkhimandritu Nikanoru (Brovkovichu), 8 sentiabria 1870 g." *Pravoslavnyi sobesednik* (January 1910): 110–117.

————. *O sisteme prosveshchenia inorodtsev i o Kazanskoi tsentral'noi kreshcheno-tatarskoi shkole. K piatidesiatiletiiu sistemy i shkoly. Predislovie i dopolnenie A. A. Voskresenskogo.* Kazan: Izd. P. V. Shchetinkina, 1913.

Imperatorskoe Obshchestvo Vostokovedeniia, sostoiashchee pod avgusteishim pokrovitel'stvom e.i.v. gosudaryni imperatritsy Aleksandry Fedorovny. Ustav, polozheniia i instruktsii. Petrograd: Tip. I. V. Leont'eva, 1917.

Iuzefovich, B. "Khristianstvo, magometanstvo i iazychestvo v vostochnykh guberniiakh Rossii." *Russkii vestnik* 164 (March 1883): 5–64.

————. *Politicheskie pis'ma. Periodicheskii sbornik po voprosam tekushchei politicheskoi i obshchestvennoi zhizni* 7 (November 1907).

Ivanov, S. "O sblizhenii gortsev s russkimi na Kavkaze." *Voennyi sbornik* 7 (1859): 541–549.

Iznoskov, I. A. "Materialy dlia istorii khristianskogo prosveshcheniia inorodtsev Kazanskogo kraia." *Pravoslavnyi blagovestnik* 13 (July 1894): 221–232.

————. "Inorodcheskie prikhody Kazanskogo uezda." *Pravoslavnyi blagovestnik* 21 (1897): 223–231.

"Iz obshchestvennoi khroniki," *Vestnik Evropy* 33 (November 1898): 421–436.

"Izvestiia i zametki: Musul'manskii s"ezd. Musul'manskaia gazetnaia literatura (iz *Novogo vremeni)." Pravoslavnyi blagovestnik* 15 (1906): 335–336.

"K chitateliam "Zavolzhskogo letopistsa." *Zavolzhskii letopisets* 1 (15 December 1916): 1–3.

"K voprosu o pan-islamisme." *Mir islama* 1, no. 1 (1913): 1–12.

Kareev, N. I. "Ideia progressa v ee istoricheskom razvitii. Publichanaia lektsiia, chitannaia v S. Petersburge v 1891 godu." In *Istoriko-filosofskie i sotsiologicheskie etiudy,* 260–299. St. Petersburg: O. N. Popova, 1895.

Katkov, M. N. *Sobranie peredovykh statei Moskovskikh vedomostei za 1864 god.* Moscow: Izd. S. P. Katkovoi, 1897.

————. *Sobranie peredovykh statei Moskovskikh vedomostei za 1865 god.* Moscow: Izd. S. P. Katkovoi, 1897.

Kaufman, K. P., von. *Proekt vsepoddannieishego otcheta Gen.-Ad"iutanta K.P. von-Kaufmana po grazhdanskomu upravleniiu i ustroistvu v oblastiakh Turkestanskogo general-gubernatorstva, 7 noiabria 1867–25 marta 1881 g.* St. Petersburg, Izd. Voenno-uchenago kom-ta Glav. shtaba, 1885.

Kazanets. "Novoe tatarskoe izdanie po geografii dlia shkol." *Sotrudnik Bratstva sv. Guriia* 12 (1910): 185–188.

Kharuzin, A. N. *Kirgizy Bukeevskoi Ordy. Antropologo-etnologicheskii ocherk.* Vol. 1. Moscow: Tip. A. Levinson i K., 1889.

Koblov, Ia. D. *O magometanskikh mullakh. Religiozno-bytovoi ocherk.* Kazan: Tsentr. tip., 1907.

Krasnosel'tsev, N. F. *Kratkaia istoriia zhurnala "Pravoslavnyi sobesednik" za 30 let ego sushchestvovaniia (1855–1884).* Kazan, 1885.

"Kratkii obzor sovremennogo sostoianiia i deiatel'nosti musul'manskogo dukhovenstva, raznogo roda dukhovnykh uchrezhdenii i uchebnykh zavedenii tuzemnogo naseleniia Samarkandskoi oblasti," *Pravoslavnyi blagovestnik* 18 (September 1898): 64–71.

"Kratkii obzor sovremennogo sostoianiia i deiatel'nosti musul'manskogo dukhovenstva, raznogo roda dukhovnykh uchrezhdenii i uchebnykh zavedenii tuzemnogo naseleniia Samarkandskoi oblasti, s nekotorymi ukazaniiami na ikh istoricheskoe proshloe." In *Sbornik materialov po musul'manstvu. Sostavlen po rasporiazheniiu i ukazaniiam Turkestanskogo general-gubernatora generala ot infanterii S. M. Duk-hovskogo,* edited by V. I. Iarovoi-Ravskii. Vol. 1, 3–47. St. Petersburg, tipo-lit. M. Rosenoer, 1899.

Kreshchenyi Tatarin [R. D.]. "Gde zhe khristianskaia fraktsiia?" *Sotrudnik Bratstva sv. Guriia* 22–23 (1910): 361–363.

Kuropatkin, A. N. *Zadachi Russkoi Armii.* St. Petersburg: Tip. V. Bezobrazov i K., 1910.

———. "Izvlecheniia iz dnevnika gen. A. N. Kuropatkina i rapport ego v fevrale 1917 g." In "Vosstanie v Srednei Azii," edited by I. Galuzo. *Krasnyi arkhiv* 3, no. 34 (1929): 39–94.

Kuznetsov, I. D., ed. *Natsional'nye dvizheniia v period pervoi russkoi revoliutsii v Rossii: sbornik dokumentov iz arkhiva byvshego Departamenta politsii.* Cheboksary: Chuvashskoe gos. izd-vo, 1935.

Larionov, S. S. *Nachal'noe obrazovanie inorodtsev Kazanskogo i Ufimskogo kraia.* Petrograd; Tip. P. P. Soikina, 1916.

Leonti'ev, K. N. *Sobranie sochinenii.* Vol. 7. St. Petersburg; izd. Russkogo knizhnogo tovarishchestva "Deiatel," 1913.

Levitskii, G. P. "Pereselenie Tatar iz Kryma v Turtsiiu." *Vestnik Evropy* (October 1882): 596–639.

Maksheev, A. I. "Prebyvanie v Vernom i vstrecha Kaufmana." *Russkaia starina* 44, no. 3 (1913): 644–649.

Malov, E. A. *O Tatarskikh mechetiakh v Rossii.* Kazan, 1868.

———. *O novokreshchenskoi kontore. Rech', proiznesennaia v torzhestvennom godichnom sobranii Kazanskoi dukhovnoi akademii 1878 g. ekstraord. prof. sviashchennikom Evfimiem Malovym.* Kazan, 1878.

Markevich, A. I. *Tavricheskaia guberniia vo vremia Krymskoi voiny. Po arkhivnym materialam* Simferopol: Tip. Tavr. gub. zemstva, 1905. Reprint: Simferopol: "Biznes-Inform," 1994.

Martianov, P. "Posledniaia emigratsiia tatar iz Kryma v 1874 godu." *Istoricheskii vestnik* 24, no. 6 (1887): 698–708.

Mashanov, M. A. *Religiozno-nravstvennoe sostoianie kreshchenykh tatar Kazanskoi gubernii Mamadyshskogo uezda. Zametka Mikhaila Mashanova, studenta missionerskogo protivomusul'manskogo otdeleniia pri Kazanskoi dukhovnoi akademii.* Kazan: Univ. tip., 1875.

———. *Obzor deiatel'nosti bratstva sviatitelia Guriia za 25 let ego sushchestvovaniia 1867–1892.* Kazan: Tipo-lit. Universiteta, 1892.

———. *Sovremennoe sostoianie tatar-mukhammedan i ikh otnoshenie k drugim inorodtsam (doklad prof. Kazanskoi dukhovnoi akademii M.Mashanova Missionerskomu s'ezdu 1910 g.* Kazan: Tipo-lit. I. S. Perova, 1910.

Materialy po istorii Tatarii vtoroi poloviny XIX veka. Vol. 1: *Agrarnyi vopros i krest'ianskoe dvizhenie 50–70-kh godov XIX veka.* Moscow-Leningrad: Izd. Akademii Nauk SSSR, 1936.

"Mestnoe obozrenie." *Sredne-Aziatskii vestnik* (March 1896): 57–70.

Mikhailov, F. "Religioznye vozzreniia turkmen Zakaspiiskoi oblasti." In *Sbornik materialov po musul'manstvu. Sostavlen po rasporiazheniiu i ukazaniiam Turkestanskogo general-gubernatora generala ot infanterii S.M. Dukhovskogo,* edited by V. P. Nalivkin. Vol. 2, 87–103.Tashkent, 1900.

Mikhno, N. "Iz zapisok chinovnika o Krymskoi voine." In *Materialy dlia istorii Krymskoi voiiny i oborony Sevastopolia. Sbornik, izdavaemyi Komitetom po ustroistvu Sevastopol'skogo muzeia*, edited by N. F. Dubrovin. Vol. 3, 1–37. St. Petersburg: Tip. Departamenta udelov.

Miropiev, M. A. "Kakie nachla dolzhny byt' polozheny v osnovu obrazovaniia russkikh inorodtsev." *Rus* 17 (1884): 24–41.

———. *O polozhenii russkikh inorodtsev.* St. Petersburg: Sinod. Tip., 1901.

Missionerskii protivomusul'manskii sbornik. Trudy studentov missionerskogo protivomusul'manskogo otdeleniia pri Kazanskoi dukhovnoi akademii. Vols. 1–24. Kazan, 1873–1914.

"Missionerskii s"ezd v Kazani 13–26 iiunia 1910 goda." *Pravoslavnyi sobesednik* (November 1910): I–VIII, 1–78.

Mozharovskii, A. F. *Izlozhenie khoda missionerskogo dela po prosveshcheniiu Kazanskikh inorodtsev s 1552 goda po 1867 god.* Moscow: Obshchestvo istorii i drevnostei rossiiskikh pri Moskovskom universitete, 1880.

Muftiizade, I. M. *Ocherk voennoi sluzhby krymskikh tatar (po arkhivnym dokumentam).* Simferopol: Tavricheskaia gubernskaia tipografiia, 1899.

Murza Alim. "Islam i magometanstvo." *S. Petersburgskie Vedomosti* nos. 180, 188, 196, 224 (1882).

Nadolny, Rudolf. *Mein Beitrag. Erinnerungen eines Botschafters des Deutschen Reiches.* Cologne: Dme-Verlag, 1985.

Nalivkin, V. P., ed. *Sbornik materialov po musul'manstvu. Sostavlen po rasporiazheniiu i ukazaniiam Turkestanskogo general-gubernatora generala ot infanterii S. M. Dukhovskogo.* Vol. 2. Tashkent, 1900.

———. *Tuzemtsy ran'she i teper'.* Tashkent, A. L. Kirsner, 1913.

Nikol'skii, N. V. *Neskol'ko poiasnenii i dopolnenii k knige: Naibolee vazhnye statisticheskie svedeniia ob inorodtsakh Vostochnoi Rossii i Zapadnoi Sibiri, podverzhennykh vliianiiu Islama. Kazan, 1912.* Kazan: Tsentr. tip., 1913.

———. *Programma dlia sobiraniia svedenii ob inorodtsakh Povolzh'ia.* Kazan: Tipo-lit. Universiteta, 1915.

N. S. "Tserkovno-prikhodskie bratstva v Pribaltiiskom krae." *Otechestvennye zapiski* CLXXV (December 1867): 422–470.

Numerov, N. V. "Kazanskii missionerskii s"ezd." *Pribavleniia k "Tserkovnym vedomostiam"* 43 (23 October 1910): 1807–1817.

Obshchestvo vosstanovleniia pravoslavnogo khristianstva na Kavkaze. Otchet za 1886 god. Tiflis, 1887.

Ostroumov, N. P. "Kitaiskie emigranty v Semirechenskoi oblasti Turkestanskogo kraia i rasprostranenie sredi nikh khristianstva." *Pravoslavnyi sobesednik* (March 1879): 256–273; (May 1879): 61–86; (July 1879): 223–259; (August 1879): 359–392.

———. *Chto takoe Koran? Po povodu statei gg. Gasprinskogo, Devlet-Kil'deeva i Murzy Alima.* Tashkent: Tip., arend. F. V. Bazilevskim, 1883.

———. *Istoricheskii ocherk vzaimnykh otnoshenii mezhdu khristianstvom i musul'manstvom.* St. Petersburg: Tip. S. E. Dobrodeeva, 1888.

———. *Araviia and Koran. (Proiskhozhdenie i kharakter islama). Opyt isotricheskogo issledovaniia.* Kazan: Tipo-lit Kaz. Universiteta, 1891.

———. *Sarty. Etnographicheskie materially.* Vol. 1, Tashkent: Tipo-lit. S. I. Lakhtina, 1890. 2nd edition. Tashkent: Knizhnyi magazin "Bukinist," 1896.

———. *K istorii narodnogo obrazovaniia v Turkestanskom krae. Konstantin Petrovich von Kaufman, ustroitel' Turkestanskogo kraia. Lichnye vospominaniia N. Ostroumova (1877–1881)*. Tashkent: Tipo.-lit. t.d. F. i G. br. Kamenskie, 1899.

———. *Koran i progress: Po povodu umstvennogo probuzhdeniia sovremennykh rossiiskikh musul'man*. Tashkent: A. L. Kirsner, 1901.

———. "Magometanskii vopros v Rossii v nastoiashchee vremia," *Khristianskoe chtenie* (September 1905): 316–329.

———. *Islamovedenie*. Tashkent: Syr-Dar'inskii oblastnoi statisticheskii komitet, 1910.

———. *Kolebaniia russkogo pravitel'stva vo vzgliadakh na missionerskuiu deiatel'nost' pravoslavnoi russkoi tserkvi*. Kazan, 1910.

———. "Kolebaniia russkogo pravitel'stva vo vzgliadakh na missionerskuiu deiatel'nost' pravoslavnoi russkoi tserkvi." *Sotrudnik Bratstva sv. Guriia* 42 (1910): 657–663 and 43 (1910): 674–679.

———. "Kolebaniia vo vzgliadakh na obrazovanie tuzemtsev v Turkestanskom krae." In *Kaufmanskii sbornik izdannyi v pamiat' 25 let, istekshikh so dnia smerti pokoritelia i ustroitelia Turkestanskogo kraia general-ad"iutanta K. P. fon-Kaufmana I-go*, 139–160. Moscow: Tipo-lit. t-va I. N. Kushnerev, 1910.

———. *Vvedenie v kurs islamovedeniia*. Tashkent: Turkestanskie vedomosti, 1914.

"Otchet o zhizni i deiatel'nosti Vostochno-kul'turnogo prosvetitel'skogo obshchestva v gorode Ufe za 1916 god." *Zavolzhskii letopisets* 6 (15 March 1917): 170–174.

Otchet po rassledovaniiu obstoiatel'stv vosstaniia tuzemtsev Ferganskoi oblasti v mae 1898 goda gospodinu Turkestanskomu general-gubernatoru. Tashkent, 1898.

"Otchet Ufimskogo eparkhial'nogo komiteta Pravoslavnogo missionerskogo obshchestva za 1891 god." *Pravoslavnyi blagovestnik* 6 (March 1893): 102–107.

"Ot redaktsii," *Mir islama* 2, no. 1 (1913): I–II.

Papkov, A. A. *Pravoslavnye prikhody v Finliandii*. St. Petersburg: Tip. A. P. Lopukhina, 1901.

———. *Tserkovno-obshchestvennye voprosy v epokhu tsaria osvoboditelia (1855–1870)*. St. Petersburg: Tip. A. P. Lopukhina, 1902.

———. *O blagoustroistve pravoslavnogo prikhoda*. St. Petersburg: Sinod. tip., 1907.

Pisarev, N. *Kazanskii missionerskii s"ezd 13–26 iiunia 1910 goda*. Kazan, 1910.

Pobedonostsev, K. P. "Chernovik vsepoddanneishego doklada K. P. Pobedonostseva. In K. Ia. Zdravomyslov, "Iz chernovykh bumag K. P. Pobedonostseva," *Krasnyi arkhiv* 5 (18) (1926): 203–207.

Pogodin, M. P. *Istoriko-politicheskie pis'ma i zapiski v prodolzhenii Krymskoi voiny, 1853–1856*. Moscow: Tip. V. M. Frish, 1874. Photocopy of the original. Ann Arbor: University of Michigan, University Microfilms, 1971.

Polnoe sobranie zakonov Rossiiskoi imperii: sobranie I (PSZ I): 1649–1825. Vol. 1–49. St. Petersburg: Tip. II Otdeleniia Sobstvennoi E. I. V. Kantseliarii, 1830.

———. *Sobranie II (PSZ II): 1825–1881*. Vol. 1–55. St. Petersburg, 1830–1884.

"Rasporiazheniia i deistviia pravitel'stva i zakonopolozheniia, otnosiashchiesia do musul'man." *Mir islama* 2, no. 4 (1913): 260–278.

"Reforma dukhovnykh musul'manskikh pravlenii." *Mir islama* 2, no. 11 (1913): 729–756.

Reisner, M. A. *Gosudarstvo i vieruiushchaia lichnost': sbornik statei*. St. Petersburg: Tip. tov-va "Obshchestvennaia pol'za," 1905.

Rozanov, V. "Pamiati E. L. Markova." *Novoe vremia* 9714 (21 March 1903): 3.

Rybakov, S. G. *Islam i prosveshchenie inorodtsev v Ufimskoi gubernii*. St. Petersburg: Sinod. Tip., 1900.

Sbornik dokumentov i statei po voprosu ob obrazovanii inorodtsev. St. Petersburg: Tip. t-va Obshchestvennaia pol'za, 1869.

Sbornik zakonov o musul'manskom dukhovenstve v Tavricheskom i Orenburgskom okrugakh i o magometanskikh uchebnykh zavedeniiakh. Kazan: Tipo-let imp. universiteta, 1902.

Semenov, A. "Vozmozhna li bor'ba s islamom i kakimi sredstvami. (Iz pis'ma na imia Preosviashchennogo Dmitriia, Episkopa Turkestanskogo)." *Sotrudnik Bratstva Sv. Guria* 4 (1909): 54–57.

Semenov, A. "Pokoritel' i ustroitel' Turkestanskogo kraia general-ad"iutant K. P. von Kaufman (materialy dlia biograpficheskogo ocherka)." In *Kaufmanskii sbornik izdannyi v pamiat' 25 let, istekshikh so dnia smerti pokoritelia i ustroitelia Turkestanskago kraia general-ad"iutanta K. P. fon-Kaufmana I-go, III–LXXXIV.* Moskow: Tipo-lit. t-va I. N. Kushnerev, 1910.

Semenov, P. P., ed. *Okrainy Rossii. Sibir', Turkestan, Kavkaz i poliarnaia chast' Evropeiskoi Rossii.* St. Petersburg: Ministerstvo Finansov, 1900.

Sergii (Vasilevskii V.). *Vysokopreosviashchennyi Antonii (Amfiteatrov), arkhiepiskop Kazanskii i Sviiazhskii. Sostavleno po lichnym vospominaniiam i po pechatnym i pis'mennym dokumentam arkhim. Sergiem (Vasilevskim).* Vol. 1–2. Kazan, Tip. okr. shtaba, 1885.

Shchegolev, P. E., ed. *Padenie tsarskogo rezhima: stenograficheskie otchety doprosov i pokazanii, dannykh v 1917 g. v Chrezvychainoi sledstvennoi komissii Vremennogo pravitel'stva.* Vol. 1–7, Leningrad: Gos. izd-vo, 1924.

Shpitsberg, I. "Tserkov' i rusifikatsiia buriato-mongol pri tsarizme." *Krasnyi arkhiv* 4 (53) (1932): 100–126.

Slavinskii, M. "Natsional'naia struktura Rossii i velikorossy." In *Formy natsional'nogo dvizheniia v sovremennykh gosudarstvakh. Avstro-Vengriia, Rossiia, Germaniia,* edited by A. I. Kastelianskii, 277–303. St. Petersburg: "Obshchestvennaia pol'za," 1910.

Smirnov, E. T. "Dervishizm v Turkestane." In *Sbornik materialov po musul'manstvu. Sostavlen po rasporiazheniiu i ukazaniiam Turkestanskogo general-gubernatora generala ot infanterii S.M. Dukhovskogo,* edited by V. I. Iarovoi-Ravskii. Vol. 1, 49–71. St. Petersburg, tipo-lit. M. Rosenoer, 1899.

Smirnov, V. D. "Po voprosu o shkol'nom obrazovanii inorodtsev-musul'man." *Zhurnal Ministerstva narodnogo prosveshcheniia* CCXXII (July 1882): 1–24.

Snouck Hurgronje, Christian. *Mohammedanism: Lectures on Its Origin, Its Religious and Political Growth and Its Present State.* New York: G.P. Putnam's Sons, 1916.

Solov'ev, V. S. *Magomet. Ego zhizn' i religioznoe uchenie.* St. Petersburg: Tip. Iu. N. Erlikh, 1902.

Svod zakonov Rossiiskoi Imperii (SZRI) Vol. 11, part I: *Ustavy dukhovnykh del inostrannykh ispovedanii.* St. Petersburg, Tip, II Otdeleniia Sobstvennoi E.I.V. Kantseliarii, 1857 and St. Petersburg: Gos. tip., 1896.

———. Vol. 12, part I. *Ustav stroitel'nyi.* St. Petersburg: Tip, II Otdeleniia Sobstvennoi E. I. V. Kantseliarii, 1857.

Ternovskii, S. A. *Istoricheskaia zapiska o sostoianii Kazanskoi dukhovnoi akademii posle ee preobrazovaniia. 1870–1892.* Kazan: Tip. universiteta, 1892.

Tolstoy, I. I., and Iu. I. Gessen. *Fakty i mysli. Evreiskii vopros v Rossiii.* St. Petersburg: Tip. t-va "Obshchestvennaia pol'za." 1907.

Tolstoy I. I., and L. I. Tolstaya. *Memuary grafa I. I. Tolstogo.* Moscow: Izd-vo Indrik. 2002.

Topchibashi, A. M. "Musul'manskie s"ezdy v Rossii." In *Iz istorii azerbaidzhanskoi emigratsii: sbornik dokumentov, proizvedenii, pisem,* edited by S. M. Iskhakov, 108–
138. Moscow: Izd-vo Sotsial'no-politicheskaia mysl', 2011.

Totleben, E. I. "O vyselenii Tatar iz Kryma v 1860 g." *Russkaia starina* 78 (June 1893):
531–550.

Tretii vserossiiskii musul'manskii s"ezd. Kazan, 1906.

"Tretii vserossiiskii musul'manskii s"ezd. Postanovleniia i rezoliutsii." In *Politicheskaia
zhizn' russkikh musul'man do fevral'skoi revoliutsii.* Oxford: Ob-vo Issledovaniia
Srednei Azii, 1987.

Ushakov, N. I. "Zapiski ochevidstsa o voine Rossii protiv Turtsii i zapadnykh derzhav."
In *Deviatnadtsatyi vek. Istoricheskii sbornik,* edited by P. Bartenev, Vol. 2, 1–242.
Moscow, 1872.

Valikhanov, Ch. "Sledy shamanstva u kirgizov" and "O musul'manstve v stepi." In *Sobranie sochineni.* Vol. 4, 48–70, 71–75. Alma Ata: Glavnaia redaktsiia Kazakhskoi
sovetskoi entsiklopedii, 1985.

Valuev, P. A. *Dnevnik P.A. Valueva, ministra vnutrennikh del.* Moscow: Izd-vo Akademii
nauk SSSR, 1961.

"Vnutrennee obozrenie." *Vestnik Evropy* 5 (October 1876): 799–823.

Volkov, A. "Islam i ego vliianie na zhizn' ispoveduiushchikh ego." *Pravoslavnyi sobesednik*
2 (1887): 218–242; 341–366.

Voronets, E. N. "Kharakter mokhammedanstva po Pal'grevu." *Pravoslavnyi sobesednik* 2
(1874): 236–262.

——. *Lamskii vopros.* Moscow: Tip. L. i A. Snegirevykh, 1888.

——. *Nuzhny li dlia Rossii muftii.* Moscow: Tip. A. I. Snegirevoi, 1891.

*Vsepoddanneishii otchet ober-prokurora Sv. Sinoda po vedomstvu pravoslavnogo ispoveda-
niia za 1905–1907 gg.* St. Petersburg: Sinodal'naia tip., 1910.

Witte, S. Iu. *Vospominaniia.* Vol. 2. Moscow: Izd-vo sotsial'no-ėkon lit-ry, 1960.

Za pervyi god veroispovednoi svobody v Rossii. St. Petersburg: Tip. "Kolokol," 1907.

Zarinskii, P. E. "Apologiia islamizma noveishei angliiskoi raboty." *Pravoslavnyi sobesednik*
26 (1878): 133–160; 252–288.

Znamenskii, P. V. *Istoriia Kazanskoi dukhovnoi akademii za pervyi (doreformennyi) period
ee sushchestvovaniia (1842–1870 gody).* Vol. 1–2. Kazan: Tip. Imp. Universiteta,
1891–1892.

——. *Na pamiat' o Nikolae Ivanoviche Il'minskom. K dvadtsatipiatiletiiu Bratstva sviatitelia Guriia.* Kazan: Bratstvo sviatitelia Guriia, 1892.

——. *Uchastie Il'minksogo v dele inorodcheskogo obrazovaniia v Turkestanskom krae.* Kazan: Tipo-lit universiteta, 1900.

——. *Pravoslavie i sovremennaia zhizn', Polemika 60-kh godov ob otnoshenii pravoslaviia
k sovremennoi zhizni.* Moscow: Svobodnaia sovest, 1906.

VI. Secondary Sources: Books and Articles

Abashin, S. N. "V. P. Nalivkin: '. . . budet to, chto neizbezhno dolzhno byt' i to, chto neizbezhno dolzhno byt' uzhe ne mozhet byt'. . .' Krizis orientalizma v Rossiiskoi imperii? In *Aziatskaia Rossiia: liudi i struktury imperii. Sbornik nauchnykh statei k
50-letiu professora A. V. Remneva,* edited by N. G. Suvorova, 43–96. Omsk: Izd-vo
OmGU, 2005.

Abdirashidov, Zainabidin. Ismail Gasprinskii i Turkestan v nachale XX veka: sviazi-otnosheniia-vliianie. Tashkent: Akademnashr, 2011.

Adam, Volker. *Russlandmuslime in Istanbul am Vorabend des Ersten Weltkrieges.* Heidelberger Studien zur Geschichte und Kultur des modernen Vorderen Orients; Bd. 29. Frankfurt am Main and New York: Lang, 2002.

Akhunov, A. "Izvestnyi i neizvestnyi Zahir Bigiev." *Gasyrlar avazy-Ekho vekov,* 1 (2006): http://www.archive.gov.tatarstan.ru/magazine/go/anonymous/main/?path=mg:/numbers/2006_1/06/06_6/.

Allworth, Edward. *Tatars of the Crimea: Their Struggle for Survival: Original Studies from North America, Unofficial and Official Documents from Czarist and Soviet Sources.* Durham, N.C: Duke University Press, 1988.

Alston, Patrick L. *Education and the State in Tsarist Russia.* Stanford, Calif: Stanford University Press, 1969.

Anan'ich, B. V., and L. I. Tolstaya. "I. I. Tolstoy i 'kruzhok ravnopraviia i bratstva.'" *Osvoboditel'noe dvizhenie v Rossii.* Vol. 15, 41–156. Saratov: Izd-vo Saratovskovo universiteta, 1992.

Anan'ich, B. V., and R. Sh. Ganelin. *Sergei Iul'evich Vitte i ego vremia.* St. Petersburg: Dmitrii Bulanin, 1999.

Anan'ich, B. V., R. Sh. Ganelin, and V. M. Paneiakh, eds. *Vlast' i reformy: ot samoderzhaviia k sovetskoi Rossii.* Moscow: Dmitrii Bulanin, 1996.

Anderson, Benedict R. O' G. *Imagined Communities: Reflections on the Origin and Spread of Nationalism.* London: Verso, 1991.

Andreeva, N. S. *Pribaltiiskie nemtsy i rossiiskaia pravitel'stvennaia politika v nachale XX veka.* St. Petersburg: Mir, 2008.

Arapov, D. Iu. *Sistema gosudarsvennogo regulirovaniia islama v Rossiiskoi imperii (posledniaia tret' 18 veka-nachalo 20 v.).* Moscow: Moskovskii gos. universitet. Istoricheskii fakul'tet, 2004.

——. "Vladimir Petrovich Nalivkin (Biograficheskaia spravka)." In *Musul'manskaia Sredniaia Aziia: traditsionalizm i XX vek,* edited by D. Iu. Arapov, 13–17. Moscow: Tsentr tsivilizatsionnykh i regional'nykh issledovanii, 2004.

——. *Imperatorskaia Rossiia i musul'manskii mir.* Moscow: Natalis, 2006.

——, V. O. Bobrovnikov, and I. L. Babich. *Severnyi Kavkaz v sostave Rossiiskoi imperii.* Moscow: Novoe literaturnoe obozrenie, 2007.

——, and N. E. Bekmakhanova, eds. *Tsentral'naia Aziia v sostave Rossiiskoi imperii.* Moscow: Novoe Literaturnoe Obozrenie, 2008.

Arsharuni, A., and Kh. Gabidullin. *Ocherki panislamizma i panturkizma v Rossii.* Moscow: Izdatel'stvo Bezbozhnik, 1931.

Ascher, Abraham. *The Revolution of 1905: Authority Restored.* Stanford, Calif: Stanford University Press, 1988–1992.

——. *P. A. Stolypin: The Search for Stability in Late Imperial Russia.* Stanford, Calif.: Stanford University Press, 2001.

Avksent'ev, A. V. *Islam na Severnom Kavkaze.* Stavropol: Stavropol'skoe knizhnoe izd-vo, 1973.

Avrekh, A. I. *P.A. Stolypin i sud'by reform v Rossii.* Moscow: Izdatel'stvo polit. lit-ry, 1991.

Azamatov, D. D. "The Muftis of the Orenburg Spiritual Assembly in the 18th and 19th Centuries: The Struggle for Power in Russia's Muslim Institution." In *Muslim Culture in Russia and Central Asia from the 18th to the Early 20th Centuries,* edited by Anke von Kügelgen, Michael Kemper, and Allen J. Frank. Vol. 2, 355–384: Inter-Regional and Inter-Ethnic Relations. Berlin: Klaus Schwarz Verlag, 1998.

———. *Orenburgskoe magometanskoe dukhovnoe sobranie v kontse XVIII–XIX vv.* Ufa, Izd-vo "Gilem," 1999.

Babadžanov, Baxtiyar M. "Dukchi Ishan und der Aufstand von Andizan 1898." In *Muslim Culture in Russia and Central Asia from the 18th to the Early 20th centuries,* edited by Anke von Kügelgen, Michael Kemper, and Allen J. Frank, 167–191. Vol. 2: Inter-Regional and Inter-Ethnic Relations. Berlin: Klaus Schwarz Verlag, 1998.

Babadzhanov B. "Andizhanskoe vosstanie 1898 goda i 'musul'manskii vopros' v Turkestane (vzgliady 'kolonizatorov' i kolonizirovannykh." *Ab Imperio* 2 (2009): 155–200.

Baldauf, Ingeborg. "Jadidism in Central Asia within Reformism and Modernism in the Muslim World." *Die Welt des Islams* 41, no. 1 (March 2001): 72–88.

Batunskii, M. A. *Rossiia i islam.* Moscow: Progress-Traditsiia, 2003.

Bassin, Mark. "Geographies of Imperial Identity." In *The Cambridge History of Russia.* Vol 2: *Imperial Russia, 1689–1917,* ed. D. C. B. Lieven. Cambridge; Cambridge University Press, 2006.

Bekmakhanov, E. *Prisoedinenie Kazakhstana k Rossii.* Moscow: Izd-vo Akademii nauk SSSR, 1957.

Bennigsen, Alexander. "Ismail Bey Gasprinskii (Gaspraly) i proiskhozhdenie dzadidskogo dvizheniia v Rossii." In Ismail Bey Gasprinkii, *Rossiia i Vostok.* Kazan: Fond Zhien. Tatarskoe knizhnoe izd-vo, 1993.

Bennigsen, Alexandre A., and Chantal Lemercier-Quelquejay. *La Presse et le Mouvement National chez les Musulmans de Russie avant 1920.* Paris: Mouton, 1964.

Bessmertnaia, O. Iu. "Russkaia kul'tura v svete musul'manstva: musul'manskii zhurnal na russkom iazyke, 1908–1911." *Odissei* (1996): 268–286.

———. "Musul'manskii Azef, ili igra v Drugogo: metamorfozy Magomet-Beka Hadjetlashe." *Kazus: individual'noe i unikal'noe v istorii.* 9 (2007–2009), (2012): 209–298.

Bobozhonov, Bakhtiyar, and Anke Kügelgen, *Manakib-i Dukchi Ishan: Anonim Zhitiia Dukchi ishana-Predvoditelia Andizhanskogo vosstaniia 1898 goda.* Tashkent: Daik-Press, 2004.

Bobrovnikov, V. O. *Musul'mane Severnogo Kavkaza: obychai, pravo, nasilie; ocherki po istorii i etnografii prava Nagornogo Dagestana.* Moscow: Izd. firma "Vostochnaia lit-ra" RAN, 2002.

———, ed. *Obychai i zakon v pis'mennykh pamiatnikakh Dagestana V—nachala XX v.* Vol. 1–2, Moscow: Izdatel'skii dom Mardzhani, 2009.

———. "Russkii Kavkaz i Frantsuzskii Alzhir: sluchainoe skhodstvo ili obmen opytom kolonial'nogo stroitel'stva?" *Imperium unter pares: rol' transferov v istorii Rossiiskoi imperii (1700–1917),* 182–209. Moscow: Novoe literaturnoe obozrenie, 2010.

Breyfogle, Nicholas B. *Heretics and Colonizers: Forging Russia's Empire in the South Caucasus.* Ithaca, N.Y.: Cornell University Press, 2005.

———. "Enduring Imperium: Russia/Soviet Union/Eurasia as Multiethnic, Multiconfessional Space." *Ab Imperio* 1 (2008): 75–130.

Brower, Daniel. *Turkestan and the Fate of the Russian Empire.* London: RoutledgeCurzon, 2003.

Buldakov, V. P. "Pervaia mirovaia voina i imperstvo." In *Pervaia mirovaia voina. Prolog 20-go veka,* 21–25. Moscow: Nauka, 1998.

Burbank, Jane. "An Imperial Rights Regime: Law and Citizenship in the Russian Empire." *Kritika: Explorations in Russian and Eurasian History* 7, no. 3 (2006): 397–431.

Cadiot, Juliette. "Kak uporiadochivali raznoobrazie: spiski i klassifikatsii natsional'nostei v Rossiiskoi imperii i Sovetskom Soiuze (1897–1939)." *Ab Imperio* 4 (2002): 177–206.

Campbell, Elena. "'Edinaia nedelimaia Rossiia" i 'inorodcheskii vopros' v imperskoi ideologii samoderzhaviia." In *Prostranstvo vlasti: istoricheskii opyt Rossii i vyzovy sovremennosti,* edited by B. V. Anan'ich and S. I. Barzilov, 204–217. Moscow: Moskovskii obshchestvennyi nauchnyi fond, 2001.

Chernukha, Valentina, and Boris Anan'ich. "Russia Falls Back, Russia Catches Up: Three Generations of Russian Reformers." In *Reform in Modern Russian History: Progress or Cycle?* edited by Theodore Taranovski and Peggy McInerny, 55–96. Washington, D.C.: Woodrow Wilson Center Press, 1995.

Chernyshev, E. I. "Prichina emigratsii Krymskikh Tatar v Turtsiiu v 1860 godu." In *Trudy obshchestva izucheniia Tatarstana.* Vol. 1, 93–128. Kazan: Obshchestvo izucheniia Tatarstana, 1930.

Chervonnaia, S. M. *Ismail Gasprinskii–prosvetitel' narodov Vostoka. Materialy mezhdunarodnoi nauchnoi konferentsii k 150-letiiu so dnia rozhdeniia.* Moscow: NII teorii i istorii izobraziteľnykh iskusstv Rossiiskoi Akademii Khudozhestv, 2001.

Christoff, Peter K. *An Introduction to Nineteenth-Century Russian Slavophilism: A Study in Ideas.* Vols. 1–4. Gravenhage: Mouton, 1961–1991.

Cooper, Frederick. *Colonialism in Question: Theory, Knowledge, History.* Berkeley: University of California Press, 2005.

———, and Ann L. Stoler. *Tensions of Empire: Colonial Cultures in a Bourgeois World.* Berkeley: University of California Press, 1997.

Crews, Robert. *For Prophet and Tsar: Islam and Empire in Russia and Central Asia.* Cambridge, Mass: Harvard University Press, 2006.

Curtiss, John Shelton. *Russia's Crimean War.* Durham, N.C.: Duke University Press, 1979.

Dolbilov, M. D. "Russification and the Bureaucratic Mind in the Russian Empire's Northwestern Region in the 1860s." *Kritika: Explorations in Russian and Eurasian History* 5, no. 2 (2004): 245–271.

———. "Prevratnosti kirillizatsii: zapret latinitsy i biurokraticheskaia russifikatsiia litovtsev v Vilenskom general-gubernatorstve v 1864–1882 gg." *Ab Imperio* 2 (2005): 255–296.

———. *Russkii krai, chuzhaia vera: etnokonfessional'naia politika imperii v Litve i Belorussii pri Aleksandre II.* Moscow: Novoe literaturnoe obozrenie, 2010.

Dorskaia, A. A. *Svoboda sovesti v Rossii: Sud'ba zakonoproektov nachala XX veka.* St. Petersburg: Izdateľstvo RGPU imeni A.I. Gertsena, 2000.

Dowler, Wayne. *Classroom and Empire: The Politics of Schooling Russia's Eastern Nationalities, 1860–1917.* Montreal: McGill-Queen's University Press, 2001.

Dudoignon, Stéfane A. "Kadimism: elementy sotsiologii musul'manskogo traditsionalizma v tatarskom mire (konets 18-nachalo 20 veka)." Translated by Aliia Akimova. In *Islam v tatarskom mire. Istoriia i sovremennost,'* edited by S. Dudoignon, D. M Iskhakov, and R. Mukhametshin, 57–69. Kazan: In-t istorii Akademii Nauk Tatarstana: Frantsuzskii in-t issledovanii v Tsentral'noi Azii (Tashkent): Tsentr gumanitarnykh proektov i issledovanii (Kazan), 1997.

Eklof, Ben. *Russian Peasant Schools: Officialdom, Village Culture, and Popular Pedagogy, 1861–1914.* Berkeley: University of California Press, 1986.

——, John Bushnell, and L. G. Zakharova. *Russia's Great Reforms, 1855–1881.* Bloomington: Indiana University Press, 1994.

Emmons, Terence. *The Emancipation of the Russian Serfs.* New York: Holt, Rinehart, 1970.

——. *The Formation of Political Parties and the First National Elections in Russia.* Cambridge, Mass: Harvard University Press, 1983.

Engelstein, Laura, *Slavophile Empire: Imperial Russia's Illiberal Path.* Ithaca, N.Y.: Cornell University Press, 2009.

Erkinov, Aftandil S. *The Andijan Uprising of 1898 and Its Leader Dukchi Ishan Described by Contemporary Poets.* Tokyo: Department of Islamic Area Studies, Center for Evolving Humanities, Graduate School of Humanities and Sociology, University of Tokyo, 2009.

Fadeeva, I. L. *Ofitsial'nye doktriny v ideologii i politike Osmanskoi imperii: Osmanizm, Panislamizm: XIX–nachalo XX vv.* Moscow: Izd-vo "Nauka." Glav. red. vostochnoi lit-ry, 1985.

Fakhrutdinov, R. R. *Tatarskoe liberal'no-demokraticheskoe dvizhenie v kontse 19–nachale 20 vv: ideologiia i politicheskaia programma.* Avtoreferat kand. dissertatsii. Kazan, 1996.

Farah, Irmgard. *Die Deutsche Pressepolitik und Propagandatätigkeit im Osmanischen Reich von 1908–1918 Unter besonderer Berücksichtigung des "Osmanischen Lloyd."* Beirut: Orient-Institut der Deutschen Morgenländischen Gesellschaft, 1993.

Field, Daniel. *The End of Serfdom: Nobility and Bureaucracy in Russia, 1855–1861.* Cambridge, Mass: Harvard University Press, 1976.

Figes, Orlando. *The Crimean War: A History.* New York: Metropolitan Books/Henry Holt, 2010.

Firsov, S. L. *Pravoslavnaia Tserkov' i gosudarstvo v poslednee desiatiletie sushchestvovaniia samoderzhaviia v Rossii.* St. Petersburg: Izd-vo Russkogo Khristianskogo Gumanitarnogo Institutata, 1996.

Fisher, Alan W. "Enlightened Despotism and Islam under Catherine II." *Slavic Review* 27, no. 4 (1968): 542–553.

——. *The Russian Annexation of the Crimea, 1772–1783.* Cambridge: Cambridge University Press, 1970.

——. "Emigration of Muslims from the Russian Empire in the Years after the Crimean War." *Jahrbücher für Geschichte Osteuropas* 35, no. 3 (1987): 356–371.

Frank, Allen J. *Muslim Religious Institutions in Imperial Russia: The Islamic World of Novouzensk District and the Kazakh Inner Horde, 1780–1910.* Leiden: Brill, 2001.

Freeze, Gregory. *The Parish Clergy in Nineteenth-Century Russia: Crisis, Reform, Counter-Reform.* Princeton, N.J.: Princeton University Press, 1983.

——. "Institutionalizing Piety: The Church and Popular Religion, 1750–1850." In *Imperial Russia: New Histories for the Empire,* edited by Jane Burbank and David L. Ransel, 210–255. Bloomington: Indiana University Press, 1998.

Gainullin, M. *Tatarskaia literatura i publitsistika.* Kazan: Tatarskoe knizhnoe izd-vo 1983.

Gammer, M. *Muslim Resistance to the Tsar: Shamil and the Conquest of Chechnia and Daghestan.* London: F. Cass, 1994.

Gankevich, V. Iu. *Na sluzhbe pravde i prosveshcheniiu: kratkiii biograficheskiii ocherk Ismaila Gasprinskogo, 1851–1914.* Simferopol: Dolia, 2000.

———, and S. P. Shendrikova. *Ismail Gasprinskiii i vozniknovenie liberal'no-musul'manskogo politicheskogo dvizheniia.* Simferopol: Dolia, 2008.

Gatagova, L. S. *Pravitel'stvennaia politika i narodnoe obrazovanie na Kavkaze v XIX v.* Moscow: Rossiia molodaia, 1993.

Gatrell, Peter. *A Whole Empire Walking: Refugees in Russia during World War I.* Bloomington: Indiana University Press, 1999.

Geraci, Robert. "Russian Orientalism at an Impasse: Tsarist Education Policy and the 1910 Conference on Islam." In *Russia's Orient: Imperial Borderlands and Peoples, 1700–1917,* edited by D. R. Brower and E. J. Lazzerini, 138–161. Bloomington: Indiana University Press, 1997.

———. "Going Abroad or Going to Russia? Orthodox Missionaries in the Kazakh Steppe, 1881–1917." In *Of Religion and Empire: Missions, Conversion, and Tolerance in Tsarist Russia,* 274–310. Ithaca, N.Y.: Cornell University Press, 2001.

———. *Window on the East: National and Imperial Identities in Late Tsarist Russia,* Ithaca, N.Y.: Cornell University Press, 2001.

———, and Michael Khodarkovsky. *Of Religion and Empire: Missions, Conversion, and Tolerance in Tsarist Russia.* Ithaca, N.Y.: Cornell University Press, 2001.

Gerasimov Il'ia, Marina Mogil'ner, and Aleksandr Semenov. *Konfessiia, imperiia, natsiia: religiia i problema raznoobraziia v istorii postsovetskogo prostranstva.* Moscow: Novoe izd-vo, 2012.

Gleason, Abbott. *European and Muscovite: Ivan Kireevsky and the Origins of Slavophilism.* Cambridge, Mass: Harvard University Press, 1972.

Glushchenko, E. A. *Stroiteli imperii. Portrety kolonial'nykh deiatelei.* Moscow: XXI vek-Soglasie, 2000.

Goldfrank, David. *The Origins of the Crimean War.* London: Longman, 1994.

———. "The Holy Sepulcher and the Origin of the Crimean War." In *The Military and Society in Russia, 1450–1917,* edited by Eric Lohr and Marshall Poe, 491–505. Leiden: Brill, 2002.

Gorizontov, Leonid. "The 'Great Circle' of Interior Russia: Representations of the Imperial Center in the Nineteenth and Early Twentieth Centuries." In *Russian Empire: Space, People, Power, 1700–1930,* edited by Jane Burbank, Mark von Hagen, and Anatoly Remnev, 67–93. Bloomington: Indiana University Press, 2007.

Grekov, B. I. "Natsional'nyi aspect vneshnei politiki Germanii v gody Pervoi mirovoi voiny (Liga nerusskikh narodov Rossii)." In *Pervaia mirovaia voina: prolog XX-go veka,* edited by V. L. Mal'kov, 67–93. Moscow: Nauka, 1998.

Gubaidullin, G. "K voprosu ob ideologii Gasprinskogo." *Izvestiia Azerbaijanskogo Vostochnogo fakul'teta,* 179–208. Vol. 4. Baku, 1929.

Hagen, Gottfried. "German Heralds of Holy War: Orientalists and Applied Oriental Studies." *Comparative Studies of South Asia, Africa and Middle East* 24, no. 2 (2004): 145–162.

Hairutdinov, Ramil. "'Mir islama': iz istorii sozdaniia zhurnala." *Mir islama* 1/2 (1999): 3–20.

Happel, Jörn. *Nomadische Lebenswelten und zarische Politik: der Aufstand in Zentralasien 1916.* Stuttgart: Franz Steiner Verlag, 2010.

Harrison, Christopher. *France and Islam in West Africa, 1860–1960.* Cambridge: Cambridge University Press, 1988.

Höpp, Gerhard. *Muslime in der Mark als Kriegsgefangene und Internierte in Wünsdorf und Zossen, 1914–1924.* Berlin: Verlag Das Arbische Buch, 1997.

Iosifova, P. "Iu. Samarin i ego 'Pis'ma iz Rigi." *Vestnik Moskovskogo Gosudarstvennogo Universiteta. 8: History* 6 (1990): 3–13.

Isakov, S. G. "Ostzeiskii vopros v russkoi pechati 1860-kh." *Uchenye zapiski Tartuskogo Gosudarstvennogo Universiteta.* Vol. 107 (1961).

Iskhakov, D. M., and R. M. Mukhametshin. *Fenomen Tatarskogo dzhadidizma: vvedenie k sotsiokul'turnomu osmysleniiu.* Kazan: Izd-vo "Iman," 1997.

Iskhakov, S. M. "Revoliutsiia 1905–1907 gg. i rossiiskie musul'mane." In *1905 god–nachalo revoliutsionnykh potriasenii v Rossii XX veka: materialy mezhdunarodnoi konferentsii,* edited by P. V. Volobuev, 192–210. Moscow: Institut rossiiskoi istorii RAN, 1996.

———. *Pervaia russkaia revoliutsiia i musul'mane Rossiiskoi imperii.* Moscow: Sotsial'no-politicheskaia mysl', 2007.

Iskhakova, R. R. *Kazanskaia tatarskaia uchitelskaia shkola i ee rol v formirovanii i stanovlenii natsionalnogo obrazovaniia.* Kazan: Novoe Znanie, 2002.

Ivanov, L. M., A. M. Pankratova, and A. L. Sidorov. *Revoliutsiia 1905–1907 gg. v natsional'nykh raionakh Rossii.* Moscow: Gos. izd-vo polit. lit-ry, 1955.

Jahn, Hubertus. *Patriotic Culture in Russia during World War I.* Ithaca, N.Y.: Cornell University Press, 1995.

Jersild, Austin Lee. "From Savagery to Citizenship: Caucasian Mountaineers and Muslims in the Russian Empire." In *Russia's Orient: Imperial Borderlands and Peoples, 1700–1917,* edited by Daniel R. Brower and Edward J. Lazzerini, 101–114. Bloomington: Indiana University Press, 1997.

———. *Orientalism and Empire: North Caucasus Mountain Peoples and the Georgian Frontier, 1845–1917.* Montreal: McGill-Queen's University Press, 2002.

Kanlidere, A. *Reform within Islam: The Tajdid and Jadid Movement among Kazan Tatars (1809–1917): Conciliation or Conflict?* Istanbul: Eren, 1997.

Kappeler, Andreas. *Russlands erste Nationalitäten: das Zarenreich und die Völker der Mittleren Wolga vom 16. bis 19. Jahrhundert.* Cologne: Böhlau, 1982.

———. *The Russian Empire: A Multiethnic History.* Translated by Alfred Clayton. Harlow, England: Pearson Education, 2001.

Karpat, Kemal. *The Politicization of Islam: Reconstructing Identity, State, Faith, and Community in the Late Ottoman State.* New York: Oxford University Press, 2001.

Kefeli-Clay, Agnès. "L'islam populaire chez les Tatars chrétiens orthodoxes au XIXe siècle." *Cahiers du monde russe* 37, no. 4 (1996): 409–428.

———. "Constructing an Islamic Identity: The Case of Elyshevo Village in the Nineteenth Century." In *Russia's Orient: Imperial Borderlands and Peoples, 1700–1917,* edited by Daniel R. Brower and Edward J. Lazzerini. 271–291. Bloomington: Indiana University Press, 1997.

Kemper, M. *Sufis und Gelehrte in Tatarien und Baschkirien, 1789–1889: der islamische Diskurs unter russischer Herrschaft.* Berlin: K. Schwarz, 1998.

Kerimova, M. M., and O. B. Naumova. "Aleksei Nikolaevich Kharuzin." *Anthropology & Archeology of Eurasia* 42, no. 2 (2003): 7–39.

Khabibullin, M. Z. *Iz istorii Kazanskogo islamovedeniia vtoroi poloviny 19-nachala 20 veka. Mikhail Aleksandrovich Mashanov.* Kazan: Făn 2004.

Khalfin, N. A. *Prisoedinenie Srednei Azii k Rossii: 60–90-e gody XIX v.* Moscow: Izdatel'stvo "Nauka." Glav. red. vostochnoi literatury, 1965.

Khalid, Adeeb. *The Politics of Muslim Cultural Reform: Jadidism in Central Asia.* Berkeley: University of California Press, 1998.

———. "Russian History and the Debate over Orientalism." *Kritika: Explorations in Russian and Eurasian History* 1, no. 4 (2000): 691–699.

———. "Pan-Islamism in Practice: The Rhetoric of Muslim Unity and Its Uses." In *Late Ottoman Society: The Intellectual Legacy,* edited by Elizabeth Özdalga, 201–224. London: RoutledgeCurzon, 2005.

Kirimli, Hakan. "Emigration from the Crimea to the Ottoman Empire during the Crimean War." *Middle Eastern Studies* 44, no. 5 (September 2008): 751–773.

Kizenko, Nadezhda. *A Prodigal Saint: Father John of Kronstadt and the Russian People.* University Park: Pennsylvania State University Press, 2000.

Klibanov, A. I. *Istoriia religioznogo sektantstva v Rossii: 60-e gody XIX v.–1917g.* Moscow: Nauka, 1983.

Klier, John. *Imperial Russia's Jewish Question, 1855–1881.* Cambridge: Cambridge University Press, 1995.

Klimovich, L. I. *Islam v tsarskoi Rossii: ocherki.* Moscow: Gos. antireligioznoe izd-vo, 1936.

———. "Na sluzhbe prosveshcheniia. O pervoi tiurkoiazychnoi gazete "Terdzhiman" i ee izdatele I. Gasprinskom." In Ismail Bey Gasprinskii, *Rossiia i Vostok,* 98–121. Kazan: Fond Zhien: Tatarskoe knizhnoe izd-vo, 1993.

Knight, Nathaniel. "Grigor'ev in Orenburg, 1851–1862: Russian Orientalism in the Service of Empire?" *Slavic Review* 59, no. 1 (Spring 2000): 74–100.

———. "On Russian Orientalism: A Response to Adeeb Khalid." *Kritika: Explorations in Russian and Eurasian History* 1, no. 4 (2000): 701–715.

Knysh, Alexander. "Sufism as an Explanatory Paradigm: The Issue of the Motivations of Sufi Resistance Movements in Western and Russian Scholarship." *Die Welt des Islams* 42, no. 2 (2000): 139–173.

Kolonitskii, B. I. "Emigratsiia. Voennoplennye i nachalnyi etap germanskoi politiki 'revoliutsionizirovaniia' Rossii (avgust 1914–nachalo 1915 goda)." In *Russkaia emigratsiia do 1917 goda– laboratoriia liberal'noi i revoliutsionnoi mysli,* edited by Iu. Sherrer and B. V. Anan'ich, 197–216. St. Petersburg: Evropeiskii dom, 1997.

Komatsu, Hisao. "The Andijan Uprising Reconsidered." In *Muslim Societies: Historical and Comparative Aspects,* edited by Sato Tsugitaka, 29–61. London: Routledge-Curzon, 2004.

———. "Dar Al-Islam under Russian Rule as Understood by Turkestani Muslim Intellectuals." In *Empire, Islam, and Politics in Central Eurasia,* edited by Uyama Tomohiko, 3–21. Sapporo: Slavic Research Center, Hokkaido University, 2007.

Kotsonis, Yanni. "Face-to-Face": The State, the Individual, and the Citizen in Russian Taxation, 1863–1917." *Slavic Review* 63, no. 2 (Summer 2004): 221–246.

Kozelsky, Mara. "Casualties of Conflict: Crimean Tatars during the Crimean War." *Slavic Review* 67, no. 4 (Winter 2008): 852–891.

———. *Christianizing Crimea: Shaping Sacred Space in the Russian Empire and Beyond.* DeKalb: Northern Illinois University Press, 2010.

Kuznetsov, O. V. *R. A. Fadeev: general i publitsist.* Volgograd: Izdatel'stvo Volgogradskogo gosudarstvennogo Universiteta, 1998.

Landau, Jacob. *The Politics of Pan-Islam: Ideology and Organization.* Oxford: Clarendon Press, 1990.

Lazzerini, Edward, "Ismail Bey Gasprinskii and Muslim Modernism in Russia, 1879–1914." Ph.D. dissertation, University of Washington, Seattle, 1973.

——. "From Bakhchisarai to Bukhara in 1893: Ismail Bey Gasprinskii's Journey to Central Asia." *Central Asia Survey* 3, no. 4 (1984): 77–88.

——. "Volga Tatars in Central Asia, 18–20th Centuries: From Diaspora to Hegemony." *Central Asia in Historical Perspective,* edited by Beatrice Forbes Manz, 82–100. Boulder, Colo.: Westview Press, 1994.

Lohr, Eric. *Nationalizing the Russian Empire: The Campaign against Enemy Aliens during World War I.* Cambridge, Mass: Harvard University Press, 2003.

——. "The Ideal Citizen and Real Subject in Late Imperial Russia." *Kritika: Explorations in Russian and Eurasian History* 7, no. 2 (2006): 173–194.

Mackenzie, David. "Kaufman of Turkestan: An Assessment of His Administration 1867–1881." *Slavic Review* 26, no. 2 (June 1967): 265–285.

Maiorova, Olga. *From the Shadow of Empire: Defining the Russian Nation through Cultural Mythology, 1855–1870.* Madison: University of Wisconsin Press, 2010.

Manz, Beatrice Forbes. "Central Asian Uprisings in the 19th Century: Ferghana under the Russians." *Russian Review* 46, no. 3 (July 1987): 267–281.

Martin, Virginia. *Law and Custom in the Steppe: The Kazakhs of the Middle Horde and Russian Colonialism in the Nineteenth Century.* Richmond, Surrey: Curzon, 2000.

Matsuzato, Kimitaka. "General-gubernatorstva v Rossiiskoi imperii: ot etnicheskogo k prostranstvennomu podkhodu." In *Novaia imperskaia istoriia postsovetskogo prostranstva,* edited by I. Gerasimov, S. Glebov, A. Kaplunovski, M. Mogilner, and A. Semenov, 427–458. Kazan: Tsentr issledovaniia natsionalizma i imperii, 2004.

McCarthy, Frank T. "The Kazan' Missionary Congress." *Cahiers du monde russe et soviétique* 14, no. 3 (1973): 308–332.

Meyer, James H., "Immigration, Return, and the Politics of Citizenship: Russian Muslims in the Ottoman Empire, 1860–1914." *International Journal of Middle East Studies* 39, no. 1 (2007): 15–32.

Michelson, Patrick Lally. "Slavophile Religious Thought and the Dilemma of Russian Modernity, 1830–1860." *Modern Intellectual History* 7, no. 2 (2010): 239–267.

Miller, Alexei. *"Ukrainskii vopros" v politike vlastei i russkom obshchestvennom mnenii (vtoraia polovina 19 veka).* St. Petersburg: Aleteia, 2000.

——. "Rusifikatsii: klassifitsirovat' i poniat.'" *Ab Imperio* 2 (2002): 133–148.

——. *Imperiia Romanovykh i natsionalizm.* Moscow: Novoe literaturnoe obozrenie, 2006.

Morrison, Alexander. *Russian Rule in Samarkand, 1868–1910: A Comparison with British India.* Oxford: Oxford University Press, 2008.

——. "'Applied Orientalism' in British India and Tsarist Turkestan." *Comparative Studies in Society and History* 51, no. 3 (2009): 619–647.

——. "Metropole, Colony, and Imperial Citizenship in the Russian Empire." *Kritika: Explorations in Russian and Eurasian History* 13, no. 2 (2012): 327–364.

Motadel, David. "Islam and the European Empires." *Historical Journal* 55, no. 3 (2012): 831–856. doi:10.1017/S0018246X12000325.

Naganawa, Norihiro. "Maktab or School? Introduction of Universal Primary Education among the Volga-Ural Muslims." In *Empire, Islam, and Politics in Central Eurasia*, edited by Uyama Tomohiko, 65–97. Sapporo: Slavic Research Center, Hokkaido University, 2007.

Noack, Christian. *Muslimischer Nationalismus im Russischen Reich: Nationsbildung und Nationalbewegung bei Tataren und Baschkiren: 1861–1917.* Stuttgart: Franz Steiner Verlag, 2000.

Nogmanov, Aidar. *Tatary Srednego Povolzh'ia i Priural'ia v rossiiskom zakonodatel'stve vtoroi poloviny XVI–XVIII vv.* Kazan: Izdatel'stvo "Fen," 2000.

Nol'de, B. E. *Iurii Samarin i ego vremia.* Paris: YMCA-Press, 1926.

Norris, Stephen M. *A War of Images: Russian Popular Prints, Wartime Culture, and National Identity, 1812–1945.* DeKalb: Northern Illinois University Press, 2006.

Novikova, I. N. *Finliandskaia karta v nemetskom pas'iantse: Germaniia i problema nezavisimosti Finliandii v gody pervoi mirovoi voiny.* St. Petersburg: izd. S. Petersburgskogo universiteta, 2002.

O'Neill, Kelly Ann. "Between Subversion and Submission: The Integration of the Crimean Khanate into the Russian Empire." Ph.D. dissertation, Harvard University, 2006.

Pelenski, Jaroslaw. *Russia and Kazan: Conquest and Imperial Ideology (1438–1560).* The Hague: Mouton, 1974.

Polunov, A. Iu. *Pod vlast'iu ober-prokurora: gosudarstvo i tserkov' v epokhu Aleksandra III.* Moscow: AIRO-XX, 1996.

———. "Church, Regime, and Society in Russia (1880–1895)." *Russian Studies in History* 39, no. 4 (2001): 33–53.

———. "The Orthodox Church in the Baltic Region and the Policies of Alexander III's Government." *Russian Studies in History* 39, no. 4 (2001): 66–76.

———. "The Religious Department and the Uniate Question, 1881–1894." *Russian Studies in History* 39, no. 4 (2001): 77–85.

Polvinen, Tuomo. *Derzhava i okraina: N. I. Bobrikov—general gubernator Finliandii 1898–1904 gg.* Translated by Gennadii Muravin. St. Petersburg: Evropeiskii dom, 1997.

Rabow-Edling, Susanne. *Slavophile Thought and the Politics of Cultural Nationalism.* Albany: State University of New York Press, 2006.

Reynolds, Michael A. *Shattering Empires: The Clash and Collapse of the Ottoman and Russian Empires 1908–1918.* Cambridge: Cambridge University Press, 2011.

Renner, Andreas. *Russischer Nationalismus und Öffentlichkeit im Zarenreich 1855–1875.* Cologne: Böhlau, 2000.

———. "Defining a Russian Nation: Mikhail Katkov and the 'Invention' of National Politics." *Slavonic and East European Review* 81, no. 4 (October 2003): 659–682.

Riasanovsky, Nicholas V. *Russia and the West in the Teaching of the Slavophiles: A Study of Romantic Ideology.* Cambridge, Mass: Harvard University Press, 1952.

Robinson, David. *Paths of Accommodation: Muslim Societies and French Colonial Authorities in Senegal and Mauritania, 1880–1920.* Athens: Ohio University Press and Oxford: James Currey, 2000.

Rodinson, Maxime. *Europe and the Mystique of Islam.* Translated by Roger Veinus. Seattle: University of Washington Press, 1987.

Romaniello, Matthew P. *The Elusive Empire: Kazan and the Creation of Russia, 1552–1671.* Madison: University of Wisconsin Press, 2012.

Rorlich, Azade-Ayse. *The Volga Tatars: A Profile in National Resilience.* Stanford, Calif: Hoover Institution Press, 1986.

Rosenberg, William G. *Liberals in the Russian Revolution: The Constitutional Democratic Party, 1917–1921.* Princeton, N.J.: Princeton University Press, 1974.

Royle, Trevor. *Crimea: The Great Crimean War, 1854–1856.* New York: St. Martin's Press, 2000.

Rozhkov, Vladimir. *Tserkovnye voprosy v Gosudarstvennoi Dume.* Rome: Pontificium Institutum Orientalium Studiorum, 1975.

Rzaev, A. K. *Muhammad Ali M. Kazem-Bek.* Moscow: Nauka, Glav. red. vostochnoi lit-ry, 1989.

Sabol, Steven. *Russian Colonization and the Genesis of Kazak National Consciousness.* Houndmills, Basingstoke: Palgrave Macmillan, 2003.

Sahadeo, Jeff. *Russian Colonial Society in Tashkent: 1865–1923.* Bloomington: Indiana University Press, 2007.

Said, Edward. *Orientalism.* New York: Pantheon Books, 1978.

Sanborn, Joshua, *Drafting the Russian Nation: Military Conscription, Total War, and Mass Politics, 1905–1925.* DeKalb: Northern Illinois University Press, 2003.

Sartori, Paolo. "The Birth of a Custom: Nomads, Sharia Courts and Established Practices in the Tashkent Province, ca. 1868–1919." *Islamic Law and Society* 18, nos. 3–4 (2011): 293–326

Schamiloglu, Uli. "The Formation of a Tatar Historical Consciousness: Shihabuddin Marjani and the Image of the Golden Horde." *Central Asian Survey* 9, no. 2 (1990): 39–49.

Schimmelpenninck van der Oye, David. *Russian Orientalism: Asia in the Russian Mind from Peter the Great to the Emigration.* New Haven, Conn.: Yale University Press, 2010.

Semyonov, Alexander. "The Real and Live Ethnographic Map of Russia: The Russian Empire in the Mirror of the State Duma." In *Empire Speaks Out: Languages of Rationalization and Self-description in the Russian Empire,* edited by Il'ia Gerasimov, Jan Kusber, and Alexander Semyonov, 191–228. Leiden: Brill, 2009.

Shevzov, Vera. *Russian Orthodoxy on the Eve of Revolution.* Oxford: Oxford University Press, 2004.

Shissler, Ada Holland. *Between Two Empires: Ahmet Agaoglu and the New Turkey.* London: I.B. Tauris, 2002.

Sinel, Allen. *Classroom and the Chancellery: State Educational Reform in Russia under Dmitrii Tolstoy.* Cambridge, Mass.: Harvard University Press, 1973.

Slocum, J. "Who, and When, Were the *Inorodtsy?* The Evolution of the Category of 'Aliens' in Imperial Russia." *Russian Review* 57, no. 2 (1998): 173–190.

Sokol, Edward. *The Revolt of 1916 in Russian Central Asia.* Baltimore: Johns Hopkins Press, 1954.

Sorenson, Thomas C. "Pobedonostsev's Parish Schools: A Bastion against Secularism." In *Religious and Secular Forces in Late Tsarist Russia: Essays in Honor of Donald W. Treadgold,* edited by Charles E. Timberlake, 185–205. Seattle: University of Washington Press, 1992.

Spidle, Jake Jr. "Colonial Studies in Imperial Germany." *History of Education Quarterly* 13, no. 3 (Autumn 1973): 231–247.

Staliūnas, Darius. "Did the Government Seek to Russify Lithuanians and Poles in the Northwestern Region after the Uprising of 1863–64?" *Kritika: Explorations in Russian and Eurasian History* 5, no. 2 (2004): 273–289.

——. *Making Russians: Meaning and Practice of Russification in Lithuania and Belarus after 1863.* Amsterdam: Rodopi, 2007.

Steinwedel, Charles. "Invisible Threads of Empire: State, Religion, and Ethnicity in Tsarist Bashkiria, 1773–1917." Ph.D. diss., Columbia University, 1999.

——. "To Make a Difference: The Category of Ethnicity in Late Imperial Russian Politics, 1861–1917." In *Russian Modernity: Politics, Knowledge, Practices,* edited by David Hoffmann and Yanni Kotsonis, 67–86. New York: Palgrave Macmillan, 2000.

Sultangalieva, G. S. *Zapadnyi Kazakhstan v sisteme etnokul'turnykh kontaktov (XVIII–nachalo XX vv.).* Ufa: RUNMTS Goskomnauki Respubliki Bashkortostan, 2001.

Sunderland, Willard. "Russians into Iakuts? 'Going Native' and Problems of Russian National Identity in the Siberian North, 1870s–1914." *Slavic Review* 55, no. 4 (Winter 1996): 806–825.

——. "Imperial Space: Territorial Thought and Practice in the Eighteenth Century." In *Russian Empire: Space, People, Power, 1700–1930,* edited by Jane Burbank, Mark von Hagen, and Anatoly Remnev, 33–66. Bloomington: Indiana University Press, 2007.

——. "The Ministry of Asiatic Russia: The Colonial Office That Never Was But Might Have Been." *Slavic Review* 69, no. 1 (Spring 2010): 120–150.

Swietochowski, Tadeusz. *Russian Azerbaijan, 1905–1912: The Shaping of National Identity in a Muslim Community.* Cambridge: Cambridge University Press, 1985.

Taranovski, Theodore, and Peggy McInerny. *Reform in Modern Russian History: Progress or Cycle?* Washington, D.C.: Woodrow Wilson Center Press, 1995.

Tarasova, V. A. *Vysshaia dukhovnaia shkola v Rossii v kontse 19-nachale 20 veka. Istoriia imperatorskikh dukhovnykh akademii.* Moscow, 2005.

Tarle, E. V. *Krymskaia voina.* Vols. 1–2. Moscow and Leningrad: Izdatel'stvo Akademii nauk SSSR, 1950.

Thaden, Edward. *Conservative Nationalism in Nineteenth-Century Russia.* Seattle: University of Washington Press, 1964.

Tolz, Vera. "Rossiiskie vostokovedy i obshcheevropeiskie tendentsii v razmyshleniiakh ob imperiiakh kontsa 19-nachala 20 veka." In *Imperium inter pares: rol' transferov v istorii Rossiiskoi imperii (1700–1917),* edited by Martin Aust, Rikarda Vilpius, and Aleksei Miller, 266–307. Moscow: Novoe literaturnoe obozrenie, 2010.

——. *Russia's Own Orient: The Politics of Identity and Oriental Studies in the Late Imperial and Early Soviet Periods.* Oxford: Oxford University Press, 2011.

Tsimbaev, N. I. *I. S. Aksakov v obshchestvennoi zhizni poreformennoi Rossii.* Moscow: Izdatel'stvo Moskovskogo Universiteta, 1978.

Tsiunchuk, Rustem A. *Dumskaia model' parlamentarizma v Rossiiskoi imperii: Etnokonfessional'noe i regional'noe izmerenie.* Kazan: FEN, 2004.

Tuna, Mustafa Özgür. "Gaspirali v. Il'minskii: Two Identity Projects for the Muslims of the Russian Empire." *Nationalities Papers* 30, no. 2 (2002): 265–289.

——. "Imperial Russia's Muslims: Inroads of Modernity." Ph.D. diss., Princeton University, 2009.

Tursunov, Kh. *Vosstanie 1916 goda v Srednei Azii i Kazakhstane.* Tashkent: Gos. izd-vo Uzbekskoi SSR, 1962.

Tvardovskaia V. A. *Ideologiia poreformennogo samoderzhaviia: M. N. Katkov i ego izdaniia.* Moscow: "Nauka," 1978.

Umbrashko, K. B. *M. P. Pogodin: chelovek, istorik, publitsist.* Moscow: Rossiiskaia akademiia nauk, Institut rossiiskoi istorii, 1999.

Usmanova, Diljara M. *Musul'manskaia fraktsiia i problemy "svobody sovesti" v Gosudarstvennoi Dume Rossii: (1906–1917).* Kazan: Master Lajn, 1999.

———. *Musul'manskie Predstaviteli v Rossiiskom Parlamente: 1906–1916.* Kazan: Faṅ, 2005.

Valeev, R. M. *Is istorii Kazanskogo vostokovedeniia serediny–vtoroi poloviny 19 veka: Gordii Semenovich Sablukov–tiurkolog i islamoved.* Kazan: Izd-vo "Kazan-Kazan," 1993.

Validi, D. (Validov). *Ocherki istorii obrazovannosti i literatury tatar.* Kazan: "Iman," 1998.

Vigasin A. A., A. N. Khokhlov, and P. M. Shatitko, eds. *Istoriia otechestvennogo vostokovedeniia s serediny 18 veka do 1917 goda.* Moscow: Izdatel'skaia firma "Vostochnaia literatura" RAN, 1997.

Von Hagen, Mark. "The Great War and the Mobilization of Ethnicity." In *Post-Soviet Political Order: Conflict and State Building,* edited by Barnett R. Rubin and Jack L. Snyder, 34–57. London: Routledge, 1998.

Von Laue, Theodore H. *Sergei Witte and the Industrialization of Russia.* New York: Columbia University Press, 1963.

Vorob'eva E. I. (Elena Campbell). "Khristianizatsiia musul'man Povolzh'ia v imperiiskoi politike samoderzhaviia." In *Imperskii stroi Rossii v regional'nom izmerenii. XIX–nachalo XX veka),* edited by B. V. Anan'ich, J. Burbank, and P. Savel'ev, 138–148. Moscow: Moskovskii obshchestvennyi nauchnyi fond, 1997.

Waldron, Peter. "Religious Reform after 1905: Old Believers and the Orthodox Church." *Oxford Slavonic Papers* 20 (1987): 110–139.

———. "Religious Toleration in Late Imperial Russia." In *Civil Rights in Imperial Russia,* edited by Olga Crisp and Linda Harriet Edmondson, 103–119. Oxford: Clarendon, 1989.

———. *Between Two Revolutions: Stolypin and the Politics of Renewal in Russia.* DeKalb: Northern Illinois University Press, 1998.

Walicki, Andrzej. *The Slavophile Controversy: History of a Conservative Utopia in Nineteenth-Century Russian Thought.* Translated by Hilda Andrews-Rusiecka. Notre Dame, Ind.: University of Notre Dame Press, 1989.

Wcislo, Francis William. *Reforming Rural Russia: State, Local Society, and National Politics, 1855–1914,* Princeton, N.J.: Princeton University Press, 1990.

———. *Tales of Imperial Russia: The Life and Times of Sergei Witte, 1849–1915.* Oxford: Oxford University Press, 2011.

Weeks, Theodore. *Nation and State in Late Imperial Russia: Nationalism and Russification on the Western Frontier, 1863–1914.* DeKalb: Northern Illinois University Press, 1996.

———. "Russification: Word and Practice 1863–1914." *Proceedings of the American Philosophical Society* 148, no. 4 (December 2004): 471–489.

Werth, Paul. "The Limits of Religious Ascription: Baptized Tatars and the Revision of 'Apostasy,' 1840s–1905." *Russian Review* 59, no. 4 (October 2000): 493–511.

———. *At the Margins of Orthodoxy: Mission, Governance, and Confessional Politics in Russia's Volga-Kama Region, 1827–1905.* Ithaca, N.Y.: Cornell University Press, 2002.

———. "Arbiters of the Free Conscience: State, Religion, and the Problem of Confessional Transfer after 1905." In *Sacred Stories: Religion and Spirituality in Modern Russia,* edited by Heather Coleman and Mark Steinberg, 179–199. Bloomington: Indiana University Press, 2007.

———. "Lived Orthodoxy and Confessional Diversity: The Last Decade on Religion in Modern Russia." *Kritika: Explorations in Russian and Eurasian History* 12, no. 4 (Fall 2011): 849–865.

———. *Pravoslavie, inoslavie, inoverie: ocherki po istorii religioznogo raznoobraziia Rossiiskoi imperii.* Translated by Nataliia Mishakova, Mikhail Dolbilov, and Elizaveta Zueva. Moscow: Novoe literaturnoe obozrenie, 2012.

———. *The Tsar's Foreign Faiths: Toleration and the Fate of Religious Freedom in Imperial Russia.* Oxford University Press, 2014.

Wortman, Richard. *Scenarios of Power: Myth and Ceremony in Russian Monarchy from Peter the Great to the Abdication of Nicholas II.* Princeton, N.J.: Princeton University Press, 2006.

Yemelianova, Galina M. "The National Identity of the Volga Tatars at the Turn of the 19th Century: Tatarism, Turkism and Islam." *Central Asian Survey* 16, no. 4 (1997): 543–572.

———. *Russia and Islam: A Historical Survey.* Houndmills: Palgrave, 2002.

Zagidullin, I. K. *Perepis' 1897 goda i tatary Kazanskoi gubernii.* Kazan: Tatarskoe knizhnoe izd-vo, 2000.

———. *Islamskie instituty v Rossiiskoii imperii: mecheti v evropeiiskoii chasti Rossii i Sibiri.* Kazan: Tatarskoe knizhnoe izd-vo, 2007.

Zaionchkovskii, P. A. *Otmena krepostnogo prava v Rossii.* Moscow: Prosveshchenie, 1968.

Zakharova, L. G. *Samoderzhavie i otmena krepostnogo prava v Rossii, 1856–1861.* Moscow: Izd-vo Moskovskogo universiteta, 1984.

Zelenogorskii, M. L. *Zhizn' i deiatel'nost' arkhiepiskopa Andreia (kniazia Ukhtomskogo).* Moscow: Terra, 1991.

Zelnik, Reginald. *Labor and Society in Tsarist Russia: The Factory Workers of St. Petersburg. 1855–1870.* Stanford, Calif.: Stanford University Press, 1971.

Zenkovsky, S. A. "A Century of Tatar Revival." *American Slavic and East European Review* 12, no. 3 (October 1953): 303–318.

———. *Pan-Turkism and Islam in Russia.* Cambridge: Harvard University Press, 1960.

Zetterberg, Seppo. *Die Liga der Fremdvölker Russlands 1916–1918: ein Beitrag zu Deutschlands antirussischem Propagandakrieg unter den Fremdvölkern Russlands im ersten Weltkrieg.* Helsinki: Finnische Historische Gesellschaft, 1978.

Index

Page locators in *italic* indicate photographs.

Abdülhamid II, sultan of Turkey, 178, 179, 185
adat, 114, 147
Afanasii (Sokolov), archbishop of Kazan and Sviiazhsk, 40
Afghanistan, 200, 207
Agaev, A. (Ahmet Ağaoğlu), 179, 199
Agafangel (Solov'ev), rector of the Kazan Theological Academy, 232n39
Akchurin, Y. (Yusuf Akçura), 139, 179, 199
Akhmerov, Sh. I., 80
Akhtiamov, I. A., 202
Aksakov, I. S., 2, 5, 49, 69
Aleksii (Dorodnitsyn), bishop of Chistopol, rector of the Kazan Theological Academy, 162
Alexander II, emperor of Russia, 2, 8, 25, 31, 40, 43, 46, 55, 61, 63, 82, 87, 111, 216
Alexander III, emperor of Russia, 8–9, 46, 68
Algeria, 202
Alien Question, alien questions, 5–7, 29, 68, 75, 104, 142, 150, 153, 159, 160, 169, 176, 184, 216
Allaev, A., 187
Altynsarin, I., 65–66
Andijan revolt, 91–92, 99, 101, 104–105, *129,* 178, 209–210
Andrei (Ukhtomskii), bishop of Mamadysh, later bishop of Ufa and Menzelinsk, *132,* 158–160, 164, 166–167, 175–176, 211–214, 220, 222–224
animists, animism, 33, 35–36, 43, 166
Antaki, P. V., 182, 185, 186, 201
Antonii (Amfiteatrov), archbishop of Kazan, 27, 42, 43, 44, 50, 120, 121, 158, 216
Antonii (Vadkovskii), metropolitan of St. Petersburg, 158
apostasy, 33–53, 145, 146, 162; and Decree on Religious Tolerance, 155–157, 160; initial response to, 35–41; legacy of, 51–52; origins, 34–35; and perceived weakness of Russian Orthodoxy, 48–51; in Reform Era, 41–48; and Russian modernization, 217–220

Arabic language, 36, 180
Armenians, 143, 222
Asian Department (Ministry of Foreign Affairs), 12
assimilation, 68, 72, 75, 78, 79, 101, 142, 152, 161, 221
Astrakhan, 114, 138
Austria-Hungary, 198, 206, 212
Azamatov, Daniil, 107

Bagin, S. A., 138–139, 160
Baiazitov, A., 74
Baiazitov, M.-S., 205, 211
Bakhchisarai, 71, *128,* 138
Baku, 138, 140, 186, 203
Balaklava, 25, *126*
Balkan crisis (1912–1913), 170, 185–186, 188
Balkan Slavs, 9, 23, 27, 29–31
Balkan uprisings (1875–1876), 177–178
Baltic Germans, 67, 163
Baltic Question, 4–5, 68, 95
Baltic region: German domination and influence in, 5, 68; Lutheranism in, 49, 156; and 1905 revolution, 137; perceived alienation of, 5; in World War I, 212
Baratynskii, A. I., 57
Bariatinskii, A. I., 26
Bartol'd, V. V., 171–176, 205
Bashkirs, 73, 74, 110, 111
Batumi province, 198
Becker, C. H., 172
Beletskii, S. P., 184, 213
Bezak, A. P., 117
Black Sea region, 23, 26, 58
Bobrovnikov, N. A., 77–78, 80, 99, 104, *131,* 149, 150, 153, 157, 163, 164, 170, 181, 187, 218, 264n3
Boiarskii, P. M., 176
Britain, 2, 4, 21, 30, 86, 215

British Muslim Society, 205
Brotherhood of St. Gurii, 43, 50–51
Brower, Daniil, 49
Buddhists, Buddhism, 38, 156, 166
Budilovich, A. S., 143–144, 148, 149, 216, 221
Bukhara, Emirate of Bukhara, 85, 87, 181, 187
Bunge, N. Kh., 68, 226n12

Catherine II (Catherine the Great), empress of
    Russia, 22, 34–35, 65, 95, 106, 107, 118, 123
Catholicism. *See* Roman Catholicism
Caucasian War, 8, 26, 29, 114
Caucasus, 26, 29–30, 198, 206, 207
censorship, 5, 31, 62, 63, 75, 76, 83, 138, 197
Central Asia: Russian imperial expansion into,
    85–86, 103–104; and World War I, 195, 206.
    See also Turkestan
"central core" of Russian empire, 6. *See also* Rus-
    sian core
Chechnya, 114
Cheremis. *See* Mari (also Cheremis)
Cherevanskii, V. P., 146–148
Cherniaev, M. G., 86, 90, 114
China, 96, 110, 207
Chicherina, S. V., 149–150, 157
Chistopol district, 36
Christianity, 29–30, 37, 39, 40, 43–44, 46, 47, 50,
    57, 58, 59, 76–77, 168
Christianization, 7, 26, 34, 51, 52, 58, 59, 67, 74,
    152, 165
Chuvash, 36, 38, 41, 57, 59, 64, 67, 156, 157, 176
Circassians, 26, 30
citizens, citizenship, 3, 10, 45, 54, 58, 59, 72, 76,
    142, 154, 165, 193, 205, 214, 216
civilizers, civilizing mission, 56, 65, 72, 84, 101,
    103, 223
clergy. *See* Muslim clergy; Orthodox clergy
Clerical Question, 3
confessional system, 14, 48, 51, 52, 59, 68, 81,
    105, 124, 147, 151, 153, 216–217, 221–223
Constitutional Democrats (Kadets), 139, 141,
    156, 210
Constitutional Question, 3
Crews, Robert, 14, 90
Crimea, Crimean peninsula, 4, 7, 8, 22, 26, 27,
    106, 115
Crimean khanate, 22
Crimean Tatars, 56, 58, 190; and Crimean War,
    22–28, 30, 31; emigration of, 25, 28; Jadadism
    and, 73; and World War I, 196
Crimean War, 1–2, 4, 21–32, 110, 177–178

Daghestan, 114
Davletshin, A.-A., 98–99, 202
Decree on Religious Toleration (decree of 17
    April 1905), 145–146, 155–157, 160
Delianov, I. D., 61–62
Department for Religious Affairs of Foreign
    Confessions, 11–12, 50, 55, 107, 121–123, 160,
    174, 184, 186, 196, 203, 209, 210
Department of Police, 12, 83, 180, 182–183,
    186, 210
Devlet-Kil'deev, A. A., 74
Dolbilov, Mikhail, 13
Dolgorukov, V. A., 23
Dowler, Wayne, 238n44
dual transcription, 151, 152
Dukchi ishan (Muhammad Ali), 85, 91
Dukhovskaia, V. F., 92–93, 97–98
Dukhovskoi, S. M., 85, 92–102, 104–105, 114–
    115, 178, 209
Duma, 12; First, *130*, 138, 141, 154; Fourth, 154,
    192; Muslim faction in, 141, 143, 186, 187,
    189, 192, 202, 210, 220–221; and Revolution
    of 1905, 137–138, 154; Second, 138, 141, 154,
    156; Third, 154, 156; and World War I, 205–
    206, 210
Durnovo, I. N., 62
Durnovo, P. N., 140
Dzhanturin, S-G. S-Kh., 185

Eastern Question, 22
Eastern Russian Society for Culture and Enlight-
    enment, 212
Ecclesiastical Assembly of the Mohammedan
    Creed, 34–35, 107. *See also* Orenburg Mo-
    hammedan Ecclesiastical Assembly; Muslim
    clergy; Muslim religious institutions
Education: and control over social change, 55–
    63; of converts, 39; and Great Reforms, 12;
    mass, 12, 54; and Muslim Awakening, 71–81;
    of Muslims, 54–83, 89–91, 111; primary, 57–
    63, 154, 164; religious, 50–51; and Russifica-
    tion policy of state, 63–71; and School Ques-
    tion, 142, 152, 192; and Special Commission
    on Education (1910–1911), 164; and Special
    commission on Education of Eastern *inoro-
    dtsy* (1905), *131*, 148–152; universal primary
    education, 56, 154, 164. *See also* schools
Egypt, 38
emancipation of the serfs, 2–3, 33, 54
empire, 3; conception of, problem of, and diver-
    sity and unity, 3–6, 14, 18, 216, 221

Enikeev, G. Kh., 201
Enlightenment, 3, 34, 54, 56, 59, 67, 71, 74, 77, 80, 89, 168, 176, 191, 216, 219
ethnography, 37, 176
Evlogii (Georgievskii), bishop of Kholm and Liublin, 156, 161
Evpatoriia, 24

Fadeev, R. A., 29, 30
fanaticism, 27, 56, 61, 70, 74, 77, 79, 86, 94, 209, 237n11
fatalism, 57
Fedor, tsar of Russia, 35
Ferghana, 92, 207, 208, 209
Filaret (Amfiteatrov), archbishop of Kazan, 36
Finland, 5, 155, 161
Finnish Question, 5, 17, 95, 166
Finns, 27, 68, 143, 161, 163, 198
Fisher, Alan, 26
France, 2, 4, 21, 172, 185, 199
Frankini, V. A., 30
Freeze, Gregory, 52

Gabiev, S., 187–188
Gasprinskii, I. Bey, *128*; and Il'minskii system, 220, 221; and Muslim Awakening, 71–83, 138, 139; and pan-Turkism, 179, 185, 187; and Petrograd Muslim congress of 1914, 203; and state policy for non-Russian education, 149–152
Georgia, 29
Georgians, 143, 198
Geraci, Robert, 13, 164–165
Germans, 27, 68. *See also* Baltic Germans
Germany, 5, 12, 198–202, 206, 212, 213, 215
Germogen, metropolitan of Kazan, 35
Gippius, A. I., 208
Girs, F. K., 90
Glazov, V. G., 149
Golovnin, A. V., 55
Gordlevskii, V. A., 75
Goremykin, I. L., 205
Great Reforms, 2–4, 8, 9, 21, 55, 217; and apostasy to Islam, 51; and assassination of Alexander II, 61, 90; and educational policies, 55, 58; issue of Muslim clergy during, 108–109; and modernization of Orthodox church, 42; mosques during, 120; and religious tolerance, 40; and Revolution of 1905, 137; and Russification, 63
Grigor'ev, D., 49

Grigor'ev, V. V., 64, 65, 89
Grigorii (Postnikov), archbishop of Kazan and Sviiazhsk, 36, 38

Hajetlashe, M. Bek, 183–184, 200, 211
Hartmann, M., 172
Holy Synod, 11, 36, 39, 43, 46, 47, 55, 68, 77, 158, 160, 161
holy war, 23, 85, 92, 93, 188, 197, 207

Ibragimov, A. (Abdurreşid Íbrahim), 139, 140, 178–179, 199
Igel'strom, O. A., 106, 107
Ignat'ev, A. P., 146
Ignat'ev, N. P., 29, 178
Il'minskii, N. I., *127*; and anti-Islamists, 99, 103, 104; and apostasy to Islam, 36–43, 47, 51–52; and educational reform, 56, 57–67; and Muslim Awakening, 71, 75–81; and policy of "ignoring Islam," 89–90; and state regulation of Islam, 115–116, 124, 217–218
Il'minskii's system, 42, 43, 78, 145, 149–152, 157–160, 167, 190, 214, 219
Imperial Decree of 12 December 1904, 144
Imperial governance, rule, 14, 26, 29, 31, 32, 34, 72, 76, 83, 84, 86, 89, 168, 169, 194, 215, 217; and danger of pan-islamism, 193; and education, 54; and islamicization, 65; and mosques, 122–123; and Russification, 66
Imperial Society for Oriental Studies, 171, 173, 256n5
imperialism, 215
Innokentii (Borisov), archbishop of Kherson and Tauride, 23
inorodtsy, 6, 43, 50, 62, 68, 70, 116, 145
Ioann (Sokolov), rector of the Kazan Theological Academy, 40
Ioann of Kronstadt (Sergiev), priest, 159
Iranian Constitutional Revolution, 10, 168, 178
Irkutsk province, 156
Iskhakov, A., 139
Iskhakov, L., 140, 174
Islam, 7, 8, 29, 30, 56–57, 59, 61, 62, 72–77, 89, 106, 168, 175; Dukhovskoi's report on, 95, 101; Il'minskii's new vision of, 36–37, 218; Ostroumov's vision of, 101; "privileges" of, 105, 124
Islamicization, 46, 64, 65, 66, 69
Istanbul, 197, 198
Ittifak (Union of Muslims of Russia), 139–140, 143, 180, 186

Iuzefovich, B. M., 46–47, 216
Ivanov, N. A., 101
Ivanov, P. P., 208
Iznoskov, I. A., 69

Jadidism, 72–73, 138–139, 144, 152, 162, 180, 181, 210, 220
Japan, 9, 204
Jewish Question, 5, 142, 143, 166
Jews, 27, 140, 144, 205, 212, 222

Kadets, 139, 141, 156, 210
Kamyshanskii, P. K., 162
Karakozov, D., 43, 55
Karashaiskii A.D., 188
Kareliia, 161
Karpat, Kemal, 178
Kars province, 198
Katanov, N. F., 176
Katkov, M. N., 5, 9, 29–30, 45, 46, 71
Kazakh language, 64–66
Kazakhs, 64–67, 111, 114, 147
Kazan, 57–61, 65, 75, 105, 115; 1910 missionary congress in, 165–167, 221; progressive movement in, 181; publishing in, 138
Kazan educational district, 56
Kazan khanate, 7, 34
Kazan province: and Alien Question, 176; apostasy movement in, 34–47; and Decree on Religious Toleration, 156; mosques in, 120; Muslim propaganda in, 160; petitions from, 144; Tatarization in, 67; and World War I, 197, 203
Kazan School for Baptized Tatars, 42–43, 51, 59
Kazan Tatars, 31, 33, 35–38, 67, 107, 190. See also Volga Tatars
Kazan Theological Academy, 36–40, 43, 45, 57, 74, 78, 150, 166, 176, 233n56
Kazan University, 41
Kazem-Bek, A. K., 36, 38, 44, 50, 110, 113, 232n24
Kerensky, A. F., 210
Khalid, Adeeb, 13, 210
Kharuzin, A. N., 160, 161–166
Kholm province, 156, 161
Khuseinov, Mukhamedzhan, 107
Khvostov, A. N., 205, 206
Kiev, 44
Kiev Theological Academy, 44
Klemm, V. O., 201
Knight, Nathaniel, 13
Koran, 57, 74, 174, 211

Korol'kov, N. I., 94
Kovalevskii, M. E., 46
Kozelsky, Mara, 26
Krachkovskii, I. Iu., 171
Kruzhok Ravnopraviia i Bratstva, 143
Kryzhanovskii, N. A., 31, 86, 87, 110–112, 121
Kun, A. L., 89
Kuropatkin, A. N., 99, 103, 207–210

Labor faction (Trudoviki), 141, 210
Larionov, S. S., 70
Latvians, 212
Le Chatelier, A., 172
Leont'ev, K. N., 70
Levitskii, G. I., 27–28
liberalism, 56, 70, 71, 151, 222
Luk'ianov, S. M., 161
Lutheranism, 49, 156

madrases, 58, 80
Makarov, A. A., 172
Maklakov, N.A., 188, 197–198
Maklakov, V. A., 156
Maksudov, M., 140
Maksudov, S., 184, 189
maktabs, 58, 72, 142, 180, 181
Malov, E., 57, 120–121
Mari (also Cheremis), 35, 38, 59, 64, 67, 156
Marjani, Sh., 73
Markevich, A. I., 22
Markov, E. L., 58
Mashanov, M. A., 49–50, 67, 166
Men'shikov, A. S., 23–24
Mikhail Nikolaevich, Grand Duke, 112–113
military draft, 28, 195, 206–207
Miliutin, D. A., 30, 87
Miller, Aleksei, 13
Ministry of Foreign Affairs, 12, 201
Ministry of Internal Affairs (MVD), 11, 12, 55; and apostasy to Islam, 44–45, 47, 48, 52; commission during Crimean War, 28, 31; courses sponsored by, 174; and educational policies, 60–62; and mosque regulation, 119–123; and Muslim press, 171–172; and "national question," 83; and pan-Islamism, 180–187; and system of spiritual administration, 107, 109–110, 116; during World War I, 195–201. See also Department for Religious Affairs of Foreign Confessions
Ministry of Public Education (MNP), 12, 55, 60, 61–63, 80, 151, 163, 164

Ministry of War, 87, 200, 210
Miropiev, M. A., 74–75, 150
missionaries, missionary activity: and apostasy
to Islam, 47–53; congress in Kazan, 165–167,
221; in 18th century, 34; and "ignoring" of
Islam, 88; and mosque policy, 118, 120, 123;
and post-1905 reforms, 157, 159–160; and
state-sponsored Muslim establishments, 115;
and Tatar Muslim propaganda, 176; and Tatarization, 64, 69–70, 74; in Turkestan, 100,
104; in Volga region, 35–45, 118, 155, 157,
159, 175
MNP. *See* Ministry of Public Education (MNP)
modernization, 3–4, 103, 168, 190, 216–219, 223
Mongolian language, 36
Morrison, Alexander, 13
mufti, 24, 107, 108, 112–118, 144, 147, 148, 197–
198, 205, 211
Muhammad Ali (Madali). *See* Dukchi ishan
(Muhammad Ali)
mullahs, 24, 42, 44, 51, 66, 88, 111–112, 114,
119–121, 163, 191, 209, 223
Murav'ev, M. N., 87
Muridism, 113
Muslim clergy, 25, 50, 60, 61; educational requirements imposed on, 111; and Fourth
Muslim Congress, 193; and 1914 interministerial commission on Muslim Question,
188–193; and 1916 revolt, 208, 209; proposed
Russian-language requirement for, 148; Russian state and defining the role of, 106–118;
and Special Commission of 1910, 163, 164;
and Third Muslim Congress, 148; and tsarist
state, 124–125. *See also specific positions:* mullahs; mufti
Muslim Congresses: First and Second, 139–140;
Fourth (St. Petersburg, 1914), 192, 201, 202,
212–213; participants of, *133*; Third, 143,
148, 152
Muslim faction (of Duma), 141, 143, 186, 187,
189, 192, 202, 210, 220–221
Muslim intelligentsia, 8, 10, 13, 71, 72, 74–79,
103, 125, 138–139, 141, 151, 168–169, 189,
195, 197, 201, 205, 210, 222
Muslim Labor Group, 141
Muslim press, 138, 171–175
"Muslim propaganda," 39–40, 44, 46–48, 50, 52,
57, 71, 76, 89, 115, 159–162, 190–191
Muslim Question *(Musul'manskii vopros)*, 1,
7–14, 215, 217, 219, 221, 223–224; in aftermath of Revolution of 1905, 9–10, 154–169;

and apostasy, 33, 46–48; Bobrovnikov on, 99;
Cherevanskii and, 146–148; "complication"
of, 81–82; Dukhovskoi's approach to, 95–98,
104–105; in early 20th century, 152–153; and
eastern part of Russia, 68, 86–87, 110; emergence of, 2, 5, 7–8, 27; Hajetlashe and, 184,
200; interministerial commission on (1914),
188–192; Kharuzin and, 161–165; Kharuzin
commission's program for study of, 170–177;
in late imperial period, 52; and mass education, 54–56; missionaries' view of, 165–168;
and mosque regulation, 120, 124; and Muslim
alienation, 81–83; and Muslim awakening,
71, 141; and Muslim clergy, 110; and Orthodox church problem, 48; Orthodox writers on, 77; and pan-Islamism, 177–179, 187;
and perceived weakness of Orthodoxy, 176;
and policy paralysis, 193–194; and reforms of
1905, 142; and Russification, 63; "solvability"
of, 215–224; Stolypin and, 168; D. A. Tolstoy
and, 55–56
Muslim religious institutions, 106–118, 123–125,
219; Kaufman's approach to, 88; mosques,
118–123; and state policies, 123–125. *See also*
Muslim clergy; Orenburg Mohammedan Ecclesiastical Assembly
Muslims: alienation of, 26–31, 54, 56, 79, 81,
108, 150, 165, 219; integration of, 53, 63, 71,
89; isolation of, 58, 71, 72, 77, 97; 1905 revolution and political awakening of, 138–144;
perceived "backwardness" of, 49, 56–58, 70–
73, 193; percentage of, by province (map),
16–18; as soldiers, *133*; "trustworthiness" of,
21–26
MVD. *See* Ministry of Internal Affairs (MVD)

Nalivkin, V. P., 79, 96, 102, 244n73
Napoleon III, emperor of France, 21
Naqshbandi order, 91, 113
Nasyri, K., 73
nationalism, 6, 45, 163, 177, 203; and Crimean
War, 23; rise of non-Russian, 221
nationalistic ideologies, ideas, goals, 6, 77, 78,
81, 163, 168, 195
nationality, 6, 7, 45, 67, 68, 82, 207
Nationality Question, 10, 142, 198, 205
native languages: instruction in, 57–58
new-method movement, 163, 181, 182. *See also*
Jadidism
Nicholas I, emperor of Russia, 4, 21, 23, 36
Nicholas II, emperor of Russia: and post-1905

reforms, 158; and Revolution of 1905, 137–138, 154; and World War I, 205

Nikanor (Kamenskii), archbishop of Kazan and Sviiazhsk, 166

Nikolai Nikolaevich, Grand Duke, 206, 207

Nikol'skii, N. V., 175, 176

Nizhnii Novgorod, 181, 186

Nogays, 22

October Manifesto, 137, 138, 141, 145, 146

Odessa educational district, 56

Office of New Converts, 34, 37, 118

Old Belief, Old Believers, 38, 40, 50, 58, 144, 158, 232n39

Orenburg, Orenburg province, 24–25, 31, 64, 65, 108, 109

Orenburg educational district, 181

Orenburg Mohammedan Ecclesiastical Assembly, 35, 60, 77, 107–112, 116, 119, 122, 123, 147, 163, 164, 191, 211

Oriental Institute (Vladivostok), 174

Orientalism, Orientalist discourse, vision, 1, 13, 84, 164, 227n33

Orthodox church, 9, 32, 63; apostates from (see apostasy); and Clerical Question, 3; and Crimean War, 21, 23; and imperial expansion, 34; and Islam, 56–57, 74; and promulgation of Decree on Toleration, 156–158; and Russian modernization, 216–219; and Russification campaign, 70; state as protector of, 118–119

Orthodox clergy: Il'minskii and, 76; Muslim clergy vs., 50, 51, 108–109, 144, 147; needs of, 49; and Parish Question, 158, 213, 216, 222; and state-sponsored Muslim establishments, 115. See also priests

Ostroumov, N. P., 71, 76–79, 99–105, *129*, 146, 166, 173, 174, 207, 218

Ottoman empire, 2, 60; and Crimea, 106; and Crimean War, 21–23, 25–28, 30–31; and pan-Islamism, 177–180, 185; and World War I, 196–200, 202, 204. See also Turkey

Palestine, 21

pan-Finnish propaganda, 161

pan-Islamism, 162, 177–189, 201

pan-Tatarism, 189–190

pan-Turkism, 179, 185–187, 189

Parish Question, 158, 213, 222

patriotism, appeals to, during World War I, 201–203; of natives in Turkestan, 208

Peasant Question, 2–3

Penza province, 156

Persia, 143, 168, 180

Pestel, V. I., 23

Peter the Great, emperor of Russia, 11, 103

Pobedonostsev, K. P., 9, 46, 47, 62, 63, 77, 156–157, 222–223

Pogodin, M. P., 23

Poland, 26, 27, 29, 33, 44, 52, 137, 155, 168–169, 190, 212

Poles, 27, 67, 68, 140, 143, 144, 161, 198, 205, 206, 212, 222

Polish Question, 5, 29, 69, 95, 166, 206

Polish rebellion of 1863, 4–6, 8, 27, 29, 33, 44, 46, 48, 52, 55, 87, 216

Popov, A. V., 36

Potulov, I. M., 109, 110

Pozdneev, D. M., 172–173

Practical Oriental Academy (St. Petersburg), 174

priests, 34, 35, 37, 42, 43, 50–52, 57–58, 60, 67, 213. See also Orthodox clergy

Progressive Bloc, 205, 210

propaganda: anti-government, 154; during World War I, 197–201, 213. See also "Muslim propaganda"

Protestantism, 34, 49

Protopopov, A. D., 209–210

Pugachev rebellion, 34

rapprochement, 26, 30, 54, 72, 74, 75, 101, 147, 150, 151, 168, 191

Rasputin, G., 213

Reisner, M. A., 68, 156

Religious tolerance, 7, 63, 68, 91, 95, 122, 146, 155, 157, 166, 192, 193, 205, 217, 220, 222

Revolution of 1905, 10, 220–221; and competing views on education of aliens, 148–152; and limited expansion of religious tolerance, 144–148; and missionaries, 165–167; and Muslim political awakening, 138–144; Muslim Question in aftermath of, 154–169; and Special Commission of 1910, 161–165; and threat of "Muslim propaganda," 155–161

Roman Catholicism, 34, 44, 55, 156, 161, 190

Rozov, E. A., 42, 120

Russian core, 153, 221

Russian intelligentsia, 48, 63

Russian language, 59–61, 79, 80, 111, 116–117, 142, 148, 151, 191

Russian Question, 7, 10, 70, 176, 195, 212, 222

Russification, 63–71, 72, 75, 82, 124, 159

Russo-Japanese War, 9, 137

Russo-Turkish War (1877–1878), 31, 60, 177–178
Rybakov, S. G., 50, 173, 174, 190–191, 201, 211

Sablukov, G. S., 39
Said, Edward, 13
Samarin, Iu. F., 4–5
Samarkand, Samarkand oblast, 87, 94, 207, 209
Samoilovich, A. N., 171, 205
Sart language, 78
Sazonov, S. D., 198, 206
Schimmelpenninck van der Oye, David, 13
Schmidt, A. E., 188
School Question, 142, 152, 192
schools, 57–63; administration of Muslim, 51; and apostasy, 51–52; for baptized non-Russian minorities, 42, 43; under Catherine II, 34; and cultural transformation among Russians, 50; elementary, 150–152; and Muslim nationalism, 150; new-method, 163, 181, 182; reform of Muslim, 79–82, 88, 105, 140–142; Russian-Native, 91; and Tatarization, 65–66, 70. *See also* education; *madrases; maktabs;* Orenburg Mohammedan Ecclesiastical Assembly
Sevastopol, 21, 24
Shakhovskoi, N. V., 83
shamanism, 64
Shamil, Imam, 26, 97, 114
Shamil, Z. Sh., 203
Sharia, 57, 74, 110, 113–115
Shestakov, P. D., 42, 57, 60
Shmidt, A. E., 171
Shuvalov, P. A., 87
Shvedov, N. K., 171, 172
Siberia, 12, 85, 86, 91, 99, 107, 124, 140, 147, 149, 156, 175, 190
Sievers, E. K., 44
Simbirsk, Simbirsk province, 31, 156
Simferopol, 25, 57, 58, 60, 71–72
Slavophiles, Slavophilism, 9, 49, 61, 64, 70–75, 81, 115, 152, 218
Smirnov, V. D., 75–76
Smolensk, 44
Social Democrats (SDs), 141, 210
Social Revolutionaries (SRs), 141
Staliunas, Darius, 13
Stasiulevich, M. M., 27
State Duma. *See* Duma
Steppe region, 114, 119, 209
Stolypin, P. A., 154–155, 161, 164, 165, 168, 171, 180, 183
Strizhevskii, M. V., 160–161

Stroganov, A. G., 25
Suleimanov, G., 117
Sultanov, M., 117
Suvorin, A. S., 139
Sviatopolk-Mirskii, P. D., 137, 144
Syria, 38
Syromiatnikov, S. M., 183

Taranovskii, G. N., 203–204
Tashkent, 85, 86, 92–93, 100, 105, 174
Tatar language, 39–40, 42, 43, 50, 60, 64, 65, 138, 211
Tatar Muslim nationalism, 10, 163, 168, 177, 213
Tatarization, 64–71
Tatars, 7, *126;* and Crimean War, 22–31; and Decree on Religious Tolerance, 157; and pan-Tatarism, 189–190; publishing by, 138; Russians' imitation of, 50. *See also* Crimean Tatars; Volga Tatars
Tauride Mohammedan Ecclesiastical Board (Simferopol), 107–108, 110, 112, 119, 122, 123
Tauride province, 22, 25, 58, 62, 74, 107, 112, 119
Temporary Muslim Committee on Rendering Assistance to Soldiers and Their Families, 202–205
Tevkelev, K.-M., 192, 210
Tevkelev, S., 24–25, 116, 117
Tiflis, 113
Timashev, A. E., 111–113, 178
Timofeev, V., 42
Tolstoy, D. A., 43, 55–57, 60, 61, 90
Tolstoy, I. I., 142–143
Tolz, Vera, 13
Topchibashev, A. M., *130,* 139, 141, 142, 192–193, 203
Totleben, E. I., 27
Transcaucasia, 22, 73, 88, 91, 112–116, 124, 137, 147, 149
Treaty of Paris (1856), 25–26
Trepov, A. F., 206
Turkestan, 84–105, 111, 114–115, 147; Andijan revolt in, 91–92, 99, 101, 104–105; and Dukhovskoi's view of "hostile" Islam, 92–99, 104; Ostroumov's tempered approach to Islam in, 99–105; and Russian imperial expansion, 85–86, 103–104; and von Kaufman's policy of "ignoring" Islam, 86–91; and World War I, 195, 196, 206–209
Turkey, 10, 24, 32, 168, 177; and pan-Islamic movement, 162, 163; and World War I, 196–200, 202, 204. *See also* Ottoman empire

Turkic languages, 71, 73, 78, 80, 205
Turkish language, 187

Udmurts, 36, 41, 64, 156
Ufa, Ufa province, 7, 25, 34, 49, 50, 61, 123, 156, 180–181
Ukhtomskii, E. A., 64
Ukrainians, 198
Union of Muslims of Russia. *See* Ittifak (Union of Muslims of Russia)

Valikhanov, Ch., 65
Valuev, P. A., 41, 86, 109, 111, 115, 117
Viatka province, 24, 162
Vladimir (Bogoiavlenskii), metropolitan of Moscow, 166
Volga Muslims, 7, 8, 32, 62
Volga Tatars: alienation of, from Russian culture, 56; and apostasy movement, 8; and Ittifak party, 140; Jadadism and, 73; as *Kulturträgers*, 69; in post-1905 period, 162. *See also* Kazan Tatars
Volga–Ural region: apostasy to Islam in, 33, 47, 54, 68, 217; Christianization efforts in, 34–35; and Crimean War, 22, 24; and Decree on Religious Tolerance, 156; Duma representatives from, 154; education in, 59; emigration of Tatars from, 25, 28–30; and modernization, 90; mosques in, 120; muftiates in, 148; Muslim reformist movement in, 73; pan-Tatarism in, 189–190; in post-1905 period, 162, 164; Russification efforts in, 63–64; Tatar Muslim influence in, 66; as transitional area, 7
von Bradke, F. M., 31
von Cosack, H., 199
von Kaufman, K. P., 86–91, 114

von Rozenbakh, N. O., 91
Voronets, E. N., 115
Vorontsov, M. S., 113
Vorontsov, S. M., 28
Vrevskii, A. B., 79
Vyrubova, A. A., 213

Weeks, Theodore, 13
Weinberglager, 198, 199
Werth, Paul, 35, 52, 145
Westernizers, 9
Wilhelm II, emperor of Germany, 201
Witte, S. Iu., 2, 98, 99, 144, 158, 178
women: education of, 58, 80; Muslim, as teachers, 58; Russian, living with Muslim men, 58
World War I, 195–214; and appeals to patriotism, 201–203; and attacks on alien separatism, 203–204; and inquiries into "true moods" of Russian Muslims, 195–201; "Muslim cause" vs. "Russian cause" in, 204–213; Muslim soldiers in, *133*
Wortman, Richard, 9

Young Turk Revolution, 10, 168, 179
Young Turks, 10, 162, 179–181, 183, 185

Zabelin, A. I., 91
Zagidullin, I.K. 241n126
Zalesskii, P.F., 167, 256n77
Zefirov, M., 67
Zelenogorskii, M. L., 159
Zhukovskii, G. V., 57
Znamenskii, P. V., 66
Zolotarev, I. M., 188
Zolotnitskii, N., 57
Zwemer, S. M., 172

Elena I. Campbell is Associate Professor of History at the University of Washington, Seattle.